Historical Dictionary of
World's Fairs
and
Expositions,
1851–1988

Historical Dictionary
of
World's Fairs
and
Expositions,
1851–1988

JOHN E. FINDLING,
Editor

KIMBERLY D. PELLE,
Assistant Editor

GREENWOOD PRESS

NEW YORK • WESTPORT, CONNECTICUT • LONDON

Library of Congress Cataloging-in-Publication Data

Historical dictionary of world's fairs and expositions, 1851–1988 /
  John E. Findling, editor; Kimberly D. Pelle, assistant editor.
    p. cm.
  Includes bibliographical references.
  ISBN 0–313–26023–0 (lib. bdg. : alk. paper)
  1. Exhibitions—History. I. Findling, John E. II. Pelle, Kimberly D.
  T395.H57   1990
  907.4—dc20   89–17217

British Library Cataloguing in Publication Data is available.

Library of Congress Catalog Card Number: 89–17217
ISBN: 0–313–26023–0

First published in 1990

Greenwood Press, Inc.
88 Post Road West, Westport, Connecticut   06881

Printed in the United States of America

The paper used in this book complies with the
Permanent Paper Standard issued by the National
Information Standards Organization (Z39.48–1984).

10 9 8 7 6 5 4 3 2 1

Copyright Acknowledgment

The publisher and editors wish to thank *World's Fair* quarterly for permission to publish Arthur
Chandler's chapters on the Paris expositions of 1867, 1878, and 1937.

FOR
Jamey and Summer
Jason and Kristen

CONTENTS

PREFACE

This book had its origin in a senior seminar on world's fairs and expositions for history majors that I taught at Indiana University Southeast in the spring of 1982. While it was a very successful venture, capped off with a trip to the Knoxville world's fair in early May, I encountered major problems in obtaining resource material for my students. John Allwood's fine book, *The Great Exhibitions* (1977), was out of print (I had plucked my one cherished copy from a remainder table at a local bookstore months earlier), and little else was readily available. Through a combination of photocopied articles and a book on American fairs written for a juvenile readership, I got through the seminar, but I regretted the lack of good reading and bibliographic information. A few years later, after the completion of another project, I made a proposal to Greenwood Press, whose editors were sympathetic, and the *Historical Dictionary of World's Fairs and Expositions* was launched. The choice of fairs to include came originally from Allwood. His list was refined by a number of authors and librarians with whom I corresponded and then finalized by the ample use of editorial discretion. Fairs not included—generally those lacking a sufficient international scope or hewing to an overly specialized theme—are listed in appendix D. In some cases, however, a fair had to be left out for lack of an author or the availability of sufficient information.

This book strives to serve two purposes. First, the essays on individual fairs and the various appendixes provide a collective body of basic information on over ninety fairs held in more than twenty countries between 1851 and 1988, as well as fairs planned but never held, fairs yet to come, and the governing body of fairs, the Bureau of International Expositions. Authors, who in many cases had published previous works on their fairs, were encouraged to emphasize features of the fairs they considered most significant. In addition, each author was asked to provide basic statistical information and prepare an annotated bibliography on the fair, indicating, where possible, the location of relevant primary sources and the quality of secondary sources. These bibliographies, along with a general bibliography at the end of the book, containing commentary on archival collections, published bibliographies and checklists, and collective or thematic works, should prove valuable for researchers who wish to go beyond the factual information provided in the essays and appendixes.

A series of grants from Indiana University Southeast enabled Kimberly Pelle to join the project as assistant editor. She contributed enormously to all aspects of the process, from writing essays to editing others' essays to carrying on correspondence with authors; in many ways, the final product is as much hers as it is mine.

Many others have rendered valuable services as well. Ron Mahoney, curator of the special collections department of the Henry Madden Library at California State University, Fresno, helped refine the list of fairs to be included, suggested the "fairs that never were" appendix, found a number of West Coast authors, and was a genial host on a research trip to his campus. Arthur Chandler, of San Francisco State University, provided many useful suggestions on all phases of the project and was a marvelous guide to former fair sites (and Mexican restaurants) in San Francisco. Raymond Clary welcomed us into his home and shared with us his knowledge of the California Midwinter Exposition of 1894, as well as his collection of artifacts from that fair. Peter M. Warner of New York facilitated the processing of many of the photographs in the book, most of them from his personal files, and also helped with the statistics. Martin Manning dug up many interesting and helpful documents on post–World War II fairs from his post in the historical library of the U.S. Information Agency. Bernard Rosenfeld of New York and Sally Mitchell also helped us find authors early in the project.

Patrick Nolan and the staff of the Hagley Museum and Library were most gracious in sharing their facilities with us, as were the staffs of the Winterthur Library and Archives and the University of Maryland library. Bob Rogers, Inc., sent us materials that enhanced our understanding of the Vancouver 1986 fair. Camille Garnier and Bohdan Bochan helped us translate fair titles. Stacy Russell and the reference librarians at Indiana University Southeast were tireless in their efforts to obtain materials on interlibrary loan, and Mary Ann Braden and the other secretaries in the Division of Social Science were instrumental in keeping the flow of official paperwork moving throughout the project. Grants from Indiana University Southeast, the President's Council on International Programs of Indiana University, and the Hagley Foundation enabled us to do research at various locations. Finally, special thanks go to Cynthia Harris, the history editor at Greenwood Press, for her patience and encouragement from the very beginning, and to all the sixty authors, whose cooperation has made this quite an enjoyable task.

Kim and I want to thank our spouses, Jay and Carol, respectively, for their tolerant support throughout. We thank our children, who were also tolerant and supportive, and dedicate this book to them in the hope that, as they grow into adulthood in the early twenty-first century, they will continue to find world's fairs to visit and enjoy.

John E. Findling

INTRODUCTION

Although the world's fairs and expositions described in this book can claim only a rather short direct ancestry prior to their beginnings in 1851, rudiments of these fairs can be traced back to ancient times. There are biblical references to great feasts held at important population centers, which also included markets, athletic games, and visiting dignitaries. The Romans held numerous festivals, usually associated with religious holidays; indeed, the English word *fair* derives from the Latin word for holiday, *feriae*. During medieval times, great fairs were held at major crossroads of trade and were a mixture of commerce, entertainment, and theater. They continued to grow as trade and communications improved.

These medieval European fairs were basically international, at least to the extent to which there were nations. In England, however, the fairs were national and were a blend of a trade show and a public entertainment, similar to a modern carnival. Although the fairs continued in England until at least the late nineteenth century, the more direct genealogical line to the Crystal Palace exhibition of 1851 may be said to have originated with the formation of the Royal Society of Arts in London in 1754.

In 1761, the Royal Society produced a show of its annual prize winners in the "arts, manufactures, and commerce," which ran successfully for seven weeks. The show included exhibits of a sort that we might understand as industrial arts. Thus, the exhibits were technological innovations—machines, mostly—such as miniature windmills, spinning wheels, agricultural implements, including a threshing machine and a cider press, various models of ships, and assorted machines of concern to the textile industry.

Little publicity was given to this exhibition, and people were not encouraged to come and see it after the first year. The Royal Society decided to put its prize winners on permanent display, much like a museum, where they continued to attract attention, but the idea of a special annual event was lost.

Thus it was left to the French, later in the eighteenth century, to hold the first industrial exhibition that had an impact on the development of subsequent exhibitions and, ultimately, world's fairs. Such an exhibition in France was the idea of the marquis d'Avèze, the commissioner of three manufacturing outlets that until 1789 had been under the authority of the king. After the onset of the French Revolution, the marquis found that business was bad and so arranged in 1797 an exhibition in Paris to display his tapestry, carpet, and porcelain products, as well as the products of other trades he had invited to the fair. This exhibition resembled a bazaar or a medieval fair in the sense that the items on display were meant to be sold.

The success of d'Avèze exhibition was so obvious that the French government took up the idea and decided to hold an annual national exhibition of French products in three specially constructed buildings. This fair was more strictly a national exhibition, state sponsored, with nothing for sale during the period of the fair. A good part of the motivation behind this scheme was to demonstrate the ability of the French to compete on favorable terms with their main rival, the British. Since the two nations were then at war, however, the British did not participate, so no direct comparisons could be made.

These French national exhibitions continued to be held intermittently, wars and governmental instability often interfering, until 1849. In that year, the eleventh and largest attracted over 4,500 exhibitors and remained open six months— four months longer than any previous fair.

In England, no such exhibitions were organized. There was no interest, and the prevailing feeling appears to have been that the French shows were nothing more than futile efforts to promote the absurd notion that French products were superior to English ones.

What did develop in England, however, were exhibitions sponsored by mechanics institutes. These institutes, designed to teach scientific principles to working-class people, began to function in English towns in the 1820s. One manner of providing this instruction was through periodic exhibitions. These exhibitions emphasized scientific inventions and mechanical devices, often miniaturized for display purposes. Often model working machines produced actual products, which were then sold to visitors. Other exhibits followed the different stages in the production of a particular item and were especially instructive.

There were other attractions at these exhibitions as well, many of which traveled around England appearing at many sites. Mr. Austin's "Happy Family," for example, featured nearly 200 different animals cohabiting peacefully in a single cage. Other attractions bordered on the miraculous—the key to the Tower of London, a bed that King Richard III slept in, and a bodice worn by Mary, queen of Scots—and were very popular.

In addition to the scientific, mechanical, and exotic exhibits, all of the mechanics institute exhibitions included a fine arts section. Little discrimination was made among artworks, and local artists vied for space with nationally known painters and sculptors.

From their beginning in Manchester in 1837, the mechanics institute exhibitions spread to nearly every town of any size in England and attracted several million visitors before 1851 and the Crystal Palace. These exhibitions were popular and successful in diffusing knowledge; moreover, they contained several attributes later found in the great international exhibitions.

Art exhibitions also form a part of modern world's fairs, although, with few exceptions, they take a back seat to the industrial and technological show. Still, the development of art exhibitions in England constitutes part of the heritage of the Crystal Palace and subsequent world's fairs.

In eighteenth-century England, there were no art museums or other public places to view art. Paintings and sculpture were held in private collections, to which public access was understandably difficult. Only when art was to be sold at public auction was it on public view, and many people attended auctions with no intent (or any means) to purchase items offered for sale. In both Italy and France, on the other hand, art was publicly displayed at this time.

In 1760, the first public art exhibition was held in England. It was the idea of a group of artists, who were encouraged by the popularity of a few portraits given by contemporary artists to a London hospital. In addition, there was a good deal of interest expressed in the annual prize winners of the Royal Society of Arts, which made awards for a variety of artistic and applied scientific achievements. The artists' show ran for two weeks in April 1760, admission was charged, and the money was used to create a fund for impoverished artists. Several thousand visitors attended this event, which stands as an important milestone in the prehistory of world's fairs. In 1768, the Royal Academy (different from the Royal Society of Art) was founded and began putting on annual art exhibitions, which were helpful in dignifying the status of British artists.

From this amalgam of industrial arts displays, art exhibitions, mechanics institute exhibitions, and French national shows emerged the Crystal Palace exhibition of 1851 and the ninety or so other fairs described in this volume. At their foundation, these fairs have never strayed too far from the object stated with respect to the Crystal Palace: "to forward the progress of industrial civilization." By including an international component, visitors to a fair could make easy comparisons of technology and craftsmanship among the industrial products of many nations.

As the essays that follow demonstrate, fairs have moved far beyond being mere showcases of industrial progress. The evolution of fairs has come to involve such things as the inclusion of special themes: the 1876 exposition in Philadelphia commemorated the centennial of the Declaration of Independence; the 1915 fair in San Francisco celebrated the completion of the Panama Canal and the rebirth of the city from the earthquake and fire of 1906. There has been a movement away from fairs contained in one big building, such as the Crystal Palace, and toward individual thematic or country buildings. Finally, one might note the inclusion of more and more nonindustrial features, such as fine art (although that was present from the beginning on a minor scale) and amusements. With these more diverse elements, fairs have come to exhibit comparative national life-styles rather than simply industrial progress.

Through it all, world's fairs have consistently demonstrated a strong streak of nationalism, or the notion of boosting the national image and the people's pride in it. Fair managers, often with government support, have strived to emphasize nationalistic features on behalf of the host country in order to make it look better than its rivals.

In the United States, there was no tradition of national industrial exhibitions or even broadly based art shows for potential fair managers to build upon. Mechanics institute exhibitions, as well as county and state fairs, certainly existed by the mid-nineteenth century and displayed some of the same attributes as world's fairs—exhibits of products, competition for awards, amusements—but these seem to have had negligible impact on the individuals who were involved in the planning of the earliest international fairs held in the United States. Rather, American fairs came about because of the experience Americans had participating in the early European fairs.

In these earliest fairs, U.S. participation was undertaken by private means; there was much resistance to government support among Americans used to a sense of isolation and nonentanglement with the Old World. Not surprisingly, then, early American fairs tended to be more frequently privately managed operations with relatively little government funding or encouragement, especially apart from an official U.S. government pavilion and exhibit.

In addition, as Reid Badger points out in *The Great American Fair* (1979), American fairs had a greater significance for their host cities than did European fairs. Hosting a fair was a great and obvious symbol of urban achievement and a matter of civic pride to the host cities, and many of the earlier American fairs witnessed intense competition among cities vying to host them.

American fairs also put a greater premium on the entertainment aspect. In part, this derived from a desire to make more money, almost always a major challenge for fair managers. In addition, managers noticed quite early that visitors needed diversion from the fatigue that accompanied a day of looking at nothing but machine tools and farm implements.

One final note. The international events described in this book are commonly called "fairs" in the United States, "exhibitions" in Great Britain, and "expositions" in France. For purposes of literary grace, we have used the three words interchangeably, as if they were precise synonyms. Language purists, however, will want to know that they are not. As Kenneth Luckhurst explains in *The Story of Exhibitions* (1951), exhibitions are similar to fairs but are quite different in one respect: exhibitions are solely for displaying or exhibiting goods, while fairs connote commerce, as in the sales of goods being displayed. Thus it is no accident that we usually refer to art exhibitions (where works of art are seldom sold) and trade fairs (where products are contracted for and sold). As for *exposition*, it is a word that etymologically bridges the gap between fair and exhibition. It was first used in 1649, with the meaning of displaying or putting on a show, but in contemporary usage, its meaning has become indistinguishable from that of *fair*, except in a connotative sense that an exposition is larger, more extensive, and perhaps more formally organized than a fair.

THE FAIRS, 1851–1988

The following table indicates currency equivalents at several different points during the time period covered in this book. The figures show the amount of French francs, U.S. dollars, Canadian dollars, and Belgian francs equal to one British pound.

Currency Equivalency Table

Year	British pounds	French francs	U.S. dollars	Canadian dollars	Belgian francs
1878	1.00	25.00	4.85	—	25.00
1889	1.00	25.00	4.85	—	25.00
1905	1.00	25.00	4.80	—	25.00
1925	1.00	101.43	4.83	4.83	101.48
1931	1.00	115.56	4.53	4.70	162.35
1937	1.00	121.96	4.94	4.94	146.32
1965	1.00	13.67	2.79	3.01	138.80
1989	1.00	10.27	1.61	1.90	63.34

Sources: John Allwood, *The Great Exhibitions* (1977); Federal Reserve System, *Banking and Monetary Statistics, 1914–1941*, Vol. 2 (1943); *Banking and Monetary Statistics, 1941–1970* (1971); *Wall Street Journal.*

LONDON 1851

THE GREAT EXHIBITION OF THE WORKS OF INDUSTRY OF ALL NATIONS

The Great Exhibition of the Works of Industry of All Nations, commonly referred to as the Great Exhibition of 1851 or the Crystal Palace Exhibition, was the first true world's fair and a supreme monument to Victorian engineering. It opened May 1, 1851, and closed five months later on October 15, 1851, having accommodated some 6,039,195 visitors. It is often taken as a symbol of the mid-Victorian age and of Great Britain's role as the workshop of the world. The exhibition organizers, who included Prince Albert (the prince consort) and Henry Cole (a promoter of many projects and at the time on the staff of the Public Record Office), intended for it not only to demonstrate British industrial supremacy but also to be a running commentary on the gospel of free trade, peace, and the virtues of democracy and the British constitution.

The idea for such an exhibition grew out of the local exhibitions that had been held in Britain from early in the century. In 1847 the Society of the Arts, with Prince Albert as president, sponsored a series of exhibits of well-designed manufactures in 1847, 1848, and 1849. Albert and Henry Cole discussed the possibility of holding another exhibition that would be international in scope. The site of the exhibition was discussed at length, with Hyde Park chosen over Albert's initial suggestion of Leicester Square, which he readily agreed was too confined an area. The queen gave permission for the use of the royal park.

To promote the enterprise, subscriptions from industries and private individuals were encouraged by means of speeches, circulars, banquets, and personal appeals. Subscriptions were slow at first, but soon the pace picked up, and Samuel Peto, the railway contractor, promised £50,000. The queen and the prince consort together donated £1,500. More modest amounts started coming in, including shillings from workmen. Altogether some 5,000 people contributed.

Because of the widespread public enthusiasm, the government appointed a Royal Commission, which by supplemental charter became a permanent body. It was chaired by Prince Albert and included a number of the most distinguished men in public service, such as the prime minister, Lord John Russell. Prince Albert was tireless in his efforts on behalf of the exhibition.

Besides the Royal Commission, a Building Committee was formed in July 1850 and solicited plans for the exhibition building. It was one of several committees that administered the exhibition. All 254 designs were rejected, and the committee set to work to produce an official design of its own. The design unveiled in 1850 proposed a building of brick, iron, and stone, with a dome much larger than that of St. Paul's Cathedral. It was heavily criticized in Parliament and the press. The *Times* was particularly hostile to the "permanent mutilation" of Hyde Park.

By this time it was July 1850, only ten months from opening day. Joseph Paxton (later Sir Joseph) submitted a hastily drawn plan for what amounted to a gigantic greenhouse three times the length of St. Paul's. Paxton at the time was a friend and adviser of the duke of Devonshire and a director of the Midland Railway. He had started his career as a gardener for the duke, and his blueprint was patterned after large greenhouses he had designed for the conservatory and the lily house at Chatsworth, the duke's estate in Derbyshire.

The design captured the public's opinion at once when Paxton had it published in the July 6, 1850, *Illustrated London News*, while the executive committee was still debating the plan. The committee accepted Paxton's design on July 15, and the construction contract went to the London-based firm of Fox, Henderson, and Company.

There was considerable opposition to the idea of an international exhibition. Memories of the 1848 Chartist disturbances in London were still fresh in the minds of the propertied classes in London, who worried about the possibility of public disorder. The presence in England of a number of refugees from failed continental revolutions of 1848, combined with the masses of foreigners who would descend on London for the exhibition, seemed a menace to many Britons. The 67-year-old Colonel Charles Sibthorp (M.P., Lincoln) was particularly vocal in his condemnation of the project. He prophesied that rioting, robbery, rape, whoremongering, and espionage would ensue. The duke of Wellington feared revolution, and Lord Henry Brougham warned of some 70,000 to 80,000 vagrants coming to London, together with foreign "specimens of Socialists and men of Red colour" to stir up the masses. Richard Mayne, the London police commissioner, expressed anxiety that many of the refugees were men of "extreme democratic revolutionary principles" who might foment disturbances. Others predicted that foreigners would bring disease and would set up brothels around Hyde Park.

On a more mundane level, there were questions about the stability of such a building: it would not be finished in time; the wind would blow it down; the heat would expand the metal, and it would crash down; the vibration from the working machinery and the walking multitudes would make it fall. Even the astronomer royal predicted that it would collapse.

The enterprise, nonetheless, went forward, and possession of the site in Hyde Park was taken on July 30, 1850. The concrete foundations were laid in August, and the first columns were raised on September 26. The whole structure was completed by January 1851, with goods being received for exhibit in February.

The exhibition building was dubbed by *Punch* the "Crystal Palace," and the term has remained. It was situated south of the Serpentine, with its west end close to what is now Exhibition Road. Remains of the concrete foundation are still under the soil of Hyde Park.

The Crystal Palace was the one purely functional building of any size in the

LONDON 1851. Joseph Paxton's Crystal Palace, shown here after its removal to Sydenham, helped guarantee the success of the first great world's fair.

Victorian period and was the world's first large edifice built of metal and glass. It was a prefabricated structure, a new technique that allowed for speedy construction and rendered a uniform aesthetic effect. The building covered about 19 acres and was 1,848 feet long, 408 feet wide, and 66 feet high, except in the transepts, which were 108 feet high. On the north side there was added an extension 936 feet long by 48 feet broad, making the building 456 feet wide at its broadest part. Most of the building measurements were either dividends or multiples of twenty-four.

Paxton modified the original design to add a transept just off-center to enclose some old elm trees that would be spared the ax. Living in the trees were sparrows, and the prospects of their remaining to shower visitors caused momentary concern. The duke of Wellington advised the queen to try sparrow hawks, but the sparrows deserted the trees en masse before the aged duke could wage his last battle.

All the material used was interchangeable: the 2,300 girders, the 3,300 columns, the gutters, and the sash bars were identical throughout the whole structure. The main supports were hollow cast-iron columns, which acted as rainwater conduits.

Many of the wrought-iron beams to span the central nave were made in the Birmingham works of Fox and Henderson, and the cast-iron columns and girders were subcontracted. In one week 316 girders were supplied, and by the end of October the average number of girder columns supplied to the site was close to 200. The raising of the main ribs began on December 4, and within a week all 16 were in place. Each casting was examined on the ground and stress-tested under considerable weight in a special machine built for the purpose, then painted and quickly hoisted into place.

Next began the task of glazing the enormous weblike structure, a project that required some 900,000 square feet of glass, made into the largest panes ever produced, which represented a third of England's glass production a decade before. The glass panes measuring $4' \times 1'' \times 10''$ were supplied by the firm Messrs. Chance of Birmingham. For glazing the roof, eighty men were able to install upwards of 18,000 panes of glass a week, using wooden-wheeled carts that rolled in the gutters.

The construction of the Crystal Palace attracted considerable attention and was attended by hordes of sightseers. A five-shilling admission fee was charged to visit the site, the proceeds going toward a workmen's accident fund. In September 1850 the number of workmen was 39, but by January an average of 2,000 labored on the project.

Owen Jones, architect, designer, and teacher of applied arts at the South Kensington School of Design, was in charge of building decoration. In keeping with the belief that in all great artistic periods only primary colors were used, blue was selected as the predominant color on the columns and girders. In fact, most of the vertical flat surfaces were blue. The undersides of the girders were red.

The overall color scheme was bright, with touches of yellow and large expanses of red behind the balconies, which made a dramatic backdrop for the exhibits. Red banners with white lettering announced the country and classification of the exhibits. The exterior of the building was either white or stone colored, with some blue touches.

Numerous committees in Great Britain and abroad chose the exhibits, which numbered over 100,000 from 13,937 exhibitors. Half the available space was allocated for foreign exhibits (6,556), and the other half of the area was occupied by Britain and its colonies (7,381 exhibits). No prices were displayed on the items. Of the many foreign nations represented, France and Germany were the most important.

The United States, at its own insistence, was given space second only to France but failed to fill it. If quantity was lacking, quality was not, for some of the most significant exhibits were provided by the Americans: a precision, mass-produced Colt revolver, the only sewing machine exhibited, a display of rubber products from the Goodyear Company, and the McCormick reaper.

All the displays inside the Crystal Palace were divided into six groups: (1) raw materials, (2) machinery, (3) manufactures (textile fabrics), (4) manufactures (metallic, vitreous, and ceramic), (5) miscellaneous, and (6) fine arts.

The machinery gallery was the noisiest and most popular; visitors could see huge marine engines, locomotives, hydraulic presses, reapers, and the like. There were models illustrating architecture and engineering; there were statues and porcelains, raw minerals and processed materials, and needlework and other crafts. In the eastern nave there was exhibited the 186-carat Koh-i-Nor diamond from India. Scientific instruments, including orreries and microscopes, musical instruments, weapons, and even an alarm bedstead that would tilt a sleeper out of bed, were on view.

An electric telegraph, connected with Edinburgh and Manchester, was installed inside. It also connected the east and west entrances with the police commissioner's office to notify him of emergencies or when the crowds inside reached more than 50,000, at which point the doors were supposed to be closed until the numbers dwindled. The police soon realized that the building could accommodate larger numbers safely, and on some days over 60,000 strolled inside at the same time. On October 7, 1851, a record of 93,224 was attained.

Instead of cash prizes for exhibit winners, medals were awarded in two categories. One hundred and seventy Council Medals were given for novelty and beauty of design, as well as for excellence of workmanship. A total of 2,918 Prize Medals were awarded for high standards of craftsmanship.

Fears that the Crystal Palace might provide a venue for criminals and disorderly crowds had prompted the authorities to take extra precautions. The police had added 1,000 men to their ranks, and police reserves were located around the area, backed up by some 10,000 military around London. Thirty-five police from other countries, as well as 24 from other British cities, were in attendance, mainly to watch for familiar pickpockets. There was actually very little crime, except for some petty theft and pocket picking.

Much to the delight of everyone, the Great Exhibition was a remarkably orderly event, and lavish praise came from all sides, where months before there had been many doubts. Class distinctions seemed temporarily on the shelf; some of the wealthy even came on shilling days, the "classes and the masses" thus mixing cordially and viewing each other with mutual curiosity. Queen Victoria was a frequent and tireless visitor and wrote about it glowingly in her diary. Since many of the objects came from abroad, and with them many foreign visitors, the cultural horizons of the English were broadened.

Admission charges varied. From the May 1, 1851, opening until May 22, the charge was 5 shillings. Then the charge was lowered to 1 shilling from Mondays through Thursdays. On Fridays it was 2 shillings, sixpence (a half-crown), and on Saturdays it was 5 shillings. There was no Sunday opening. No smoking was permitted, and no alcohol was served in the restaurants—only soft drinks. Filtered water was provided free. There were three entrances, with the principal one located on the south side, opposite the Prince of Wales Gate.

A triumph of Paxton's design was the ability to dismantle and reassemble the building. Since few could bear the thought that it would be gone forever, the Crystal Palace was reerected to a modified design in Sydenham between 1851 and 1854. Surrounded by gardens and fountains, the structure served as a pleasure garden and cultural center for South London until it was destroyed by fire in 1936. In its use, it was a successor to the defunct Vauxhall Gardens.

The commissioners of the Great Exhibition used the £186,437 surplus to buy 87 acres in South Kensington, which would be devoted to the establishment of teaching institutions and centers for the encouragement of science and art. Museums like the Natural Science Museum and the Victoria and Albert Museum are only two of the many intellectual establishments in the South Kensington area that are a legacy from the Great Exhibition of 1851.

BIBLIOGRAPHY

Richard Altick, *The Shows of London* (1978), is a massive study, useful for the history of entertainment in London, as well as for other fairs and spectacles. Charles Babbage, *The Exposition of 1851* (1968), was first published in 1851. Asa Briggs, "The Crystal Palace and the Men of 1851," in *Victorian People: A Reassessment of Persons and Themes, 1851–1867* (1970), is an excellent essay to illuminate the larger social and political setting. See Roger Dixon and Stefan Muthesius, *Victorian Architecture* (1978); also Charles R. Fay, *Palace of Industry, 1851: A Study of the Great Exhibition and Its Future* (1951). C. H. Gibbs-Smith, *The Great Exhibition of 1851* (1981), published by the Victoria and Albert Museum, is a full factual account, accompanied by photographs and many excellent illustrations. The *Official Descriptive and Illustrated Catalogue*, 3 vols., and a supplementary volume (1851), is the official catalog with a history and description of the whole exhibition. The *Official Catalogue* (1851) is a one-volume guide that sold for a shilling and was not illustrated. The *Popular Guide* (1851) is a small official guide that sold for twopence. Sir Nikolaus Pevsner's *High Victorian Design: A*

Study of the Exhibits of 1851 (1951) views the displays from an aesthetic angle. See also Christopher Hobhouse, *1851 and the Crystal Palace* (1950), and Eric de Maré, *London 1851. The Year of the Great Exhibition* (1973) for other descriptive accounts that place the Great Exhibition into its historical context.

Phillip T. Smith

DUBLIN 1853

THE GREAT INDUSTRIAL EXHIBITION

While the 1853 International Exhibition is regarded as Dublin's first world's fair, it followed in a long tradition of Irish industrial and scientific exhibitions. The Royal Dublin Society (RDS), an educational and scientific body founded in the eighteenth century, sponsored biennial national exhibitions from 1834 until the famine year of 1847. The success of London's Great Exhibition of 1851 encouraged a more ambitious approach, and in 1852 during the course of a national exhibition in Cork, the possibility of holding a major international exhibition in Dublin was first mooted.

Some days later William Dargan, a pioneer of Irish railway development, wrote to the Royal Dublin Society urging that such an exhibition should be given "a character of more than usual prominence" and offering the society a sum of £20,000 to erect a suitable exhibition building. Dargan and his co-organizer, Dublin businessman Richard Turner, received considerable support from Irish railway interests, who saw the fair as a means of promoting tourism and restoring confidence in the Irish economy following the devastating famine of the 1840s; they also wished to assist economic development by publicizing the extent of Irish natural resources and introducing people to the wonders of new technology. While the committee's purpose was primarily utilitarian, it was also seen as an opportunity for expressing Irish patriotism by displays of ancient artifacts and by spreading an awareness of foreign artistic achievements.

The exhibition was held on the lawn of Leinster House (then the RDS head-quarters, now the Irish parliament building), a 2½-acre site, where a large glass building, modeled on London's Crystal Palace and designed by Cork architect Sir John Benson, was erected. It was opened by the Lord Lieutenant, the earl of St. Germans, and was subsequently attended by Queen Victoria. Despite the organizers' contacting every individual who had exhibited in London and other strenuous efforts, the international component of this fair was slight; over 1,500 exhibits came from the British Isles (including Ireland), 254 from overseas with only France, Belgium, Netherlands, the Zollverein, the United States, Dutch East Indies (modern Indonesia), and British Guiana contributing. Exhibits were organized on a national basis and then subdivided between art and industry, with the industrial exhibits further categorized according to their raw materials. Most foreign exhibits were artistic rather than industrial—the Netherlands sent a display of Japanese antiques, and one-third of the British and Irish exhibition space was also devoted to the fine arts.

Overall attendance was 1,156,232, a figure achieved by progressively radical reductions in admission charges. As a result the exhibition incurred an overall loss of approximately £9,000, which was offset by Dargan's donation. The fair, however, did bring long-term benefits to the arts and sciences. The enthusiasm engendered by the fine arts exhibition led to efforts to secure a permanent art gallery. This movement ultimately joined forces with independent proposals to honor William Dargan's contribution. The result was the construction, with government assistance, on the site of the 1853 exhibition, of the National Gallery of Ireland, and, on the other side of Leinster Lawn, of the Natural History Museum, both completed in 1864.

BIBLIOGRAPHY

John Sproule was the official historian for this fair. He edited a fair "newspaper," the *Exposition Expositor*, that ran for twenty-five weeks during the run of the fair and contained lengthy feature articles, reprinted pieces from other papers, and illustrations. The material from this paper formed the basis for the official history of the fair, published as *The Resources and Manufacturing Industry of Ireland* . . . (1854), a series of essays on raw materials, machinery, and manufactured goods of various kinds, as well as detailed information about the exposition.

Information is also available in the *Official Catalogue of the Great Industrial Exhibition* . . . (1853), which contains a sixty-one-page art supplement. William J. Battersby, *The Glories of the Great International Exhibition of All Nations in 1853* (1853), describes the opening ceremony, Queen Victoria's visit, and the exhibition itself in rather florid language. Thomas D. Jones, *Record of the Great Industrial Exhibition 1853* (1854), provides more factual information on such matters as attendance charges and exhibits. *The Illustrated Record and Descriptive Catalogue of the Dublin International Exhibition 1865* (1866), by Henry Parkinson and Peter Lund Simmonds, contains many useful comparative statistics on the 1853 and 1865 expositions. *Erin's Fairy Spell* (1853), by William Scribble (pseudonym of William Smith), a writer of comic verse, presents a more whimsical view of the fair.

Modern scholarship on this fair is scant. Alun C. Davies has two articles touching on the event. In "The First Irish Industrial Exhibition, Cork, 1852," *Irish Economic and Social History* 11 (1975), he discusses the interest shown in Irish exhibitions during the 1850s, while "Ireland's Crystal Palace, 1853," in J. M. Goldstrom and L. A. Clarkson, eds., *Irish Population, Economy, and Society* (1981), 249–70, deals specifically with the Dublin exposition. Finally, John Allwood, *The Great Exhibitions* (1977), briefly discusses this fair.

Mary E. Daly

NEW YORK 1853–1854
EXHIBITION OF THE INDUSTRY OF ALL NATIONS

In 1853–1854, New York City hosted the first world's fair ever held in the United States. The inspiration for that fair was the 1851 Great Exhibition at the Crystal Palace in London. Businessmen from the United States who attended the Great Exhibition were favorably impressed by the fair and by the successes of American exhibitors, who won a large number of prizes. Many left London convinced that a similar exhibition should be held in the United States.

There was little doubt that if the United States were to have a world's fair, it would be held in New York City. The project was promoted primarily by New Yorkers, among them Horace Greeley, who, in a May 1851 *New York Tribune* article about the London Crystal Palace, proposed erecting a similar structure in New York. The most active early promoter of such an exhibition was Edward Riddle, a Massachusetts auctioneer, who also advocated a New York site. Mid-nineteenth-century New York fancied itself, and was widely regarded as, the London of America; if London hosted a great international exhibition, New York surely would have to follow suit.

The site originally chosen for the fair was Madison Square, but opposition from local residents and others resulted in its location at Reservoir Square. This square was bounded by Fortieth and Forty-second streets, Sixth Avenue and the Croton distributing reservoir, and is now the site of Bryant Park. Clearly this was not the best place for the fair; it was far from the center of the city, and the huge reservoir provided a poor backdrop for the building that was to be erected.

Several plans for the structure were submitted, the most interesting coming from Leopold Eidlitz, a prominent New York architect, Joseph Paxton, the designer of the London Crystal Palace, and James Bogardus, the New York architect credited with originating the use of cast-iron exteriors for business buildings. However, the plans chosen were those of Georg J. B. Carstensen and Charles Gildemeister. Carstensen was the designer of Copenhagen's famous Tivoli amusement park, and Gildemeister was a New York architect and lithographer.

Emulating the building housing the London exhibition, the New York structure also was constructed of iron and glass, though its configuration was quite different. The New York Crystal Palace was in the form of a Greek cross, with a 100-foot-diameter dome at the intersection of the arms. The total exterior height of the building was 149 feet, and the arms of the cross were 365 feet long. The angles formed by the intersection of the cross were filled with 24-foot-high triangular lean-tos. At each of the eight corners of the building was an octagonal tower, 8 feet in diameter and 75 feet in height. The exhibition area of the New York Crystal Palace was approximately 4 acres. As applications from prospective exhibitors poured in, its promoters realized that this space would be insufficient. Therefore, an additional two-story building was erected in the space between the main building and the reservoir. This building was used to house a machine arcade and a picture gallery. To lessen the heat and glare from the sun, the Crystal Palace's glass walls were enameled. The London structure had not been so treated, and so the interior of that building had to be covered with canvas.

The Exhibition of the Industry of All Nations opened with great ceremony, attended by President Franklin Pierce, on July 14, 1853. Although the total number of exhibitors varied from month to month, no fewer than 4,000 were represented at the fair. More were from the United States than from any other country, and the largest single category of American exhibits was that of machinery. Generally the classification of articles was patterned after the system used at the London exhibition. There were four divisions, each representing a nation or a group of nations. Each division occupied one-quarter of the space on the first floor of the Crystal Palace. These divisions were further divided into "courts"—twenty-nine for each division—each representing a category of products. In addition to the displays of products relating to industry, the Crystal Palace housed a significant collection of sculpture—probably the largest such display in the United States until then—and a picture gallery. While the quality of the paintings exhibited in the picture gallery was questioned by many contemporaries, the inclusion of that gallery was significant: the New York Crystal Palace exhibition was the first world's fair to include an exhibit of this type. Visitors seeking entertainment beyond that offered by the industrial and artistic exhibits at the Crystal Palace would have to leave the fair's grounds, for unlike later world's fairs, this one contained no midways or sideshows. However, various forms of popular entertainment were to be found in the surrounding area.

The opening festivities for the Crystal Palace attracted considerable attention, but the attendance figures were disappointing until the fall months. Still, between July 15 and November 30, nearly 700,000 people were admitted to the Crystal Palace, and more than $300,000 was collected; but in December and January attendance fell off precipitously. In January, the organization's president, Theodore Sedgwick, handed in his resignation but agreed to stay on until a successor could be found. P. T. Barnum was persuaded to take over that office. Although he announced that the exhibition was to become a permanent institution, even that celebrated showman could not rejuvenate it. On July 10, he resigned the presidency. The Crystal Palace Exhibition officially closed on November 1, 1854, leaving a debt of $300,000.

Although a financial failure, the Exhibition of the Industry of All Nations was of considerable significance. It was, after all, the first world's fair held in the United States and the first anywhere to include an exhibit of paintings. It was a source of some pride to New York, and it surely added to that city's economy. Further, like many other world's fairs, it served as a proving ground for new concepts. Most significant, at a time when the police of New York wore no distinctive attire, the special police at the Crystal Palace were outfitted with uniforms and before the end of 1853, the city police were required to be similarly clothed. It is perhaps ironic that the most celebrated day in the history of the Crystal Palace was October 5, 1858, several years after the close of the world's fair. On that day, while the building was being used for the annual exhibit of the American Institute, a fire broke out. In less than half an hour, the building was consumed in a spectacular blaze.

BIBLIOGRAPHY

The principal manuscript collection relating to the Exhibition of the Industry of All Nations is the Crystal Palace Papers at the New-York Historical Society. The papers of Samuel Francis du Pont and his wife in the Henry Francis du Pont Winterthur Collection at Longwood Library near Wilmington, Delaware, also contain a significant number of items related to the Crystal Palace.

The most extensive description of the Crystal Palace may be found in Georg J. B. Carstensen, *New York Crystal Palace* (1854). Several catalogs of the exhibits were published by the Association for the Exhibition of the Industry of All Nations, including: *Official Catalogue of the New York Exhibition of the Industry of All Nations, 1853* (1853); *Official Catalogue of the Pictures Contributed to the Exhibition of the Industry of All Nations in the Picture Gallery of the Crystal Palace* (1853); and *Official Awards of Juries, 1853* (1853). These do not contain illustrations depicting any of the items exhibited. Other catalogs and guides do contain illustrations and are generally more interesting. Of these, the most important are: Charles R. Goodrich, ed., *Science and Mechanism: Illustrated by Examples in the New York Exhibition, 1853–54* (1854); Horace Greeley, *Art and Industry as Represented in the Exhibition at the Crystal Palace, New York, 1853–54* (1853); William C. Richards, *A Day in the New York Crystal Palace, and How to Make the Most of It* (1853); and Benjamin Silliman, ed., *The World of Science, Art, and Industry, Illustrated from Examples in the New York Exhibition, 1853–54* (1854).

No books have been written about the New York Crystal Palace exhibition, but a few articles have been published. Earle E. Coleman provides a brief history of the fair and an extended discussion of manuscript and published materials dealing with it in "The Exhibition in the Palace: A Bibliographical Essay," *Bulletin of the New York Public Library* 65 (September 1960): 459–75. A lengthy description of the exhibition, its exhibits, and contemporary reaction to it may be found in Charles Hirschfield, "America on Exhibition: The New York Crystal Palace," *American Quarterly* 9 (Summer 1957): 101–16. Grace M. Mayer, "The New York Crystal Palace," *Museum of the City of New York Bulletin* 2 (March 1939): 50–55, is too brief to be of much value. A more recent article is Richard Reinhardt, "The Dubious Glory of New York's 'Great Exhibition,' " *World's Fair* 6, no. 1 (Winter 1986). Two articles by Ivan D. Steen discuss the New York Crystal Palace exhibition, including its significance to New York City, at some length: "America's First World's Fair: The Exhibition of the Industry of All Nations at New York's Crystal Palace, 1853–1854," *New-York Historical Society Quarterly* 47 (July 1963): 257–87, and "New York's Crystal Palace: Symbol of a World City," *NAHO* 13 (Spring–Summer 1981): 68–71. The fullest discussion of the fair is to be found in Steen's master's thesis, "The New York Crystal Palace Exhibition" (New York University, 1959).

Ivan D. Steen

PARIS 1855
EXPOSITION UNIVERSELLE

Like the Crystal Palace Exhibition that preceded it and the international exhibitions that would follow it, the Paris exposition of 1855 served as a vehicle for a series of soon-to-be familiar messages. One was the benefits of ever-advancing industrial technology, even though by the middle of the nineteenth century only a tiny proportion of the labor force of even the most modern economies worked in factories and only a handful of industries had as yet adopted the steam engine. Another was the advantages of international cooperation—the exposition was intended to celebrate forty years of peace in Europe since Waterloo—demonstrated by expanding international trade, encouraged in part by agreements on currency, river tolls, and reductions in tariff barriers. The exposition was also to be a showcase for the regime of the host country—that of Napoleon III, which had been installed after the coup d'état of December 1851—and for the host city of Paris, now with over a million inhabitants and the second largest of European cities after London. Already, then, though only the second major international exhibition, the 1855 exposition was conceived as a celebration of, and a stimulus to, international understanding and production, both material and cultural.

The Paris exposition possessed features that set it apart from other international exhibitions. First, while the London exhibition of 1851 had included only sculpture among its exhibits, its Parisian successor built a separate pavilion devoted to the fine arts. Second, between the inception and the opening of the exposition, war had broken out in the Crimea between Great Britain, France, Turkey, and Sardinia, on the one hand, and Russia on the other. As a result, Imperial Russia was not officially represented in Paris, though individual Russian businessmen were invited to participate and Russian prisoners of war were allowed to attend. In addition, the event was used to cement the new Franco-British alliance: French and British exhibits naturally predominated in both numbers and importance, and there were reciprocal state visits between the two countries. Victoria's visit to France in August was the first by a reigning British monarch since Henry V in 1422. If it was used to reinforce the entente, though, the exposition also highlighted industrial and wider cultural differences—and rivalries—between the two nations. Third, the exposition indicated, and in a minor way accentuated, the economic, cultural, and political primacy of the French capital. A rapidly growing Paris was already responsible for over a third of national industrial production by value. The completion of the major rail links in the 1850s and the beginning of the monumental public works program under Georges Haussmann, who became prefect of the Seine in 1853, reinforced the city's attractive power. Nearly a million visitors a year, for example, came to Paris during the Second Empire. Culturally, too, the exposition served to signal the vibrancy of

Parisian artistic life. At the end of April 1855 Hector Berlioz conducted his *Te Deum* in Paris, and, at the closing ceremony of the Exposition, he conducted his *L'Impériale* cantata with twelve hundred performers. In June 1855, Giuseppe Verdi presented the *Sicilian Vespers* that he had recently composed in Paris. As for the plastic arts in the capital, the exposition itself eloquently demonstrated their vitality. Politically, too, 1855 and 1856 were benchmark years for Paris and the Second Empire regime: the arrival of half a million tourists for the exposition and the signing of the treaty that ended the Crimean war enhanced the capital's international status, while the Treaty of Paris and the birth of the prince imperial, the heir to the throne, both in March 1856, marked what was to prove the apogee of the regime's popularity.

The exhibition had a fourth distinction. Although the immediate stimulus to the holding of the Paris exposition was the Great Exhibition of 1851, it was the French rather than the British who had a recent but already well-entrenched tradition of holding national industrial exhibitions. Beginning in the 1790s under the Directory, these had continued the public festivals of both the Old Regime and the Revolution and, indeed, had usually been held on the sites where these rites had been celebrated. Successive French governments, and officially sponsored organizations, like the Société d'encouragement pour l'industrie nationale (established in 1802), recognized not only that industrialization constituted the puberty of nations and separated nations in terms of national power and well-being, but also that bringing industrialists together and giving medals to the most meritorious would stimulate innovation and emulation. Though the first industrial exhibition, held in 1798 (the Year VI), had attracted only 110 exhibitors, chiefly from the Paris region, precisely twice that number of industralists, representing more departments, exhibited at the second held in 1801 (the Year IX) and while only 23 prizes had been awarded at the first, 80 awards were made at the second. By the time of the tenth exhibition in 1844, 3,960 industrialists participated, and 3,253 medals were awarded. It had frequently been suggested that Paris industrial exhibitions take place annually, and it had even been proposed that the one to be held in 1849 be made international. Political events prevented this, but the international exhibition the British organized in 1851 was closely modeled on the French example and on the 1849 show in particular.

Planning for the 1855 exposition began even before the Crystal Palace had closed its doors. French motives for wanting to organize a similar event in Paris were mixed. One aim, of course, was to seize back the initiative from the British. Another was to use the exposition to enhance the stature of the new regime and to trumpet French prowess in cultural and material domains. There was also a profit motive. On March 27, 1852, the government approved the formation of a private company that would build and operate a permanent structure to house future industrial exhibitions (previous exhibitions had been held either in temporary buildings or in space allocated in the Louvre). The state donated the land and guaranteed a minimum 4 percent annual return on the original capital; in return, it would gain possession of the building in 1898. Though the exposition

itself lost money, the company that built and operated the chief exhibition building earned a profit.

The holding of an exposition that would include both industrial and fine arts
exhibits was announced in imperial decrees of March 8 and June 22, 1853, and
the following December, a commission of thirty-seven was put in charge of organizing the event. This body, which was divided into two sections, one for
agriculture and industry and the other for the fine arts, included leading political figures, such as Jules Baroche and the duc de Morny, as well as artists like
Jean Ingres and Eugène Delacroix. Responsibility for detailed planning, however, rested with a smaller group that included the emperor's cousin, Prince
Napoleon, who proved an effective chair of the commission, Frédéric Le Play,
a prominent social thinker, Michel Chevalier, an economist, and Emile Pereire, a financier.

It was originally intended that the entire exhibition would be housed in the
Palais de l'Industrie, which the private company was to build on the Grand Carré
de Marigny, a promenade and recreation area along the still little developed
Champs Elysées, a site now occupied by the Grand and Petit Palais, themselves
built for the 1900 exposition. The structure that was erected had two remarkable
features. One was the speed with which it was completed. The other, more
important, was the innovative use that its engineer, Alexandre Barrault, and, to
a lesser extent, its architect, Jean-Marie Viel, made of modern materials to give
height and light to the building. They designed an iron frame, 250 meters long,
108 meters wide, and 35 meters high, and incorporated reinforced glass in the
roof. The Palais de l'Industrie thus resembled Paxton's Crystal Palace. Barrault
also drew on the examples of the metal and glass canopies of the first Parisian
railroad stations; its design prefigured that of the department stores that were to
develop rapidly in the Paris of the Second Empire. The Palais de l'Industrie,
though, also had two signal disadvantages. One was that, like Victor Baltard's
original design for the new Paris central market that Napoleon III had rejected
in 1853, and like what was already happening to Parisian railroad termini, the
daring engineering was sadly hidden behind a facade that was a pastiche of past
architectural styles; the metal frame was encased in heavy stone facing. The
other was that the hall proved ill suited to meet the needs of the 1855 exposition.
Not only did inadequate ventilation make the building too hot, a problem that
the fitting of muslin screens only marginally alleviated in the warm summer of
1855, but insufficient space obliged organizers to build two additional temporary
structures: a long gallery along the quai de Billy, parallel to the Palais de
l'Industrie, and, at the end of the avenue Montaigne, a building in the French
Renaissance style, designed by the architect Hector Le Fuel, which was to house
the fine arts exhibits.

Despite the delays and the additional buildings that had to be hastily erected,
the exposition that opened on May 15 and closed on November 15, 1855, was
in many respects more successful than its London predecessor. It occupied a site
that, at 117,000 square meters, was over half again as large as that of the Crystal

Palace and at 11 million francs (not counting the main building paid for by the private company) cost nearly 50 percent more. It also attracted a much higher number of exhibitors: 20,839 came from thirty-four countries. Nearly half of the exhibitors were French, with the British easily outdistancing all other nationalities. The fine arts exhibition alone included 5,000 works by 2,054 artists representing twenty-nine states. Here, France's numerical domination was even more pronounced: 3,634 of the paintings and sculptures were by French artists. In one other respect, though, the Paris exposition was not as successful as its London predecessor. Although it attracted 5,162,330 visitors, the great majority of whom came on Sundays when the admission charge was reduced to a minimal 20 centimes, this total was nearly a million fewer than that for the Crystal Palace. The exposition, indeed, suffered a loss of 8.3 million francs, as compared to the profit that was put to such practical use in London.

The layout of the exhibits in the Palais de l'Industrie and in the glass gallery along the quai de Billy is noteworthy for two reasons. First, exhibits were arranged according to a classification devised by Frédéric Le Play. This proved too elaborate to be fully effective, however, and visitors complained they could not follow it. Second, the exposition had the beginnings of thematic displays. One of these was a theme for which Napoleon III had long professed concern: the living conditions of the working classes. Articles destined for workers' consumption were prominently displayed, as were models of projected workers' housing. A second featured theme was European expansion in general and overseas colonies in particular. Though not given the prominence they were later accorded, colonies were presented in the same way as at some later fairs: exhibits on the extra-European world stressed cultural differences, especially exoticism, and they also emphasized the vast potential colonies possessed for supplying Europe with agricultural and mineral products. Understandably, the British gave pride of place to their vast Indian possession and presented a reconstitution of an Indian court, furnished with rich rugs, hangings, and craftwork. The French stressed the potential offered by Algeria, their more recent colonial conquest.

As at London in 1851, greatest emphasis in the two main pavilions was laid on the increasing capacity to harness nature, on what was a vital element in the spreading nineteenth-century faith in progress: technology. Technology dominated the glass gallery, where machines were driven by a common transmission belt, thus symbolically demonstrating the interdependence of the different processes and branches of advancing industrial capitalism. The exposition came too soon on the heels of the Crystal Palace Exhibition for there to be major new technical advances on display. New machines and processes there were, though, and among the more notable were the Singer sewing machines from the United States that successfully synthesized previous developments, the Ruolz silver electroplating process—Napoleon III purchased a 1,200-place dinner service of silver plate—and the production, albeit in small quantities, of a newly discovered metal, aluminum. The technology on show, as well as the distribution of medals of excellence, demonstrated two points about British and French industry, which dominated the exposition. First, the technology gap, which had been considerable immediately after the ending of the Napoleonic wars, had narrowed by 1855. Tariff reformers in France, indeed, sought to use the success of French exhibitors as an argument to persuade their government to follow Britain's lead and lower or even abolish customs barriers. Second, the exposition showed that if there was rivalry between British and French industrialists, there was also complementarity: if British technology was more successful in heavy engineering, metallurgy, and the preparatory, spinning, and weaving processes in textiles, the French excelled in textile finishing processes and in producing high-quality goods that required significant design and flair.

The pavilion on the avenue Montaigne attracted only one in five of the visitors to the exposition, but the million people who visited the fine arts exhibition still made it an exceptional success. It also attracted the most critical attention in the press. The exposition organizers had early decided on a new departure. There would be a fine arts exhibition that would be retrospective; all artists living in June 1853 were eligible to show, with national juries choosing the works they wanted to represent their country. The French expected to be able to demonstrate to the world the prowess of their artists. They were not disappointed. Sculpture was dominated by Frenchmen: François Rude, Francisque Duret, and Augustin Dumont were each awarded the highest medals. French painters were even more prominent, and whole sections of the pavilion were devoted to the works of Ingres, Delacroix, Alexandre DeCamps, and Emile Vernet. At the same time, however, the exposition also revealed strains in the French art world. The French jury still favored the morally uplifting art that successive governments patronized and, although it accepted some of the works of Gustave Courbet, it rejected two that posterity would consider two of the finest of this young realist painter: *Burial at Ornans* and *The Studio of the Painter*. In retaliation, Courbet organized his own rival exhibition in a tent set up opposite the fine arts pavilion, producing a catalog and charging admission. When viewed in a longer perspective, his gesture, mocked by critics at the time, becomes one of a number of symbolic challenges to the power of the salon and government patronage. Complacency about the easy supremacy of French art was also shaken by the popular success enjoyed by the foreign, and particularly British, art. With John Constable and J.M.W. Turner both dead, Britain did not possess living artists of the stature of Ingres and Delacroix, and French critics were often scathing about British genre painting and the absence in their works of what they considered proper historical subjects. However, both they and the French public were brought into contact with some of the finest early Victorian artists—William Powell Frith, Edwin Landseer, William Holman Hunt, John Everett Millais—who until then had been very little known across the channel. Besides, critics could not hide their envy that British artists were more widely supported by private patrons than were their French counterparts, still overwhelmingly dependent on government support. And whatever art critics wrote, British, and to a lesser extent Belgian and German, painting enjoyed considerable popular success. In yet another respect, then, the exposition served to open contemporaries' eyes to new realities.

BIBLIOGRAPHY

Like other world's fairs, the 1855 exposition has not yet received the attention from scholars that it deserves. In consequence, the most useful and informative sources remain the government-sponsored atlases, guides, and, especially, the reports of the commission set up to organize the exposition, all published between 1855 and 1857. These are: *Exposition universelle de 1855. Atlas descriptif. Dressé par ordre de S.A.I. le prince Napoléon* (1855); *Catalogue officiel publié par ordre de la Commission imperiale* (1855); *Rapport sur l'Exposition universelle de 1855 présenté à l'Empéreur par S.A.I. le prince Napoléon* (1857); and *Rapports du jury mixte international publiés sous la direction de S.A.I. le prince Napoléon*, 2 vols. (1856). For Canada's participation at the exposition, see *Canada at the Universal Exhibition of 1855* (1856), published by the Canadian Executive Committee for the Paris Exhibition.

Those wishing to go beyond contemporary published sources should know that the archives of the Seine Department and the Prefecture of Police contain little on the Paris exposition, mainly because they suffered irreparable losses when the Communards burned the Hôtel de Ville and the police headquarters in 1871. The Archives Nationales, however, has a number of important dossiers on the planning of the event, on bringing exhibits to Paris, and on the awards made (especially in the F^{12} series from the Ministère de commerce et de l'industrie and the LH series from the Grande chancellerie de la Légion d'honneur).

Three kinds of secondary works are available on the 1855 exposition. One consists of studies of the nineteenth-century exhibitions in general and of Paris expositions in particular. These have generally been written without consulting archives or attempting to use exhibitions as windows to study technology, culture, or values. The most useful of these is Werner Plum, *Les Expositions universelles au XIXe siècle, spectacles du changement socio-culturel* (1977). Less helpful are Pascal Ory, *Les Expositions universelles de Paris* (1982), and Raymond Isay, *Panorama des expositions universelles* (1937).

The second type of study deals with ancillary aspects of the exposition. Achille de Colmont, *Histoire des expositions de l'industrie français* (1855), which gives a descriptive analysis of French industrial exhibitions, has still not been superseded, an indication of the poverty of the historiography. Madeleine Rebérioux, a leading social historian, has suggested paths future research might take in "Approches à l'histoire des expositions universelles à Paris, du Second Empire à 1900," *Bulletin du Centre d'histoire économique et sociale de la région lyonnaise* 1 (1979): 1–17. François Laisney has published a brief and superficial article on the architecture of the French expositions, "L'Architecture industrielle dans les expositions universelles," *Monuments historiques* 3 (1977): 41–45.

The fine arts exhibits are the only facet of the 1855 exposition to have been examined seriously by scholars. The most recent and detailed of this type of study is Patricia Mainardi, *Art and Politics of the Second Empire: The Universal Expositions of 1855 and 1867* (1987). Still useful, though, are Marcia Poynton, "From the Midst of Warfare and Its Incidents to the Peaceful Scenes of Home," *Journal of European Studies* 11 (1981):

233–61; Elizabeth G. Holt, *The Art of All Nations, 1850–1873: The Emerging Role of Exhibitions and Critics* (1981), which deals with the impact of the fair on art; and Guillemette Delaporte, "L'Exposition universelle de 1855 à Paris: Confrontations de cultures et prises de conscience," *L'Ecrit-Voir* 6 (1985): 5–10. A recent and well-written survey of the exposition is Arthur Chandler, "Fanfare for the New Empire: The Paris Exposition Universelle of 1855," *World's Fair* 6, no. 2 (Spring 1986), 11–16.

Barrie M. Ratcliffe

LONDON 1862

INTERNATIONAL EXHIBITION OF 1862

Does a palace of glass cast a shadow? The members of the Royal Commission that supervised the International Exhibition learned the hard way that it did. They sought to follow up on and surpass the success of the 1851 Crystal Palace Exhibition. They promised a larger exhibition (a building covering 23½ acres), with more exhibitors (26,336), more foreign representation (17,851 exhibitors), more colonies participating (35), more money expended. Following the successful examples of the Paris 1855 exhibition and the Manchester 1857 art exhibition, they widened the scope of their exhibition to include fine arts, as well as raw materials, manufactured goods, and machinery in motion. In fine arts as in industrial arts, they promised more: twice the wallspace of the Manchester show, 6,529 works of painting, sculpture, and engraving by 2,305 English and European artists. The commission counted on the progress of industry not only to be the main feature of the exhibition but also to facilitate its success; transportation networks and print media had expanded rapidly over the decade. Prince Albert himself predicted in 1861 that the success of 1851 would be "rivalled, and, I trust, surpassed, by the beauty and success" of the following year's exhibition.

But the commissioners failed. Almost all commentators compared the exhibitions of 1851 and 1862. All agreed the successor was bigger, that no collection of goods could be compared to that found there, that in its halls world progress was much evident. Few preferred it. The press covered it richly but often critically. The crowds came but not in substantially larger numbers (6,211,103 as compared to 6,039,195 eleven years before). The commissioners who had so successfully collected guarantees for £450,000 by advance subscription and had spent more than that putting it on, barely broke even. But the 1862 exhibition had to contend with death and war as well as with memories of the Crystal Palace.

The death was that of Prince Albert in December 1861. His death and Victoria's deep widowhood meant, most obviously, that the 1862 exhibition would open without the presence of royalty. The commissioners stood in for the absent queen, and the temporary throne erected for the ceremony stood empty, with busts of the mourning monarch and the late prince on either side. Albert's death had deeper significance because of the central role he had played in the 1851 exhibition; he was less involved in the preparations for 1862, but his symbolic presence and support meant much. The measure of the loss can be found in the opening day's ceremonies: the beginning lines of every speech referred to Albert's death. The choral ode that Alfred Tennyson, the poet laureate, penned for the occasion addressed the "silent father of our Kings to be" and insisted the exhibition's "world-compelling plan was thine." Every newspaper article about the opening enlarged upon the theme.

Further, the Crystal Palace had been taken by many as the symbol of a new era of world peace. But, as a writer in *Fraser's* put it, "No sooner had the doors of the Exhibition of 1851 closed than the nations of the earth rose to war." The overthrow of the French republic, the mutiny in India, the Crimean War, and conflicts in Lombardy and Sicily had marked the decade. In the United States, the Civil War raged. To the needs of war industry responded, and many visitors to the exhibition noted that one of the most visible forms of industrial progress was in the machinery of war. For instance, the Birmingham small arms trophy could not be disguised by the *Illustrated London News*'s attempts to describe it as art: "a cornice enrichment is also formed . . . with bayonets . . . The angles of the roof are rendered ornamental by being crocketed with heavy pistols." Dreams of world peace could in no way enrich the industrial display of London's second exhibition.

For the loss of that ideal, the exhibition had nothing to substitute but industrial progress itself. "The whole thing will be treated more in a spirit of business, and less as a novel entertainment," the *Illustrated London News* promised, "the competition between foreigners and ourselves will be more real, painstaking, energetic, and critical." This could, however, also be seen as the "portentious Bedlam of peddlar sovereignty" that Frederick Greenwood lamented in *Cornhill's*. Against the proud claim of the *Times* that "the only real jury in the question of manufactures is the consumer," the *Quarterly Review* countered that "while art has certainly made progress, so also has puffery and shoppiness." Without an ideal vision of peace through commerce, the exhibition could claim more practicality but not more luster.

The U.S. Civil War had even more direct effects on the exhibition. It was for a time questionable whether the United States would participate at all, especially since the war raised tensions between the United States and Great Britain. In congressional debate, Congressman Roscoe Conkling (R-New York) argued against participation because "we have a World's Fair now in session on this continent"; Congressman Owen Lovejoy (R-Illinois), more vociferously anti-British, insisted, "I think it is enough for us, in all conscience, to have been humbugged, and dishonoured, and disgraced by the British nation, without now appropriating $35,000 for the purposes of an American Exhibition there." The United States did finally participate, but on a small scale and at such short notice that its exhibition space was limited to a small corner.

In Britain, meanwhile, the Civil War's disastrous impact on the textile industry was felt in the exhibition hall. The display from Spitalfield, the *Times* noted, "was on a small scale" because of the shortage of cotton. Reporting on the first day of shilling admissions, *Chambers's Journal* observed that "the mechanical crowd" was "somewhat lacking" among the visitors; they "have not even shillings to spend this year" because of the war's impact. The exhibition even lost its general manager, Colonel Lawrence Shadwell, to the war, when in the wake of the *Trent* affair, involving the forced removal of two Confederate commissioners by U.S. naval forces from a British ship, British reserves were sent to Canada.

To judge from the conduct of the commission, the manager's loss was sorely felt. What the *Quarterly Review* called the "bungling inefficiency" of the Royal Commission affected almost every detail of the exhibition. The reasons for the failure are not evident in the composition of the commission the queen appointed in 1860; Earl Granville had served on the commission of 1851 and Wentworth Dilke on its executive committee; William Fairbairn, a successful civil engineer and a founder of the British Association for the Advancement of Science, had been involved with the Manchester Art Exhibition; the marquis of Chandos and Thomas Baring, M.P., were both successful businessmen. They had the support of the Royal Society of Arts, the financial backing of many prominent citizens, and the cooperation of both the 1851 commission, whose grounds they leased, and the Royal Horticultural Society, whose gardens their plot of land abutted. But bungle they did.

The exhibition building was their most colossal blunder. The massive structure, designed by naval engineer Captain Francis Fowke after all proposals by architects were rejected, consisted of an ironwork nave cut across by two transepts, with gigantic glass domes at each intersection; a picture gallery of brick, intended to be permanent, that ran the full 1,250-foot length of the front facade; and two temporary annexes, one for machines in motion and one for agricultural produce. The structure had the advantage of being large; otherwise it was not well received. The *Art Journal* called it a "wretched shed" and a "national disgrace"; *Fraser's* termed the "monstrous piles" an "architectural fungus"; *Illustrated London News* thought it "would be absurd" to call it architecture. The domes, bigger than St. Paul's Cathedral, were "as useless as unsightly" (*Art Journal*), "truly ludicrous" (*Once a Week*), "colossal dish covers" (*Fraser's*). *Quarterly Review* called it an "ignorant, presumptuous, tasteless, extravagant failure." Its defenders made rather a weak case for it. A French correspondent opined to the *Times* of "the big dome built on boards and half hid by the big shed," that if his emperor visited, "I hope in charity you will bring him into building blindfooled," and that "even the little boy the guide he say 'dam ugly,' " and the *Times*'s defense was at best tepid: "That the exterior is very ugly no one denies," but it was large, cheap, effective for display purposes, and had "a fine interior." The commissioners themselves insisted on its utilitarian value, its cheapness, the speed with which it had been built, and the potential to change it later.

The building was only the first difficulty the commissioners encountered. During preparations, complaints arose about poor access to the Brompton site and about space assignments by both nations and individual exhibitors. Interior decorations were critiqued for "show[ing] a lamentable lack of taste" (*Temple Bar*). The *Times* lamented haphazard construction, the array of packing boxes, and the permission granted the French court to wall off its portion of the nave. There was confusion about press privileges, rights of season ticket holders, the order, reserved seating, and proper dress for the opening. On the musical side, Giuseppe Verdi's composition for the opening ceremony was refused by the commissioners because it was a chorale instead of a march, and musical director Michael Costa's refusal to conduct Sterndale Bennett's choral setting of Tennyson's ode became public knowledge. Pains were taken to build the hall around a living tree, but the commissioners then assigned that space to the Sheffield exhibitors, and the tree was cut down because watering it would rust the iron objects on exhibit.

After opening day, the commissioners did no better. The "trophies" they had allowed exhibitors to construct even the usually temperate *Times* called "very large and very ugly things" producing a "hideous anarchy" in the arrangement of the nave. Most of them were removed, but not without objection from the exhibitors and expense for the commission. The official illustrated catalog, issued by the commissioners and financed with paid pages by exhibitors, was, when it belatedly came out, dismissed by the *Times* as "dull and most unsatisfactory . . . two volumes of tradesmen's advertisements." Francis Palgrave's catalog of the fine arts collection had to be withdrawn when the commissioners realized— after the *Times* pointed it out—that it was "of a character likely to be painful to the feelings of artists who have been invited to exhibit their works." Columnists criticized the state of unpreparedness on opening day, the refreshment service for bad service and high prices, ticket arrangements, and crowd handling. There was at least one fatality in the machines-in-motion annex. Even the perfumed waters of the fountain received complaints; the *Illustrated London News* demanded a scent with "a less cloying and sickly effect." More critical to the financial outcome of the exhibition, the commissioners overestimated attendance, scheduled too few of the popular shilling days, sold too few of the unpopular catalogs, and continued to find themselves faced with unexpected expenses.

But the International Exhibition did open on May 1, as scheduled. The opening featured a ceremonial procession (a "meagre pageant," the *Art Journal* called it) and music by Daniel-François-Esprit Auber, Sterndale Bennett, and Giacomo Meyerbeer if not Verdi (many complained that they could not hear it). Surveying the vast collection illustrating the industrial and artistic progress of nations, the *Illustrated London News* declared, "Let us look at ourselves as we are in the mirror of this Exhibition."

In that mirror each nation saw, above all else, itself. "No other country but this," the *Times* claimed, "could have built it in the time and, above all, no other country could pay the enormous cost." In his account for *Revue des deux mondes*, Alphonse Esquiros wrote: "The idea of a universal exposition,—as the English themselves admit,—is a French idea: it is bound up with the principles of the revolution of '89." Of his country's steel industry, German journalist Lother Bucher wrote, "It will be seen that England has fallen behind Germany." The internationalism of the exhibition, whatever the general claims made about universal progress, was above all else nationalistic, an internationalism of competing nations.

The competition began before the opening, in the very preparations for the exhibition. The *Times* cast the progress of exhibitors in terms of national struggle, warning "that the building will be open with the foreign courts complete and beautifully arranged, while the English will have their counters and cases but half-finished, and their displays, of course, proportionately ill-arranged and ill-shown." After almost daily harping, the English exhibitors finally progressed at a rate the paper approved, and by the week before the opening the British were "very far in advance of their foreign competitors," especially the French. The French wall—the partitioning of the French court from the nave to increase display space—seemed an emblematic display of nationalistic insularity, and, reversing the conventional cliché, the *Times* complained that it would "break up what should be one grand Exhibition into a number of detached courts as distinct from each other as so many shops." Also part of the competitive struggle were warnings that the goods of other nations would triumph over domestic products unless the exhibitors prepared well.

In the industrial department, the nationalistic aspect of the exhibition took the form of claims of superior workmanship. The *British Quarterly*, for example, claimed that "no people has invented so much that is useful and necessary to man as the British race," and specified superiority in civil engineering, agricultural implements, ironwork, machine making, pottery, and furniture. The French tended to cede machinery to the British but to claim precedence in ornamental work. Esquiros wrote that the English were masters at "applying the resources of industry to the needs of science and commerce" but that the French were "an artistic race, which masters above all charm, sobriety, and taste in ornament." For precisely the reason that their accomplishments in the field were less assured, British commentators emphasized their achievements in the ornamental industrial arts, especially pottery, furniture, and jewelry. Other countries' efforts were belittled. Only when a nation's industrial progress did not threaten major industrial powers could it be safely celebrated: the potential industrial rebirth of a newly united Italy was celebrated by the British press.

Apparently more international in character was the role the 1862 exhibition played in the diffusion of technical knowledge; most notably, it is often credited with the spread of the Bessemer process to Germany. Also noteworthy is the fact that the nations of divided Germany participated together as the Zollverein. Even here, though, nationalism played a part. On a small scale, the Zollverein department remained subdivided into individual, competitive units. On a larger scale, these processes of economic centralization contributed to the *Grossdeutsch* ideology of German unification. The process was recognized as one of nationalistic consolidation at the time of the exhibition by Edmund Yates, who wrote in *Temple Bar* that the continued progress of German industry would be impossible without unification.

The fruits of empire provided another vehicle for nationalistic display, especially by Great Britain. Although the 1862 exhibition lacked the blatant imperial display of later exhibitions, it already featured the major elements of imperialist ideology: an ethnological approach to subject people and a division of labor between industrial and nonindustrial underpinned by the ideology of free trade.

Esquiros, guiding his readers through the exhibition, rearranged its map: "Would it not be interesting to take industry as a point of departure, to follow the stages in the development of the races, and see how human power appears but by successive degrees among the groups around the world?" His tour moves from black to "stagnated" Asian to European, culminating with France and England. The tour simultaneously moves from raw materials to mining and small manufactures to full-scale industry. Similarly, Robert Hunt, in the *Synopsis* of the official handbook, treats Australian aborigines, Indians, and settler colonists as successive levels of development. Journalistic accounts took the ethnographic approach to the displays not only of colonies but also of non-Western nations (especially Liberia and Japan).

It was the role of colonies to supply the raw goods European industry needed; that role was underlined by the dominance of raw materials in the displays of colonial possessions. Free trade reinforced the system by making the division of labor part of the natural law of economics. As Esquiros put it, "The system of free trade has the effect . . . of reinforcing the spirit of specialization that applies to local production." Attempts on the part of colonists to resist such classification were ignored. Thus in the 1862 exhibition, fine arts contributions by New South Wales and India, including oil painting, were relegated to the national courts and not shown with other fine arts works. Only those forms of art specifically designed for Western consumption were not so despised; thus the *Times* approved of Bengali ivory carvers introducing perspective in their landscapes under the influence of Western forms and markets. The *Synopsis* said of a gilt-framed mirror in the New Brunswick collection that it was included "as if to mark the march of refinement in the colony." Colonial manufacture could only be described in quaint, not productive or artistic, terms.

Of all the displays at the 1862 exhibition, the fine arts galleries most blatantly reinforced nationalism. The arrangements lent themselves to the display of national schools of art. With the general theme of "progress and present condition of the arts," each country was permitted to select not only its own artists but also the time period covered. This allowed each country to select a founder for its national school of art and to trace "progress" from the founder to the present. The French alone chose to exhibit only recent work, a gesture that seemed to reflect their confidence in their established preeminence in fine arts.

The British, on the other hand, began their selection in 1762 in order to include William Hogarth, whom Theodore Gautier called "absolutely original" and "thoroughly English." Hogarth was represented by thirty-three works and was followed by generous collections of Joshua Reynolds and Thomas Gainsborough. This founding trio established the basis for the English national school as in-dividualistic, strongly based on nature, and defiant of academicism and classicism. Its strengths were thus in portraiture, landscape, and genre painting, its weaknesses in "higher" forms like history paintings. Commentators traced the sociopolitical roots of the national school to the rise of commerce, the independence of art from state patronage, and the "free thought and political agitation" that came with the move to a more democratic government after the Glorious Revolution of 1688. The successors were then measured against this standard. Those whose styles seemed conventional, continentally influenced, "high," or academic tended to be dismissed, as did those whose works departed from naturalism. A line of naturalists, from Richard Wilson to John Constable to David Wilkie to the contemporary pre-Raphaelites, carried on the English tradition.

Similar assessments, slanted by a bias in favor of naturalism as a more progressive mode, were made of other national schools. The French were conventional, their individuality trained out of them. This gave them confidence and formal precision, which equipped them for history painting and monumental art, but it removed them from the study of nature and made their works artificial and potentially decadent. The Germans were consistently criticized for being too philosophical, for sublimating art to ideas, and for being too rigorously academic. The Russian czar's attempt to import European art forms failed for lack of indigenous roots, leading to mere imitation. Dutch domestic scenes and Norse nature studies perfectly fitted their national characters. The progress of nations was abundantly mirrored in their arts.

When the 1862 exhibition closed in November, it had not succeeded in making a profit or in supplanting the Crystal Palace in people's memories. It may have succeeded in diffusing technical knowledge more widely, with such innovations as the Bessemer process and Babbage's calculating machine. But it most certainly succeeded in cementing the institutional structure of world exhibitions; as intended, it established a decennial pattern for future English exhibitions. And above all else, by dissolving the visionary ambitions of the 1851 fair and substituting its own more worldly aims, it succeeded in confirming the nature of international exhibitions as fields for competitive nationalism.

BIBLIOGRAPHY

The catalog to the British Museum collection lists over a hundred official publications and unofficial guides to the 1862 exhibition, including separate catalogs for many foreign and colonial displays and for many specific classes of objects; thirty-five of these are also held in the Library of Congress. Official handbooks sold at the exhibition site and published in 1862 include a two-volume *Industrial Catalogue;* a *Fine Arts Catalogue*; an *Official Illustrated Catalogue* in thirteen parts; a *Concise History of the International Exhibition* by John Hollinshead; *Robert Hunt's Handbook to the Official Catalogue (Natural Products) and the International Exhibition of 1862* in ten parts, or bound in one volume; *A Synopsis of the Contents of the Industrial Department of the Exhibition* also by Robert

Hunt; and a *Synopsis of a Complete Guide to the Contents of the International Exhibition of 1862*, again by Robert Hunt. All official catalogs featured brief descriptions, names and addresses of exhibitors, and large numbers of paid advertisements. They were generally panned by contemporary critics, and, judging from the last-named of them, their brief descriptions cannot be very useful to historians. In addition, Francis Palgrave wrote *Handbook to the Fine Arts in the International Exhibition of 1862*, but because of its harsh treatment of some exhibiting artists, the royal commissioners withdrew it; an independent edition was also sold, however. Contemporary critics most often mention the unofficial guides: *Routledge's Guide to the International Exhibition*, edited by George Frederick Pardon; *A Plain Guide to the Exhibition*, published by Sampson and Low, and aimed at those planning a one-day visit; and *Penny Guide to the International Exhibition*. A fairly accessible alternative guide was the well-illustrated *Art Journal Catalogue to the International Exhibition of 1862*, published both as a single bound volume and as part of *Art Journal*. Curiously, it did not treat the fine arts but only the ornamental aspects of the industrial arts and those industrial displays that applied to art materials.

The exhibition was thoroughly covered in both the *Times* and *Illustrated London News*. The *Times* featured practically daily general accounts from early 1862 on, as well as columns on particular aspects of the exhibition, and the letters to the editor serve well as a good guide to ongoing controversies. *Illustrated London News* did features on the exhibition nearly every week, with especially rich coverage in May and June, including general updates, detailed discussions of particular exhibits, descriptions of individual pictures, exhibition gossip (in its "Echoes" column), and an irregular column on the fair from "a feminine point of view." There were, of course, many pictures, including foldout maps and illustrations and tinted inserts.

Contemporary periodicals also covered the fair extensively. The most detailed criticism of exhibition arrangements can be found in [A. J. Beresford] Hope, "The International Exhibition," *Quarterly Review* 112 (1862), 179–214; other good but hostile accounts include John Horner's two pieces in *Once a Week* and several pieces in *Fraser's* and *Bentley's Miscellany*. An interesting sympathetic view is Esquiros's extended treatment, "L'Exposition universelle de 1862," in *Revue des deux mondes* 40 (1862). The best treatment of the fine arts can be found in Atkinson's series of columns on national arts in *Art Journal*, the two features on art in *London Society* (the nonart articles in the same volume are less interesting), W. M. Rossetti's article in *Fraser's* (restricted to living artists), and the three translated excerpts from Theodore Gautier in *Temple Bar* (on English art only). For sheer quirkiness, "How a Blind Man Saw the Exhibition" in *Temple Bar* and the serialized fictional feature, "Mossoo's Visit to the International Exhibition," about two Frenchmen visiting the exhibition, in *Bentley's* should not be overlooked.

Secondary sources have largely overlooked the 1862 Exhibition or dismissed it as a failed Crystal Palace. Paul Greenhalgh's *Ephemeral Vistas* (1988) gives 1862 regular, if not prominent, treatment and is in general a solidly organized discussion of major themes of exhibitions. Evelyn Kroker's *Die Weltausstellungen im 19. Jahrhundert* (1975) is possibly the only work that claims the 1862 exhibition was more central than 1851 (and in Paris 1867 was more central than 1855). The grounds for the argument, however, are for the most part restricted to German national and economic development.

Thomas Prasch

DUBLIN 1865

INTERNATIONAL EXHIBITION OF ARTS AND MANUFACTURES

The Dublin exhibition of 1865 was initiated by a group of wealthy and influential citizens, among them, the duke of Leinster, Lord Talbot de Malahide, and Dublin brewer Benjamin Lee Guinness, who wished to extend the city's cultural and educational facilities. They proposed to erect a large complex comprising a winter garden, concert hall, art gallery, display area for manufactures, and facilities for lectures on the arts and sciences. Dublin, despite being the second largest city of the British empire, had no institution providing such resources for all social classes. To achieve these ends, they established a private company: the Dublin Exhibition Palace and Winter Garden Co., with a capital of £50,000 and decided to hold an international exhibition as a way of launching the new venture. The enterprise was undoubtedly influenced by the success of London's 1862 exhibition and by the value of the Crystal Palace facilities.

The company acquired the former Coburg pleasure gardens, a 17-acre site leased on nominal terms by Guinness. This site was in the fashionable southeast section of the city, close to railway lines and to Dublin's most exclusive suburbs. The London architect A. G. Jones constructed a building in two parts. The main building consisted of three separate floors; the ground floor was framed by a piazza with Doric columns that contained lecture rooms, exhibition rooms, and a concert hall. Above this, there was a sky-lighted hall surmounted by a dome with two levels of galleries. The winter garden directly adjoined the rear of the building.

The exhibition attracted substantially more foreign interest than the 1853 exhibition. Twenty-one foreign countries and twenty-two British colonies participated, supplying more than 2,300 exhibits; a conscious decision was made to restrict British and Irish exhibits in favor of foreign contributions; more than two-thirds of all exhibits were foreign. The committee, however, also sought to display the progress made by Irish industry since the previous exhibition.

The display was organized in a manner similar to the London exhibition of 1862 with exhibits divided into five industrial categories plus fine arts but with exhibits shown in national groups. The winter garden area provided fountains, mazes, and cascades in addition to wonders such as a column of coal from Nova Scotia. Despite the more elaborate attractions and the keen promotion of railway season tickets, attendance, at 956,295, was 200,000 below the 1853 figures, possibly due to the fair's coinciding with economic depression. Receipts amounted to £45,000, sufficient to cover all operating costs and to pay a rent of £10,000 for the building. It was felt, however, that Ireland needed a longer interval between international exhibitions in the future.

Dublin's first tramline, laid between the exhibition hall and a distant railway station, was removed. The company continued to organize further smaller national exhibitions in subsequent years and attempted without success in the 1880s to mount a permanent national industrial exhibition on the current wave of Irish patriotism. When this venture failed, the company folded, and the buildings became the property of the Royal University. Today, however, much rebuilt on this site is Ireland's National Concert Hall.

BIBLIOGRAPHY

Henry Parkinson and Peter Lund Simmonds, *The Illustrated Record and Descriptive Catalogue of the Dublin International Exhibition 1865* (1866), provides a detailed account of the initiatives that led to the 1865 exhibition. It also includes line drawings and detailed descriptions of buildings and exhibits. *Dublin International Exhibition 1865. Official Catalogue* (1865) is also useful. William F. Wakeman, *Tourist's Guide through Dublin and Its Interesting Suburbs Specially Suited to the Visitors of the International Exhibition* (1865), as the name suggests, devotes more attention to the Dublin area than to the exhibition. There is also a comic treatment: *Dublin International Exhibition 1865, Comic Catalogue* (1865).

Mary E. Daly

PARIS 1867
EXPOSITION UNIVERSELLE

In 1867, 7 million people came to see Emperor Napoleon's answer to the challenge of the 1862 London International Exhibition. Eleven years after the first Great Exhibition of 1851, the British had proved to the world that it was no easy matter to repeat a resounding success. Napoleon decided, twelve years after the first French Exposition universelle, that the French could and should surpass the efforts of their ancient rival.

What the visitors saw was more than just a bigger and better show. In its attempt to classify and organize every branch of human activity and to invest that activity with moral purpose, the 1867 Exposition universelle symbolized the encyclopedic ambitions of the Second Empire. Every aspect of the Parisian exposition, from the overall plan for exhibits to the final awarding of medals, would proceed from a single conviction: the bounty of nature could be transformed into universal harmony for the human race.

To spread this message, the Empire enlisted some of the best talent in France to proclaim Paris not only the host of the exposition but the seat of a new order for the human race. Victor Hugo was commissioned to write the introduction to the *Paris Guide* for 1867; Théophile Gautier, to introduce visitors to the treasures of the Louvre; Alphonse Viollet-le-Duc to show the proud heritage of the cathedrals of Paris. Hippolyte Taine, Alexandre Dumas *fils*, Ernest Renan, Sainte-Beuve—all contributed the powers of their pens to promote the glory of France. The *Paris Guide* that year was a showcase for the intellectual power of France's writers, just as the great oval palace on the Champ de Mars would be the showcase for its industrialists and artists. The Exposition universelle would be a vast choral symphony, with the best talents of France harmonizing under the baton of Napoleon III.

Engineers and painters, Parisian laborers and colonial sultans all worked to make the exposition not merely a success but a triumph, a living proof that France was the leader of the world and Paris the capital of the new civilization. In the closing words of his *Paris Guide* essay, Hugo rang out the most noble aspiration of the age:

Down with war! Let there be alliance! Concord! Unity! . . .

O France, adieu! Thou art too great to remain merely a fatherland. To become a goddess, thou must be separated from motherhood. Soon thou shalt vanish in a transfiguration. Thou shalt no longer be France: thou shalt be Humanity! No longer a nation, thou shalt be Ubiquity. Thou art destined to dissolve utterly, radiating outward, tran-

This article was originally published in *World's Fair* in somewhat altered form and is printed here with the permission of the publisher.

scending thy frontiers. Resign thyself to thy immensity. Adieu, O people! Hail, Humankind! Submit to thy sublime and fateful enlargement, O my country; and as Athens became Greece, as Rome became Christianity, thou, France, become the world! (Vol. 1, 1867: xliii-xliv)

Hugo was a great visionary but no prophet. He could not foresee the coming of the Franco-Prussian War, the brutal siege and capitulation of Paris and France, the capture and disgraced exile of Napoleon III, the Prussian troops marching down the Champs Elysées, the massacres of the Commune Revolt. Dazzled by the brilliance of a revitalized Paris and the splendors of the world's fair, Hugo was temporarily blinded to the old blood rivalries between nations—antagonisms that could not be banished by words or expositions. In 1867 Paris was a harvest banquet, a rich repast where all the fruits of autumn were there on the Champ de Mars for all to enjoy.

By the end of the fifth act in 1872, Parisians were reduced to trapping rats for food.

Few visitors to the exposition of 1867 went directly to the central exhibit hall. Surrounding the main building was a vast four-sectioned park. The area was originally meant to be a continuation of the interior exhibition space: a place where nations could erect large pavilions or displays that could not conveniently be housed inside.

Such was the plan. In reality, the effect of the park was "picturesque confusion," if one found it charming and amusing to visit or "a trivial game," if one thought it contrary in spirit to the tone of high seriousness espoused by the Imperial Exposition Commission.

Most visitors apparently wandered among the wonders of the park without too much thought for deeper meanings. One could amble contentedly from a rustic American one-room schoolhouse—representative of the ideal of free education for everybody—to the replica of the Tunisian "Bardo of the Bey" (king's palace), pass through the underground grottos of the aquarium, then relax beneath an ornate kiosk with its novel zinc roofing, iron railings, and curiously carved wood. From this vantage point, one could admire the series of trophy vases awarded to medal winners at previous expositions, placed along the path that led to the "glavanoplastic" exhibit in the French section of the park.

But Victor Fournel, a contemporary critic and merciless deflater of what he considered the pretensions of the exposition, could see little value in the entire park:

From the Trocadero you can see the colossal amusement park, installed by the city of Paris for the diversion of everyone. The distractions of this park are a stumbling block for most visitors. Only the most stoic characters can resist the seductions they find here ... In their desire to complete the grand Exposition, the planners have risked watering it down, or turning it from a serious lesson into a trivial game. In spite of the number of serious and useful exhibits that make up a true supplement to the Exposition, the double character of a bazaar and a pedlar's festival dominate the mood of the park.

All the exhibits that border the grand avenue summarize, in a striking manner, everything incoherent, sloppy and fantastic in this decorative ensemble, where it seems as though a gigantic fairy has jumbled and dumped all his theatrical sets. (*Le correspondent*, April 1867)

Even writers such as François Ducuing, who found pleasure in the variety of the park, also found much to object to in the individual exhibits. He especially despised the English lighthouse, which to our eyes so strangely presages the Eiffel Tower. "The English have put up their electrical tower," Ducuing wrote, "and it dishonors the Champ de Mars with its fleshless skeleton."

But perhaps Ducuing was only writing patriotically. The French, too, had erected a lighthouse in the park. Almost 50 meters in height, the towering structure illuminated the Parisian sky every night for the duration of the exposition. Perhaps it was the memory of this sky-reaching illumination that inspired the commissioners of the 1889 world's fair to propose a 300-meter tower as the spike for the exposition of that year.

One of strangest additions to the park was a full-sized Gothic cathedral, designed by a Monsieur Leveque of Amiens. Its intent was to afford suitable exhibition space for a number of arts connected with such a setting. There was a collection of altars, representing styles from the the twelfth century onward; a grand organ by the master organ builder of the nineteenth century, Cavaillé-Coll; painted glass, chandeliers, candelabra, ivory figurines, and wax images of saints. The total effect, all writers agreed, was quite lovely. But the unintentional symbolism of the placement of this cathedral equated it with the Egyptian temples and cast-iron lighthouses surrounding it. The Catholic religion, as embodied in its most venerable form, the Gothic cathedral, was thus reduced to the level of one exhibit among many. Visitors entered Leveque's edifice not to worship but to study. Appreciation of styles took precedence over worship. The church, once the sponsor of fairs, now became a fair exhibit.

Once past the fairyland setting of the park itself, the stoic visitors had still another round of temptations to brave before actually entering the exhibit hall. The series of international restaurants that ringed the palace of industry were the special favorites of fairgoers, who could linger until 11:00 P.M. (the main hall closed at 6:00 P.M.), hear evening concerts, and dine in the glow of gaslight. As always, the critic Fournel was offended: "No matter where you enter, the long line of refreshment stands embraces the main building with a belt of bottles, hams, and lobsters, and gives the whole affair the vulgar air of a marketplace" (*Le correspondent*, May 1867).

The innovations of the park would be copied in virtually every subsequent world's fair. All previous international expositions in Europe had been thoroughly serious affairs, or at least festive in a sober manner. The park and the ring of restaurants brought a carnival atmosphere to the 1867 exposition—an atmosphere that would be present, in varying degrees, at all world's fairs thereafter. Since many entrepreneurs were beginning to see international expositions as golden opportunities to make money, it was no surprise that enterprising speculators began to offer inside the gates the kinds of popular entertainment of Parisian cafés and cabarets, many of which had grown up in conjunction with the old medieval fairs of Paris.

Even so, the park was not so vulgar or inappropriate as Fournel would have us believe. The park did help fulfill the grander and more noble goals of the exposition by allowing exhibitors to build on a larger and more innovative scale then they could within the strict confines of the main exhibit hall. Lovely or logical as the exhibit palace was, it could not hold everything. And the park structures—lighthouses, school buildings, palaces and all—could not distract from the overwhelming presence of the main exhibit hall. In many subsequent world's fairs, the park structures would come to dominate all others and often remained in the host city as permanent monuments.

Once past the attractions of Tunisian palaces and spiced hams, the visitor confronted the Palais du Champ de Mars, the main exhibit hall: a vast iron-and-glass ellipse a mile in circumference. From the first, its architecture was heavily criticized by contemporary observers. Eugéne Rimmel, himself an exhibitor at the exposition, gave voice to the prevailing opinion:

The external appearance of the structure is far from attractive; much as the [British] Exhibition of 1862 was open to criticism, its two noble domes atoned for the heaviness of the edifice, whilst in this instance the monotony of the grey dull building is but poorly relieved by the meagre flagstaffs which form its only ornament.

The interior of the palace is not more striking than the exterior; its continual curves so fatiguing to the eye, do not offer at any point those long vistas which usually form the beauty of this species of building; the only spot which really presents a pretty aspect, is the central garden, whence the different courts radiate. (*Recollections of the Paris Exhibition of 1867*, London 1868, p. 8.)

The report of the American commissioners echoed this sentiment but went on to point out why the palace departed so radically from traditional architectural practice:

The buildings erected for previous great exhibitions are generally known as *palaces*, but the structure on the Champ de Mars had nothing in its appearance, as our previous remarks have hinted, suggestive of the name. In its plan and construction architectural effects were subordinated to the great end in view—the exhibition of the objects of all nations in such a manner as to invite and facilitate comparison and study. (*Report of U.S. Commissioners to the Paris Exposition*, Washington, D.C., 1870, Vol. 1: 13)

The Palais du Champ de Mars was conceived by Frédéric Le Play, general commissioner for the 1867 Exposition universelle. But the task of design was given to Jean-Baptiste-Sébastien Kranz, an experienced engineer, who in turn contracted Gustave Eiffel to carry out his plans. The palace did indeed defy tradition insofar as it did not try to be a church, a city hall, or an aristocratic chateau in the accepted historical styles. Nor did it attempt to be a greenhouse or a railway station—the two most common types of structures that employed glass and iron. It was a structure designed first and foremost as an exposition building, whose dimensions would be determined solely by the requirement of its contents. The domes, interior barrel vaulting, and incidental ornamentation of all previous exposition palaces had drawn their models and inspiration from past structures, as the very term *palace* indicates. But the 1867 palace turned its back on tradition and resolutely faced the necessity of rational classification in an exposition. Hear the voice of Chief Commissioner Le Play:

> The Imperial Commission had, as its point of departure, a methodical classification, at whose base there is a double grouping of products: by the nature of the objects, and by their nationality. This condition has been achieved by a circular arrangement with two systems of division. The first is formed by concentric zones, which will house similar products of all nations; the second, of radiating sections, each one given over to a particular nation. (*Rapport sur l'exposition universelle de 1867 à Paris*, 1869, p. 164)

The palace design represented a serious effort to classify the bewildering variety of the products of human ingenuity. All previous—and subsequent—expositions have had to deal with the problem of organizing their offerings in such a way as to help visitors find and understand what they were seeing. During the fairs of the Middle Ages and later, it was the nature of the product alone that mattered. One visited the cloth section or the toys section of the fair, where members of all nations displayed their wares. Since the time of the first world's fair at London in 1851, the guiding principle was the exhibition of products by nations. Within the confines of the space allotted to them, nations could display whatever they wanted and in whatever manner they pleased. In the Palais du Champ de Mars in 1867, however, the first effort was made to integrate these two organizing principles—nations and products—into one coherent system. As such, the system represents more than a convenient arrangement of products. It is a philosophy, realized in architectural space, about the nature and purpose of human achievement.

The classification system of the 1867 Exposition universelle recognized ten fundamental divisions of human endeavor, each group divided into classes, or subgroups:

Group I: works of art (subdivided into five classes).

Group II: apparatus and application of the liberal arts (eight classes).

Group III: furniture and other objects for use in dwellings (thirteen classes).

Group IV: clothing, including fabrics and other objects worn upon the person (thirteen classes).

Group V: industrial products, raw and manufactured, of mining, forestry, and so forth (seven classes).

Group VI: apparatus and processes used in the common arts (twenty classes).

Group VII: food, fresh or preserved, in various states of preparation (seven classes).

Group VIII: livestock and specimens of agricultural buildings (nine classes).

Group IX: live produce and specimens of horticultural works (six classes).

Group X: articles whose special purpose was meant to improve the physical and moral conditions of the people (seven classes).

In general, the classification scheme worked well. Thoughtful people might pause, though, at seeing grouped together, in the industrial products section, India-rubber baths and corkscrews, fishing tackle and pills. Guns were classified as types of clothing and housed in Group IV, a fact that reveals much about the nature of life in nineteenth-century Western civilization. Perfumers were surprised to find themselves in the section devoted to furniture and other objects for use in dwellings, a classification that reveals the vision, held by the Imperial Commission, that attractive fragrances were domestic in their location and domesticating in their purpose.

All entries were on display for the general public and for the judges who would award prizes in all ten groups. Agricultural and horticultural exhibits were located on Billancourt Island in the Seine. Exhibits too large to fit in the main exhibition hall were erected in the park. Groups I through VII were housed in the palace. The innermost ring of the ellipse contained a special exhibit, the "History of Labor." In the courtyard at the very center of the palace were a garden and two pavilions devoted to a display of weights, measures, and monetary currencies of the world.

The most striking feature of the classification system was Group X. Products in this category were arranged not by national origin or nature of material but by the intentions of their creators. Emperor Napoleon himself entered a design for a workers' housing project in the competition and was awarded a grand prize. That the emperor should win a grand prize surprised no one, of course, but it was a matter of universal comment that the emperor had deigned to enter at all. Such an act clearly gave the signal that France, through the personage of the emperor, set great store by this "physical and moral improvement" category. Group X represents the *bon marché* classification of the 1855 exposition carried to the next higher power. These special categories clearly represent the legacy of Bonapartist reform and the conviction of the exposition commissioners that international exhibitions should do more than promote rivalry among businesses, nations, or cultures, do more than educate or entertain. If future expositions could persuade the nations of the world to dedicate themselves to the physical and moral improvements of the human race, one of the major ideals of the emperor and his commissioners would be fulfilled.

If Group X represented the peaceful universal aspirations of the Second Empire, the outer ring of the Palais du Champ de Mars represented the realities of Europe in the nineteenth century. Here, in the highest, widest, and longest section, the great machines loomed over fairgoers, and the setting perfectly matched the nature of the exhibits.

Since it was here, in the heavy machinery section, that each nation put forth its largest and technologically most impressive inventions for the control and application of mechanical force, this gallery constituted the main arena of the

1867 Exposition universelle. It was here that the United States made its first truly impressive showing as a force to be contended with in future industrial development. Among the Americans' proudest achievements was the telegraphy exhibit under the supervision of Samuel F. B. Morse, and Chicago's Lake Water Tunnel exhibit. In previous world's fairs, the United States had little serious attention from the leading European nations. In 1867, though, American manufacturers were determined to make their presence felt, though they knew they ranked below France, Prussia, and England as major industrial forces. Grand prizes went to Cyrus Field and the Anglo-American Transatlantic Telegraph Company; David Hughes, for his novel printing telegraph; C. H. McCormick for his reaping machines; and to the U.S. Sanitary Commission for the exhibit of ambulances and other materials used for the relief of those wounded in war.

The most impressive French display was the Suez Maritime Canal exhibit. A large working model showed the details of this monumental engineering feat. The success of French engineers, particularly with the colossal dredging machines, promised a great future for the construction of canals in the years ahead and concomitant improvements of maritime commerce. (Smaller versions of the hydraulic machinery were being used to bring water and ventilation to the exposition building itself.)

One of the strangest machines in the French section was a contraption that turned rabbit skins into felt hats. One observer reported (humorously, we hope): "They put in a live rabbit at one end of the machine, and it emerged at the other end as a trimmed, embellished, and garnished hat."

The exhibit that most forcibly captured popular attention was the one mounted by the Krupp ironworks of Prussia. The Krupp company was awarded a grand prize for its innovative methods of steel production—methods so far in advance of previous procedures that this company alone produced more steel in 1861 than the entire world had produced by the time of the first English international exposition of 1851. At the Krupp display in the outer gallery, visitors could see a single 80,000-pound cast-steel ingot, whose fracture at the exposed end showed a flawlessly uniform grain.

But it was not the gigantic ingot that gathered the largest crowd. The most awe-inspiring feature of the Krupp exhibit was the 50-ton steel cannon, capable of firing 1,000-pound shells. Notices in front of the cannon proclaimed that the titanic guns were intended primarily for coastal defense, since their shells could pierce and destroy iron-plated ships. Victor Hugo's noble scorn of this instrument of war seems, in retrospect, a sad instance of cultural myopia: "These enormous shells, hurled from the gigantic Krupp cannons, will be no more effective in stopping Progress than soap bubbles blown from the mouth of a little child" (*Paris Guide*, Vol. 1, 1867). This gigantic Krupp cannon was the very 50-ton monster that would, in three years, hammer Paris into the quickest, most humiliating defeat in its history and force Emperor Napoleon III into an ignominious capture and disgraced exile.

As visitors moved from the outer gallery through the inner circles of the

palace, they beheld a collective display of ingenuity and inventiveness unequaled
in the history of the human race. One visitor calculated the time it would take
to make even a cursory examination of the exhibits:

The gates were opened every morning at eight o'clock and closed every evening at
six. By giving a single minute to each exhibitor and by employing faithfully all the
intervening time, it would have been possible to dispose of six hundred in a day. But
even at that rapid rate, it would have taken three months of unintermitted labor to complete
the list. Many of these exhibitors, moreover, presented not single objects, but scores and
hundreds. There is no extravagance at all in the assertion that the number of objects in
the Exhibition, each individually interesting and worthy, if time allowed, of a separate
examination, amounted to several million. (*Report of U.S. Commissioners to Paris Exposition*, 1867, Vol. 3, 1870: 2)

Mark Twain made essentially the same observation: "To tell the truth, we saw at a
glance that one would have to spend weeks—yea, even months—in that monstrous
establishment to get an intelligible idea of it" (*The Innocents Abroad*, 1869, chapt. 13).

The orderly two-part classification of all exhibits helped save the exposition
from lapsing into a chaos of unrelated impressions. But even with this system
there were problems in laying out the exhibits. France received the majority of
space. The amounts allocated to other nations were in direct proportion to the
esteem or respect in which the French government held each country. After
France, the next six countries, judged by the exhibit space they received, ranked
as follows: Great Britain, "Prussia and north Germany," Austria, Belgium, the
United States, and Russia. Many countries complained of their cramped quarters.
Some observers noted that the system—prestige plus the requirements of the
twofold classifications within the ellipse of the Palais—had assigned some nations
far more room than they needed, others not enough. Prestige and logic were
often at odds.

Although the 1867 exposition avowedly centered around the industrial arts,
it was the fine arts that held the most prestige. An atmosphere of grime still
seemed to hover over even the most prodigious mechanical displays. The fine
arts exuded an aura of refinement and dignity. Beside the thoughtful and polished
canvases of the painter, such metallic monsters as the Krupp cannon seemed
like swaggering bullies from the iron mills.

The drama of the art exhibit at the 1867 exposition resembled surprisingly the
scenario played out at the 1855 fair: two official practitioners battled for top
honors, while the eventual winner—in the eyes of most later art historians, at
any rate–lurked outside the fairgrounds, outside the pale of official acceptance.
In 1855, it had been Jean-Auguste Ingres versus Eugène Delacroix, with Gustave
Courbet opening his own one-man show apart from the Palais des Beaux Arts.
In 1867, Jean-Louis-Ernest Meissonier and Jean-Léon Gérome contended for
top honors within the gates, while across the quay in his own gallery, Edouard
Manet displayed the works he was sure the exposition art committee would have
rejected.

Viewed more than a century after the event, the fine arts competition of the

1867 Exposition universelle evokes yet another image of autumn: the fall of academic art. Meissonier and Gérome were two of the most highly regarded artists of their time. The death of Ingres in 1867 left vacant the throne of "king of painters." After Meissonier won top honors at the exposition, there seemed no doubt that he was the monarch of the fine arts. His clever genre scenes and dramatically staged historical canvases brought him great wealth and international acclaim. Who–except Emile Zola, for years a champion of the cause of new and unconventional artists—could have guessed that the painter of *Déjuner sur l'herbe* and *Olympia*, both exhibited by Manet in his gallery on the avenue de l'Alma across the quay from the exposition, would in time utterly displace his rivals? In 1867, at the twilight of the Second Empire, the *ancien régime* of art still enjoyed its applause, its medals of honor, its wealthy patrons. In the wars and revolutions to follow, the old art and empire would fall like the last leaves of autumn.

Far from the glittering restaurants, away from the banging and clanging of machines in the outer gallery, the works of art clustered close to the center of the Palais du Champ de Mars. But the innermost ellipse, surrounding the open-air garden and central pavilion, offered a novel display: the Gallery of the History of Labor. Here was yet another attempt by the Second Empire to win the hearts of the working people by granting dignity to their enterprise. The Gallery of the History of Labor gave archaeological justification for the elevation of the common man.

The History of Labor showed, in its successive displays, the advance of the human race from the Stone Age down to the year 1800. Almost entirely French in its makeup, the exhibit could have been seen as equating the rise of civilization with the rise of France. But even patriotic foreign visitors had to admit that this retrospective, with more than 5,000 artifacts drawn from private collections around the world, was a noble undertaking. Though Francocentric in its selection of objects, the History of Labor evinced genuine internationalism. Visitors were invited to reflect not only on the superiority of the products of their nation or their professions but on the eons-long rise of human civilization.

Although universal in its scope, there was one patently aristocratic assumption in this panorama of human labor: that the most worthwhile products of human labor were the applied arts. The selections in the part of the exhibit devoted to prehistoric and ancient cultures did show tools and other instruments of labor; but in the main, the displays of objects dating from the Middle Ages to the year 1800 featured decorative works almost exclusively. Jewelry settings, book bindings, huge and ornate vases, delicate bonbon boxes, chimney ornaments, and ivory fans—this view of the products of labor dominated the gallery.

Reflections and echoes of this archeological impulse could be encountered everywhere in the 1867 exposition. From kiosks in the park to the furnishings and fine arts in the palace, the past imposed its compelling fascination on the minds of artists and artisans throughout nineteenth-century Europe. It was almost as if the designers of the History of Labor, surrounded by the overwhelming

feats of mechanical ingenuity at the exposition, desperately turned to the ornamental embellishments of past styles for assurance. In 1867 there was only an
inchoate sense that the new world of steam and steel would someday generate
its own international aesthetics and economics, immensely greater in scope than
achieved by the European luxury products so proudly set forth in the Gallery of
the History of Labor.

At the heart of the 1867 Exposition universelle was a garden. After weary
visitors had wended their way past cannons and corsets, statues and stone axes,
they could relax in the fragrant garden courtyard in the center of the Palais du
Champ de Mars. But even here one final pavilion offered itself for inspection
and contemplation. It featured an assemblage of money, weights, and measures
from various countries around the world.

The placement of this pavilion was a masterpiece of planning. After the vast
collection of objects at the exposition—gathered from all over the world and
from every era of human history—this exhibit invited the visitor to reflect on
concepts and systems that bound them all together. Every country had a different
kind of currency, it was true, but every country did have some medium of
exchange. Every culture had its unique system of weights and measures, but all
peoples used some system for weighing and measuring. The exhibition commissioners hoped that this display would prompt influential people, especially
those engaged with international commerce, to formulate an international standard for money, weights, and measures. The commission's optimism was jus-
tified. Partly as a result of this exhibit, the International Bureau of Weights and
Measures was constituted in Paris in 1875.

During the summer and autumn months of 1867, the photographer Nadar
(Felix Tournachon) took passengers and his camera up over the Champ de Mars
in his hydrogen-filled balloon. From this spectacular overview, visitors had time
and space to survey the entire exposition without being overwhelmed by the
sheer number and diversity of objects, the exotic attraction of the international
costumes and cuisine, or the carnival concert of steam engines, carillons, and
street hawkers all sounding off together.

What they saw was a Paris resplendent with new boulevards and fountains,
cafés and parks. Baron Haussmann had given the city a new raiment, and Victor
Hugo had envisioned a new role for the queen city in the emerging world-nation.
Paris was prosperous, the emperor was victorious, France was the leader of the
new world. From the Suez to Indochina, the new French empire seemed to
reduce even the Sun King's light to a pale dawn compared to the brilliant promise
of the Second Empire. As they watched Nadar snap photographs from his aerie
in the heavens, it must have seemed, to old-timers especially, that a golden age
had truly come to pass. Paris had never seemed lovelier.

But the practiced eye could see thunderheads gathering on the horizon. Polish
patriot Antoni Berezowski attempted to assassinate Czar Alexander II while he
visited Paris in 1867. In June of that year, Emperor Maximilian was executed
by insurgents in Mexico, and the sad presence of his widow, Charlotte, in Paris

during the summer and autumn months gave a melancholy cast to some of the official ceremonies at the exposition. Victor Emmanuel II of Italy, angered at France's attempts to intervene in Italian internal affairs, conspicuously stayed away from the exposition. Opposition to Emperor Napoleon's domestic and foreign policies grew stronger every month. Industrialists began to complain of the renewed foreign competition that followed free-trade legislation. The political ardor of the working classes soared with the impassioned speeches of republicans and revolutionaries. Opponents of the empire began to speak out more boldly, denouncing the direction in which Napoleon was taking the country. Adolph Thiers, from the beginning the most insistent critic of the Second Empire, felt that there were no blunders left to commit. And in this year, General Helmuth von Moltke of Prussia published *The Campaign of 1866 in Germany*, which recounted the story of his crushing defeat of the Austrians and presaging what was in store for the French in 1870.

It was easy to ignore the distant thunder, so beguiling were the wonders of Paris in the year of its second international exposition, in the autumn months of the Second Empire. Throughout the bitter years that followed, the sweet optimism of the 1867 Exposition universelle would haunt the memories of the millions of visitors who had tasted its vanished delights.

BIBLIOGRAPHY

For primary sources, the reader must consult Michel Chevalier, *Exposition universelle de 1867 à Paris. Rapports du jury internationale publiés sous la direction de m. Michel Chevalier*, 13 vols. (1868), and Frédéric Le Play, *Rapport sur l'Exposition universelle de 1867 à Paris* (1869). The most thorough contemporary account in English is the *Report of the United States Commissioners to the Paris Exposition 1867*, 6 vols. (1870). Most other participating nations also published catalogs or reports of their participation. Many of these are scarce, but the Hagley Museum and Library (near Wilmington, Delaware) holds *Catalogue des objets exposés par la République du Salvador, rédigé par M. le Dr. David J. Guzmán . . .* (1878), from which the reader learns that the small Central American nation displayed everything from insects to liquor.

There are a number of contemporary travelers' accounts of this fair. Two of the more literate are George Augustus Henry Sala, *Notes and Sketches of the Paris Exhibition* (1868), and Eugene Rimmell, *Recollections of the Paris Exhibition of 1867* (1868). Sala, a correspondent and illustrator from the *London Daily Telegraph*, provides witty commentary and speaks highly of the American bar and restaurant. Rimmell, an Englishman in the perfume business who had also visited the London fair in 1862, liked the park and the Gallery of the History of Labor but felt the fair as a whole was too commercial.

Apart from significant mention in John Allwood, *The Great Exhibitions* (1977), the Paris fair of 1867 is central to an important modern work, Patricia Mainardi, *Art and Politics of the Second Empire: The Universal Expositions of 1855 and 1867* (1987), which contains a fine discussion of the social and aesthetic issues raised by the fine arts sections of the expositions with which it deals and the influence they had on the development of modernism in art.

Arthur Chandler

LONDON 1871–1874

LONDON INTERNATIONAL EXHIBITIONS

The London International Exhibitions of 1871–1874 began with a proposal made on July 18, 1868, by the Provisional Committee of the Royal Albert Hall to Her Majesty's Commissioners for the Exhibition of 1851. To commemorate Prince Albert's involvement with the Great Exhibition of 1851 and his commitment to industrial education, the committee proposed that the commissioners organize a series of annual international exhibitions on the commissioners' estate in South Kensington, adjacent to the Royal Albert Hall and the Royal Horticultural Gardens. Pursuing the recommendations of the commissioners of the Paris exhibition of 1867, the committee suggested that the size of the exhibitions be limited, that no prizes be awarded, and that goods be organized by class, not nationality. Each exhibition would focus on a class or small number of classes of manufactured goods and on significant scientific discoveries and works of art.

After consulting with chambers of commerce, the Royal Society of Arts, the Institute of Mechanical Engineers, and other relevant groups, the commissioners declared sufficient public interest to support the exhibitions. On July 8, 1869, they approved a plan for sponsoring the exhibitions, established committees to carry out various tasks, and elected additional commissioners. The General Purposes Committee, which served as the executive committee until it was replaced by the Committee of Management in 1872, was chaired by the marquis of Ripon and included the marquis of Lansdowne, earl of Devon, duke of Edinburgh, and Earl Granville. Henry Cole (later Sir Henry) was also a key organizer, as he had been for the exhibitions of 1851 and 1862.

Influenced by the Great Exhibition's Crystal Palace, the commissioners briefly considered building a large glass structure in the ante garden of the Royal Horticultural Society, but the cost proved prohibitive. Instead two brick halls were built on the commissioners' strips of land south of the Royal Albert Hall and east and west of the Horticultural Gardens. Annexes and temporary wooden exhibition halls were added in the remaining space. The total cost for buildings and fittings was £126,383. Although the commissioners intended the exhibition halls, the Royal Albert Hall, and the Royal Horticultural Gardens to function as a unified exhibition site, the public did not like having exhibits separated into two halls on opposite sides of the gardens. When the Royal Horticultural Society withdrew its support after the first year and limited access to the gardens, the separation of the two halls became even more of a problem.

The halls were built under the supervision of General Henry Young Darracott Scott and James Wild, based on the design proposed by Richard Redgrave and executed by Francis Fowke at the South Kensington Museum and the exhibition of 1862. Thirty feet wide, each hall was built of red brick and decorated with terra-cotta. The ground floors were 20 feet high, and the top galleries were 30 feet high with 15 feet of skylight.

In each exhibition the top-lighted galleries featured fine arts, the south and east sides of the ground floors displayed manufactured goods, and the west side exhibited machinery in motion. Except for the exhibition of 1871, which included Horticulture as a fourth category, each exhibition had three categories: Fine Arts, Manufactures, and Recent Scientific Inventions and New Discoveries of All Types. Dividing the category of Manufactures into specific classes of goods, the commissioners published a plan for ten annual exhibitions. The exhibitions closed in 1874 because of financial losses after the first year. The following classes of manufactured goods were exhibited between 1871 and 1874:

1871 pottery, woolen and worsted fabrics, educational works and appliances.

1872 cotton and cotton fabrics, musical instruments, acoustic apparatus and experiments, paper, stationery, and printing.

1873 silk and velvet, steel, surgical instruments, carriages not connected with rail or tram roads, food and cooking.

1874 lace, civil engineering, architectural and building contrivances, heating, leather, bookbinding, and foreign wines.

Music was an integral part of the exhibitions. In 1871 the commissioners invited noted organists from eight of the participating European countries to perform on the Royal Albert Hall's organ. In 1872, when musical instruments comprised a class of manufactured goods, instruments on display were played in the hall. That same year a series of concerts featuring oratorios, popular music, choral arrangements, and operatic and miscellaneous works was held in the hall. In 1873 a fifty-piece orchestra performed daily, and organ recitals were given frequently—daily in 1874. A military band played twice a week toward the end of the 1874 exhibition.

Because the exhibitions were intended to encourage industrial education, lectures were given on many of the displays, but the only well-attended lectures were those on cooking. In 1873 three £50 scholarships were offered, and two were awarded to people who passed the Royal Society of Arts's examinations on the Exhibition's technological subjects.

Although the exhibition of 1871 was generally considered a success, those of the following three years registered increasingly steep declines in gross receipts and attendance and showed financial losses. Gross receipts dropped from £76,433 in 1871 to just £16,399 in 1874; attendance shrunk from 1,142,154 to 466,745 over the same period. A £17,671 profit in 1871 turned into a £17,821 loss in 1874.

The financial decline is also reflected in the decreasing amount of ceremony associated with the exhibitions from year to year. In 1871 the prince of Wales and Princess Helena opened the exhibition in a formal state ceremony. In 1874, the exhibition opened with no ceremony at all. An article in an 1874 number of the *Practical Magazine* described the closing of that year's exhibition as the "most inglorious ending of any Industrial, especially any International, Exhibition. . . . Not an atom of ceremony, not a word of leave-taking or explanation."

After receiving the financial results of the 1873 exhibition, the commissioners met in March 1874 and decided, on the advice of the earl of Caernarvon, chair of the Board of Management, to discontinue the series of exhibitions unless the first two months of the 1874 exhibition proved extremely popular. They were not, and the commissioners agreed to end the series after the exhibition's close.

The commissioners provided several explanations for the exhibitions' financial losses. Lord Caernarvon pointed to the competition with the Vienna exhibition of 1873 and to the Royal Horticultural Society's lack of cooperation. Henry Cole blamed the severe decline in receipts in 1873 and 1874 on the Horticultural Society's excluding visitors from the gardens and demanding payments from the commissioners for the use of a pathway between the two exhibition halls. Other deficiencies he cited included the lack of a railway link with the exhibition, the lack of a connection with the South Kensington Museum, and insufficiently convenient refreshment rooms.

Cole speculated that the arrangement of goods by class instead of by national origin may have discouraged visitors since such an arrangement is less strikingly interesting. In a twentieth-century critique of the exhibitions, Kenneth Luckhurst added that this nongeographic arrangement obscured the international nature of the displays, deprived foreign countries of the chance to arrange their goods, and confused the general public with its scientific nature. Other theories explaining the exhibitions' failure include the lack of juried awards, the interference of the Franco-Prussian War in 1871, and controversy over the right to sell exhibited goods.

While some of the exhibitions' problems were unavoidable, others stemmed directly from the commissioners' adoption of the recommendations made after the Paris exhibition of 1867. The policies of limiting the size and expense of the exhibitions, arranging goods by class, and not awarding prizes were intended to make the exhibitions more affordable and educational; unfortunately, they also made them less dramatic. Beginning only twenty years after 1851, this series was inevitably compared with the Great Exhibition. While no British exhibition, no matter how exciting, could have eclipsed that of 1851, the London exhibitions of 1871–1874 never even came close.

BIBLIOGRAPHY

The most complete source of information on the exhibitions is Henry Cole, Her Majesty's Commissioners for the Exhibition of 1851, *A Special Report on the Annual International Exhibitions of the Years 1871, 1872, 1873, and 1874*. Appendixes, C. 2379 (1878–1879). This command paper includes copies of documents, lists of commissioners, and other pertinent materials. Another helpful parliamentary report is Her Majesty's Commissioners for the Exhibition of 1851, *Sixth Report*, Appendixes (1879). For detailed information on the 1871 exhibits, see *Official Reports on the Various Sections of the Exhibition of*

1871, ed. Lord Houghton [Richard Monckton Milnes], 2 vols. (1871). Copies of Lord Houghton's report are available in the British Museum (London), the Newberry Library (Chicago), Yale University (New Haven), and University of British Columbia (Vancouver).

In addition to these official reports, contemporary journalistic accounts of the exhibitions provide useful information. The *Journal of the Royal Society of Arts* 19–23 (1871–1874) contains many detailed articles on the exhibitions. For an overview and evaluation of the 1871 exhibition, see "The International Exhibition," *London Times*, October 2, 1871. For a good analysis of why the exhibitions failed, see "International Exhibitions from 1851 to 1874: A Retrospect," *Practical Magazine* 4 (1874): 454. A more recent explanation of the exhibitions' failure is contained in Kenneth W. Luckhurst, *The Story of Exhibitions* (1951).

Catherine Dibello

VIENNA 1873

WELTAUSSTELLUNG 1873 WIEN

The Vienna world's fair of 1873 was organized to boost the tarnished image of the Austro-Hungarian Empire, which had lost a considerable amount of territory and prestige since the mid–1850s. Originally planned for 1859, war with France and a tenacious power struggle with Prussia, as well as internal social and economic upheavals, delayed the fair for years. Following the decisive victory of Prussia over Austria in 1866, the Austro-Hungarian empire intended to celebrate its spectacular economic recovery in the wake of a newly established balance of power in Central Europe.

In 1870 the Lower Austrian Trade Association submitted the proposal for an international exhibition with the pledge of 6 million gulden to the Austrian government. The plan was accepted by Emperor Franz Joseph and the date set for 1873. Wilhelm von Schwarz-Sendborn, the experienced organizer of Austria's participation at the previous international exhibitions of 1855, 1862, and 1867, was named general director of the fair. Following the examples of England and France, peace and progress were to be the guiding principles of this potentially largest world's fair to date.

The twenty-fifth anniversary of Emperor Franz Joseph's coronation was deemed to be a suitable occasion to show the world the results of the most ambitious reconstruction and urban planning of any European city in recent history, expect perhaps for Paris. The medieval moat and wall, a ring of fortification around the inner city, was opened by imperial decree in 1857 to connect old Vienna with its growing suburbs. The old wall was leveled and turned into a boulevard of tremendous proportions, lined with grandiose buildings in an array of eclectic styles: neo-Gothic, Renaissance, baroque, and neoclassical. Predominantly financed by the newly rich bourgeoisie, the Ring became a showpiece of capitalism.

Another huge project of civil engineering was the relocation of the Danube Canal. For centuries, the city had been plagued by regular severe flooding of the low-lying meadows along the Danube. One of the worst of these floods, in 1862, prompted Vienna to relocate the canal closer to the city itself. It now bisects its northeastern end and in effect created an ideal site for the fair within Vienna's immense public park, the Prater. The site was five times larger than the Champ de Mars in Paris and was easily reached by rail, boat, roads, and on foot. The mature trees of the park served as an excellent backdrop for the numerous buildings and exhibits. The beauty of the fairgrounds was enhanced by lavish plantings of flowers, shrubs, and exotic introductions. Expanses of lawns provided open vistas and lent perspective to the buildings.

It had become apparent at the 1867 exposition in Paris that it was no longer possible to house and exhibit the accumulation of products by the various participating nations in one single, albeit enormous, exhibition hall. Instead, the Austrian government built separate Palaces of Industry, Machinery, Agriculture, and Art, all of them in an Italian Renaissance style. Throughout the fairgrounds were scattered a large number of other structures of various sizes and styles, the majority in what was called the Swiss style (wooden chalets). These included coffeehouses, arcades, dance pavilions, ethnic restaurants, and authentic farmhouses from the diverse nations present at the fair.

The Palace of Industry, designed by Karl Hasenaur, with its immense rotunda by the English engineer John Scott Russell, was the central focus of the fair and became its signature building. Using Elizabeth G. Holt's and Burton Benedict's comparison, the monumental dome of the rotunda was greater "than twice the diameter of St. Peter's" in Rome. It provided the definitive symbol of the exhibition. The rotunda was built to last and was intended to house the future Corn Exchange of Vienna, according to John Allwood. It remained in use as an exhibition hall for various trade fairs until 1937 when it was destroyed by fire. At present, a complex of multipurpose trade fair exhibition halls occupies the site of the former Palace of Industry.

Lyman Bridges, in his report as member of the U.S. Commission to the fair, describes specific engineering requirements for the exhibition buildings. Since the fair site was located on an alluvial floodplain of the Danube, it was necessary to drive deep piles into the ground to ensure the stability of the foundations of the main buildings. The walls were made of brick, reinforced with pilasters, and covered on the outside with cement stucco. For the Palace of Industry, Vienna adopted a plan of one long main nave, 2,953 feet in length, running east-west to the central rotunda, and crossed by shorter transepts. This construction created a series of twenty-eight galleries with connecting arcades or open courtyards in between. This so-called herringbone system allowed for greater flexibility in space arrangement by individual exhibitors. Another innovation used by the Viennese fair organizers was the systematic allocation of space according to Mercator's projection; the participating countries were arranged from east to west in their natural geographical proximity to each other, with Austria significantly occupying the center and, incidentally, the largest amount of space.

The central rotunda, 354 feet in diameter and 284 feet high, was the largest structure of this kind ever built. The great dome, made of wrought iron, weighed 4,000 tons. It was supported by thirty-two pairs of 80-foot-high double columns, encased in sheet iron. This huge circle of columns formed the base for an iron ring, or girder, that had been assembled in sections on the ground before being hoisted by hydraulic pressure into place atop the columns. A special railway track was laid inside the ring to carry the completed sections to be inserted into the girder. Two-hundred-foot-long girders, at an angle of 35 degrees (the slope of the cone), rested on the circular girder and bore the weight of the roof of the dome. The roof consisted of 360 tapering iron plates, riveted together. The main dome supported a very large lantern, 100 feet in diameter and 50 feet in height, with thirty clerestory windows and an outside walkway, allowing visitors a magnificent view of the fairgrounds as well as the city, the surrounding countryside, and the Alps in the distance. The lantern itself was topped by a smaller lantern, 25 feet in diameter, which in turn was capped by a "gigantic copy of the Austrian crown, made from wrought iron plate, gilded and decorated with glass imitations of the crown jewels."

Four grand entrances provided access to the Palace of Industry, the most elaborate being the southern main portal, a huge triumphal arch, bearing Emperor Franz Joseph's motto, "Viribus Unitis" ("with forces joined"), a conciliatory maxim for a world's fair.

The Machinery Hall stood parallel with and to the north of the Palace of Industry. It too was built to last and was intended to be used as a storage building for the Great Northern Railway. Essentially similar in construction to the Palace of Industry (brick and iron), the exterior paint of the stucco facade gave it the appearance of bluestone. Its length was 2,060 feet and accommodated two parallel railway tracks. These were connected to outside railway lines to allow for easy shipping of heavy equipment and displays.

To the east and southeast of the Palace of Industry stood the "Kunsthalle" (Arts Building) and the Floral and Horticultural Exhibition Halls, respectively. The Arts Building was relatively small, 600 feet long and 100 feet wide, but had a large corridor at its center as well as at each end to enhance the display of statuary. It was well lighted from the roof and divided into individual galleries and studios. Numerous pieces of plastic art were exhibited in open wooden pavilions connected to the Arts Building. Other pavilions surrounding the principal halls included the Imperial and Jury pavilions to the east and west of the grand entrance to the fair.

To contrast with the rather matter-of-fact soberness of the buildings of the Paris exposition of 1867, Vienna placed considerable emphasis on the visual attractiveness of all of the fair structures. Especially the triumphal arches and entry portals reflect this desire for ostentatious ornamentation executed in a variety of historical styles.

The *Internationale Ausstellungs Zeitung*, a daily supplement to Vienna's *Neue Freie Presse* and printed directly on the fairgrounds, gives a detailed account of the intended purpose of the exhibition and of various setbacks and problems. It was reported that despite frantic efforts and the help of 4,000 soldiers from the Austrian army, the grounds were not completely ready when Franz Joseph officially opened the fair on May 1, 1873, as scheduled. It may have stung to have yet another example added to the prevailing European view of Vienna's perpetual unpreparedness, but Franz Joseph, with customary dignity and reserve, presided over his imperial city's most spectacular event in the style of the monarch of a great empire. The day was cold and raw, with a biting wind blasting down from the northeast. The emperor's opening address termed the fair as a "friedlicher Wettstreit aller Culturvoelker der Erde" ("a peaceful competition among all of the cultured peoples of the world"). Accompanied by a 170-piece orchestra, a 720-member chorus performed Handel's Oratorium *Judas Maccabaeus* with the rousing words, "See, the conquering hero comes!" Franz Joseph then received the report from the fair's protector, Archduke Charles Louis, and declared the exhibition officially opened.

Two major themes governed the exhibition. The idealism of improvement of the education, taste, and quality of life of all people was juxtaposed to the reality of the industrial age with its vast numbers of manufactured products and the wealth of raw materials. Despite the idealistic expectations in regard to intellectual and humanistic goals, Austria, to quote Benedict, followed the British example of 1851 by placing raw materials first and ending with the arts.

August Oncken, a contemporary German observer, wrote that the exhibition was subdivided into twenty-six distinct categories. These included the ownership of ideas, the cultivation of good taste, the healing arts, the education of children and women, distribution of food products, and cottage industry. Also covered were the improvement of transportation, best exploitation of machine power, forestry management, mining, engineering, the new science of chemistry, the army and navy, the living conditions of common people, and, finally, the arts. Numerous international congresses were busy examining various aspects within these diverse categories.

Although 70,000 exhibitors from over thirty countries were invited and expected, the three major nations of the world, Britain, France, and the United States, were not well represented. The United States apparently did not comprehend the magnitude of the fair in time to send a suitable number of exhibits. It did, however, send an official group of government commissioners, headed by Robert H. Thurston, to the fair. This commission prepared an extensive four-volume report that was studied with great interest in preparation for the exhibition planned for Philadelphia in 1876.

Much was expected of Great Britain; however, it did not exhibit anything radically new or outstanding in regard to new inventions or manufacturing processes. Rather, it was British India, as well as the independent countries of China and Japan, that dazzled with their rich collection of artifacts. According to Herbert Fux, it was Japan that enjoyed a tremendous success in its first major participation at an international exhibition. The Japanese delegation of more than sixty technical engineers, craftsmen, and highly skilled artisans arrived with a hoard of national treasures that filled two steamers. They effectively presented to the world a comprehensive sample of Japan's potential and productivity. Japan's main goal at this event, however, was to observe, study, and absorb as much as possible of the current industrial achievements and organization of social institutions of Western nations. The delegation returned to Japan with enough material to compile a ninety-six-volume report that served as an informational foundation for Japan's astonishing rise among the ranks of industrial world powers in international commerce.

By contrast, a certain lack of interest, even fatigue, is easier to understand with regard to France, which still suffered from the crushing defeat by the

Prussians the year before and struggled with internal problems as a new republic. Even so, out of the grand total of 26,000 medals and awards distributed at the fair, France achieved third place overall with 3,142 (240 of them for fine arts, the highest number awarded in this category).

As expected, Austria, most likely because of the sheer number of entries, claimed first place with 5,991 medals, followed closely by Germany with 5,066. Italy, Hungary, Spain, England, and Russia managed to obtain just over 1,000 each. The United States trailed Turkey in thirteenth place, with merely 442 medals.

An international jury system was retained to award the prizes. In all, there were five categories of medals: Art, Good Taste, Progress, Cooperation, and Merit. Each portrayed allegorical figures in classical attire distributing laurel wreaths. The reverse of all portrayed the head of Franz Joseph, crowned with laurel.

In addition to the numerous and very popular ethnic food restaurants at the fair, the Strauss orchestra provided one of the greatest attractions to people of all classes. Vienna had no desire to compete with the high tone of the Paris 1867 exposition and the attempts to integrate serious music as part of the overall art scene. The daily concerts in the open air Strauss Pavilion entertained the fairgoers with typical selections ranging from overtures to operas, romantic music, marches, tunes from operettas, and, of course, Viennese waltzes. The greater part of the nineteenth century in Vienna was dominated by the lighthearted music of the Strauss family. According to William Johnston, Johann Strauss, Jr., gained world fame at the International Exposition in Paris in 1867 with his lilting "Blue Danube Waltz," which he had composed specifically for this occasion. The fair directors were well aware of the immense popularity of Vienna's indigenous specialty and incorporated the charming and unpretentious waltz music as one of the fair's great assets. Throughout the fairgrounds the Strauss orchestra was augmented by military bands and gypsy ensembles.

According to the *Official Art Catalog* of the fair, the art exhibits were divided into three categories: the fine arts, religious art, and the "Exposition des amateurs." Twenty-one countries participated in the display. Not surprisingly, France was represented with the largest number of paintings (1,573 in all). Germany, Austria, Italy, Russia, Belgium, Hungary, Switzerland, and Britain followed in descending order of number of entries. The German and Austrian exhibits centered mainly on historicism and religious art. The United States was represented with fifteen paintings, two of them Albert Bierstadt landscapes.

The decorative arts and crafts played an enormous role with regard to their application to the manufactured articles of the industrial age. Except for the first world's fair in London in 1851, the quality of European taste in the decoration of consumer goods was dictated by France, as demonstrated at the fairs in Paris. In Vienna in 1873, however, Austria asserted itself competitively on the international scene in the fields of glassware, porcelain, pottery, leather, and metalwork. The same admiration for beauty of line and design, together with meticulous craftsmanship and attention to detail, brought Japan international recognition for her exquisite objects.

Despite the pomp and high expectations, the fair had a rocky start. Just nine days after the grand opening ceremonies, the Viennese stock market crashed. Not all of the frenzied building and resulting speculation of the past decade of free enterprise rested on a solid foundation. The Vienna exhibition represented the apex of industrial and economic progress at the brink of a sensational collapse. It was a tremendous setback for the city and caused a rash of suicides among financiers and speculators. A severe financial depression gripped the city and country and caused widespread unemployment.

To compound Vienna's troubles, an outbreak of cholera in the summer of 1873 caused an estimated 2,000 deaths and scared would-be visitors away. Bad weather plagued the fair throughout the early months, and a tremendous down-pour flooded the Prater and damaged the fair buildings at the end of June.

As Allwood suggests, perhaps the greatest deterrent to visitors from abroad was the unbridled greed of hotel keepers, restaurant owners, and cab drivers, who charged such outrageous prices for their services that even the wealthiest visitors were discouraged from traveling to or spending time in Vienna. Overall, the loss amounted to 15 million gulden (reported by Franz Herre), branding the Vienna International Exhibition, in Allwood's words, as "one of the great financial failures of the nineteenth century."

Vienna, however, is known for its resilience. As the weather improved during the summer, the attendance figures increased in tandem. Allwood claims that by the end of the six months during which the fair was open, more than 7¼ million visitors saw this potentially most spectacular exhibition to date. They had the unique opportunity to inform themselves of the latest advances in science and industry, education, the decorative and the fine arts. Perhaps they came away with a greater understanding of and tolerance for other nations, other ways of living, and differences in thought and expression.

Vienna itself could relax in the knowledge of being spared the yearly inundations by the Danube. The Danube Canal, together with the impressive reconstruction of the old city, represent the culmination of a successful urban renewal program. The international exhibition was the Austro-Hungarian empire's final celebration at the height of its cultural grandeur before its gradual but inevitable decline early in the following century.

Although the fair was initially to be called a *Welt-Industrieausstellung* (International Industry Exhibition), the term was changed to the more universal *Weltausstellung*. The official program aimed to represent the cultural life of the present time, as well as the totality of the industrial and economic status, and to further the progress of both. Since this particular exhibition was dominated by the German-speaking nations, however, one is left with the impression that the expectations of equitable and worldwide representation of all nations fell somewhat short of these high ideals. Another problem became apparent in regard to the overwhelming number of exhibits. It was impossible for any one visitor to experience the exhibition in its entirety. In this sense, the fair in Vienna served to illustrate a newly emerging phenomenon: the limits of the individual to comprehend and deal with the sum total of society's industrial processes, manufactured goods, and artistic and social diversity.

BIBLIOGRAPHY

Much detailed information on the Vienna exhibition can be found in the daily issues of *Internationale Ausstellungs Zeitung*, a supplement to *Neue Freie Presse*, between May 2 and November 1, 1873. The paper contained in-depth articles regarding any number of subjects pertaining to the fair, daily minutiae, and detailed information about special events and feuilletons, as well as a fascinating glimpse of life in Vienna at this time. A bound collection of these newspapers is located in the Larson Collection at the Henry Madden Library, California State University, Fresno, California. Another contemporary article, particularly valuable for its information on exhibits, is August Oncken, "Die Wiener Weltausstellung 1873," in *Deutsche Zeit-und Streitfragen, Flugschriften zur Kenntis* [sic] *der Gegenwart* (1873): 30–39.

The U.S. role at the Vienna fair is detailed in Robert Thurston, ed., *Reports of the Commissioners of the United States to the International Exhibition Held at Vienna, 1873*, 4 vols. (1876). These reports contain the excellent engineering study by Lyman Bridges on the problems encountered in constructing the exhibition buildings on an alluvial flood plain. See volume 4, section Aa. 8. Further information gathered by the commissioners may be found in Record Group 43 of the National Archives. This material consists of letters, reports, minutes of meetings, and newspaper clippings concerning U.S. participation at Vienna. Also included are lists of exhibitors and commissioners of the participating nations, as well as catalogs and lists of foreign exhibits.

The British role at the exposition was published in four volumes as *Reports on the Universal Exposition of 1873* (1875). Students interested in architecture and engineering should consult William H. Maw and James Dredge, *A Record of the Vienna Universal Exhibition of 1873* (1874). This oversized book contains illustrations and line drawings of the major exposition buildings, as well as many of the principal industrial exhibits.

Modern scholarship concerning this fair includes John Allwood, *The Great Exhibitions* (1977), whose chapter titled "Vienna International Exhibition, 1873" provides a general overview and summary of the most noteworthy events and exhibits. It also contains an illustration of the central section of the Palace of Industry with the rotunda. In addition, Herbert Fux, *Japan auf der Weltausstellung in Wien 1873* (1973), details the extravagant effort the Japanese made participating in their first major international exposition. William M. Johnston, *Vienna, Vienna: The Golden Age 1815–1914* (1980), discusses the music of the exhibition, and Burton Benedict, et al., *The Anthropology of World's Fairs: San Francisco's Panama Pacific International Exposition of 1915* (1983), also treats this fair as an important forerunner to the San Francisco exposition.

Leila G. Sirk

PHILADELPHIA 1876
CENTENNIAL INTERNATIONAL EXHIBITION

On the initiative of Congressman D. J. Morrell of Pennsylvania, the U.S. Congress acted in 1871 "to provide for celebrating the One Hundredth Anniversary of American Independence, by holding an International Exhibition of Arts, Manufactures and Products of the Soil and Mine" in Philadelphia in 1876. The originator of the idea was Professor J. L. Campbell of Wabash College, Indiana, who in 1866 conveyed his thoughts in a letter to the mayor of Philadelphia. The Congress was pressed into action after the idea won the support of the Franklin Institute, the Academy of Fine Arts, the select and common councils of the city, and the state legislature.

To oversee the first major U.S. world's fair, Congress created the Centennial Commission, to be appointed by the president from nominees of the governors of each of the existing states and territories. But it offered no money for the commissioners and specifically disclaimed federal liability for the expenses of the exhibition. (Nor has the United States accepted financial responsibility for any other world's fair held in the country since the Centennial.)

The city of Philadelphia put up $50,000 for the commission's operating expenses, but aside from deciding that the exhibition would be held in Fairmount Park, the commission could accomplish little without sufficient funds. Once again Morrell prevailed on the Congress, and this time they chartered the Centennial Board of Finance, which had the power "under the Centennial Commission" to sell up to $10 million in stocks. This sum was never realized, however. Ultimately the board sold $2.5 million in stocks, almost all of it to local supporters; the city produced $1.5 million (not for stocks); and in 1875 Congress loosened up sufficiently to loan $1.5 million to finance the completion of the buildings. The federal government also spent more than a half-million dollars on its building and its exhibits. An additional $2 million was expected from admissions and payments from concessionaires.

With 2,740 acres (today more than 4,000), Fairmount Park in Philadelphia was the world's largest urban reserve and surely one of the most beautiful. On July 4, 1873, the park's commissioners handed over 450 acres to the Centennial Commission, of which 285 became the fairgrounds. North and west of Independence Square, some 115 feet above the Schuylkill River, the grounds filled a plateau that rose toward George's Hill on their western edge. Pleasing views of the river and the city, modest ravines, running water, and a small lake contributed to the attractions of the site.

The commission entrusted the layout of the fair to an ambitious 27-year-old German immigrant with an engineering and architectural background, Hermann J. Schwarzmann. He had been instrumental in designing the park and had de-

PHILADELPHIA 1876. By this time, fair exhibits were located in thematic buildings. The Horticultural Hall was one of five main buildings at this fair. (Courtesy Peter M. Warner)

signed its splendid zoo. For the fair he envisioned several main buildings and many separated pavilions placed within an efficient and handsome landscape. It was the grandest scheme of any world's fair held so far and fixed the pattern that has persisted to this day. An architectural competition to choose the design of the main building produced a number of plans by some of the most famous architects of the time. The winners, the Philadelphia firm of Collins & Autenrieth, did not receive the commission, however, because their plans followed the official specifications and, if realized, would have proved too costly. The Centennial Commission eventually abandoned all the competitors and in 1874 assigned the Main Building and the adjacent Machinery Hall to Henry Pettit and Joseph M. Wilson, engineers connected with the Pennsylvania Railroad. They entrusted the design of the exhibition's two permanent buildings, Memorial Hall (the art gallery) and Horticultural Hall, to the ever-ready Schwarzmann.

By early summer 1875, construction was underway on the large buildings and some 250 pavilions and auxiliary structures. Although all the major buildings were completed more or less on schedule, the inside work lagged, as did the fitting out of some exhibits. Four days before the scheduled opening of May 10, the *New York Times* noted that in Memorial Hall, "the larger half of the great plaster pilasters have yet to be placed in position, and much of the marble work, such as the cornices and plinths, is still undone." And even two days after the opening, Agricultural Hall was "in a deplorably backwards stage," with "empty showcases." Three days after, workers were trying to complete exhibits in the Main Building, and in the Memorial Hall paintings and statuary were still being installed. Six days after the opening, a huge shipment of exhibits from Russia and China arrived.

On May 9, the fairgrounds were soggy from two days of steady rain. The entire Congress and high officials in the other branches of the government had come up from Washington on three special trains. Visitors jammed the downtown hotels. Workmen struggled through the night to clear debris from the fairgrounds. It was raining at 7:00 A.M. on opening day, but the weather soon lifted. The sun came out at times. The *Times* was confident the Centennial would "present the grandest monument ever offered to the world of the industrial progress of the English-speaking race." The *Philadelphia Inquirer*, by contrast, brooded that the government had "refused to vote a dollar or to render help in any way, until our own citizens had completed the work and assumed obligations so vast as to shame the national authority into doing something."

The opening ceremonies were in front of the neoclassic Memorial Hall, where a platform had been fitted out for the dignitaries, with a program affixed to each seat. The plans had been carefully laid, but some attendees were not happy. Congressmen disliked the seating arrangements, soldiers were disgruntled that their uniforms had been splattered with mud, and diplomats found themselves lost and struggling in the crowd of 200,000 (altogether, thirty-seven nations had accepted the U.S. invitation to participate in the fair). The program began with a march composed for the occasion by Richard Wagner. The critic for the *New*

York Tribune called it "one of the most original things Wagner has written since Tristan," but it was inaudible to the reviewer from the *Inquirer*, even though, he said, "Wagner bears the reputation of being the noisiest of composers."

A lengthy invocation, a hymn with words by John Greenleaf Whittier, and speeches by John Welsh, president of the Board of Finance, and Joseph R. Hawley, president of the Centennial Commission, preceded the address of President Ulysses S. Grant, who modestly downplayed the American exhibits ("Our necessities have compelled us to chiefly expend our means and time in felling forests, subduing prairies, building dwellings, factories, . . . machinery") and commended displays that demonstrated "the skill and taste of our friends from other nations." Then he declared the exhibition open, and in the ensuing tumult, Dom Pedro, the emperor of Brazil, the only foreign head of state who was in attendance, stood up and waved his hat. The ceremony ended with a rendition of "The Hallelujah Chorus" and a 100-gun salute.

After a noontime reception, the officials proceeded to the center of Machinery Hall for the most remembered moment of the entire exhibition. Beneath the towering twin cylinders of the largest of all steam engines, devised for the fair by American inventor and manufacturer George Corliss, the president and the Brazilian emperor each turned handles setting the engine in motion. Other machines in the hall, connected to the giant by 23 miles of shafting and 40 miles of belting, began heaving, clanking, and whirring. The power and potential of American industry were at once made plain to all the world.

Visitors to the Centennial felt overwhelmed. The developed portion of the grounds was inside what might be described as a large triangle, with a narrow-gauge railroad around its periphery. Across its southern base stretched the Main Building and Machinery Hall, end to end some 4,000 linear feet of warehousing. The Main Building, framed in cast iron, had brick walls 6 feet high, with two bands of windows above. It enclosed 20 acres of land. Square towers at the central entrances and at each corner diverted attention from the low-slung effect, as did colorful flags and streamers that flew above the length and breadth of the hall. Archways above the entrances echoed the three grand arches of Memorial Hall just across the Avenue of the Republic.

The Main Building was devoted mainly to manufactures of the United States and other countries; those of the United States occupied about a third of the space. Products arrayed in eye-catching patterns filled row on row of tall, glassed-in display cases: glassware, silverware, scientific instruments, clocks, dental instruments, and ceramics. Furniture—carved, tassled, cushioned in needlepoint—was mixed with ornate examples of industrial art: caskets, carriages, textiles, musical instruments, revolving pistols, vases, chandeliers, beer mugs, chimney pieces, and a steel gun weighing 100 tons, turned out by Friederich Krupp of Essen, the largest ever made. Most items were grouped according to their countries of origin—the United States, Austria, Britain, France, Japan, and so forth. But everything at the Centennial was also classified in one of eight departments (Mining and Metallurgy, Manufactures, Education and Science,

Art, Machinery, Agriculture, and Horticulture), subclassified and subclassified again, in a logical scheme that later became a model for the Dewey Decimal System used in libraries. In contrast with earlier exhibitions, the Centennial made no hierarchical awards; the judges handed out more than 13,000 identical bronze medals to exhibitors in the various categories.

Machinery Hall, framed in wood, was similar in configuration to the Main Building. Most of the mechanical marvels gathered here, produced by the United States and thirteen other nations, were in actual operation (except the steam plant that powered the Corliss engine, which was in a separate annex): mining equipment, typesetters and printing presses, locomotives, drills, lathes, fire trucks, electric engines, looms, and magic lanterns, to cite a few examples. Although many articles were first introduced to the public at the Centennial—typewriters, a mechanical calculator, Bell's telephone, Edison's quadruplex telegraph, machines for agricultural use and heavy industry—the cumulative impression of industrial power must have been the most stunning of all. And the United States, whose exhibits filled 80 percent of Machinery Hall, was at the center of progress.

The 700-ton Corliss engine proved to be the most popular attraction of the fair and its most celebrated artifact. At midday it would be shut down for an hour, and after the repast the crowds would gather to see the behemoth wheeze back to life. During the summer when, as contemporary historian James McCabe expressed it, "the exhibition buildings were like ovens, and the concrete paths through the grounds burned the feet like lava," fairgoers gravitated to an annex of the hall, in which the latest in hydraulic pumps sent plumes of cooling water into a tank.

The exhibit of fine art in Schwarzmann's granitic, square-domed Memorial Hall also turned out to be exceedingly popular. An extra building had to be built hastily to accommodate some of the thousands of paintings, statues, and photographs from some twenty countries. It was the first full-fledged international art exhibit in the republic and has been credited with bringing about a strong American interest in the arts, even though, as Walter Smith in *Masterpieces of the Centennial* (1876) grumbled, it included nothing from the Louvre or the Vatican. The British sent a fine collection from the Royal Academy; French and Italian works depicting large-breasted women in various stages of deshabille as allegorical figures had a large following. America had brought some of its best, including works by Frederick E. Church, Edward Moran, Winslow Homer, and Albert Bierstadt. The building itself, topped by a colossal zinc statue of a gloomy Columbia bestride a globe, dominated the Centennial. Envisioned as a permanent museum for the city, it spawned numbers of beaux-arts-style galleries and libraries throughout the United States. The hall still stands, empty of exhibits except for a scale model of the Centennial in the basement, which may be viewed in the summer.

The elaborately detailed Moorish-style Horticultural Hall was a conservatory for the display of native and exotic plants, some of great rarity. Around it and along walkways leading from it were beds of plants and flowers. The building was finally torn down in 1955, a victim of neglect and damage from the elements. The fifth major building, at the top of the triangle, was Agricultural Hall, with roofs and windows pointed heavenward in Gothic peaks. The tillers of the soil, their animals, and producers of farm equipment were much exalted at the Centennial, as befitted a largely agricultural nation.

On the west side of the grounds were twenty-four state buildings, each in a regional style. The states generally showed their manufactures in the main exhibit halls, reserving these small houses as resting places and greeting centers for dignitaries and visitors from "home." The Ohio Pavilion, built of stone, along with Memorial Hall, are all that remain today of the Centennial buildings. Some states of the Confederacy, notably Virginia, Georgia, Louisiana, and Texas, had no buildings and were unable to contribute much in the way of exhibits. Nor did they participate in the festivities, causing the Centennial Commission's president, General Joseph R. Hawley, to lament, "Had the Governor of Virginia appointed a day for his people to meet here he would have received the warmest greeting he ever saw in his life."

The Declaration of Independence was on view in a good-sized U.S. government building, along with exhibits from the Smithsonian Institution (Indian artifacts, mineral samples), the War and the Navy departments (artillery, model boats), the Interior Department, the U.S. Post Office, and others. The Women's Building, presided over by Elizabeth Duane Gillespie, displayed items of art, crafts, and inventions by women. It represented an early achievement in the feminist struggle for suffrage and equal rights.

The Pennsylvania Railroad had built a depot on Elm Avenue, across from the main entrance to the grounds. Before entering or after leaving the fair, visitors might tarry along the avenue and its side streets for amusements provided in beer halls, cheap hotels, and sideshows. One establishment claimed to recreate the 1870 siege of Paris by the German army (with its Krupp cannon); another, calling itself a "museum," featured the fierce and unregenerate "Wild Men of Borneo." (Soon after, P. T. Barnum brought this act into his circus. His wild men, if not the ones at the Centennial, were gentlemen who had grown up on Long Island). Thus the precincts of Elm Avenue were an unofficial midway at a time before amusement zones were incorporated into the fairs.

Beside the lake near Machinery Hall was a piece of Bartholdi's Statue of Liberty—its arm, hand, and torch. Visitors helped fund the statue's completion by paying to climb to the observation platform below the flame. The exhibit attracted much interest, but art critic Edward Strahan was not enthusiastic about the "titanic Hand of Liberty whose tremendous fingernails were reflected in the shuddering waters of the Lake." Another unusual structure was a public comfort station that provided reading rooms, access to the telegraph, umbrellas, messengers, barbers, hairdressers, and baths, in addition to toilets. Restaurants and soda fountains were available throughout the grounds. Fairgoers could enjoy exhibits in many small pavilions erected by brewers, dairymen, shoe manufacturers, carriage makers, and others. Fireworks, concerts, and parades were regular activities, and sporting events, such as an international rowing regatta on the Schuylkill, accompanied the fair. Both presidential candidates that year, Rutherford B. Hayes and Samuel J. Tilden, spoke before large crowds on the fairgrounds.

In the summer when the weather was unusually hot, attendance was low. The daily average in July was just 15,207, and on the Fourth only 50,000 arrived for the country's hundredth birthday. The throngs and the enthusiasm grew in the fall. Pennsylvania Day in September brought in 257,165. By nightfall on the final day, November 10, the fair had drawn 9,789,392 visitors, of whom 8,004,325 paid to get in. If it had not been for the heat, the Sunday closings, a turn in the economy, and, perhaps, the reluctance of the railroads to lower their rates, who knows how high the attendance would have gone? The Centennial suffered a loss of $1.9 million. The federal government demanded repayment of its $1.5 million, so the stockholders had to accommodate the entire loss.

"We had a nation to show," said General Hawley, and the Centennial gave ample evidence of American progress in education, industry and the arts. According to Congressman Morrell, foreign visitors saw "a polite, orderly, self-respecting and self-governing people . . . What [they] may be lacking in form is made up in substance." In the United States, the effect of the Centennial was deep and lasting. Sales were made through the fair; foreign trade received a definite boost. Americans could observe firsthand how their best work compared with that of others. They came to know people from other lands and to admire their accomplishments (even though, as Frank Leslie reported, the Americans' "vulgar curiosity" discouraged foreigners at the fair from wearing their native costumes). At a time when the scandals of the Grant administration had undermined the people's confidence in their leaders, the administration of the fair, led by director general Alfred T. Goshorn, showed itself to be efficient, honest, and deserving of the public trust. The entire fair, in fact, boosted the pride and self-confidence of the sponsoring nation.

BIBLIOGRAPHY

A great deal of primary source material for the Centennial Exhibition of 1876, including the records of the U.S. Centennial Commission and the Board of Finance, is in the Philadelphia City Archives. Other original material is located in the Historical Society of Pennsylvania in Philadelphia, and in the National Archives and Smithsonian Institution, both in Washington, D.C. The U.S. Centennial Commission published *International Exhibition 1876. Official Catalogue* (1876), as well as several volumes in 1879: *International Exhibition 1876: Report of the Director General*, 2 vols.; *Appendix to the Reports of the Director General*; *Reports of the Officers*; and *Reports and Awards*, 2 vols.

Contemporary publications of value include *The Masterpieces of the Centennial International Exhibition*, 3 vols. (1876); *Frank Leslie's Historical Register of the United States Centennial Exposition, 1876* (1877), filled with vivid wood engravings and much information; James D. McCabe, *The Illustrated History of the Centennial Exhibition* (1876); and Thomson Westcott, *Centennial Portfolio* (1876), with engravings and thumbnail descriptions of the buildings. Two more whimsical works are David S. Cohen, *Our Show: A Humourous Account of the International Exposition* . . . (1876), and A. G. Sedgwick, "The Restaurants at the Centennial," *Nation* 23 (1876): 22.

Among modern works, one should begin with John Maass, *The Glorious Enterprise: The Centennial Exhibition of 1876 and H. J. Schwarzmann, Architect-in-Chief* (1973), which contains an excellent bibliography. A book published in conjunction with an ambitious exhibit mounted at the Smithsonian in 1976 to mark the centennial of the Centennial contains many informative essays about the original exhibit halls: Robert C. Post, ed., *1876, A Centennial Exhibition* (1976). Intended as a "microscopic recreation" of the world's fair, the exhibit still stands in the Arts and Industries Building on the Mall in Washington, D.C. At the site of the fair in Fairmount Park in Philadelphia, many of the fair's roads and walkways remain, as does Memorial Hall.

Alfred Heller

PARIS 1878

EXPOSITION UNIVERSELLE

Seven years after "the terrible year" of 1870–1871, France was ready to transcend the Franco-Prussian war and the Commune Revolt. To forget those tragic years would be impossible. But to the leaders of the Third Republic, it was equally impossible for France to remain an object of pity and scorn, a has-been power with no sense of national purpose. The 1878 Exposition universelle was a proclamation, to the nation and the rest of the world, that France was ready once again to assume its traditional role as a great civilizing force in human culture. "The time had come," wrote Alfred Picard a decade after the event, "for France to lift the veil of sorrow and mourning, and to invite the world to a public festival."

"The advocates of monarchy have always been boasting of the fêtes of the Royalty and the Empire," wrote the staunch republican Francisque Sarrey. "Well, here are the fêtes of the Republic. Are they less worthy than the others?" Throughout the journals and official reports of 1878, there runs a common theme: whatever the Empire did, the Republic can do better.

Comparisons with the 1867 exposition were everywhere. Newspapers reported with pride that, in the first nine days of the 1867 exposition, there were 38,363 paid visitors. But after nine days of the 1878 exposition, 258,342 had paid to see the wonderworks of the Third Republic's fair. Even when, at the close of the exposition, it became apparent that the fair would lose money, most people and government officials agreed that the price paid for the confirmation of confidence in the new Republic was not excessive.

There were dissenting voices, however. Some critics cried out that the exposition was a monstrous extravagance that France could ill afford at the time. The country had paid off its 5 billion franc indemnity to Germany only a few years previously. The money, they argued, should not be gouged out of the French people just to prove that the Republic could outdo Napoleon III as an international host.

Members of the clergy also objected strongly to the fair. The Empire expositions had always been opened with a religious ceremony. The Republic, taking its first steps to separate affairs of government from the power of the church, pointedly refused to include any religious statement, implicit or explicit, in the opening ceremonies. Many parish priests told their congregation to stay away from this "atheist exposition," a prohibition that perhaps contributed to the

This article was originally published in *World's Fair* in somewhat altered form and is printed here with the permission of the publisher.

lower-than-expected final attendance figures and the financial loss suffered by the 1878 fair.

In the 1878 exposition, more than any previous such event, engineering was married to art. Visitors who toured the exposition grounds before opening day were surprised to see a miniature railroad built underneath the Palace of Industry and the Trocadéro Palace. These trains greatly accelerated both the building process and the removal of debris after the exhibition closed. Before the fair opened, the tracks and cars were covered with planking. Visitors were amazed to learn that, wherever they went in the Palace of Industry, they were walking 10 feet over a hidden railway.

But the greatest feat of engineering at the 1878 Exposition universelle was the virtuoso control of water. Four gigantic hydraulic pumps fed the waters of the Seine through 23 miles of cast-iron and lead pipe to all corners of the exposition. First the water surged up to the summit of Trocadéro Hill and into the palace towers, where it powered elevators so swift that speedometers were mounted on the walls to show astonished passengers the velocity of their ascent and descent. Some of the waters then flowed over the top of a pond that was elevated and supported by three arches in front of the Trocadéro Palace, plunged down 29 feet into a fountain, then glided over terraced steps into a large basin. Another pipe carried water more swiftly beneath the earth, then launched towering 62-foot-high jets that flanked the central fountain like liquid pillars. Still another pipe carried water in a quiet, constant pulse to the aquarium in the Trocadéro Park.

From the basin, the water flowed down again through the iron and lead pipes, surged beneath the Seine, then emerged quietly in peaceful ponds in the Champs de Mars. Other pipes carried water silently beneath the floorboards of the Palace of Industry and kept the building several degrees cooler than the outside air, even on the warmest days. The harnessing of the Seine to elevators and fountains, aquarium and air-conditioning, the orchestration of the force of water to unite the river with the Palace of Industry on the left bank and the Trocadéro Palace on the right—this was the triumph of French engineering at the 1878 Exposition universelle.

Not all the hydraulic virtuosity of France could redeem the Trocadéro Palace, designed by Gabriel Davioud and Jules Bourdais. Davioud, the chief architect of the Trocadéro building and fountains, had worked with Baron Haussmann during the glory years of the Second Empire and was serving, at the time of the exposition, as the inspector general of architecture for the city of Paris. He helped create the landscaping of the Bois de Boulogne and the Parc Monceaux. Several squares, gardens, and fountains in Paris were Davioud's handiwork. His touch with plants and water was deft and sure. But his talent did not redeem the Trocadéro Palace. Even to contemporary observers sympathetic to eclecticism in architecture, Davioud's pastiche of Romanesque columns, Spanish-Moorish arches, the Giralda Tower, and polychrome decor was an unqualified failure. The wide sweep of the two flanking colonnades was impressive enough but the

PARIS 1878. The Champ de Mars was the site for this fair, housed in one principal building, representing France's effort to redeem its reputation after the Franco-Prussian War. (Courtesy Peter M. Warner)

Trocadéro Palace itself looked squat and proportionless. Parisians put up with the building for fifty-six years before demolishing it to make way for the Chaillot Palace at the 1937 Exposition universelle.

The building seemed cursed even before its completion. It was unfinished on the opening day of the exposition, though over 800 workers had labored diligently for a year on the building and its site. Even when the exterior was finished and the internal exhibits mounted, the opening day of the music festival had to be delayed because the *grande salle des fêtes* was still not finished in June. Then, less than a month after the concert hall was finished, a careless workman left a water tap running all night on one of the top floors of the building. The ceiling of the hall was damaged and once again, the music festival had to be delayed.

When the difficulties were cleared up, however, the Trocadéro quickly became a major center of cultural activity at the exposition. The concert hall itself was glorious, even if the vast space became a sea of echoes during the performances. This was an epoch that loved the grand gesture in art and life, and the Trocadéro auditorium was a fitting realization of the era's delight in colossal effects. Concerts were held almost every night, and the main hall, which held 4,500 people, was usually filled to capacity. On the walls, 4,500 gaslights made every musical performance a visual spectacle as well. The sights and sounds of the International Choral Competition, in which thousands of singers at a time performed before thousands of spectators, were among the most overwhelming events of the entire exposition.

Taking up several other large rooms in the Trocadéro was the retrospective exhibit. Here visitors could see choice works of decorative art culled from government and private collections all over France. Arms and armor, crowns, fans, metal and woodwork, Sèvres porcelain—over a thousand years of French craftsmanship was gathered into a single show, which continued for several months after the exposition itself was officially closed in November.

In other halls of the Trocadéro Palace, members of the international conferences discussed a wide range of topics. The International Congress on the Rights of Women featured discussions and debates on the place and rights of women in all phases of society. There were technical conferences for engineers and psychologists, gatherings of Alpine climbers, meetings for "discharged prisoners' friends," sessions on gas-tar, a convocation of the International Peace Congress. One congress even had to take up a problem created by the world's fairs themselves: how to deal with dishonest manufacturers who falsely advertised medals claimed to have been won at international exhibitions.

Some of the meetings had immediate and far-reaching results. Victor Hugo headed the Congress for the Protection of Literary Property, which led to the eventual formulation of international copyright laws. Similar congresses dealt with the problems of protecting industrial property and of governing the rights to reproductions of works of fine arts. An international postal union was established to facilitate communication by letters among the nations of the world. The International Congress for the Amelioration of the Condition of Blind People led to the worldwide adoption of the braille system of touch reading. By incorporating these meetings into the official agenda of the exposition itself, the commissioners were consciously attempting to offset the charges of frivolousness that had been leveled at the 1867 exposition.

Sloping down from the Trocadéro Palace to the Seine was the Parc. Here visitors could find restaurants, an aquarium, and some of the foreign pavilions too large to fit into the Street of Nations inside the Palace of Industry. The Parc on Trocadéro Hill was the 1878 exposition's answer to the 1867 exposition's open-air amusements and outdoor exhibits. At the 1878 exposition, any nation that felt it had been given too little space in their main exhibit off the rue des Nations could construct a secondary structure here in the Trocadéro Park. There were fewer such outlying buildings at the 1878 fair than in the 1867, since this time most nations were given space for their architectural statements on the rue des Nations inside the Palace of Industry. But there was still the same arbitrary, scattered quality about the placement of structures on the grounds: a Japanese farm wedged incongruously between an Egyptian temple and a Spanish restaurant; a Norwegian clock tower striking the hour over potters in an Algerian village where women made pots using ancient Etruscan techniques.

Crossing the pont d'Iena from the Trocadéro Park, the fairgoer confronted Léopold-Amédée Hardy's impressive facade (constructed by Gustave Eiffel) of the main exposition building. The stark iron beams of the Palace of Industry were painted blue and decorated with red and yellow lines. Ranged along the lower story of the entranceway and facing the Seine were twenty-two "Statues of the Powers"—allegorical sculptures that represented the twenty-two other nations that the French officially recognized as the significant forces in world affairs. These statues signified more than complimentary bows toward sister nations; they were explicit statements of esteem by the French government. Several important features of French foreign policy can be detected at once: South America is treated as a single nation, presumably including Mexico and Central America; Canada does not appear, nor do many African and Asian nations; India is represented as "British India," an avowal that, even for republican France, India was reckoned important only by virtue of its status as a British colony. Most significant of all is the absence of a statue representing Germany. France was not yet willing to forgive or forget the Franco-Prussian War. It would have been too painful for the French government to erect a statue to the nation's bitterest enemy.

Once inside the Palace of Industry, the fairgoer saw a range of displays that had by now become familiar types in international exhibitions: huge machines, elaborately decorated furniture, works of fine art—everything from cut glass to corset stays. The exhibits were organized on a modified version of the 1867 system of classification: perpendicular to the Seine, products were ordered by their nature; parallel to the Seine, products were identified by their country of manufacture.

The exhibits and their arrangement at the 1878 Exposition universelle were not just modifications of the earlier fair, however. Perhaps the most innovative and most widely admired feature of the fair was the Street of Nations, planned and executed by Georges Berger, director of foreign sections. In the central courtyard of the Palace of Industry, each participating nation was invited to build an entranceway to its exhibits. The result was a splendid row of facades that announced, in architectural terms, the character and aesthetic values of every nation. The Street of Nations not only gave the visitors a prelude to the exhibits within the palace. The whole ensemble taken together allowed fairgoers to see, at one glance, the eclectic nature of the world in 1878. What a lesson, to see the Slavic sumptuousness of the Russian facade—a model of the house where Peter the Great was born—close by the quiet geometry of the Japanese entranceway.

An astute observer who had attended the 1867 Exposition universelle might have detected some subtle but decisive changes in the nature of the exhibits. The steam engines and the decorative arts still dominated the 1878 exposition, as they had in all previous world's fairs. But now there were a number of smaller machines whose ingenuity and potential for universal usefulness captured the imagination of the public even more than the metallic monsters that hummed and banged in the heavy machinery section. One booth displayed the first personal printing machine, the typewriter. Another featured a novelty that promised to make carriage rides more endurable: rubber tires. And in the American section, visitors could marvel at a staggering array of personal appliances.

In the arena where entrepreneurs sought to make small machines available to the widest possible audience, the Americans were clearly emerging as the leaders. Typical was their dominance in the sewing machine business. The Wheeler and Wilson Sewing Machine Company repeated its performance at the 1867 exposition by winning the grand prize in its class, amid universal praise of the fine workmanship and versatility of their products. The Singer Company was demonstrating its sewing machines for home use and announcing its multinational distribution networks (over 280,000 machines had been sold in 1877).

The most dramatic embodiment—for Europeans, and especially for the French—of this quality of technological enterprise was Thomas Alva Edison. He was hailed as a universal talent who had grown up with no formal education, no advantages of aristocratic privilege or patronage. For the French people, who were still working through the first tentative stages of their Third Republic, Edison symbolized the potential of human genius unhampered by artificial social constraints.

For the hard of hearing, Edison had invented the megaphone. Fairgoers were astonished to hear how sound could be amplified with Edison's device. Even more acclaimed was the phonograph. The recording machine on display at the 1878 exposition was a simple mechanical device that used a mouthpiece for activating a notched disk, which in turn made indentations for playback on tinfoil wrapped around a brass cylinder. First shown at the Philadelphia exposition two years before, this device sent European journalists into ecstasies. In 1877, Edison showed his machine to British audiences, where they heard "God Save the Queen" sing forth from the strange device. One Parisian gazette even predicted (perhaps with malice) that the phonograph would render useless the tenors of the opera.

But for all Parisians and visitors to the fair, the most dazzling display of Edison's genius came in June of 1878. Electric lighting had been installed all along the avenue de l'Opéra and the place de l'Opéra. And when the switch was thrown, flooding these famous places with a brilliance that no gaslight could achieve, Edison's triumph was complete. The Wizard of Menlo Park had changed forever the very complexion of the night.

Although the Trocadéro Palace was the fine arts building of the fair, contemporary painting and sculpture were housed across the Seine in the Palace of Industry. In fact, the 1878 Exposition universelle hosted two artistic competitions: the annual salon, where French artists competed for prizes, and the exposition salon, where international artists vied with each other for medals.

For most art historians today, the 1870s are known as the impressionist years, when the practitioners of the new style exhibited their works in defiance of reactionary academic tradition. But even official art at the exposition showed a remarkable variety. Pierre Bonnat and Ernest Meissonier were the grand old men of the show, as Ingres and Delacroix had been in 1855. Adolphe Bouguereau's exquisitely rendered religious and mythological scenes and Alexandre Cabanel's *Death of Francesco da Rimini* were the rage of the day. Who would have predicted, in 1878, that after a hundred years, the names of these four most prominent French artists of the day would have sunk into obscurity?

But the greatest public outcry of the day was not created by the impressionists or the accepted salon entries: it was the refusal by the Exposition Committee to allow any battle scenes that referred to the Franco-Prussian War. France at that time was the home of a number of talented painters of battle scenes. "The organizers of the 1878 Exposition," wrote art critic Edward Strahan, "seemed to these ambitious young painters to be pushing French politeness to the limits of the incredible when they invited the military artists to withdraw from the competition to which the rest of Europe was bidden."

Although the German government was not invited to participate in the 1878 exposition, German artists were allowed exhibition space. Exposition commissioners were understandably anxious to avoid an embarrassing incident that might arise from showing pictures in which French and German soldiers were shooting each other. Scenes from other French military engagements, even Waterloo, were allowed, but none of the spirited and patriotic canvases of Alphonse de Neuville, Edouard Detaille, or several other young painters, was admitted to the exposition salon. The Goupil Gallery in the rue Chaptal offered the young artists exhibition space. And what foreigners most often visited the gallery? The Germans, of course. One German artist commented that he saw nothing as good in the Champ de Mars as what he had encountered at Goupil Gallery. Strahan aptly sums up the symbolism of the entire episode:

It was not to be wondered at that the interdiction which came to upset the young French school of military art at the moment when it was putting on its armor for the tournament of the Champ de Mars, should have aroused lively revolts. A prompt feeling of resentment sprang up in the world of the studios, and the ardent hearts of the painters boiled over with what they considered patriotic ardor. Was it not a painful insult to exclude that graphic and youthful school, so popular and so French, which had found a way to extract a kind of victory out of defeat? (Edward Strahan, ed., *The Chef-d'Oeuvre d'Art of the International Exposition, 1878*, p. 86)

At the 1878 exposition, though, it was not painting, but sculpture that most forcibly captured the public's attention. Since the deaths of Jean-Baptiste Carpeaux and Antoine Barye in 1875, the "throne of sculpture" had been vacant. The man who seemed destined to replace them was Marius Jean Antonin Mercié, the grand prize winner at the exposition. His statue of *Fame* surmounted the Trocadéro during the months of the exposition. His *Génie des Arts* had already been picked to replace the statue of Napoleon III in the Louvre. But it was Mercié's *Gloria Victis* ("Glory to the Vanquished") that emerged as one of the most popular works at the fair and one of the most revered sculptures of the whole decade. This was the kind of statement about the Franco-Prussian War that the exposition commissioners were willing to honor: idealized, classical in its narrative references and modeling technique, designed to arouse a sentiment rather than to express an emotion. *Gloria Victis* announced, in suitably symbolic terms, that France had accepted the burden of defeat and was on the way to complete recovery.

In the garden of the Champ de Mars, visitors were astonished to find not merely an oversized sculpture but the head of a colossus that would rank as one of the wonders of the world: Auguste Bartholdi's *Liberty Enlightening the World*. Every day visitors by the hundreds lined up to travel into the head of the Statue of Liberty. There were many ways to admire the work as it loomed over the gardens of the Champ de Mars: for the splendid view it afforded of the exposition grounds; for Gustave Eiffel's ingenuity in accommodating the rigors of structural mechanics to the demands of art; for Bartholdi's skill in modeling correct and noble proportions on a scale never before attempted in art (it is still the largest sculpture in the world). But in 1878, the deepest point to ponder was what the statue symbolized about the relation between the new republic of the old country of France and the century-old republic in the youthful country of America.

Bartholdi's *Liberty*, though, is more than a monument to the maturing friendship between the nations of France and the United States. It was and remains a votive statue to democracy. It is an announcement that a republic can survive and thrive—heroically, on a superlative level—in a world encrusted with despotism.

Here, *Liberty* merges with the more intensely national message of the 1878 exposition. Just as the United States had shown in 1876 that it was once again a nation healed and whole, a country that had overcome the tragedy of civil war and emerged stronger than ever, so France proclaimed its recovery from the twofold disaster of military defeat and civil dissension. When the exposition lights were extinguished on November 10, 1878, the streets of Paris blazed forth with fireworks, candles, gaslights, and Edison's electric bulbs. France was well.

BIBLIOGRAPHY

The official reports are the standard source of information about statistics and descriptions. See especially the *Rapport administratif sur l'Exposition universelle de 1878, Paris*, ed. Jean-Baptiste Krantz (1881) and the *Exposition universelle de 1878, Paris, Rapports du jury international*, ed. Jules Simon. The five-volume *Reports of the United States Commissioners to the Paris Universal Exposition, 1878* (1880) is an excellent source of information, particularly for details concerning U.S. participation at the fair.

For the student of the times and the city of Paris, however, the unofficial reports written up by professional journalists and sightseers make for much livelier reading. A. Bitard, ed., *L'Exposition universelle de 1878, Journal Hebdomadaire*, issued weekly for forty issues and then published as a bound volume, offers a wonderful potpourri of anecdotes and statistics, along with excellent engravings of the fairgrounds and exhibits. The English-language counterpart to this volume is the delightful *Illustrated Paris Universal Exposition* (1878). Like its French counterpart, the London journal is wonderfully opinionated and loves to relate humorous tableaux at the fair. Also not to be missed is *The Chefs-d'Oeuvre d'Art of the International Exhibition*, edited by Edward Strahan (n.d.). Among the many virtues of Strahan's volume is a detailed and thoughtful series of discussion of many works of art considered masterpieces in their own time and all but forgotten now. For the dissenting voice, see especially Emile Zola's advocacy of the impressionists in his "Lettres de Paris, l'Ecole française de peinture à l'Exposition de 1878," in *Le Messager de l'Europe* (July 1878).

The best twentieth-century assessment of the 1878 exposition remains Raymond Isay's *Panorama des Expositions universelles* (1937), esp. pp. 137–75. Isay is more than a chronicler; he is a critical reader of the symbols, intentional and unintentional, that expositions present to the thoughtful student. Philippe Bouin and Christian Chanut's *Histoire française des foires et des expositions universelles* (1980), esp. pp. 97–110, while not as penetrating as Isay's work, offers a lively, almost whimsical view of the achievements and ironies of this exposition. Especially valuable is their summary of other fairs, major and minor, in the years preceding and following the 1878 exposition. Pascal Ory's *Les Expositions universelles de Paris* (1982) contains useful and imaginative insights into this and other expositions; but its disorganization and lack of an index make this a difficult volume to use.

Arthur Chandler

SYDNEY 1879–1880

SYDNEY INTERNATIONAL EXHIBITION

The Sydney International Exhibition was formally opened by His Excellency Lord Augustus Loftus, governor of the Colony of New South Wales and also president of the Exhibition Commission. The exhibition ran from September 17, 1879, to April 20, 1880, and over a period of seven months the total attendance amounted to 1,117,536, of which 850,480 were paid admissions. As one of the earliest exhibitions in Australia (along with the Melbourne fair, in the planning stage at that time), the Sydney exhibition critically demonstrated that this distant colony had come into its own after eighty-five years of existence. Although exhibits and awards covered six departments and a range of classes within each department (the synopsis of the classification was borrowed from the 1876 Philadelphia exhibition), the focus of the exhibition was primarily on agriculture and livestock production. Awards in all fields were given not only for exhibits from other Australian colonies but also to fifteen other countries and nine British colonies, which took an active interest in demonstrating agricultural and technological developments.

The exhibition buildings, which also contained restaurants, art galleries, and musical theaters, covered 650,000 square feet (15 acres); however, the total exhibition ground was nearly 24 acres. The Garden Palace was modeled after London's Crystal Palace and was considered immense for its time in terms of what was covered and contained under one roof. The principal dome was in the center of four towers and was constructed in masonry; the galleries extending from the dome were built of wood. Construction started in January 1879, with an employment force of 800, but by May of that year the labor force was increased to 3,000, after electricity permitted work throughout the night. Buildings adjacent to the palace housed moving machinery, agricultural implements, and exhibits of cereals, wool, plants, fruits and flowers, and livestock. An art gallery was proposed in August 1879 and was completed later that year. The commission stressed musical performances, which took place throughout the seven-month period. It appears that Handel's compositions were the most popular. The organizers also commissioned an opening cantata dedicated to the prince of Wales, with lyrics by the Australian poet Henry Kendall and music by Paola Giarza.

The cost of construction and other financial expenditures were met by the colonial government of New South Wales. The initial budgeted amount was £25,000 but the final expenditures came to nearly double that amount. Overall the exhibition lost money. The Official Exhibition Record of 1881 notes that the exhibition lost £103,615 (US$504,605); however, the large sums of money spent in Sydney compensated for this loss.

The significance of the exhibition, besides symbolizing Australia's existence among the nations of the world, encouraged non-British commercial interests to seek Australia as a market for industrial products, as well as consumer goods. Throughout the years after 1880, steamship lines initiated runs between Australian ports and France and Germany and, at the same time, non-British capital, mainly through French investment and banking institutions, appeared in Melbourne and Sydney.

Within two years after the exhibition closed in April 1880, the exposition buildings burned to the ground. Although rumors abounded as to the cause, Allwood notes that the dominant rumor was that the central exhibition buildings were allegedly the depository of convict records and thus destroyed. To this day these rumors have not subsided.

BIBLIOGRAPHY

The major primary source for the Sydney International Exhibition, 1879–1880, is the *Official Record* (1881). This massive 1,154-page report contains the history of the fair, a complete list of exhibits, reports of the judges, and awards, with colored plans of the exhibit hall and grounds. Small catalogs and handbooks were published, as well as guides to specific national exhibits. All of these works are difficult to find. Secondary sources include the excellent articles on exhibitions in *Encyclopaedia Britannica*, vol. 11, 11th ed. (1910), M. Tamir's *Les Expositions internationales à travers les âges* (1939), and John Allwood's *The Great Exhibitions* (1977). There is also a short article in C. B. Norton's *World's Fairs from London, 1851 to Chicago, 1893* (1893).

Aram A. Yengoyan

MELBOURNE 1880–1881

MELBOURNE INTERNATIONAL EXHIBITION

Exuding the "dishevelled air of a frontier town," Melbourne welcomed the world as its first international exhibition opened on October 1, 1880. Leaders were proud of the city's growth in just thirty years from a small township to a metropolis of 250,000, and they hoped to encourage world trade by displaying its products in open competition with the thirty-seven nations represented. As an extravagant entertainment, even the severest critics admitted that it was a great success. During seven months, 1,458,896 visitors viewed more than 13,000 exhibits before the exhibition closed on April 30, 1881.

Australians, relatively isolated from world developments, were especially eager to both see and be seen during the 1880s. Victorian manufactures had been successfully promoted in local and intercolonial exhibitions in Melbourne in 1854, 1861, 1866, 1872, and 1875, fostering a general acceptance for the idea of an international fair. Deliberations in the Victorian legislature (1877–1880), however, coincided with violent political conflicts between small property owners and local manufacturers, and the larger mercantile and landed interests. Sir Graham Berry, Victorian premier, hoped by hosting the fair to revive the sagging Victorian economy, while his free-trade opponents accused him of promoting selective Victorian interests at the expense of general prosperity. Ultimately, successful Victorian participation in the Paris exhibition of 1878 and rival Sydney's hosting of Australia's first international exhibition in 1879–1880 brought a favorable vote of the legislature.

Exhibition Hall, the focal point of the 21-acre site in Carlton Gardens, was designed by Joseph Reed according to ecclesiastical architectural principles then in vogue. The hall featured a dome 217 feet high, second highest in the world, and reminiscent of classical models such as London's St. Paul's Cathedral, while the vistas along the arched nave and buttresses gave "something of a Gothic character to the structure." Eastern and western perpendicular annexes formed a courtyard, which was temporarily covered to house exhibits. Although detractors declared the building, largely the cause of the £277,292 deficit the exhibition sustained, "a dead loss" at the exhibition's close, it has since been used, with additions, as an exhibition hall, printing office, seat of the state parliament, and aquarium, and it stands today as one of the architectural landmarks of Melbourne.

The Melbourne exhibition was primarily a display of manufactured goods, advertising Australian products and providing a focus for negotiations to open new channels of trade, particularly with France. Increased trade specifically related to the fair, always difficult to measure, in any case remained a small fraction of Australia's total trade. Culturally the exhibition had little impact. By the admission of the trustees themselves, the paintings displayed were third and fourth rate, and the music was effusive and banal, despite the accompaniment of a huge and much-vaunted organ built especially for the hall. The exhibition was most significant as a patriotic and symbolic identification of Australia with prevailing economic and cultural movements of the European world.

BIBLIOGRAPHY

Graeme Davison discusses all the Australian exhibitions, including Melbourne 1880, in "Exhibitions," *Australian Cultural History* (1982–1983): 5–21, a thoughtful appreciation of the symbolic manifestations of the art, architecture, and exhibits associated with international competitions. More straightforward accounts are John Parris and A.G.L. Shaw, "The Melbourne International Exhibition 1880–1881," *Victorian Historical Journal* (November 1980): 237–54, and Elizabeth Barrow, "The Melbourne Exhibition: Its Relationship with and Place in the Cultural Life of 'Marvellous Melbourne'" (bachelor's thesis, University of Melbourne, 1968). Historical context is provided in Graeme Davison, *The Rise and Fall of Marvellous Melbourne* (1978).

Among primary materials, the *Official Record of the Melbourne International Exhibition 1880–1881* (1882) is the most thorough, displaying the Victorians' passion for statistics. The original drawings of the Melbourne Exhibition Building are collected in the Bates Smart and McCutcheon Collection of the University of Melbourne archives. Reports of events at the fair were regular features in the Victorian press during its run, but the "Exhibition Supplement" to the *Argus* of October 2 and 6, 1880, is particularly useful, containing the history of Australian exhibitions, descriptions of the various courts and their exhibits, statistics on Australia's wealth and economic condition, and plans and illustrations of the exhibition site.

For a great deal of representative bad verse associated with the exhibition's cultural pretensions and marketing techniques, see [Edward Glick] "The Fairies at the Exhibition: an Extravaganza in Eight Scenes, Including a Fairy Cantata (Without Music)," *Great International Advertiser of 1880* (Melbourne), October 18, 1880. In a similar vein, though with imperialistic feelings, Leon Caron, *Victoria Cantata* (1880), is a composition first performed at the Melbourne exhibition that hails Victoria as the Queen of the South.

John Powell

ATLANTA 1881

INTERNATIONAL COTTON EXPOSITION

The idea of holding the International Cotton Exposition of 1881 in Atlanta originated with Edward Atkinson, a Boston textile mill magnate. Atkinson saw the exposition as a means of educating southern cotton farmers about ginning techniques so that cleaner bales would be sent to northern mills. But promoters of Atlanta, especially Henry W. Grady and others associated with the *Atlanta Constitution*, channeled Atkinson's idea into a different direction. They saw the exposition as an opportunity to demonstrate to the nation that the New South, and particularly Atlanta, had abandoned the plantation ideal and was now ready to worship the Yankees' industrial gospel.

Planning for the fair began in earnest when the International Cotton Exposition Association was incorporated in April 1880. The incorporators turned to the city's most flamboyant booster, Hannibal Ingalls Kimball, to organize the crusade for the exposition. Kimball, a native of Maine and a controversial figure in Reconstruction politics in Georgia, had earlier led a successful drive to build the state's largest cotton factory in Atlanta in 1879. Appointed chairman of the association's executive committee, Kimball immediately began looking for the funds. He and others argued that outside capital could not be found for the venture unless local citizens first indicated their support. He suggested that at least one-third of the association's capital stock issue (initially set at $100,000 and later raised to $200,000) would have to come from Atlanta. Within a 6-hour period on March 15, 1881, Kimball and his friends raised $36,600 in the city. Kimball shrewdly relayed news of this dazzling success to newspaper offices across the country. When he and other organizers of the exposition went on a whirlwind tour of northern cities later in the spring, they had no trouble finding additional Yankee capital.

When the exposition opened on October 5, 1881, attendance lagged at first because of inadequate hotel facilities. The executive committee addressed this problem by building a 300-room hotel adjoining the fair grounds (at Oglethorpe Park) and canvassing the city to enroll local citizens willing to shelter visitors in their homes. In response to the committee's request, many elegant residences along Peachtree Street were opened to strangers. Attendance picked up as a result of these actions. In all, more than 290,000 people eventually went to the fair before it closed on December 31, 1881.

Those who visited the fair saw 1,113 exhibits from thirty-three states and seven foreign countries. The exhibits were displayed in four buildings; most were items associated with cotton cultivation or textiles manufacturing, though just about everything usually seen at world's fairs of the era was available for viewing. On October 27, visitors saw an unusual demonstration. Shortly before sunrise on this day, enough cotton was picked and ginned on the grounds to make two suits of clothes. By the end of the day, the cotton had been woven into cloth, and the suits were given to the governors of Georgia and Connecticut during an evening reception.

After the exposition ended, its main hall (designed in the shape of a Greek cross for the purpose) was turned into a cotton factory, the Exposition Cotton Mills, which opened for business in 1882. This was not the only legacy of the International Cotton Exposition of 1881, often referred to as the South's first world's fair. It spawned a number of successors in the late nineteenth- and early twentieth-century South: two in Atlanta (the Piedmont Exposition of 1887 and the Cotton States and International Exposition of 1895); one in New Orleans (the Cotton Centennial Exposition of 1884–1885), one in Nashville (the Tennessee Centennial Exposition of 1897); and one near Norfolk (the Jamestown Exposition of 1907). All were expressions of the New South's urban-industrial ethos. While the region failed to industrialize as much or as profitably as the organizers of these expositions desired, it did succeed in demonstrating that its economic leadership had accepted the need for manufactures.

BIBLIOGRAPHY

The best source is H. I. Kimball, *International Cotton Exposition, Atlanta, Georgia, 1881: Report of the Director-General, H. I. Kimball* (1882). A good comparison of this fair with the later Cotton States and International Exposition may be found in Mary Roberts Davis, "The Atlanta Industrial Expositions of 1881 and 1895: Expressions of the Philosophy of the New South" (master's thesis, Emory University, 1952). A short summary of the event is provided by Jack Blicksilver, "The International Cotton Exposition of 1881 and Its Impact upon the Economic Development of Georgia," *Atlanta Economic Review* 7, no. 5 (May 1957): 1–5, 11–12, and 7, no. 6 (June 1957): 1–5, 11–12. Blicksilver overemphasizes, however, the economic spinoff from the exposition for Atlanta and Georgia. There is an adequate summary of Kimball's role in the undertaking in Alice E. Reagan, *H. I. Kimball: Entrepreneur* (1983). Many of the details and events of the fair are described most accurately in Franklin M. Garrett's *Atlanta and Environs: A Chronicle of its People and Events*, 3 vols. (1954), 2: 29–34.

James M. Russell

AMSTERDAM 1883

INTERNATIONALE KOLONIALE EN UNTVOERHANDEL TENTOONSTELLUNG

In the first half of the nineteenth century, the Netherlands experienced bleak times, characterized by little economic growth. By the 1860s and 1870s, this began to change, especially after 1876, when the Noord Canal was completed, bringing oceangoing vessels to Amsterdam. At the same time, the national rail system was rapidly improving, and in 1879, Amsterdam's new central station was completed. By this time, international expositions were commonly known to promote economic growth and tourism, and in 1880, a French entrepreneur, Edouard Agostini, saw potential in a fair in the Netherlands.

Agostini mailed brochures and information to a group of influential Amsterdam business leaders, describing the possibilities of an exhibition to be held in their city. A local organizing committee was formed and brought Agostini to Amsterdam as a technical adviser. Because the Netherlands was not well known except for the wealth of its colonial empire, the committee decided to organize the fair as a colonial exhibition, giving it the formal name of Internationale Koloniale en Untvoerhandel Tentoonstellung te Amsterdam.

A preliminary report was given to King William II, who endorsed the plan, but this was about all the help the organizers received from the government. Although the committee was unable to obtain national government funding, the city of Amsterdam donated the use of 62 acres of land in the western section of the city for use as an exposition site. After some difficulty, the committee contracted a Belgian firm to develop the site and build the large exhibition hall.

Behind the newly completed Rijksmuseum rose the main building of the fair. Measuring about 1,000 by 420 feet, the building covered some 13 acres. A temporary structure, it was built of wood, with a glass roof, but it was covered with plaster and painted canvas to give the impression of marble. The facade was decorated in a grotesque Indian motif, featuring large elephant heads and other animals, all cast in plaster. Other major exhibit halls were the Colonial Building, measuring 417 by 250 feet, and the Machinery Hall and the Art Palace, both 667 by 100 feet. There were many other buildings on the site, including a pavilion for the city of Amsterdam, a Japanese bazaar, and many small shops and restaurants. A canal, traversed by a bamboo bridge, ran through the grounds, providing a home for a Chinese junk.

The newly crowned King William III formally opened the exhibition on May 1, 1883. Although only the Netherlands and Belgium had comprehensive exhibits, other participants included most of the other countries of Europe, as well as China, Japan, India, Siam, the Dutch East Indies, New South Wales, and Victoria. Persia, Turkey, Egypt, Tunisia, and Mauritius represented the Middle

East and Africa, and the United States, Canada, Jamaica, Haiti, Brazil, Uruguay, and Venezuela came from the Western Hemisphere. Major attractions at the fair were model villages with natives brought to Amsterdam from Dutch colonies in the Caribbean and Southeast Asia. The natives displayed their way of life, foreshadowing the larger anthropological exhibits using Filipinos that were a staple of U.S. fairs in the early twentieth century.

By the time the exhibition closed on October 31, just over a million visitors had attended. This was the last major international exhibition held in Amsterdam.

BIBLIOGRAPHY

There is no record of primary materials surviving from the Amsterdam exhibition. The official report of the French commissioner, Oliver Claude Augustin Poullain Saint-Foix, *Rapport sur l'Exposition internationale industrielle d'Amsterdam en 1883* (1885), contains much general information about the fair, its theme, exhibits, and other participating nations. A much narrower account is Louis Roux, *Conference faite per L. Roux . . . le 17 aout 1883* (1883), which describes a conference held at the fair on the process of manufacturing dynamite. The Hagley Museum and Library, near Wilmington, Delaware, has a number of other catalogs or official reports from this fair. A contemporary account in English is ''The Amsterdam Exposition,'' *Nation* 37 (1883): 350–51. The only modern work dealing with this fair is Ileen Montijn, *Fair of Commerce* (1983), a short pamphlet published for its centennial.

Michael L. Gregory

BOSTON 1883–1884

THE AMERICAN EXHIBITION OF THE PRODUCTS, ARTS AND MANUFACTURES OF FOREIGN NATIONS

Known to Bostonians simply as the Foreign Exhibition, the American Exhibition of Products, Arts and Manufactures of Foreign Nations came as a result of the dogged determination of Boston's business leaders. In late May and early June 1881, these business leaders began discussing the idea of holding a world's fair in 1885. Ideas of economic growth and the potential for increased exports and imports were central to the argument of holding a world's fair in Boston.

By January 1882, however, it had become clear that the funds needed for the undertaking would not be raised, and plans were put on indefinite hold. Almost a year later, in December 1882, committed business leaders formed the Foreign Exhibition Association in an effort to keep the world's fair idea alive but on a much smaller scale. It was proposed to have an exhibition of foreign arts, products, and manufactures only. This idea proved to be much more realistic, and the Foreign Exhibition was officially opened on September 3, 1883.

Conducted entirely by the Foreign Exhibition Association, a private organization, the exhibition did not have financial assistance from the U.S. government. The government supported the goals of the exhibition by sponsoring official contact with foreign representatives, and by an act of Congress in June 1883, all objects intended for the exhibition were allowed to enter free of duty and remain so while on exhibit.

The exhibition was held in Mechanics Hall of the Massachusetts Charitable Mechanics Association. Designed by William G. Preston in 1880 and completed in 1882, this permanent structure was built for the association's triennial exhibitions, not specifically for the Foreign Exhibition. Mechanics Hall occupied a triangular piece of land at the intersection of Huntington Avenue and West Newton Street in Boston. It covered 92,000 square feet and was erected at a cost of $500,000. Mechanics Hall was equipped with many modern conveniences, including electric lights, which allowed the fair to remain open into the evening.

Featuring nearly 680 exhibits from forty countries, which was one of the largest foreign representations at a nineteenth-century world's fair, the exhibition was noteworthy in that none of the exhibits displayed objects from the host country. The displays consisted mainly of decorative objects, such as fabrics, porcelain, pottery, furniture and jewelry, as well as fine art objects. Products that could be easily sold were more prevalent than industrial products or machinery—hence the unofficial title, "The Grand Bazaar."

For the admission price of fifty cents, visitors could view the entire exhibition, including attractions such as the Japanese Tea House or the Vienna Beer Vaults, or listen to music from international bands performing at the bandstand in the central hall. The Western Art Gallery, containing European paintings and sculpture, was one of the most popular exhibits at the fair.

The Foreign Exhibition was scheduled to close January 5, 1884, but at the request of the foreign exhibitors, the board of directors voted to extend the fair for an additional week, lowering the admission price to twenty-five cents. On January 12, 1884, the exhibition officially closed.

During the four and one-half months the exhibition remained open, visitors numbered a disappointing 300,000. Charles Benjamin Norton, secretary of the Foreign Exhibition Association, estimated that four-fifths of the visitors came from outside the city of Boston and only 5 percent of Boston's population visited the exhibition. The fair was considered a financial failure, with unofficial newspaper accounts setting the losses at $25,000. Although the monetary loss was substantial, both foreign exhibitors and exhibition officials pronounced the fair a success in the intangible areas of increased education and commerce between nations.

BIBLIOGRAPHY

A limited number of primary sources are available in the Robert A. Feer Collection of World's Fairs of North America at the Boston Public Library. The holdings include sporadic daily programs, as well as assorted catalogs and guides to the exhibition. See, for example, *Lee and Shepard's Illustrated Catalogue, 1883–1884* (1883), Morris and Company, *The Morris Exhibit at the Foreign Fair, Boston, 1883–1884* (1883), and C. B. Norton, ed., *Official Catalogue Foreign Fair, Boston, 1883* (1883). The Massachusetts Historical Society in Boston holds a copy of the official catalog and another excellent primary source, *Minutes of the Committee on Exhibits of the Foreign Exhibition Association.* Bound in one volume, these minutes were recorded by C. B. Norton between December 1882 and April 1883 and contain much of interest on the planning of the foreign manufactures exhibit.

Good accounts of the exhibition can be found in the *New York Times*, June 2–3, October 14, 1881, January 17, 1882, January 13, September 4, 1883; and the *Boston Globe*, September 2, 18, 1883, January 13, 1884. Contemporary information about the design and building of Mechanics Hall, as well as additional accounts of the proposed 1885 world's fair and the 1883 exhibition, may be found in *American Architect and Building News*, May 21, June 4, 1881, January 27, 1883.

Andrea Witczak

CALCUTTA 1883–1884

CALCUTTA INTERNATIONAL EXHIBITION

India's first international exhibition, staged in the full flush of an age of exhibitions, opened to great pomp in Calcutta on December 4, 1883. A procession of dignitaries, led by the viceroy, the marquess of Ripon, and the duke of Connaught marched into the India Museum building at 4:30 P.M., attended by the Royal Warwickshire regiment, band, and colors. After a specially prepared cantata, addresses by noted individuals, and an invocation by the lord bishop of Calcutta, the duke of Connaught officially opened the exhibition. The buildings were then electrically lighted, no small wonder in 1883, a trumpet bray was sounded, and a thirty-one-gun salute was fired from the ramparts of Fort William. During the following three months about 1 million people viewed the exhibits. On March 10, 1884, Augustus Rivers Thompson, lieutenant-governor of Bengal, proclaimed the exhibition an almost unqualified success before it was officially closed by the viceroy.

The Calcutta exhibition was largely the private project of Jules Joubert, a naturalized citizen of New South Wales and an entrepreneur who became a leading promoter of international exhibitions in the 1880s. In December 1882 he presented a plan to Thompson, who agreed that the government of Bengal should provide 50,000 rupees for the purchase and display of provincial products and manufactures, arrange for the use of portions of the India Museum for display, and authorize the Public Works Department to erect additional buildings at Joubert's expense. Thompson, mindful of the successes of the great London exhibition of 1851 and of more recent colonial exhibitions in Sydney, Melbourne, and Christchurch, primarily hoped to encourage trade by advertising Indian products, particularly in the Australian colonies.

The main entrance to the exhibition was through the vestibule of the India Museum, a two-story structure built in the form of a quadrangle enclosing a courtyard. A permanent building (180 feet by 32 feet), which eventually housed the art gallery and jewelry court, was erected beside the museum on the east side of Chowringhee Road in order to shield from general view six "extemporized" annexes. In addition, on the west side of Chowringhee Road the Indian Court (488 feet by 120 feet), Machinery Court (410 feet by 144 feet), and several smaller buildings were temporarily erected according to designs utilized previously by Joubert in Christchurch. The unexpectedly large response from exhibitors forced the executive committee to expand into areas not previously designated until the exhibition comprised almost 22 acres, about 7 acres (300,000 square feet) of which was enclosed. A total of 2,500 exhibitors displayed over 100,000 articles, which were judged in 149 classes. Austria-Hungary, Great Britain, France, Germany, Italy, Belgium, Turkey, Japan, the United States, a number of European and British colonies, and the various Indian provinces were represented, although Austria-Hungary was the only country to appoint an official delegation. The Japanese court drew special attention to the artistic skill of "that remarkable people."

The Calcutta exhibition was hailed by promoters as a harbinger of India's integration into a world economy. It was in fact more important in introducing many Indians to non-Indian and non-British influences. The primary beneficiaries, however, were Joubert, a few tradesmen, and the local hotel and boarding-house industry.

BIBLIOGRAPHY

Relatively little has been written about the Calcutta International Exhibition of 1883, thus making the *Official Report of the Calcutta International Exhibition, 1883–84*, 2 vols. (1885) essential. Brief notices are given in C. E. Buckland, *Bengal under the Lieutenant Governors*, 2 vols. (1901), and H.E.A. Cotton, *Calcutta Old and New* (1907). General guides to Calcutta during the nineteenth century include M. Massey, *Recollections of Calcutta for Over Half a Century* (1918), and W. K. Fiminger, *Thacker's Guide to Calcutta* (1906).

The Indian and Anglo-Indian press, preoccupied during 1883 and 1884 with Lord Ripon's internal reforms, took relatively little interest in this exhibition, which was viewed largely as an entertainment. Scattered references, however, may be found in all of the Calcutta newspapers. See particularly Qui Vivra Verba, "The Exhibition," *Statesman and Friend of India*, November 20, 1883, 1640; "Opening Ceremony," *Hindoo Patriot*, December 10, 1883, 582; Gamin De Bon Accord, "The International Exhibition: Its Influence," *Statesman and Friend of India*, December 25, 1883, 1821–22; "Closing of the Calcutta International Exhibition," *Englishman*, March 11, 1884, 4; and "The Close of the International Exhibition," *Bengalee*, March 15, 1884, 124.

John Powell

LOUISVILLE 1883–1887
SOUTHERN EXPOSITION

Organized ostensibly "to advance the material welfare of the producing classes of the South and West" and "to exhibit the products and resources of the southern states to northern and eastern manufacturers," the Southern Exposition was a central element in Louisville's strategy to capture control of the southern market during the post-Reconstruction era. The concept of a Louisville exposition was first suggested in 1880 by Boston financier Edward Atkinson. The idea won the immediate endorsement of *Courier-Journal* editor Henry Watterson, but Atlanta preempted the notion by holding its Cotton States Exposition in 1881.

After the Atlanta exposition closed, Watterson resurrected the concept and in August 1882 gained the support of the Louisville Board of Trade. Two months later, the board appointed a committee headed by merchant J. H. Lindenberger to incorporate the Southern Exposition at Louisville. Paper manufacturer Bidermann du Pont was elected exposition president, and J. M. Wright, superintendent of the Board of Trade, was appointed general manager. To raise the projected $300,000 budget, the exposition directors initiated a stock subscription campaign, offering 12,000 shares at $25 per share. Sales progressed well, but there is no record that the entire offering was subscribed.

The exposition site was a vacant tract located between Fourth and Sixth streets, about 1 mile south of the central business district. Situated immediately to the north was Central Park, then owned by exposition president Bidermann du Pont and his elder brother, Alfred V. du Pont. When the du Ponts loaned the park for exposition use, the grounds approximated 45 acres.

Louisville architects Cornelius Curtin and Kenneth McDonald designed the exposition buildings. The main exhibition hall, constructed of wood and glass over a steel frame, measured 300 by 600 feet, enclosed 13 acres of floor space, and cost $200,000. Central Park served as a promenade and picnic ground and provided sites for a 3,000-seat Music Hall and an art gallery, which eventually housed works from the collections of New York financiers J. P. Morgan and August Belmont and former Louisville & Nashville Railroad president Victor Newcomb.

President Chester A. Arthur opened the Southern Exposition on August 1, 1883. The *Courier-Journal* predicted that the fair's influence would be "felt for years in cutting new channels for commerce, in opening new avenues of industries, and furnishing new sources of wealth and power." Over fifteen hundred exhibitors paid the $25 exhibit fee. Oriented largely toward southern industry and agriculture, exhibits gave particular emphasis to sawmilling, mining, sugar refining, and textile machinery. Much space was devoted as well to grape, hemp, tobacco, grain, silk, and rice cultivation. Fairgoers witnessed an electric lighting system that consisted of 4,600 16-candlepower incandescent lamps powered by fifteen dynamos furnished by the Edison Company of New York. Complementing this innovation was an electric railway that carried passengers on a narrow track that circled Central Park and passed through an artificial tunnel lighted by incandescent bulbs.

Although primarily a regional event, the exposition had a limited international dimension as well. The Museum of Natural History included specimens such as a mammoth from the Royal Museum in Stuttgart, Germany, an orangutang from Borneo, and the fossilized remains of a megatherium discovered in Argentina. Ethnological exhibits included a Japanese village installed in 1886, and the art gallery displayed a large number of paintings, sculptures, tapestries, and objects of art by international artists, mainly from American collections.

By the time the exposition closed its first season on November 10, 1883, it had attracted 770,129 paid guests and an additional 200,933 admitted on passes. The exposition operated through 1887, usually from August to October.

Along with bringing Louisville's economic advantages to national attention, the exposition was a catalyst for urban development. In 1885 alone, 260 large Victorian houses were constructed in the neighborhood. In 1890 William H. Slaughter developed the vacant fair site as St. James Court, an exclusive residential subdivision, which soon housed some of Louisville's most illustrious citizens.

BIBLIOGRAPHY

The most comprehensive contemporary source on the Southern Exposition is the *Southern Exposition Guide* (1883). The official program of the event, it includes an extensive narrative detailing the range of exhibits, activity schedules, descriptions of buildings and grounds, and aims of the exposition. It also contains extensive information about Louisville itself, such as an analysis of local economic conditions and lists of visitor accommodations and entertainment opportunities. A similar publication, which appeared three years later, is *The Great Southern Exposition of Art, Industry & Agriculture*. In addition to recapitulating much of the information contained in the *Southern Exposition Guide*, it contains data on the costs of buildings and grounds, local economic advantages, ethnological and historical exhibits, and exhibitor rules and regulations. The publication claims that the exposition was a financial success, but it provides no evidence to support the statement.

Useful secondary accounts are Carl E. Kramer, *Old Louisville: A Changing View* (1982), and George H. Yater, *Two Hundred Years at the Falls of the Ohio: A History of Louisville and Jefferson County* (1979). Kramer's pamphlet focuses on the neighborhood in which the Southern Exposition was located, exploring the event's impact on the area's growth and development, as well as describing the fair's exhibits and facilities. Yater's history of Louisville provides a concise analysis of the city's desire to strengthen its control of the southern market, the primary motive behind the Southern Exposition.

Carl E. Kramer

NEW ORLEANS 1884–1885
THE WORLD'S INDUSTRIAL AND COTTON CENTENNIAL EXPOSITION

The stagnation of despair has, by some magic transformation, given place to the buoyancy of hope, of courage, of resolve. The silence of inertia has turned into joyous and thrilling uproar of actions. We are a new people. Our land has had a new birth.

These words from a *New Orleans Times-Democrat* editorial of December 4, 1881, capture the emotional essence of the New South movement, which swept the southern business community in the closing decades of the nineteenth century. Impelled by a fervor very much akin to the Born Again Christian movement of our own day, the New South idea suggested that the old sectional quarrels be put aside and that henceforth the region should devote itself to commerce and industry—in a word, progress. It was also the impetus for the several expositions, including the World's Industrial and Cotton Centennial Exposition of 1884–1885 in New Orleans, which the region mounted during these years.

Not surprisingly, the men most closely associated with promoting the New Orleans exposition, or Cotton Exposition as it came to be commonly called, were all New South zealots. The most prominent of these were F. C. Morehead, a Vicksburg editor and president of the National Cotton Planter's Association, Edmund Richardson, described by a contemporary as the largest cotton planter in the United States, and with the exception of the khedive of Egypt, the largest in the world, and Major E. A. Burke, Bourbon Redeemer, treasurer of the state of Louisiana, and not least, editor of the *New Orleans Times-Democrat*. Given the support of such powerful men, the notion of a New Orleans cotton exhibition would prove to be an idea whose time had come.

In a letter of August 10, 1880, to the *New York Herald*, the economist Edward Atkinson urged that the centennial of the cotton industry in the United States be celebrated with an exhibition in New York. He asserted that the staple had first been exported from the country in 1784 and that the celebration therefore should be held in 1884. Nothing came of the New York idea, but in 1881 a cotton exhibition was held in Atlanta. Convinced that the Atlanta exhibition failed to achieve the potential inherent in Atkinson's idea, Morehead, Richardson, and Burke began a concerted campaign for a cotton exhibition to be held in New Orleans in 1884. In 1882 a resolution supporting their proposal was passed by a convention of the National Cotton Planter's Association, and on February 10, 1883, Congress gave legal existence to the proposal by an act creating the World's Industrial and Cotton Centennial Exposition.

In addition to various technical provisions, the congressional act placed the exposition under the joint auspices of the federal government, the National Cotton

Planter's Association, and the host city. On April 24, 1883, the executive committee of the association chose New Orleans as the site.

The act also provided for a thirteen-member board of management to be appointed by the president of the United States from nominations submitted by the National Cotton Planter's Association and the subscribers in the city where the exposition would be held. Edmund Richardson was chosen as president of the board of management, Samuel Mullen as its secretary, and Major E. A. Burke as the director general. The other board members were prominent local business and professional men.

Subscription to exposition stock opened in the spring of 1883 with initial pledges of about $225,000, payable in installments, from railroads, banks, businesses, the Cotton Exchange, and individuals. The city of New Orleans contributed $100,000 to erect the Horticultural Hall, which would remain as a permanent structure. In a report to his government, the British consul stated, "With this capital the Direction commenced work in March, 1884, as their own contractors and builders."

The location chosen for the exposition was a site of 249 acres comprising what was then called Upper City Park and is today called Audubon Park. Through a complicated series of highly questionable but profitable transactions, a cabal of entrepreneurs and legislators had sold the property to the state during Reconstruction, but it remained undeveloped. By 1884 this chicanery was all but forgotten when creditors suddenly threatened to foreclose on the property for unpaid notes just as work was commencing on the exposition. The state legislature rescued the property by hastily enacting legislation allowing the city to refinance a $108,000 balance due for twenty years.

Although plans called for opening the exposition on December 1, 1884, construction was not begun until December 1883, and only in March 1884, with one building begun, was construction on the main building started. Even then, no sense of urgency seems to have existed, and work was carried forward, according to an observer, by "sheer manual labor" without benefit of "one labor-saving appliance, not even a tramway for moving timber."

As a result of these conditions, construction on the physical plant had hardly begun when the enterprise reached its first financial crisis. Solution to the problem came in the form of a congressional loan of $1 million. This was subsequently supplemented by Congress with appropriations of $300,000 for the government display and $15,000 for a Woman's Department. To meet congressional requirements for the loan, the state legislature made a grant of $100,000 to the exposition.

These funds solved the immediate crisis, but they probably contributed to the financial failure that finally overtook the exposition. According to a contemporary observer, previous fears "of [not] completing even the main building . . . gave way to a species of madness which appears to have seized the management." It enlarged the plans, and if the money was sufficient for the original undertaking, it certainly was not adequate for the expansion. The expansion also caused delays in the completion of the various structures and in the installation of displays, which in turn required that the scheduled opening be changed from December 1 to December 16, 1884.

Even so, at the conclusion of the opening day's ceremonies, it soon became apparent to the visiting throng of 14,000 that the exposition was largely unfinished. The grounds, which for weeks had been described in newspapers as a veritable Shangri-la, were in reality a bleak landscape relieved only by some groves of ancient oaks, with here and there a hastily planted giant cactus. Indeed, a combination of heavy rains and a lack of gravel paths forced the visitors on opening day to walk ankle deep in mud. Conditions in the various exhibition halls were generally no better. The Woman's Department lacked flooring, and Louisiana's exhibit consisted of no more than an allotted area of empty space. Elsewhere in the vast halls, numerous displays from manufacturers, states, and foreign governments remained in their shipping cases. The consequence of such conditions was immediate. Telegraph wires that had carried the opening morning's confident speeches were soon busy with reports to the north and east about the unhappy state of the exposition. Attendance, both local and national, slackened sharply.

By spring, the exposition had overcome much of its earlier chaos. Asphalt walks finally permitted visitors to move freely from one building to another while enjoying the bright flower beds planted in the immediate vicinity of the buildings. And if many of the exhibits were less than had been promised, they at least revealed some sense of order.

In the center of the grounds on what is today a golf course stood the exposition's Main Building. Built entirely of wood, it covered over 31 acres and was credited by contemporaries with being one of the largest buildings ever erected. Attached to one of its sides was the Factories and Mills Building, with a floor area of 67,500 square feet. Actually an extension of the Machinery Hall in the Main Building, it housed displays of heavy machines used primarily in cotton, sugar, and rice processing. To the northeast of the Main Building stood the United States and States Building with a floor area of 500,000 square feet, also constructed of wood.

In addition to these mammoth halls were four other large buildings: the Horticulture Hall, the Art Gallery, the Grand Rapids Furniture Pavilion, and the Mexican National Headquarters. Ranged about the grounds were numerous small structures, including the Mexican iron pavilion, public comfort houses, stables, sawmills, and concession stands. Most of the exposition's buildings were designed by G. M. Torgerson, a Swedish architect who had come to the United States about fifteen years earlier. Architecturally, their style was typical of late nineteenth-century Victorian eclecticism.

The exhibits in the Main Building consisted of foreign and domestic displays, with a majority of the latter coming from private firms. These last were composed of raw and manufactured products and included ores, woods, fabrics, clothing, furniture, machinery, and educational materials.

Although exhibits were sent from many nations, including all of the major powers, many governments did not participate officially, and were represented only by private firms. Of the thirteen European displays, only the Belgian exhibit appears to have been extensive and truly representative of an advanced manufacturing country. Other European countries represented by displays were Great Britain, France, Italy, Austria, Russia, Germany, Denmark, Sweden, Norway, Portugal, Spain, and Hungary.

The remaining foreign exhibits were from Japan, China, Siam, Jamaica, Hawaii, Mexico, British Honduras, Venezuela, Brazil, Guatemala, Colombia, Nicaragua, Costa Rica, and El Salvador. Most of these non-European exhibits consisted of native artifacts and natural resources. In degree of completeness and quality, these exhibits ranged from very good to poor, with Japan and Mexico being the best. Indeed participation by Mexico was official and extensive. It erected two major structures and sent a military band and cavalry squadron to participate in the festivities.

The playing out of the exposition's life was highlighted by increasing financial difficulties and the erosion of public support. The large attendance so confidently predicted during the exposition's formative period did not materialize, and as a result, admission money was not sufficient to pay current operating expenses. By early February the debt had climbed to $360,000, and in desperation a committee went to Washington in the hope of obtaining a congressional loan. These efforts proved at least partially successful when on March 3, 1885, Congress appropriated $335,000 to aid the exposition. Though less than requested, the appropriation was made as a gift rather than a loan.

The World's Industrial and Cotton Centennial Exposition closed on June 1, 1885. As closely as can be determined, its debt in the end stood at $470,000. Of the originally predicted 4 million visitors, only 1,158,840 materialized. Nor was there any significant increase in the city or state's commercial and industrial development, which had been promised with such confidence by the New South advocates promoting the exposition.

Measured against those promises, the exposition was a failure. In an unintended way, however, it was a catalyst for important changes in the city. Visiting journalists, bored by the exposition and its too often dull exhibits, turned their attention instead to the city itself and the strange ways of its inhabitants. This attention would make New Orleanians for the first time aware of their own culture and its unique aspects. Simultaneously, articles in the national press about the city and its exotic way of life aroused the interest of a large and growing public just then acquiring sufficient leisure and surplus capital to permit travel. The exposition's unintended but very real legacy would be the inception of the city's tourist industry.

BIBLIOGRAPHY

The World's Industrial and Cotton Centennial Exposition prompted a considerable body of printed material. Although government documents, both state and federal, comprise only a small fraction of such material, they do include a number of important items. The most important of these are the various enabling and funding acts found in *U.S. Statutes at Large for the Period 1883–1885* and in *Acts Passed by the General Assembly of . . . Louisiana at the Regular Session . . . 1884*. One of the most revealing of such documents is a report to the British Parliament in May 1885 by that government's consul in New Orleans, A. de G. de Fonblanque, reprinted in the *Commercial*, no. 11, pt. 2 (1885).

By far the largest portion of printed material on the fair consists of the numerous pamphlets, catalogs, and guide books, with works devoted to individual displays greatly outnumbering the more general guides. In terms of reliability and utility, most of these publications contain useful and otherwise unavailable information, which may in general be relied upon. One of the best of these guides is Herbert S. Fairall, *The World's Industrial and Cotton Centennial Exposition, New Orleans, 1884–1885* (1885). The spirit of the times may be gauged by study of "The World's Cotton Centennial Exposition," an epic poem by Mary Ashley Townsend, read at the inaugural ceremony and published as a pamphlet.

Newspapers, both local and national, are an important source for studying the exposition. Local press stories should be read with the understanding that such accounts are often colored by boosterism and a desire to put the best light on the subject. Surprisingly, the reports on the exposition in the *Mascot*, a local scandal sheet, are generally accurate and among the most informative of all local press accounts.

A modern article that summarizes the fair and gives special attention to its organization and the role of women is Samuel C. Shepherd, Jr., "A Glimmer of Hope: The World's Industrial and Cotton Centennial Exposition, New Orleans, 1884–1885," *Louisiana History* 26, 3 (1985): 271–90.

D. Clive Hardy

ANTWERP 1885

EXPOSITION UNIVERSELLE D'ANVERS

The closing of the Schelde River linking Antwerp to the North Sea after the Belgian revolution of 1830 had also closed Belgium to the world. In October 1831, the major powers (France, Great Britain, Austria, Prussia, and Russia) signed a treaty ensuring free navigation on the Schelde River and also establishing a fee structure that benefited the Netherlands. Belgium, however, was to benefit from this agreement only seven years later when William I of the Netherlands agreed to sign the treaty. This action meant that Antwerp was to become what it had not been since the sixteenth century, a port open to all nations. At the same time, Belgium was opened up to the world on all borders. By 1883 the first dry dock was completed, allowing new expansion, and in 1885 the port received 4,798 ships with a capacity of 3.4 million tons. With this, there came the idea of inviting the world to join in the joy of the commercial metropolis of Belgium by means of a world's fair.

On January 21, 1884, at the urging of industrialists and shipbuilders from Antwerp, a committee was formed to organize a maritime, industrial, commercial, and artistic exposition. The government agreed, and the president of the Council of Ministers, Auguste Beernaert, accepted the post of director of the committee. The fair cost 4 million francs and received 3½ million visitors during a period of six months (May 2–November 2). It was inaugurated on May 2, 1885, in the presence of King Leopold II and Queen Marie-Henriette. The site (54.3 acres) was along the Escaut River in the proximity of the Gare du Sud. In fact, some of the buildings of the railroad station housed the exhibition of machines. A basin served the maritime section of the exposition. The classification of exhibits followed that of the Paris 1878 exposition. There were 14,472 exhibitors, of which 3,411 were Belgian. France and its colonies made up nearly one-third of the exhibits, with 4,361. Besides agricultural and industrial exhibitions, Antwerp welcomed those related to commerce and, above all, navigation.

Contrary to custom, the exhibitions were not located in one central pavilion but rather spread throughout several pavilions. The grand facade of the exposition was striking. It rose 66 meters and did not belong to any particular style but rather gave the impression of one of those prodigious Indian monuments where fantasy dominates, reminding visitors of a palace out of the "Thousand and One Nights."

Among the many participating countries was the Independent State of the Congo, born out of the International Association of the Congo founded by Leopold II in order to control the immense territories discovered by Henry Stanley and his collaborators between 1879 and 1884. Although it could not afford its own section, the Congo provided ethnographic exhibits.

One of the major attractions of the exposition was an international display of mechanical and electrical traction that featured all the types of motor vehicles existing at the time. Also, long-distance telephone communications between Brussels and the main cities of the country were inaugurated. To show the application of the telephone, the exposition committee organized concerts to be heard at a distance; from Antwerp some thirty people could hear a concert given in Brussels, more than 30 miles away. After attending one of these, Queen Marie-Henriette had such a telephone link established joining the Royal Chalet at Ostende, the Castle of Laeken, and the Theatre Royal de la Monnaie. In Ostende, on September 7, 1885, she listened to the opera *Faust*, given at the Theatre de la Monnaie in Brussels, 80 miles away.

BIBLIOGRAPHY

The best source is René Corneli and Pierre Mussely, *Anvers et l'Exposition universelle de 1885* (1885), published in both French and German. This book, dedicated to Leopold II, has a large section on the history of Antwerp. It also contains much information on the local artistic scene, as well as the city's military, commercial, and industrial importance. The second half of the book describes the contributions of the twenty-six participating countries. A Cockx and J. Lemmens, *Les Expositions universelles et internationales en Belgique de 1885 à 1958* (1958), is a good general reference on all the fairs that have taken place in Belgium. The *Catalogue officiel général* lists all of the entries but gives no descriptions of the exhibits, but the *Rapport du Comité de l'industrie* (1887), the official report of the industrial committee, contains descriptions of the exhibits. This publication is available at the Larson Collection at California State University at Fresno.

Maurice Gendron

EDINBURGH 1886

INTERNATIONAL EXHIBITION OF INDUSTRY, SCIENCE, AND ART

Launched by the Merchant Society of Edinburgh as an exercise in public relations for the city's commercial interests, the International Exhibition of Industry, Science, and Art was the largest of its kind ever staged in Scotland. It followed on the heels of the successful Fisheries Exhibition of 1883 and the Forestry Exhibition of 1884.

On May 6, 1886, the gates at the Grand Entrance were unlocked by Prince Albert Victor, and the buildings, designed by John Burnet and Charles Lindsay of Glasgow, were officially declared open. From that day until October 30, the 1,500 exhibits assembled in West Meadows Park amused and amazed well over 2 million visitors.

Through the main entrance at Brougham Street, past the fountain, and up a series of granolithic steps, lay the Grand Hall—the visual focal point of the exhibition and the only permanent structure on the site. Monumental statues depicting the arts and sciences flanked the main portal to the Grand Hall, and a panel portraying Minerva was stationed above. A 96-foot-high dome rose overhead, crowned with a gilt winged figure of Fame. Inside, the 38,400-square-foot Grand Hall housed the Fine Arts Section and concert hall, fitted out with its own pipe organ and orchestra platform.

Behind the Grand Hall stood an enormous temporary wooden structure, providing 230,000 square feet of exhibition space. This edifice was connected to the Grand Hall by way of a broad central avenue, which stretched the full 970-foot length from the main door of the Grand Hall to the far reaches of the exhibition courts.

In the *Prospectus* the Executive Council stated that its goal was to display the "Material Resources, Manufacturing, and Art Treasures of Scotland," proposing exhibits of machinery in motion, a department of fine art, a section dealing with the work of women, a section on artisans' work highlighting the talent and ingenuity of the working class, and a section featuring Edinburgh's ancient architectural heritage.

This last section, called Old Edinburgh, was a mock street composed of reconstructions of demolished fourteenth-, fifteenth-, and sixteenth-century buildings. Designed by architect Sydney Mitchell, Old Edinburgh was a pastiche of corbels, stringcourses, and gargoyles, all meticulously rendered in wood and plaster in imitation of weathered stone. Attendants in period costume completed the illusion.

In addition to the main buildings, West Meadows Park was dotted with other attractions. To the right of the entrance stood a model block of workmen's dwellings. Various types of Scottish building stone were on display. An electric railway ran along the northern periphery to shuttle spectators from one end of the grounds to the other. A small lake, fountains, a bandstand, numerous refreshment kiosks, and restaurants were provided.

The Edinburgh exhibition was a success. It was Scotland's largest as of that date; it marked Scotland's first use of electric lighting on such a grand scale; it amassed a £5,555 surplus; and its profitability served to encourage several noteworthy successors in Glasgow.

BIBLIOGRAPHY

Information from primary sources is available in abundance in the Edinburgh Room of the Edinburgh City Library. Among the official publications of the Exhibition Committee and popular commercial programs and guides are *Cameron's Guide Through the International Exhibition of Industry, Science, and Art (and Old Edinburgh)* (1886), *International Exhibition of Industry, Science, and Art, Edinburgh 1886: Daily Programme of Exhibition Arrangements, Amusements and Music* (1886), *International Exhibition of Industry, Science, and Art, Edinburgh 1886: The Official Catalogue* (1886), *International Exhibition of Industry, Science, and Art, Edinburgh 1886: The Official Guide to the Exhibition with Notes of What to See in Edinburgh* (1886), and *Pictorial Souvenir of the International Exhibition and Old Edinburgh 1886* (1886).

The Edinburgh Room holds the original prospectus for the exhibition, *Prospectus, International Exhibition of Industry, Science, and Art, Edinburgh 1886* (1886), which was developed in the planning stages and sets out the goals of the committee. Also in the Edinburgh Room is *The International Exhibition, Edinburgh, 1886: Abstract of Accounts* (1887), with financial information.

Good descriptive accounts of the exhibition are found in a series of contemporary articles that appeared in the *Builder* and *Building News*. See the *Builder* for May 8, May 15, June 5, July 31, August 21, and October 30, 1886, and *Building News* for May 7, May 14, June 4, and June 25, 1886.

Ken Carls

LONDON 1886

COLONIAL AND INDIAN EXHIBITION

The Colonial and Indian Exhibition (CIE), 1886, was the first fair devoted solely to imperial themes. The last in a series of four thematic exhibitions that had begun in 1883 and had surveyed fisheries, health, and music, the CIE was promoted under the patronage of the prince of Wales (the future Edward VII) during a period of great colonial rivalry. He realized the importance of British colonies and was struck by the attractiveness of their exhibits at the Paris 1878 exposition. He wanted millions of Britons to see that the colonies had advanced from frontier to civilized states and had contributed to the commonwealth, and he wanted to strengthen British ties with its colonies. To create public support for colonialism, it was necessary to demonstrate colonial economic importance to, and commercial ties with, Great Britain and to dispel the idea that colonies were liabilities. To this end, the CIE emphasized colonial economic, cultural, and political life.

The CIE was held in the Royal Horticultural Society Gardens, South Kensington, London, on 24 acres owned by the Royal Commission for the Exhibition of 1851. It leased the arcades from the International Fisheries Exhibition (1883) and added a few galleries for the Indian Palace, Australian exhibit, and colonial market. A contemporary described the architecture of the exhibition halls as "mere sheds, put up for convenience only," the interior defects of which were hidden from public scrutiny by art displays. Prince Albert Hall was leased, and the India Museum was included. A special Native Compound for visiting indigenous craftsman was erected.

Unlike previous exhibitions, the CIE employed no scheme of classification because it felt that recently founded colonies should have an equal footing with established colonies and because it was not easy to determine rules for classifying the varied colonial products and manufactures. Only colonial indigenes or businessmen were allowed to exhibit. Space was allocated on the basis of relative importance of colonies, and each colony determined what and how it would display. India received the largest interior floor space (about 26 percent), followed by Canada (22 percent), and Australasia, five colonies in Australia and one in New Zealand (25 percent). The other participating colonies divided the remaining space (about 27 percent). Each colony exhibited its exports, heritage and history, political and social life, geography, and ethnography. This included crafts, literature, art, architecture, minerals, woods for furniture and construction, and agricultural products such as wines, tea, coffee, cocoa, sugar, fruits, vegetables, cereals, meats, and fibers. Canada stressed its industrial products, India its tremendous variety of artware and fabrics, and Australasia its mineral and agricultural wealth, including meat. Many colonies had ethnographic exhibits that emphasized natives in their natural environments or working at indigenous crafts.

In addition to the exhibits, there were dining halls that served colonial cuisine; a bar for tasting wines and spirits; stalls to serve coffee, tea, and cocoa; and markets that sold colonial fruits, vegetables, and meats that had been shipped frozen. These displays and markets underscored the practicability of shipping produce and frozen meat to British markets. In the gardens, where band concerts were held, there were promenades and illuminated fountains that created a fairy-like atmosphere. The Royal Botanical Society sponsored flower and fruit shows. Numerous popular and professional lectures were presented. In July, in response to many inquiries, an emigration office was opened.

The exhibition was very successful. Between May 4 and November 10, 1886, over 5½ million visitors attended. To ensure that all social classes could participate, there were excursions from the provinces and, from mid-July, cheaper admissions on certain days for London workingmen and their families. Financially, the CIE made a profit at about £35,000, enough to pay the £5,964 debt of the International Instrument and Music Exhibition and to provide £25,000 to underwrite the founding of the Imperial Institute (today the Commonwealth Institute). The exhibits were to be the foundation of a permanent exhibit at the proposed Imperial Institute, but this came to naught.

BIBLIOGRAPHY

There are over fifty books and pamphlets on the Colonial and Imperial Exhibition: eight published by the Royal Commission and at least thirty-five by the colonies. The key works include the *Official Guide* (1886), which provided visitors with a highlighted tour, and the *Official Catalogue* (1886), which contained essays on each colony and a listing of the exhibits. *Her Majesty's Colonies: A Series of Original Papers Issued Under the Authority of the Royal Commission* (1886) provides historical, geographical, geological, and educational essays about each colony. *Reports on the Colonial Sections of the Exhibition* (1887), which was commissioned by the Royal Commission for the Colonial and Indian Exhibition and produced by the (Royal) Society of Arts, has twenty-six chapters covering key economic and natural resource topics. The *Report of the Royal Commission for the Colonial and Indian Exhibition* (1887) contains the major reports and statistics describing the exhibition. In addition to the more general and comprehensive catalogs covering the whole exhibition, there were handbooks describing the colonies and catalogs listing the colonies' displays. These were published by the individual colonies and served as promotional material. The 1887 *Proceedings* of the Royal Colonial Institute printed the papers of four conferences, and the *Journal of the [Royal] Society of Arts* 34–35 (1886–1887) printed additional papers. There are numerous articles in the *Times* of London in 1886 and in the *Westminster Review* (July 1886): 29–59, that cover the exhibition. In addition, there is excellent material on the connection between imperialism and exhibitions in chapter 4, "The Imperial Exhibitions," of John MacKenzie's *Propaganda and Empire: The Manipulation of British Public Opinion, 1880–1960* (1984), and William Golant's *Image of Empire: Early History of the Imperial Institute, 1887–1925* (1984).

The British Museum *General Catalogue of Printed Books* has the most complete bibliography. Unfortunately, the British Library's collection suffered severe damage in World War II, some of which has been replaced with microfilm copies of the Bodleian Library's originals. Most of the works are available in London in collections at the British Library, the Victoria and Albert Museum Library, and the Royal Commonwealth Society Library. The Bodleian Library at Oxford University possesses most of the significant works. It seems that only *Her Majesty's Colonies* and *Reports on the Colonial Sections of the Exhibition*, as well as several colonial catalogs, are available at the Library of Congress, and the *Report of the Royal Commission for the Colonial and Indian Exhibition* is at the University of Chicago. The Greater London Record Office possesses the papers of the (Royal) Society of Arts, which contain Reception Committee financial accounts.

Vladimir Steffel

ADELAIDE 1887–1888
JUBILEE INTERNATIONAL EXHIBITION

The origins of the Adelaide exhibition lay in intercolonial rivalry. Sydney had had an international fair in 1879 and Melbourne one a year later. A successful local show in 1881 using material from the eastern capitals' events encouraged plans for Adelaide's own international exhibition. The parliament of South Australia sanctioned the idea in November 1882, but persistent opposition came from country areas, which feared that public funds would be diverted from rural infrastructure to a metropolitan extravaganza. Rising estimates coincided with economic depression, and the scheme was abandoned in July 1884. However, Edwin T. Smith, mayor of Adelaide and a member of parliament (and to become Sir Edwin for his part in promoting the exhibition) was determined to revive the project, and, by having it underwritten by members of the Adelaide business elite, he persuaded the government once more to authorize the venture, this time to celebrate jointly the jubilees of South Australia and Queen Victoria.

Eighteen acres of the parkland surrounding the city center were given over to the exhibition. The project architects, Withall & Wells, had already designed several public buildings in Adelaide. Only the main building was intended to be permanent; paid for by the government, it was later used for exhibitions, concerts, and public service offices before its demolition in 1962. The only noteworthy feature of the layout was the use of electric lights, which made the building the largest in Australia to be so illuminated.

Twenty-six countries were represented, but most foreign exhibits came from sister colonies and from Great Britain. The late renewal of plans had militated against wider participation, and indeed, many displays were actually en route to Melbourne's Centennial International Exhibition of 1888. That the government increased tariffs and made no exception for exhibits did not help.

The exhibition was open for 172 days and was visited by 766,880 people. Few came from overseas, though there was a large intercolonial presence. Season tickets were only a guinea, respectively a half and a third of the Melbourne and Sydney prices. Daily tickets cost a shilling for adults, sixpence for schoolchildren, and threepence for state school pupils on organized visits. Inmates of charitable institutions were admitted free. The crowds were entertained by regular concerts, occasional military and firework displays, and one "tableaux of savage life" featuring aborigines from two mission stations.

The private sector had guaranteed £20,000 to cover any shortfall in revenue provided that the government budgeted £32,000 for the erection of the exhibition building itself. Receipts actually covered the other costs, and the guarantors were not called upon.

The exhibition paid for itself in more ways than balancing the books. It assisted recovery from a severe economic depression by providing employment to over 2,700 construction workers and attendants, by stimulating local business through visitors' spending, and by generally raising morale. That one of the least populated Australian colonies could successfully put on an exhibition of this magnitude showed that South Australia had come of age, though its maturity was set firmly within an imperial context, as the sentiments of the official speeches clearly demonstrated.

BIBLIOGRAPHY

The only writing by historians on the Adelaide Jubilee International Exhibition is Carmel McKeough and Norman Etherington, "Jubilee 50," *Journal of the Historical Society of South Australia* 12 (1984): 3–21. This article provides substantial detail on the background to the exhibition, the exhibition itself, and its aftermath. Some material on the exhibition site and buildings can be found in J. M. Daly, "The Adelaide Parklands: A History of Alienation" (master's thesis, University of Adelaide, 1980).

Contemporary material is also sparse, except for regular reports in the South Australian press, particularly the *Advertiser* and the *Register*. These are especially useful for details of the opening (*Register*, June 22, 1887) and closing (*Advertiser*, January 7, 1888) ceremonies and the presentation of awards (*Register*, December 1, 1887). This material, however, is reproduced in the official publication, *The Adelaide Jubilee International Exhibition 1887: Reports of Juries and Official List of Awards* (1889), which also contains lists of promoters, officials, guarantors, and jurors, as well as the Exhibition Ode, the final report to the promoters, and the balance sheet of the project. In the Larson Collection at the library of California State University, Fresno, is J. C. Neild, *Report of the Executive Commissioner for New South Wales to the Adelaide Jubilee International Exhibition, 1887–88* (1890). In addition to the official report of New South Wales's participation, this document contains site and building plans for the exhibition. A contemporary guide, H. J. Scott, *South Australia in 1887* (1887), includes a short description of the Adelaide fair and a longer sketch of the history and present state of South Australia. Additional information is available in the *South Australian Parliamentary Debates* and the *Notice Papers of the Adelaide City Council* for the years 1886–1888.

Wray Vamplew

BARCELONA 1888

EXPOSICIO UNIVERSAL DE BARCELONA

Spain's first international exposition dramatized Catalonia's resurgence as an industrial, commercial, and cultural center. The exposition celebrated regional power and international commerce while orienting the city of Barcelona and the surrounding region toward an apparently prosperous economic future.

Catalonia had declined from medieval splendor as Spanish interests shifted from the Mediterranean to the New World. After military repression in the eighteenth century, agriculture, textiles, and colonial trade spurred new industrialization during the nineteenth century. Economic growth funded cultural revival and nationalism. The population of Barcelona mushroomed from 34,000 in 1717 to 273,000 in 1887, and the city became a center for culture, finance, industry, and politics.

Eugenio Serrano de Casanova initiated the exposition as a private venture in 1886. When he failed, Mayor Francesc Ruis i Taulet adopted the idea, enlisting leaders from the newly emergent urban elites. Although the fair had been scheduled to open in 1887, Serrano's troubles and strikes postponed the inauguration until the following year.

The fair's 115-acre site, the Ciudadela Park, carried historical and urbanistic importance. The Ciudadela had been built in 1716 to dominate the city, which hated it as a symbol of state repression. In 1869, Barcelona regained the site from the Spanish government. Josep Fontseré produced plans to develop it in 1873, opening Barcelona beyond its constraining medieval walls and creating its largest park space. The exposition incorporated Fontseré's work, including the *Umbracle*, an arched cast-iron pavilion, and a monumental fountain designed by Antoni Gaudí.

Josep Vilaseca's Arch of Triumph crowned the exposition entrance, which led visitors along park avenues and by statuary before they reached the main buildings. Twenty-four naves in the 17-acre Palace of Industry housed international exhibits. Nearby were the Palace of Fine Arts (designed by Font Carreras) and the Hall of Colonies. Barcelona's finest architects contributed buildings. Lluís Domenech i Muntaner created his first major work in the still-extant café-restaurant, a neo-Gothic edifice ornamented with ceramic shields. Antoni Gaudí built a pavilion for his patrons, the López family. Companies, clubs, and cities erected smaller pavilions. Across cast-iron bridges, a harborside maritime section included naval, trade, and electricity pavilions. Outside the park, Domenech's hotel for international visitors drew comment for its style and extraordinarily rapid construction time of sixty-nine days.

The infant King Alfonso XIII and his regent-mother Maria Cristina inaugurated the exposition on May 8. The royal visitors also witnessed Jochs Florals, a historic Catalan literary competition. This event was boycotted by some Catalanists, who had opposed the exposition, fearing that it would fail and bring ridicule on the region and its national movement. Others, however, used the Jochs and the exposition to support Catalonia's cultural and nationalistic revitalization.

One peseta bought admission to the marvels of 12,203 exhibitors from twentyseven countries, including the United States, China, and Japan, whose displays were especially popular. Exhibits from Europe and Latin America were prominent beside those of Spain's possessions in the Caribbean, the Far East, and Africa. International naval squadrons plied the harbor. Triptyches by Hieronymus Bosch, loaned from Madrid, joined local art treasures. Concerts were frequent, with Isaac Albéniz, already a mature virtuoso and later one of Spain's major composers, playing in France's section. National congresses of archaeology, economics, and medicine met during the exposition; lighter entertainments included magic fountains, photographers, and a "captive" (tethered) balloon.

The Universal Exposition closed on December 9 after receiving more than 2 million visitors. Yet as a modern historian notes, "One chapter of the evolution of Barcelona closed while there opened that of the great European and cosmopolitan Barcelona whose adventure would reach our day." The arch, a few buildings, and the park remain, but the fair's legacy was more significant as a statement of bourgeois Catalan expectations. Subsequent growth faced bitter class conflict and state oppression, yet the Exposició Universal marked Barcelona's reemergence as a modern European capital.

BIBLIOGRAPHY

Josep María Garrut's *L'Exposició universal de Barcelona de 1888* (1976) was, until 1988, the only monographic study of the exposition, based on primary documents from the exposition in the archives of the Institut Municipal d'Història de Barcelona. This short study is nonetheless comprehensive regarding the origin, structure, and experience of 1888, and it is well illustrated. The Institut is the primary repository for original sources, newspapers, published guides, and an excellent photo collection. Published guides include *Catálogo de la sección oficial del Gobierno, Exposición universal de Barcelona de 1888* (1888), *Catálogo General Oficial* (188), and *Estudios sobre la Exposición Universal de Barcelona* (1888).

The historical context of the exposition can be explored in Vicens Vives, *Industrials i polítics del segle XIX* (1962), and for the ruling strata, in Gary McDonogh, *Good Families of Barcelona: A Social History of Power in the Industrial Era* (1986). *Barcelona y sus exposiciones*, a supplement to the newspaper *Las Noticias* published on the occasion of the 1929 fair in the city, has many interesting comparative presentations of daily life in Barcelona in 1888 and 1929. Eduardo Mendoza, *La ciudad de los prodigios* (1986), is a detailed novelistic reconstruction of the life of the lower classes of Barcelona in relation to the exposition.

The centennial of the 1888 Exposició has produced new major studies of the fair, its context, and its influence. *Exposició Universal de Barcelona: Libre del Centenari 1888–1988* (1988) is a lavishly illustrated 600-page text by leading historians and geographers under the editorship of Ramon Grau. Pere Hereu Payet and others consider history and urbanism in *Arquitectura i ciutat a l'exposició universal de Barcelona* (1988).

Gary W. McDonogh

GLASGOW 1888
GLASGOW INTERNATIONAL EXHIBITION

Civic-minded Glaswegians put on a show in 1888 that left little doubt that the Scottish city was indeed flourishing. Glasgow, an important trade center in the textile, heavy engineering, and coal markets, sought to capture an even greater slice of the international export pie. Besides, it was appropriate that the world's attention should be drawn to the birthplace of James Watt's steam engine, which had revolutionized industrial production.

From the inaugural fanfare heralding the prince and princess of Wales's visit to unlock the gates in the spring of 1888, through to the high spirits of the closing day throngs that same autumn, the site along the River Kelvin in Kelvingrove Park was a testament to Victorian achievement. Though there were a limited number of foreign exhibitors, thus qualifying the event as technically international in scope, Scottish industrial products, processes, and culture figured predominantly into the exhibition offerings.

James Sellars of Glasgow won the competition for exhibition building design, and with James Barr, he contrived a monumental structure in the Moorish style. The picturesque building featured a 150-foot-high dome at its center, surrounded by four square towers, each topped with a minaret.

The building was arranged along two major interior avenues. The Main Avenue connected the Grand Concert Hall, the Fine Art Galleries, and the Women's Industries Section, which were located at the east end of the building near the Gray Street entrance, with the Machinery Section, which was housed at the west end. Perpendicular to the Main Avenue, the Transverse Avenue ran from the southerly Sandyford Street entrance through the building and out to the grounds. Towering over the intersection of the two avenues was the great dome, painted golden yellow with red and green arabesques.

Four figures—"Industry," "Science," "Art," and "Agriculture"—gazed down from the arched dome supports, each presiding over its respective discipline represented in the exhibition. Exhibits were divided into twenty-one classes covering such far-ranging topics as agriculture, natural resources, engineering, transportation, machinery, weaponry, chemistry, food science, fishing, education, and the fine and decorative arts.

Additional attractions were the Bishop's Castle, exhibiting relics of Glasgow's past; an 85-foot-high terra-cotta fountain by Doulton & Company; an illuminated electric fountain 120 feet in diameter; a switchback railway; a display of the Queen's Jubilee presents, 799 in number; and various boating events on the river, ranging from submarine launches to rides on gondolas brought to Glasgow from Venice by sea.

The *Daily Programme* on October 16, 1888, announced a welding exhibition,

Indian artisans at work, a working dairy, a diamond-cutting demonstration, machinery in motion, an organ recital in the Grand Hall, and three military band concerts. Or one could try one's luck at the curling rink or in the shooting galleries, which lay within the exhibition grounds in Kelvingrove Park.

Enthusiasm for the undertaking was reflected in a total attendance of 5,748,379 persons, many from other parts of Great Britain, having taken advantage of special exhibition rail fares; others were local season ticket holders. In the final accounting, the exhibition realized a £41,000 surplus. All buildings constructed for the exhibition were removed, though profits were used to build the Glasgow City Museum and Art Gallery, which still stands in Kelvingrove Park.

BIBLIOGRAPHY

A wealth of primary sources is available in the Glasgow Room of the Mitchell Library, Glasgow. Among the holdings are the following catalogs, programs, and guides to the exhibition, some official publications by the Exhibition Committee and other popular commercial versions (most include maps of the exhibition buildings and grounds): *Elliot's Popular Guide to Glasgow and the Exhibition with Excursion Notes* (1888); *How to View the Exhibition: Hints to the Casual Visitor* (1888); *International Exhibition Glasgow* (1888); *The Official Catalogue* (1888); *The Official Daily Programme* (1888); *Invention: A Weekly Journal for Manufacturers, Engineers, Capitalists, and Scientists,* 10, no. 482 (August 4, 1888); *MacDonald's Guide to the Glasgow International Exhibition of Industry, Science, and Art* (1888); *Tourists' Guide to the City* (1888); *Program of the Royal Visit to Glasgow and the Exhibition* (1888); *Sneddon's Guide to Glasgow International Exhibition* (1888); *Souvenir of the Glasgow International Exhibition, 1888* (1888); and *Wilson's Penny Guide to Glasgow and the Exhibition of 1888, Comprising Notices of Every Object of Interest to Strangers and All About Town* (1888).

The Glasgow Room also holds special exhibition numbers of contemporary periodicals, which give accounts and illustrations of the exhibition. Among these are the following: *Mail Exhibition Extra, "Supplement to the North British Daily Mail,"* no. 1, April 19, 1888; no. 2, April 26, 1888; no. 3, May 3, 1888; no. 12, November 14, 1888; and *Pen and Ink Notes at the Glasgow Exhibition* (1888).

A series of contemporary articles on the exhibition written for the edification of those with interest in matters of building, design, and aesthetics is found in the *Builder.* See issues for April 9, October 22, and December 17, 1887, and May 6, May 26, June 16, August 4, and November 17, 1888.

Secondary sources that contain both summarization and interpretation of the Glasgow exhibition are Alastair L. Goldsmith, "The Glasgow International Exhibitions, 1888–1938" (thesis, University of Strathclyde, 1985), and Juliet Kinchin and Perilla Kinchin, *Glasgow's Great Exhibitions: 1888, 1901, 1911, 1938, 1988* (1988). John Allwood, *The Great Exhibitions* (1977), contains a brief discussion of the Glasgow fair.

The Glasgow Museum and Art Galleries holds among its collections a large oil painting by Sir John Lavery that depicts the visit of Queen Victoria to the exhibition in August 1888. The museum holds many of Lavery's 150-odd portrait studies of persons depicted in the audience at the queen's visit.

Ken Carls

MELBOURNE 1888–1889
CENTENNIAL INTERNATIONAL EXHIBITION

The Centennial International Exhibition was among the most natural of all international festivals. Opening on August 1, 1888, it coincided with an age of exhibitions, with the celebration of Australia's centennial anniversary, and with the apex of Melbourne's remarkable material prosperity of the 1880s. The exhibition, like the pageant poems produced for it, celebrated Melbourne's unprecedented progress, "its vigorous business and social life, its widening repute." More than 10,000 people, including the governors of all the Australian colonies, assembled to witness patriotic ceremonies performed in the quasi-religious atmosphere of the vast Exhibition Building, surrounded by the "florid imagery" of international brotherhood. Figures representing the principal applied arts and sciences covered the eight interior faces of the pillars supporting the second-highest dome in the world. The seasons were represented on the four panels below the cornices. Four large tableaux above the main arches featured Peace in a white robe and the colony of Victoria personified welcoming the nations. In keeping with Victoria's exuberant spirit, space and electrical power were provided free of charge to those it welcomed, leading to a £238,000 deficit and the resignation of Chief Justice George Higinbotham as president of the Exhibition Commission. However, to most of the commissioners, including Sir James MacBain who succeeded to the presidency, this seemed a small price to pay for the goodwill engendered and the business brought to the colony. Almost 2.2 million persons attended the exhibition before its closing by Sir Henry Loch, governor of Victoria, on January 31, 1889.

The Centennial International Exhibition originated in anticipation of Australia's centennial entertainments. With Victoria's economy booming, its prime minister, Duncan Gillies, realizing that New South Wales had waited too late to prepare, pushed forward with plans for a fair in Melbourne. Although officials in Sydney were only moderately enthusiastic about the proposal, few denied that an international fair would complement Australia's hundredth anniversary. Melbourne's great advantage lay in an already developed site, centering around the Exhibition Hall in Carlton Gardens, built and landscaped for the Melbourne International Exhibition of 1880–1881 at a cost of more than £150,000. Between 1880 and 1888 various parts of the hall had been in use as a concert hall, government printing shop, and aquarium. The quadrangle formed by the main hall and its perpendicular eastern and western annexes was once again roofed and was expanded toward the back to provide for more than 35 acres of exhibition space.

Visitors found Melbourne flat and dusty, with little discernable charm, yet nonetheless impressive, boasting more large public buildings than any other British city outside London and flaunting an air of animation befitting a burgeoning land. Most visitors were fascinated by the fast and silent cable trams, and electric lighting was new enough to attract considerable attention. Like Melbourne's earlier international fair, the Centennial Exhibition featured trade and mechanical exhibits designed to promote commerce and to improve the "technical education" of Australians.

The United States, Great Britain, France, Germany, and Austria-Hungary were the major nations officially represented among ninety-three participating states. Great Britain contributed an "imposing display" ranging from machinery to Wedgewood. The largest and most interesting of the French exhibits was reckoned to be that of the minister of public education, illustrating the painstaking steps the French government had taken in education. German exhibits of porcelain and a variety of manufactured goods were handsomely displayed through the efforts of an architect sent from Berlin for the purpose of decorating the German court with "triumphal arches and gonfalons, colossal busts of the three emperors, and an imposing statue of Germany typified as a female figure surmounting the Globe." Austria was represented by Bohemian glass and furniture displays. The leading features of the U.S. court were the Singer Sewing Machine Company display, which incorporated huge mirrors to display its machines to advantage, and the large-scale model of the Anheuser-Busch brewery in St. Louis, complete with working railroads, trams, and steamboats. About half the floor space was taken by Australian exhibitors. Victoria's contributions alone covered nearly eight acres and featured gold, wool, wheat, and wine. The exhibits of New South Wales included wool and large samples of a variety of mineral resources, including quartz, silver ore, tin, copper, lead, and mercury. Despite the emphasis on natural products and machinery, however, the most popular attractions of the exhibition were sideshows such as the switchback railway and musical concerts. These were all the more attractive because there were so few diversions for a public that quickly tired of technical exhibits.

Unlike the Melbourne exhibition, the centennial commissioners determined that theirs should be a cultural celebration. To this end they paid the distinguished English conductor, Frederick Cowan, £5,000 to create an orchestra that performed more than 260 concerts over a period of six months for approximately a half-million persons. The art exhibits, housed in a continuous gallery encircling the main hall, were popular, displaying more than 2,000 paintings on loan from Britain, France, and other countries.

The Centennial International Exhibition was a symbol of Australia's patriotism and achievement. It is not surprising that Australians, relatively isolated from the rest of the world, flocked to Melbourne in large numbers to take part in a display of national pride and to be entertained. Despite intercolonial cavils offered up by the press, the fair was considered by most to be a great success in what proved to be the twilight of Melbourne's golden age of prosperity.

BIBLIOGRAPHY

Graeme Davison's excellent article, "Exhibitions," *Australian Cultural History* (1982–1983): 5–21, includes this exhibition in a discussion of the symbolism associated with the art, architecture, and exhibits seen at all the Australian fairs. The exhibition is also treated in "Centennial Celebrations," in Graeme Davison, J. W. McCarty, and Alisa McLeary, *Australians 1988* (1988). A straightforward narrative account of the fair is J. R. Thompson, "The Melbourne Centennial Exhibition, 1888–1889" (bachelor's thesis, Monash University, 1968). Geoffrey Serle provides historical context for the exhibition in *The Rush to Be Rich: A History of the Colony of Victoria, 1883–1889* (1971).

The basic primary source is the *Official Record of the Centennial International Exhibition, Melbourne, 1888–1889* (1890), full of factual data and statistics. The local press gave regular coverage to the exhibition, but the "Exhibition Supplement" to the *Argus* of August 2, 1888, is especially valuable for its background information on the exhibits of the various courts as well as on Australia's wealth and economic condition. The supplement also includes illustrations and site plans for the exhibition.

The U.S. role is best covered in the *Reports of the United States Commissioners to the Centennial International Exhibition at Melbourne 1888* (1889) and in a wide range of official documents contained in the National Archives, Record Group 43.

John Powell

PARIS 1889

EXPOSITION UNIVERSELLE

Few other world fairs have come to fruition under less auspicious circumstances than the Paris Exposition universelle internationale of 1889. Yet of the great exhibitions of the nineteenth century, only the Crystal Palace of 1851 and the Paris exposition of 1867 rivaled the unmitigated success, acknowledged by friend and foe alike, of the Exposition universelle.

Although opponents decried ever-growing expenses, dislocation of life and work, frequency of financial failure, risk of imitation, and the unwritten law of "bigger is better," associated with world's fairs, it was clear by the late nineteenth century that certain states—and manufacturers—were most adept at exhibiting and believed that the prestige, as well as economic benefit, derived from a good showing was worth the effort. France had proven exhibition skills, a generally supportive leadership, and a capital city that was unquestionably one of the best sites in the world for a fair. While the exhibition foes could point to the great deficit of 1878 as reason enough to forgo another such venture, there was a general consensus that the tradition of holding an international exhibition in Paris every eleven years would be honored. There was only minimal apprehension that the exposition year would coincide with the centennial of the French Revolution of 1789, a date by no means dear to European monarchies or to every Frenchman.

In the summer of 1884, when France's commerce minister, Anne-Charles Hérisson, launched preliminary studies for an exposition in 1889, arguments, pro and con, proliferated in the press. To the traditional objections about stolen secrets, frequency, inflation, crime, and the influx of foreign workers was added the new voice of socialism grumbling that money would be better spent improving the living conditions of French workers. Other concerns were expressed about additional burdens on a depressed economy and the date's coinciding with the centennial of the Revolution. Exposition advocates countered with the usual lists of benefits (even the socialists, though theoretically committed to the overthrow of the capitalist system epitomized by expositions, could not ignore the job opportunities offered by a great fair in a decade of depression and chronic unemployment), but the relationship of the exposition to the centennial was especially divisive and troubling. There was serious consideration of a purely national fair in 1889 (to avoid inevitable monarchical snubs) and postponing a grand international exposition until 1900. The government ended discussion on November 8, 1884, with a decree announcing a "universal" exposition in 1889, following the tradition of eleven-year intervals and noting, almost as an aside, the anniversary of the Revolution. Accompanying decrees specified dates (May 5 to October 31, later changed to May 6 to November 6, 1889) and established a commission under the presidency of Antonin Proust to work out preliminary problems of site, financing, and design.

On March 14, 1885, the Proust commission submitted its report to the minister of commerce, but cabinet changes and the subsequent preoccupation of the government with other matters eventually gave rise to rumors and doubts concerning the status of the exposition. Fortunately for the fate of the exposition, Edouard Lockroy became minister of commerce in December 1885 and proceeded with plans for a fair despite disturbing reports that Europe's monarchies would refuse to participate and amid continued indecision about a national versus an international festival. Finally, the government decided to stage an extravaganza that the world could not ignore. On July 6, 1886, the National Assembly approved an appropriation of 17 million francs to be used along with 8 million from the Paris Municipal Council and 18 million provided by a group of capitalists organized as the Association de garantie to finance a projected cost of approximately 43 million francs. The unpopularity of not being able to offer free tickets as stipulated by the Association de garantie (2,270,000 had been admitted free in 1878) forced an adjusted financial arrangement as late as March 1889. The government accepted a proposal from the Crédit Foncier to provide 21.5 million francs instead of the original 18 million, and to allow free tickets by issuing 1.2 million *bons* of 25 francs each, containing twenty-five admission tickets and eighty-one lottery drawings distributed over seventy-five years. This was a successful arrangement; the government gained 3.5 million francs, and the Crédit Foncier made a profit of 3 million.

Lockroy, aware that the "clou" or central attraction of the exposition must be especially enticing in 1889, generally followed the Proust commission's recommendations for the exhibition halls and focused his attention on proposals for the world's tallest structure to be built on the Champ de Mars. A competition for the designs of the major buildings of the exposition was announced on May 1, 1886, with the most detailed specifications for a 300-meter iron tower, 125 meters square at the base, thus matching precisely the design of Gustave Eiffel. (Despite only two weeks for project preparations, over 100 tower designs were submitted, including a gigantic guillotine and a 350-meter stone pyramid bearing sculptures of the heroes and main events of the Revolution.) Ferdinand Dutert's design for a Galerie des Machines and Jean Formigé's companion Palais des Beaux-Arts and Arts Libéraux were also accepted. In July 1886, the administrative structure of the fair was finalized with the minister of commerce as general commissioner, three executive directors (of works, management, and finance), an executive committee, departmental committees, and lists of regulations for exhibitors.

The official decrees of July 1886 carefully described the intent to commemorate the economic progress of the century, and in the months following, the government sought to disassociate the centennial of the Revolution from the exposition. The artifice did not work. Formal invitations, issued through the diplomatic corps after March 17, 1887, brought disappointing—though not unexpected—results.

Only Greece, Switzerland, Norway, and Serbia had accepted by January 1888, although the United States, the South and Central American republics, Japan, Morocco—some twenty-nine states in all—accepted during the year. The major European states, as well as most of the smaller European countries declined (only Great Britain and Russia openly objected to the commemorative date). Yet when awards were distributed to exhibitors in September 1889, only the flag of the German empire was missing. The refusals, as France had hoped, were merely official, with no restrictions upon private exhibits. Special committees were formed in nearly every country to coordinate exhibits from private parties both with and without government support (only Germany, Montenegro, Sweden, and Turkey had no committees, and exhibitors eventually came from all of these except Montenegro). Thus, the world of business paid little heed to the political implications of the exposition or to the official or unofficial support of their governments.

The typical French response was to blame German hegemony for the snubs and firmly resolve to prove France's great power status with a magnificent achievement. The rejections, in fact, freed the politicians to sanction special exhibits and fêtes commemorating the centennial outside the exposition grounds. Determined to maintain the fair's apolitical designation, neither exhibits nor the numerous congresses planning to meet in conjunction with the exposition were allowed to portray specifically religious or political topics.

The exposition, despite its attempts to attract exhibits from all parts of the world, was distinguished by its national character. More resolutely French than any other major exhibition, it would be regarded as a great credit to the perseverance, confidence, and genius of France. The nation, divided from the Revolution, divided at the onset of the centennial year, and soon to be rent asunder again in the 1890s, came together in the summer of 1889 with an unprecedented display of artistic and technological achievement bolstered and magnified by fervent patriotism and national pride. Yet a more insidious threat to the success of the exposition was forming just when international participation seemed assured. Frequent cabinet changes always invited speculations of French political instability, but the phenomenal rise of General Georges Boulanger seemed positive proof.

As minister of war in 1886, Boulanger won popular recognition with proposals for republicanizing and reforming the army. The dashing general's talented demagoguery elicited almost frenzied support from diverse, and often incompatible, elements of the population. While substantial endorsement for Boulanger's electoral campaigns came from the nationalist and monarchist right, the movement's democratic and almost revolutionary overtones also appealed to some radical and socialist groups. Boulangism was essentially a protest movement incorporating both conservative political opposition and widespread popular disillusionment toward the Third Republic's opportunist leaders.

By the spring of 1888, Boulanger's immense popularity and the near hysteria that accompanied his movement provoked fears of an increasing momentum toward political crisis and even violence. The implications of Boulangism for the exposition were therefore potentially more destructive than the monarchical rejections and politicized the fair far more than did its concurrence with the centennial of the Revolution. Alarmed by the general's broad support, the government sought to strengthen its position and to dispel doubts concerning national security by associating the exposition with the preservation of France's republican institutions. When Boulanger's foes tried to damage his reputation by accusing him of opposing it, the general replied that the exposition was the last thing in the world he would harm. Boulanger's popularity crested in January 1889, however, and began to dissipate with his unexpected flight to Belgium in April. Public preoccupation with the exposition was without doubt a major factor in his defeat.

In the tradition of great fairs, the exposition was not quite ready on the designated opening day of May 6, and the opening ceremonies drew few plaudits. From the day of least attendance (May 10 with 36,922), the exposition's popularity peaked on October 3 when 387,877 crowded the gates. A grand total of over 32 million (some 16 million more than in 1878) came to see 61,722 exhibitors, more than half (33,937) from France, spread over a site of 228 acres extending from the Champ de Mars and the Trocadéro, down the quai d'Orsay to the esplanade des Invalides. Industry and the arts were housed on the Champ de Mars; horticulture on the Trocadéro; agriculture on the quai d'Orsay; and colonies, war, health, and social welfare on the Esplanade, with restaurants and other attractions interspersed throughout. "Le monde est venu à nous," wrote the literary critic for the *Revue des deux mondes*. Most especially, the world came to see its tallest tower—the "gigantic and hideous skeleton . . . reared by Cyclops," the "newest wonder of the world," this "useless and monstrous" tower, the "nouvelle Babel," this "abomination and eyesore," this grand success!

Paris had watched the construction of the giant metal tower for two years with mixed emotion. A protest signed by forty-seven leading artists and writers was received by exposition authorities in February 1887, deploring the profaning of the city with the tower "which even commercial America would not have," this "factory chimney" that would crush the great monuments of the city beneath its "barbarous mass" and hide the genius of centuries like a giant inkblot. Minister Lockroy replied caustically that the protest was received too late to save the part of the city that was in danger: the "incomparable sand pile called the Champ de Mars."

Not even Gustave Eiffel, who predicted that the tower would be the chief attraction of the exposition, expected the intense interest that it inspired. The impressive structure attained its final 300.51 meters (986 feet), with three platforms at 57.63, 115.73, and 276.13 meters, respectively, just two years and two months after construction began, at a cost of 7,799,401.31 francs ($1,505,675.90 or 6 percent less than the initial budget of $1.6 million) with the loss of only one workman (showing off for his girlfriend after hours). Almost

2 million people paid 5,919,884 francs ($1,142,834.70) to ascend the tower during the exposition, queuing—some 20,000 daily—from 8:30 to wait, usually until noon, for the five elevators (two from the American Otis company and three from France) to take them aloft. Among the visitors were the prince of Wales, eight African kings, Sarah Bernhardt, Thomas Edison, and Buffalo Bill.

Whereas the Eiffel Tower dominated through shadow, height, and popularity, it was complemented by another extraordinary architectural feat in the colossal iron and glass Galerie des Machines located at the opposite end of the Champ de Mars. The largest structure at the exposition, spanning a rectangle of 15 acres (1,452 feet long and 380 feet wide), the Galerie des Machines reached a height of 148 feet at the apex and employed almost twice the iron and steel tonnage of the tower. Influenced by Eiffel's new technology introduced in his bridge structures, the architect, Ferdinand Dutert, and engineer, Victor Contamin, were able to span an unprecedented 377 feet with a gigantic glazed roof balanced on twenty arches without intermediate support. Two-story galleries, extending around the sides, added to the imposing interior. An electrically operated platform could carry 200 visitors down the length of the building at a height of 22 feet to provide a panoramic view of the mechanical marvels displayed, and usually in motion, from noon until 6:00 P.M.

Cycles (including a 400-pound steam tricycle), the first gasoline-powered car (a Benz), and a machine that made 9,000 paper bags per hour were just a few of the attractions in a massive exhibit noted more for excellence than for innovation. Despite the great variety and number of machines displayed, there were few important new inventions (except in electricity), although the quality of workmanship and design showed considerable progress.

Ironically, the architectural triumphs of the Galerie des Machines engendered some criticism. There were complaints that its gargantuan proportions dwarfed even the largest machines and that the floor sweltered from intense heat admitted through the glass roof on warm summer afternoons. Yet the largest exhibit within the massive gallery did not fail to attract favorable attention. At a personal cost of over $100,000 (supervised by Major W. J. Hammer and forty-five assistants), Thomas Edison displayed all of the 493 inventions that had earned him the title King of Light and the hearty respect of the French. The crowds were especially fascinated with the phonograph ("Mr. Edison has taught inanimate wax to echo our music and reproduce at will the voices of our friends").

Between the Galerie des Machines and the Eiffel Tower, the companion "clous" of the exposition, over eighty structures on the Champ de Mars housed a variety of other attractions. Facing the tower from the gallery, railroad exhibits occupied a large space on the left toward the avenue de Suffren. Then came row upon row of industrial courts (the Palais des Industries Diverses) constructed with wrought-iron columns supporting glazed iron roofs. A sumptuously decorated Galerie de Trente Metres, extending from the Galerie des Machines through the center of the courts, led to the grand central dome—195 feet high with an exterior diameter of 120 feet and surmounted by a 30-foot statue of France by

Eugène Delaplanche. The rotunda, elaborately decorated with a frieze representing the procession of the nations, was the central point of the exposition and the site of the official opening ceremony on May 6. In front of the dome and to the sides paralleling the avenue de Suffren and the avenue de la Bourdonnais, extended more galleries holding the industrial exhibits of visiting nations. The two-story Galerie Desaix on the left (which held a huge balloon under its dome) and Galerie Rapp on the right divided the industrial groups from Jean Formigé's palaces of fine arts and liberal arts. The principal facades of these buildings formed a giant U around the central garden, and their ground floors housed some of the fifty-odd eating establishments on the grounds.

Across the Seine were the horticultural exhibits—including Dutch tulips, a Japanese garden, and 4,500 roses in bloom—among the fountains and walks of the Trocadéro garden ($500,000 was spent on the parks and gardens of the exposition), and more exhibits were housed in the Trocadéro Palace, a relic of the exposition of 1878. Back across the pont d'Iéna on both sides of the tower along the quai d'Orsay were forty-nine small, highly detailed constructions designed by the eminent architect of the Paris Opéra, Charles Garnier, depicting the history of human habitation. Extending eastward for almost half a mile along the quai, more galleries of wrought-iron columns and glazed roofs housed the world's food products and agricultural exhibits. Perhaps most impressive in this popular section was a huge oaken wine barrel capable of holding the equivalent of 200,000 bottles, elaborately carved and gilded with the coats of arms of the principal wineries of Champagne. This gigantic cask had made a dramatic entrance into Paris on its specifically designed wagon pulled by ten pairs of oxen, a fitting tribute to the premier role of France in the international wine market.

More recent developments by France in other areas of the international economy could be viewed on the eastern side of the esplanade des Invalides. For the first time, the French people could witness the exotic cultures of their colonial empire displayed in an attractive jumble of huts, bazaars, and cafés attended by thousands of natives plying their crafts.

It befitted the epoch, though not without irony, that the exhibition relating to "war" and "health," and a new category entitled "Social Peace," shared the esplanade with the colonies. Having announced that it would not show anything new in armament, France mounted a magnificent historical exhibit instead. Thus, military innovations were conspicuous by their absence. Even the United States, whose commissioner decried the lack of "friendly competition" in developing the engines of war, entered no exhibit in this class. Social Peace, or "Social Economy," was a carefully structured, somber display emphasizing the well-being of French industrial workers. The exhibit was the government's proud response to escalating labor problems and social unrest. That it elicited little support from organized labor, no support from socialist groups, and only slightly reflected true working conditions were probably not matters of major interest to the average visitor. Almost unnoticed amid the hoopla of the exposition, two socialist congresses—one moderate and one Marxist—met in midsummer to discuss their own plans for social peace and justice in the world. Although the moderates drew the largest numbers of delegates (principally from French and English trade unions), the Marxists attracted the important names of international socialism, formed the founding congress of the Second International, and designated May Day as an international labor holiday. Neither were the socialist organizations part of the sixty-nine recognized congresses—on topics ranging from women's work, celestial photography, alcoholism, carrier pigeons, stenography, syphilology, to dermatology—that met as adjuncts of the exposition.

If the average visitor did not tarry long in the severe halls of Social Economy, he or she was likely going to one of the major delights of the exposition. Where the avenue de la Motte-Piquet met the avenue de Suffren at the side of the Galerie des Machines was the famous rue du Caire, a reproduction of a Cairo street and an attraction second only to the Eiffel Tower. The seductive *danse du ventre* (belly dance) became an international sensation, and repeated calls for censorship only increased its appeal. Sophisticated Parisians claimed to find more pleasure in the nubile beauty and exotic movement of the Javanese dancers performing in the Dutch pavilion. Fatigue might be somewhat alleviated by the Decauville, popular miniature trains that departed every 10 minutes from the Champ de Mars for a 2-mile journey around the exhibition perimeter. This small-gauge portable railway supported 37,000 train trips carrying 6,342,670 people in 180 days for a profit of 1,542,600 francs.

Edison's most recent invention, the incandescent bulb, made it possible to open the gates at night for the first time in exposition history and introduce the special dexterity of the French with the art of illumination. The Eiffel Tower ablaze as "a molten giant," capped with a tricolor searchlight that lit up half the city at once, was a moving sight. Huge crowds assembled each evening in the Champ de Mars's garden to wait for the jewellike spectacle of the illuminated fountains to flow at 9:00 P.M. Considered by many to be the supreme attraction of the exposition, the enchanting colors of the fountains (created by an intricate set of nozzles and lights behind colored lenses set in the pool's bed) added to the fairyland quality of the fair after dark.

The charms of the main exposition grounds dominated, but all of Paris was *en fête*. A museum of Revolution memorabilia was housed at the Louvre, and a model of the Bastille (forbidden on the Champ de Mars in order to maintain the apolitical character of the exposition) was located just outside the grounds, and special musicals, balls, and spectacles occurred regularly. In addition to the Edison exhibit in the Galerie des Machines, the Americans provided another popular spectacle in the Neuilly Hippodrome with Buffalo Bill's Wild West Show, starring Annie Oakley and an assortment of cowboys and Indians who played to packed houses twice a day. While the voluptuous amazons, cupids, and photographic realism of the academic school of fine art dominated the exposition, a few impressionist paintings hung among them in the Palais des Beaux-Arts. Nearby, however, Paul Gauguin persuaded a café owner to exhibit almost one hundred works of his impressionist synthetist group for a constant stream of visitors, while Gauguin himself slipped away to watch the Javanese dancers.

The end of summer did not diminish the exposition's popularity; the largest crowd (387,877) attended on October 3, with 370,354 thronging in on the closing day. The awards ceremony on September 29 was a grand affair where 33,138 certificates were awarded and impressively dressed commissioners paraded before President Sadi Carnot, dipping their national flags in salute. This ceremonial gesture illustrated the success of the exposition and, thereby, the French Republic. Only one week before, national elections resulted in a solid republican majority and a dramatic defeat for the Boulangists.

Originally scheduled to close on October 31, the exposition remained open until November 6 to placate popular demand. When the final cannon shot was fired from the Eiffel Tower (a sound Eiffel recorded and sent to Edison), crowds still clamored at the gates. It was too beautiful to end: this charming palette of colors and impressions—the gold of the Eiffel Tower; the flowered crystals of the Nancean potter Emile Gallé (a prophesy of the art nouveau style yet to come); the enchanting hues of the luminous fountains; yellow beauties; brown beauties— here was an "impressionistic fairyland," "a polychrome symphony," the tricolored exposition. Yet the serious purposes of the exposition were not hidden by its sensual fascinations. It illustrated French vitality, strength, and talent to the world and thereby reaffirmed France's self-confidence. More significant, the exposition crowned a century of unprecedented scientific achievement, the last age of optimistic faith in a utopian future. The great expositions of the nineteenth century sought both to instruct and entertain, and much of the success of the Paris exposition of 1889 was that it achieved a remarkable balance between the two. Inadvertently it was a tastefully lighthearted celebration of liberalism and its economic companion, capitalism. It was therefore fitting that this was one of the very few great expositions to make a profit—estimated at $600,000.

BIBLIOGRAPHY

Although no recent comprehensive analytical study of the Paris Exposition of 1889 has been written, the exposition has a voluminous literature. Virtually every newspaper and periodical in France, Great Britain, and the United States (and no doubt elsewhere) contained regular articles about the exposition throughout 1889. A plethora of details, descriptions, impressions, and anecdotes may be found in the *New York Times, Le Temps, L'Illustration*, and many other journals from 1887 to 1890.

There is a vast amount of unpublished literature in Série C (Procès-verbaux des assemblées) and Serie F (Administration générale de la France) in the Archives Nationales, Paris. For an extensive list of sources, as well as an excellent account of the political climate in which the exposition took place, see Brenda Flo Nelms, *The Third Republic and the Centennial of 1789* (1987). Documents pertaining to the U.S. exhibit are found in the National Archives, Record Group 43, "Miscellaneous Records of the United States Commission, 1889–1891," and "Photographs of American Exhibits, 1889." In addition, the Brackett Collection, located in the Library of Congress Manuscripts Division, has a collection of 215 photographs of U.S. exhibits.

The most important published primary sources are Adolphe Alphand and Georges Berger, *Exposition universelle internationale de 1889 à Paris. Monographie. Palais—Jardins—Constructions diverses—Installations générales*, ed. Alfred Picard (1891–1895), *Exposition universelle internationale de 1889 à Paris. Catalogue général officiel*, 8 vols. (1889); Alfred Picard, *Rapport général. Exposition universelle internationale de 1889 à Paris*, 10 vols. (1891–1892); and *Reports of the United States Commissioners to the Universal Exposition of 1889 at Paris*, 5 vols. (1893). Significant contemporary articles are those by Henri de Parville, Henry Fouquier, Henri Chardon, and Jules Clarétie in vol. 2 of *Les Annales politiques et littéraires* (1889), and a series by Eugène-Melchior de Vogüé, "A Travers l'exposition," in vols. 94–96 of *Revue des deux mondes*. Researchers should also consult *La Construction moderne*, an architectural journal published weekly in 1889–1890 that devoted much space to the exposition.

Among secondary works, the most informative are Merle Curti, "America at the World's Fairs, 1851–1893," *American Historical Review* 55 (July 1950): 833–56; Joseph Harriss, *The Tallest Tower: Eiffel and the Belle Epoque* (1975); Arthur Chandler, "Revolution: The Paris Exposition Universelle of 1889," *World's Fair* 7, no.1 (Winter 1987): 1–9; and Joy H. Hall, "Sheetiron, Syphilis, and the Second International: The Paris International Exposition of 1889," *Proceedings of the Western Society for French History* 11 (1984): 244–54.

Joy H. Hall

DUNEDIN 1889–1890
NEW ZEALAND AND SOUTH SEAS EXHIBITION

Dunedin's 1889–1890 exhibition marked the return of business confidence after the lean years of the long depression. The colony of New Zealand had already hosted two small international exhibitions (Dunedin 1865 and Christchurch 1882), but the third venture was far greater in size and importance.

The 1887 Adelaide Jubilee Exhibition provided D. Hastings Harris (advertising, press, and financial agent, and secretary of the local chamber of commerce) with initial inspiration, but business support was lukewarm until R.E.N. Twopeny (an influential newspaper editor who had been involved in the Christchurch Exhibition) lent his voice to the cause.

In October 1888 a guarantee company was formed with an initial capital of £10,000. Twopeny was quick to find support from the central government. It came in the form of a £10,000 grant, free use of the state-owned rail and postal services, and recognition of the exhibition as the official celebration of the colony's jubilee (fifty years since New Zealand's annexation by Great Britain and the signing of the Treaty of Waitangi). Government officials also used their influence to obtain exhibits from the 1888–1889 Melbourne exhibition.

A 12½-acre site a mile from the city center was donated by the Otago Harbour Board. James Hislop, a local architect, designed the buildings, which covered 75 percent of the site. They were temporary, the main building material being corrugated iron. Construction was functional in nature, with an entrance dome and four turrets providing the only ornate touch. A large open-air garden was enclosed by the pavilions, art gallery, and amusement arcade.

Exhibitors came from Europe, America, and Asia, but the most important were from New Zealand, Australia, and the South Pacific. This balance reflected the desire of the organizers to promote "closer relations with the Australian Colonies and the Pacific Islands." Most of the exhibits were arranged by country and province, with a few courts set aside for specific subjects. The most popular of the latter were the Natural History Court, featuring New Zealand flora and fauna, the Early History, Maori and South Seas Court (the most comprehensive display of such material ever assembled), and the government-backed Armaments and Fisheries Courts. The exhibition company had been successful in its bid to secure the best paintings from Melbourne, and these were displayed alongside New Zealand works. The small amusement area contained a well-patronized switchback railway together with a number of small sideshows.

A mining conference was held in conjunction with the exhibition, providing a reminder that Dunedin's wealth was, to a large extent, a legacy of the Otago Province's gold rushes of the 1860s. The conference, held in March, attracted delegates from New Zealand and Australia. By the time the exhibition closed in mid-April, 625,248 people had passed through the gates. The largest attendance in one day was 18,434, recorded at the closing. The total population of New Zealand at this time was just over 660,000. Shareholders lost much of their investment, but most were local businessmen whose losses had been more than compensated for by increased spending in the city during the exhibition. Including the capital provided by local investors, the exhibition did earn a profit of £579.

The 1889–1890 New Zealand and South Seas Exhibition was an important event in New Zealand. It was the official celebration of the colony's first fifty years under British rule. More tangibly it was a gesture of confidence in the future, signaling hope after fifteen years of depression.

BIBLIOGRAPHY

Primary sources are housed in the Hocken Library, University of Otago, Dunedin, New Zealand, and include letterbooks and minutes of the exhibition company. Secondary sources are found in both the Hocken Library and Dunedin Public Library. The exhibition was covered extensively in the *Otago Daily Times* and *Evening Star* newspapers, runs of which are held at both libraries. These libraries also hold the two official works: O. H. Harris, *Official Record, New Zealand and South Seas Exhibition, Dunedin, 1889–90* (1891), and W. M. Hodgkin, *Official Catalogue of the Exhibits* (1889). The other useful source is Miriam Smith, "The History of New Zealand Exhibitions, with Particular Reference to the New Zealand and South Seas International Exhibition, 1925—1926" (thesis, Auckland University, 1974), which can be found in the Hocken Library and Auckland University Library.

David Thomson

KINGSTON 1891
JAMAICA INTERNATIONAL EXHIBITION

The success of the Jamaica Court at the Colonial and Indian Exhibition held in London in 1886 encouraged A. C. Sinclair, superintendent of the government's Jamaican Printing Office, to campaign for an exhibition in Jamaica. In 1889, he persuaded the chairman of the Institute of Jamaica, William Fawcett, to approach Sir Henry Blake, the new governor of the island. The exhibition would demonstrate Jamaica's natural resources and products, encourage trade, and exhibit foreign machinery useful in developing the island's natural resources. The event could also attract winter tourists from the United States. Sir Henry enthusiastically supported the idea, and, to anticipate the World's Columbian Exposition scheduled to begin in 1892, he planned for the Jamaica fair to open in 1891. Prince George (later King George V), the son of the prince of Wales, was on duty with the West Indian squadron and agreed to open the exhibition. The £30,000 needed to pay for the exhibition was fully funded from money raised on the island, and a professional exhibition manager, S. Lee Bapty, was brought from Edinburgh to supervise the event. A local architect, George Messiter, was hired to design the exhibition buildings.

The main building was built of wood and glass in the popular cruciform floor plan with a Moorish-styled exterior of minarets and a central dome. The building was painted and illuminated at night with electric lights and a searchlight. Originally the main building was to have been prefabricated in the United States and erected by Americans. But enough local craftsmen were eventually located on the island so that only the raw materials of lumber and iron were obtained in the United States. Native trees and plants were gathered from throughout the island and used extensively inside and outside the building, and exotic gardens were laid out. An illuminated cascade was planned but never built; however, a large fountain was constructed in the front of the building and illuminated with a searchlight mounted on one of the minarets. Behind the main building were located smaller annex buildings erected to accommodate any unplanned expansion, a machinery building to power the exhibition and exhibit machinery, a separate Canadian overflow building, a poorly lighted exhibition hall for theatrical and musical performances, a tiny fine arts gallery consisting of regionally collected artworks, a vivarium (small zoo), and an industrial village containing a model school, an apiary, a working dairy, and several self-supporting native families occupied in local cottage industries. Several small amusements were available for diversion.

The primary purpose of the exhibition was to encourage and develop trade between Jamaica and the United States, Canada, and Great Britain. Although 66 percent of Jamaican exports went to the United States and the island received

34 percent of its imports from America, the United States was not officially represented because of a diplomatic misunderstanding regarding the invitation. However, hastily gathered displays were sent by a group of New England businessmen attempting to take some advantage of the exhibition. Canada eagerly filled the void created by the lack of official U.S. participation. Although the Canadian products were considered inferior by U.S. standards, the Canadians did show that they were interested in Jamaican trade. Canada was by far the largest and most enthusiastic foreign supporter of the fair, although it was not able to develop the hoped-for trade with the island. Sixteen foreign nations, as well as the British Caribbean colonies, exhibited, but only Canada, Great Britain, Barbados, and St. Vincent offered other than minor displays. A special exhibition postal cancel was available from January 27 to May 16 at the branch post office located in the main building. (In 1930, a commemorative 1/2 pence postage stamp was issued depicting the exhibition building in 1891.)

The 23-acre exhibition was held on the grounds of "Quebec Lodge" in northern Kingston from January 27 to May 2. Typical of the times, the fair was closed on Sundays. Opening day was full of parades and pomp to impress and honor the prince royal. Nearly 8,000 people visited the fair on that day. By the close of the exhibition, 302,831 visitors had been admitted (the island population was only 650,000). The final receipts showed a £4,500 loss and a bleak trade forecast. The recently enacted McKinley tariff, an island depression the following year, and the disastrously run Jamaican hotels ruined any hope for a favorable economic reward from the exhibition.

One purpose of the fair was to bring together all the people of the island in their support of the endeavor. However, the response expected from the governor's call throughout the island for a vigorous promotion of the island's local crafts was dampened by fear created among the rural population. This fear was based on rumors circulated by obeahmen (local sorcerers) and village merchants that slavery was to be reintroduced into the island or that the natives would be taxed heavily for bringing their products to Kingston. The governor was never able to dispel these rumors fully, and the expected benefits to Jamaica and its people from exposure to this exhibition were never realized.

BIBLIOGRAPHY

There are almost no publications or other records relating to the International Exhibition available in the United States. The National Library of Jamaica has significant runs of Jamaican newspapers of the period on microfilm. Of these newspapers, *Gall's Newsletter* and the *Daily Gleaner* seem to be the most entertaining and informative. The *Official Catalogue* (1891), compiled by S. Lee Bapty, apparently was to have been revised, but only the first printing is recorded. The *Jamaica Exhibition Bulletin* was published at least until a few months before the exhibition opened. There are photocopies of three issues (December 1889 to June 1890) in the Larson Collection at the Henry Madden Library, California State University, Fresno. This collection also holds *Report of the Honorary Commissioner (Mr. Adam Brown) representing Canada at the Jamaica Exhibition, Held at Kingston, Jamaica, 1891* (1891), which contains sixty-eight pages and two reproduced photographs. There are no references to any other official government reports.

The Larson Collection also has photocopies of the *Official List of Awards* (1891), *Regulations* (1891), [with classification system], and the *Handbook of Jamaica, 1890–1891* (1891), which contains preexhibition information. The London newspapers carried little on the fair, but the *New York Times* found it newsworthy. The only modern study of the exhibition is Karen Booth, "When Jamaica Welcomed the World: The Great Exhibition of 1891," *Jamaica Journal* 18, no. 3 (1985): 39–51, which is well written, illustrated, and contains a twenty-three-item bibliography.

Ronald J. Mahoney

CHICAGO 1893

WORLD'S COLUMBIAN EXPOSITION

The World's Columbian Exposition, also known as the Chicago World's Fair of 1893 and—in culturally more revealing terms—the "White City," was the most elaborate and extensive public exhibition produced by the United States in the nineteenth century. It may even be argued, as several scholars have done, that (all things considered and with the possible exceptions of the great world's fairs held in Paris, New York, and Chicago in the 1930s) the World's Columbian Exposition was the greatest world's fair of all time.

Although it is probably impossible to determine the individual responsible for first publicly proposing that the United States sponsor a world's fair to honor the four hundredth anniversary of Columbus's discovery of the New World, the success of the Philadelphia Centennial Exhibition in 1876 naturally encouraged suggestions that a similar event be considered as part of any festivities in 1892 that celebrated Columbus's achievement. In 1882, the *Baltimore Sun* endorsed such a plan, and that same year the *Chicago Times* carried a letter arguing not only that an international exposition would be an appropriate way to commemorate the discovery of the Western world but also that the city of Chicago—because of its central location, physical capacity, and remarkable growth—was the most appropriate site. The idea gained national interest over the next three years as local business and civic groups in various cities—New York, Philadelphia, St. Louis, Cincinnati, and Washington, D.C., as well as Chicago—began promoting their respective cities.

Following glowing reports describing the third universal exposition being planned for Paris in 1889, however, it became clear that in the United States, only New York, and perhaps Chicago, possessed the private financial and physical resources required even to approach, much less surpass, the extensiveness and artistic elegance of the French standard. The subsequent battle that was fought out in the newspaper editorials of the established eastern urban giant and its younger western challenger was one of the most bitter and vitriolic in American history, but it served to stimulate national interest in a prospective fair and to spur organizational efforts in both cities. In the fall of 1889 in Chicago, a corporation entitled the World's Columbian Exposition of 1892 was established with members appointed by the mayor from its leading professional and business men and chartered with an initial capital of $5 million. New York had established a similar group somewhat earlier.

In December, as the U.S. Congress assembled to begin its regular session, the scene of the debate among the competing cities shifted to Washington, D.C. Numerous world's fair bills were immediately introduced, and special committees of each house were appointed to begin consideration in early 1890. Although there was now general agreement as to the desirability of holding a world's fair in the United States in 1892, the question of the site was very much unsettled, and hearings continued until February 24, when the House committee announced that it had endured all the arguments it could stand and that, due to the intensity of the debate, a roll call of the entire House would settle the issue. Finally, after eight ballots, Chicago, the most vocal representative of the newer western states, received a majority. The Senate soon followed suit. Even so, the bill that officially authorized the exposition and designated Chicago as the city was delayed while the Chicago corporation convinced the Congress that its stock subscriptions were valid (New York, in a last-ditch effort, offered to underwrite the fair by $10 million—twice what the Chicago corporation had originally guaranteed—and the Chicagoans were forced to match that amount). Eventually, on April 28, 1890, President Benjamin Harrison signed the bill authorizing an international exposition to take place in Chicago during the spring and summer of 1893, rather than 1892, in order to provide an additional year for preparation.

The provisions of the world's fair bill of 1890 made it clear that doubts existed about the ability and appropriateness of Chicago to produce a major international world's fair that would represent and be a credit to the entire United States. In particular, the bill established a national commission to oversee and approve all significant decisions relating to the choice of physical site in Chicago, design of the grounds, construction of the buildings, and conduct of the exposition. Thus two different organizations—the local Chicago corporation and the National Commission—were charged with the responsibility for deciding what kind of a fair it was to be and for putting those decisions into effect. This duplication of authority considerably complicated the process of producing the fair. The additional problem of raising another $5 million by the Chicago Corporation was eventually solved by enlisting the aid of both the state of Illinois and the city of Chicago. The most immediate and practical problem facing the world's fair officials in the summer of 1890, however, was to determine the specific physical site for the fair.

During the spring and summer, while the Chicago Corporation and the National Commission were being organized and the financial backing was being confirmed, the initial steps were being taken toward deciding upon an appropriate location. At least some of the space needed could be obtained from the system of city parks, which had been established following the great Chicago fire of 1871, several of which remained undeveloped. The lakefront area was also attractive because of its scenic setting beside Lake Michigan. The Chicago Corporation brought in Frederick Law Olmsted, who had been involved in planning the original park system, to advise it and, although Olmsted favored the use of the lakefront, difficulties in obtaining rights to that property coupled with the unwillingness of the city's park board to allow the fair to be built on previously improved parkland eventually led to the decision to make Jackson Park, an unimproved 600-acre site alongside the lake and 8 miles south of the city's center, the principal location of the fair.

On November 25, 1890, the National Commission certified that the Chicago Corporation had met the requirements of the congressional act, and a general plan for the exposition was adopted. The basic features of the November plan for Jackson Park were primarily the work of four individuals: Daniel H. Burnham and John W. Root (of the Chicago architectural firm of Burnham and Root), and Frederick Law Olmsted and Henry S. Codman (of Olmsted's Boston company). The initial plan envisioned taking advantage of the natural characteristics of the site by utilizing water as a major element in each of the two principal aspects of the physical design. The first of these, probably a result of Olmsted's influence, was a large lagoon surrounding a wooded island. The second, undoubtedly inspired by the recent French exposition, called for a grand architectural Court of Honor surrounding a formal basin, with a system of interconnecting canals and lagoons. All of the major exhibition buildings constructed around the large lagoon and the basin were to be provided with water as well as land frontage. Also in November, the National Commission approved a classification system for the major departments (agriculture, horticulture, livestock, mines and metallurgy, fisheries, manufactures, machinery, transportation, electricity, fine arts, liberal arts, ethnology, and miscellaneous exhibits) under which the exhibits would be organized and arranged. This system, which dictated to a large degree the major buildings to be constructed on the fairgrounds, was developed primarily by George Browne Goode, an assistant secretary of the Smithsonian Institute in Washington, D.C., who was brought in as an adviser to the National Commission.

The responsibility for recommending the architects and the architectural style for the major buildings logically fell to the consulting architects, Burnham and Root. Given the time limitations, Burnham's recommendation of five leading national firms (Richard Morris Hunt, McKim, Mead and White, Van Brunt and Howe, George Post, and Peabody and Stearns) to design the buildings in the Court of Honor and five Chicago firms (Adler and Sullivan, S. S. Beman, Burling and Whitehouse, Jenney and Mundie, and Henry Ives Cobb) to design the others was approved in January 1891. Burnham and Root decided not to design any buildings themselves but would, in their capacity as consulting architects, supervise and coordinate the overall plan. John Root was expected to play an important role in determining the overall architectural style, but during the first gathering of the architects in Chicago in January, he was suddenly struck down by pneumonia, and his influence on the fair was lost. Whether Root's presence could have changed the eventual outcome remains a matter of conjecture, but it is true that following his death, the formal, symmetrical, and monumental stylistic values—those expressing authority and order—gained prominence, especially in the central Court of Honor where a uniform neoclassical style and color (white, thus the "White City") were agreed upon. It is also true that with the loss of his partner, a greater amount of direct responsibility and authority for constructing the fair was concentrated in the hands of Daniel Burnham, who was appointed chief of construction. Burnham selected Charles B. Atwood, an academically

CHICAGO 1893. The U.S. Government Building, like all the other buildings at the fair, stunned visitors with its neoclassical architecture and pure white color.

trained New Yorker, to replace Root as designer in charge, and it was in this capacity that Atwood came to have a major influence on the overall architecture of the exposition, designing the formal peristyle group that closed off the lake end of the Court of Honor, the Art Building (320' × 500'—now the Museum of Science and Industry and the sole surviving structure), plus dozens of lesser buildings. Final assignments for designing the other major buildings were as follows: Hunt—Administration (262' × 262'—the dominant structure of the court and the entrance point to the fair); Peabody and Stearns—Machinery Hall (492' × 846'); Post—Manufactures and Liberal Arts (787' × 1687'—the largest enclosed building ever constructed); Van Brunt and Howe—Electricity (345' × 690'); Beman—Mines and Mining (350' × 700'); Adler and Sullivan—Transportation (256' × 960'); Cobb—Fisheries (165' × 335'); Jenney and Mundie—Horticulture (250' × 998'); McKim, Mead and White—Agriculture (500' × 800'). Due largely to the influence of Augustus Saint-Gaudens, America's leading sculptor who had been brought in as an adviser, and Frank Millet, Burnham's director of color, many of the best-known artists and sculptors in the United States (Phillip Martiny, Lorado Taft, Mary Cassatt, Gari Melchers, Kenyon Cox, Elihu Vedder, and Karl Bitter among them) were enlisted to produce the finishing decorative details. Extensive use of a novel plasterlike substance, called "staff" and first introduced at the French exposition in 1889 (thus "plaster of paris"), permitted the artists an "architectural spree." Daniel Chester French (perhaps best known for his statue of the seated Lincoln in the Memorial at Washington, D.C.) was commissioned to create the statue of the Republic for one end of the Grand Basin, and Frederick MacMonnies was chosen to provide the Columbian Fountain to balance it at the other. A greater number of American artists and architects were drawn into the creation of the World's Columbian Exposition than had ever been brought together to work on a single project before, and perhaps since. Aided by the most extensive use of electric lighting ever attempted, the imposing and elaborate visual impression of the formal exposition buildings and grounds (the Court of Honor and the Lagoon) was undoubtedly the greatest exhibit of the Chicago world's fair.

Financial problems and construction difficulties plagued fair officials throughout the period prior to opening in May 1893, and it was only through great perseverance and an additional $2.5 million appropriation from the federal government (in the form of souvenir coins) that the exposition was ready to receive the public at all. One of the major problems, recognized early on, was that Chicago, unlike New York or Philadelphia or Paris, was only vaguely known by most Americans living in the East and hardly at all by citizens of other countries. If the fair was to attract the numbers of visitors and exhibitors required to rival the exposition in Paris or to have any expectation of financial success, serious effort would need to be expended to circulate information and awaken interest. In December 1890, the Department of Publicity and Promotion was established under the leadership of Moses P. Handy, a highly successful eastern newspaperman who had a modern appreciation of the importance of the press in molding public opinion. Handy immediately organized a staff of writers and translators to produce a weekly newsletter and to provide pictures and articles about the fair for a mailing list that grew to some 50,000 foreign and domestic organizations, newspapers, and magazines. There had been other publicity bureaus at earlier world's fairs, but the extensiveness and efficiency of the Promotion Department of the Columbian Exposition was something quite new. R.E.A. Dorr, Handy's chief assistant, estimated that one-third of all that was printed about the fair by the newspapers, at home and abroad, was written by the department itself.

There was one group, however, that needed little convincing to become excited about the opportunities of a world's fair in Chicago. Long before the exposition was formally announced in December 1890, the Chicago Corporation had begun receiving scores of requests from amusement vendors, restaurateurs, circus acts, musical troupes, and speculators of all sorts for space on the grounds. Fair officials had expected from the beginning to allow for an amusement and concessionary side to the exposition; recent experience had shown their value in drawing crowds and providing revenue. But as the plan for the exposition developed—with its emphasis on the formal and classical—what to do with the show business element became a real question. The solution was to locate the amusement features along the narrow strip of land called the midway plaisance, connecting Jackson and Washington parks. Under the supervision of a young entrepreneur, Sol Bloom, who replaced the less commercial-minded Harvard ethnologist F. W. Putnam, the midway at Chicago became one of the most successful and famous amusement areas of any of the world's fairs, and it established a pattern for mass entertainment that soon found application in such independent parks as Coney Island.

Within the midway were to be found such exotic and popular attractions as German beer halls, Turkish bazaars, Egyptian jugglers, Dahomean drummers, Algerian hootchy-kootchy dancers, the World's Congress of Beauty ("40 Ladies from 40 Nations"), balloon rides, wild animal shows, and ostrich omelets. Here, also, was to be found George Ferris's giant mechanical marvel, the ferris wheel, which took as many as 2,000 people at a time 264 feet in the air. The Barnumesque eclecticism and "exuberant chaos" of the midway provided visitors with an alternative to the refined order and beaux-arts neoclassicism of the Court of Honor, but it also offered a relief from the almost overwhelming complexity of the 65,000 exhibits of human progress displayed in the major exhibition halls. There were displays of book publishers, architectural firms, schools and universities, chemical and pharmaceutical products, paints, dyes, typewriters, paper, agricultural implements, furniture, ceramics, art metal work, glass, railroad cars, jewelry, clothing, toys, leather goods, hardware, printing presses, refrigerators, the 46-foot Krupp cannon, the "largest gold nugget in existence," a 22,000-pound block of Canadian cheese, and a 1,500-pound chocolate Venus de Milo. In the Fine Arts Building the seventy-four galleries of sculpture and paintings (some 9,000 in all) from Europe and the United States made it nearly impossible

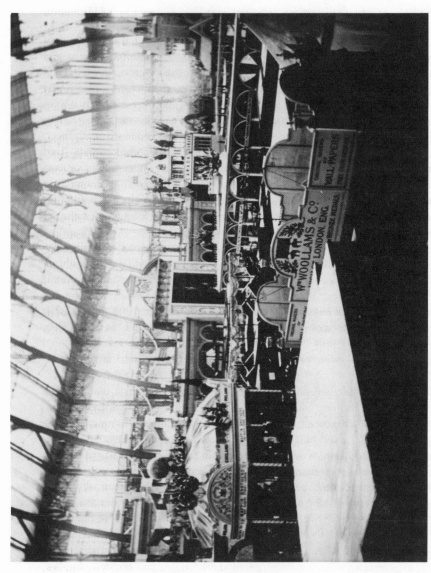

CHICAGO 1893. This photograph of the interior of the Manufactures Building gives some idea of the clutter and density of the exhibits.

to locate any particular work, in spite of the division into nationalities and the extensive cataloging. Given this situation, the small collection of French impressionists was obscured by the more traditional military, historical, and mythological romantic allegories. The diversity and extensiveness of the exhibits in Machinery Hall and in the Electricity Building, however, did announce in their aggregate that the United States had entered a new technological age. Add to this the exhibits provided by eighty-six foreign nations, colonies, and principalities (including those housed in the separate buildings that nineteen foreign governments erected), and it is not difficult to understand why many visitors felt overwhelmed.

In addition to the main exhibition halls and those of foreign countries, there were some thirty buildings erected by federal, state, and territory governments (the United States and the state of Illinois were given the better sites around the lagoon), and nineteen foreign nations erected their own structures. One building that drew special attention during the course of the fair was the Women's Building (199' × 388'), designed by Sophia G. Hayden of Boston. Indeed, due especially to the efforts of Susan B. Anthony, women played a more visible and active role in the Columbian Exposition than in any previous world's fair. Not only was there the Women's Building, housing exhibits demonstrating women's accomplishments in education, the arts, science, and industry, and a separate Women's Department, but also a 115-member national commission (labeled the "Board of Lady Managers") was established. "More important than the discovery of Columbus," Bertha Honoré Palmer, president of the Board, told her audience of over 100,000 at the dedication ceremonies in October 1892, "is the fact that the General Government has just discovered woman."

Participation of women in the Columbian Exposition was especially prominent in the World's Congress Auxiliary, an organization presided over by Charles C. Bonney, which sought to provide a comprehensive series of intellectual conferences to be held concurrently with the fair's demonstration of material progress. The auxiliary, whose motto was "Not Matter, But Mind: Not Things, But Men," was eventually organized into some twenty departments, which sponsored an unprecedented series of 1,283 sessions on such subjects as the public press, medicine and surgery, temperance, moral and social reform, commerce and finance, music, literature, education, and labor, and which drew an extraordinary number of prominent national and several international leaders to Chicago during the course of the exposition. John Dewey, Woodrow Wilson, William Jennings Bryan, Henry George, Hamlin Garland, George W. Cable, Charles Dudley Warner, Samuel Gompers, Josiah Royce, Charles Francis Adams, James McCosh, Seth Low, John Fiske, and Lester Ward were among the American luminaries who delivered addresses during the summer of 1893. One of the most significant presentations occurred in the Congress of Historians (presided over by Henry Adams) where Frederick Jackson Turner presented his paper "The Significance of the Frontier in American History," which changed the course of American historiography.

Overall, the most extensive, and most internationally representative, of the World's Congresses were the World's Congress of Representative Women, which began May 15, and the World's Parliament of Religions, which convened during the last month of the exposition. May Wright Sewell, president of the National Council of Women of the United States, was chosen as chair of the women's congress, and an advisory council of over 500 women representing twenty-seven countries was selected to organize the eighty-one meetings held at the Art Institute downtown and at the Women's Building on the grounds. Some 330 women (including Jane Addams, Frances Willard, Elizabeth Cady Stanton, Lucy Stone, and Susan B. Anthony) addressed the congress, whose total attendance exceeded 150,000. The World's Parliament of Religions, headed by John Henry Barrows of Chicago's First Presbyterian Church, began its even more notable conference on September 10. From then until the last session on September 17, almost every conceivable theme of a religious nature was discussed, and almost every conceivable sect or persuasion was given an opportunity to be heard. As historian David Burg has written, it was "the longest, most ambitious, most visited, most admired of the many congresses; and it evoked the most extensive comments in books, newspapers, and magazines." The published speeches and reviews from the congress alone required four separate volumes and thousands of pages.

When the World's Columbian Exposition of 1893 closed on October 30, over 21.5 million paid admissions had been registered. Even more remarkable was the fact that the Chicago Corporation was able to realize a small surplus with which to repay its private investors—and this was accomplished during a year that witnessed one of the most crippling depressions of the century. But the tangible results, financial or otherwise, were insignificant compared to the value of the fair as a great cultural event. To many Americans at that time, the fair was considered a massive demonstration of the coming of age of the United States as a world power, the cultural as well as material equal of any of the great imperial powers of the Old World. Writers in search of answers to the confusing multiplicity and cutthroat competition of the modern age, like Henry Adams and William Dean Howells, believed they saw in the White City the first expression of unity and utopian cooperation. For Chicagoans, the fair became a landmark in the history of their city, changing former opinions of Chicago as "Porkopolis," and opening up a new era of civic commitment and cultural flowering in the Midwest.

More specifically, the White City did exert an influence on American architecture—classicism dominated American public building into the 1930s—and upon urban planning in what became known as the City Beautiful movement. Daniel Burnham played a leading role in the movement, designing unified city plans for Chicago, Washington, San Francisco, and Cleveland. The debate over the architectural style of the White City began with the opening of the exposition, but the most sweeping condemnation came later, in 1922, from one of the fair's architects, Louis Sullivan. Sullivan, whose nonclassical Transportation Building with its gilded "Golden Door" was not widely admired at the time, pronounced the White City an authoritarian, academic "virus," which "penetrated deep into the constitution of the American mind, effecting there lesions significant of dementia.''

Several recent historians have agreed with Sullivan's assessment but have found the authoritarian disease manifest in the fair's centralized organization and operation, as well as in the architectural design. Others have emphasized the significance of the exposition as both providing a new model of democratic urban recreation (the midway) and as perpetuating, in its demeaning presentation (or exclusion) of ethnic groups, including American blacks and Indians, Western imperialism, and "scientific" racism. Because the fair was as extensive as it was and attracted as much attention as it did, the World's Columbian Exposition of 1893 will likely continue to be seen as one of the most culturally revealing events of the period, which Henry Steele Commager has called the "watershed of American history."

BIBLIOGRAPHY

Published material about the 1893 fair is voluminous. Newspapers and magazines in the United States especially covered the fair closely from the early planning stages up to closing day, and literally hundreds of guidebooks, photograph albums, and memorial and souvenir volumes were issued. Among the most informative are Rand McNally's *A Week at the Fair* (1893), and William E. Cameron, ed., *The World's Fair, Being a Pictorial History of the Columbian Exposition* (1893). The publicity department printed its own eight-page paper, the *Daily Columbian*, during the fair's operation, and a large number of exhibit catalogs, collections of speeches and papers from the World's Congresses, and official documents were published at the time or shortly after. U.S. government partic- ipation is documented in National Archives holdings, which contain the final report of the president of the National Commission and the list of exhibit awards (Record Group 43), and the Smithsonian Institution Archives (Record Groups 70, 95, and 192). In Chicago, archival material may be found at the Art Institute and the Chicago Public Library. Several of the major participants in the fair also recorded their experiences. See, for example, Daniel H. Burnham and Francis D. Millet, *The World's Columbian Ex- position: The Book of the Builders* (1894).

Contemporary histories of the fair include Hubert Howe Bancroft, *The Book of the Fair* (1894); Rossiter Johnson, ed., *A History of the World's Columbian Exposition* (1898); and Ben C. Truman, *History of the World's Fair* (1893). Julian Hawthorne, *Humors of the Fair* (1893), and Denton J. Snider, *World's Fair Studies* (1895) take a broader, somewhat more interpretative view.

David F. Burg, *Chicago's White City of 1893* (1976), and Reid Badger, *The Great American Fair: The World's Columbian Exposition and American Culture* (1979) are more recent studies, which place the exposition in a larger, primarily American, cultural context. The fair also figures prominently in Alan Trachtenberg, *The Incorporation of America: Culture and Society in the Gilded Age* (1982), where it is seen as an illustration of the emergence of a more highly structured and hierarchical society; Robert W. Rydell, *All the World's a Fair: Visions of Empire at American International Expositions, 1876– 1916* (1984), which documents the coincident messages of nationalism and scientific racism, especially in the midway exhibits; and John E. Kasson, *Amusing the Million:*

Coney Island at the Turn of the Century (1978), which views the commercial amusements of the midway as symbols of a new American cultural order at the turn of the century. William D. Andrews, "Women and the Fairs of 1876 and 1893," *Hayes Historical Journal* 1 (1977): 173–83, and August Meier and Elliot Rudwick, "Black Man and 'White City': Negroes and the Columbian Exposition, 1893," *Phylon* (1965): 354–61, address the issues of women and blacks, respectively, at the exposition. Maurice F. Neufeld, "The White City: The Beginnings of a Planned Civilization in America," *Journal of the Illinois State Historical Society* 27 (1934): 71–93, is the strongest argument for seeing the fair as a significant influence on modern urban planning. Stanley Appelbaum, *The Chicago World's Fair of 1893: A Photographic Record* (1980), offers a wonderful selection of photographs from the collections of Columbia University and the Chicago Historical Society.

R. Reid Badger

ANTWERP 1894
EXPOSITION INTERNATIONALE D'ANVERS

As early as 1891 Desire Janssens, administrator in charge of the Société anonyme du Palais de l'Industrie, des Arts et du Commerce (a private group whose members had contributed to the 1885 Antwerp exposition) had thought of organizing another international exposition. They wanted it to follow the Chicago 1893 exposition so that the European exhibitors returning to Europe would be able to show their wares on the Continent. This international exposition would also celebrate the continuous expansion of the maritime installations in Antwerp. Twenty-six nations and 12,095 exhibitors participated in the exposition, which drew some 3 million visitors.

Mostly due to the participation of the Independent State of the Congo, the Colonial Section of the Exposition attracted particular interest. Besides the Dutch colonies, the Independent State of the Congo showed off twenty years of progress. On November 18, 1889, Leopold II had convoked an international Anti-Slavery Conference in Brussels. It lasted until April 1892, when it was agreed to undertake a nineteen-month campaign to end the slave trade. In the spring of 1894 a definitive victory was won by Lieutenant Dhanis over the Arab slavers of Zanzibar. Public opinion had been reticent to support and even hostile to this African engagement but it soon changed. The exhibits were guarded by black soldiers. There were ivory sculptures by sixteen Belgian and seventeen Congolese artists; elsewhere there were display samples of various products, including rubber, copal, cotton, coffee, and cacao, as well as prototypes of prefabricated modular houses. The John Cockerill Society exhibited models of steamers navigating on the Congo River along with statues representing natives transporting pieces of a cannon and a modular boat. Drawings by native children were displayed in one of the courtyards of the pavilion. A native artist had engraved on an ivory plate the signatures of the delegates of the seventeen nations that had signed the antislavery act of Brussels (July 2, 1890).

The most striking architectural exhibit was the replication of a neighborhood of old Antwerp. Besides taking great care to follow art and archaeology of that period, the builders of the houses used furnishings and utensils of the sixteenth century, and craftsmen dressed in period costumes were at work. At 10:00 P.M. each evening, all festivities stopped as the trumpets and drums of the watch sounded to announce the curfew.

The success of this exhibit was such that no longer would there be a Belgian international exposition without the reconstruction of an old neighborhood: Bruxelles-Kermesse (1897, 1910), Old Liège (1905), Old Belgium (Antwerp, 1930), Old Bruxelles (1935), and Belgium 1900 (Brussels, 1958).

BIBLIOGRAPHY

There are two primary sources for this exposition. The first one is by Alphonse Nertogs, a councilman of Antwerp in charge of the public works of the city and also the vice-president of the executive committee of the exposition. His book, *Exposition universelle d'Anvers, 1894. Revue retrospective par Alph. Hertogs* (1896), gives ample information about the exposition, as well as a detailed budget on receipts and expenditures. The only other source of information is A. Cockx and J. Lemmens, *Les Expositions universelles et internationales en Belgique de 1885 à 1958* (1958), which gives a rather brief summary about this particular exposition but provides a good overview of Belgian expositions.

Maurice Gendron

SAN FRANCISCO 1894
CALIFORNIA MIDWINTER INTERNATIONAL EXPOSITION

That the California Midwinter International Exposition of 1894, the first international exposition to be held on the West Coast, came into being was largely due to the immensely popular and critically acclaimed World's Columbian Exposition held in Chicago the previous summer. Michael H. de Young, owner and publisher of the *San Francisco Chronicle* and a man often accused of using his newspaper to blackmail others, had been an official of the Chicago exposition and commissioner of its California exhibit.

Returning from Chicago, de Young met with some friends, including San Francisco businessmen Philip Lilienthal and Louis Sloss, and a rapid decision was made to organize an international exposition in California to be held in midwinter so as to contrast California's climate at that time of year with the rest of the snow- and ice-bound United States.

De Young, who was named president and director general of the exposition, began, along with the Executive Committee, to solicit funds for the fair in June 1893. By July 10 a site had been chosen: San Francisco's Golden Gate Park, not long claimed from the sand dunes of the city's wind- and fogswept western reaches. Ground was broken at the 160-acre site on August 24. Five principal buildings were planned around a quadrangle: Manufactures and Liberal Arts, Mechanical Arts, Horticulture and Agriculture, Fine Arts, and Administration. Scheduled to open on January 27, 1894, the exposition was to run until June 30.

Within the quadrangle was a series of spaces joined by a system of terraces and steps. In the center was a 266-foot electric tower topped by a searchlight. Other important exhibits included an allegorical fountain featuring an academicized figure of California—*Young and Fruitful*, a Japanese tea garden, a recreation of a '49er gold rush camp, a ferrislike wheel, called, in this case, a firth wheel, after J. Kirk Firth, its developer, a buffalo paddock, an ostrich farm, and a Chinese pagoda.

The architecture of the fair was the product of a local competition. Not surprisingly, the results brought to mind the familiar eclectic congeries of styles characteristic of the age. There were Romanesque halls, Moorish-looking mosques, Renaissance palaces, Egyptian temples, and—in a bow to the West—an adobelike festival hall complete with simulated viga or log rafters. Inside were exhibits of produce and manufactures from California's counties, as well as from several foreign countries.

Foreign exhibits, particularly paintings from France and Poland, were strongly represented in the Fine Arts Building—a pseudo-peripteral Egyptian temple. In fact, impressionist paintings by Auguste Renoir and Edouard Manet were the first to be publicly exhibited in the West. The whole art exhibit was so diverse and so well attended that one observer deemed it to mark a "rebirth" in art interest from the doldrums of more than a decade.

On closing day, June 30, the exposition was given a rousing farewell. During its five months it had attracted 1,355,889 patrons, and revenues exceeded the $1,193,260.70 it cost to produce by $66,851.49. In addition, the park was left with the Fine Arts building, assorted statuary, and eleven hundred benches as permanent improvements.

BIBLIOGRAPHY

The most valuable and useful publications on the California Midwinter International Exposition are the *Official Guide to the California Midwinter Exposition* (1894) and the *Official History of the California Midwinter International Exposition* (1894). Also valuable is the *Official Catalogue, Fine Arts: California Midwinter International Exposition* (1894). Copies of these publications can be found in the Bancroft Library at the University of California, Berkeley. A pictorial view of the fair is found in Adolph Witteman, *Souvenir of the California Midwinter International Exposition* (1894).

Newspaper coverage of the event was extensive in a time when several morning and evening daily papers were published in San Francisco. An extensive collection of clippings is held by the California State Library in Sacramento.

A recent descriptive article on the fair is Arthur Chandler, "San Francisco's Fantastic Midwinter Fair of 1894," *World's Fair* 6, no. 1 (Winter 1986). Another useful secondary account may be found in Raymond H. Clary, *The Making of Golden Gate Park: The Early Years: 1865–1906* (1984). Clary, a San Franciscan who is the preeminent collector of memorabilia from this fair, is writing a longer book dealing exclusively with the exposition.

Raymond L. Wilson

HOBART 1894–1895
TASMANIAN INTERNATIONAL EXHIBITION

Hobart's idea for an international exhibition stemmed from the successful 1891–1892 exhibition in Launceston, Tasmania. The larger capital city hoped to outdo Launceston's results and profits. With hopes of stimulating Tasmania's depression-mired economy, plans got underway in 1892. Jules Joubert, a well-known exhibition entrepreneur, was named general manager of the Exhibition Association, the organizing body of the fair. Joubert, a Frenchman, had organized over fifty exhibitions worldwide by the time he died in 1907.

Joubert selected the Queen's Domain, Hobart's renowned park, as the exhibition site because it was visible from most of the city. The citizens most affected by the depression, however, did not want their recreation area used for what they viewed as a largely middle-class endeavor. Public outrage, in the form of disorderly conduct (including the throwing of rotten eggs) at the planning meeting, forced a compromise: the land could be used but only if it would be returned to its original condition.

In 1893, judges chose Melbourne architect Thomas Searell's design as the winner of a competition held to solicit designs for the exhibition complex. The temporary buildings, erected during the depression's most difficult period, provided many welcome jobs.

The exhibition complex was triangular, with all buildings contained within the complex. Its main building, in Italian Renaissance style, housed the concert hall, art exhibits, and a restaurant. The surrounding triangular area intersected the main building and formed the annexes, which were divided into the Tasmanian, Foreign, British, and Machinery and Mines sections. In the center of the triangle was the cross-shaped Colonial Section. The gardens, sideshows, and large engines and machinery were located in the center of the triangle.

In spite of diligent efforts, soliciting exhibits proved difficult. Economic considerations and Tasmania's remote location discouraged most European and U.S. concerns. Tasmania's neighbors were equally reluctant. Although Tasmania had always participated in their exhibitions, courting Tasmania's economic potential did not seem worthwhile to the others. The Exhibition Association responded by granting economic concessions to surrounding countries. For instance, freight incentives were arranged with a New Zealand steamship company, and the customs and licensing fees were waived for the Vinegrowers' Association of South Australia. It was argued later that these concessions should have been granted to all potential exhibitors. Nevertheless, they did increase participation among countries to which they were available.

Although relatively few foreign manufacturers participated, Italian and Japanese concerns were among them. Additionally, the Royal Academy in London and the French government sent art exhibits. Local musicians provided top-quality music programs. The exhibits were classified in twenty-four groups, including furniture, handicrafts, jewelry, textiles, chemistry and apparatus, women's industry, cutlery and ironmongery, and electricity. Tasmania later added additional ethnohistorical and other local items to mask the somewhat bare exhibition areas. As a result, the exhibition took on a cultural, historical, and local flavor.

The Tasmanian International Exhibition opened on November 15, 1894. Attendance, however, mainly local, soon waned. When the exhibition ended on May 15, 1895, attendance figures totaled 290,000. Six months later, the site had been restored to its original condition, in keeping with the pledge made to the public.

Although not profitable, the exhibition boosted employment and morale, and it created a sense of community unity. Some blamed its lack of success on expensive customs duties and exhibitors' fees. Others blamed poor management or lack of support from the sheep industry.

The exhibition's legacy was its contribution to art appreciation. In fact, many of the paintings on display were subsequently purchased for local collections. Although largely forgotten, the Tasmanian International Exhibition reflected the isolated condition of the island itself and thus provides a microcosm of late nineteenth-century Tasmanian society.

BIBLIOGRAPHY

Because of the relatively minor role that the Tasmanian International Exhibition played in Tasmania's history, primary sources comprise the bulk of available information. The most valuable primary source is the *Mercury*, Hobart's main newspaper, which chronicles the exhibition from inception to end. In addition to daily articles, the Exhibition Supplement in the November 15, 1894, edition provides a thorough overview of the exhibition, with attention given to the people involved, as well as the exhibits and architecture. Although unavailable in U.S. collections, the newspaper can be obtained on microfilm from Pascoe's Microfilm, New South Wales, Australia. Other primary sources include *The Prospectus of the Tasmanian International Exhibition Association Ltd.* (1894–1895) and the *Tasmanian International Exhibition Association Profit and Loss Account 30 June 1896* (1896), both available in Tasmania's State Library in Hobart.

Most secondary sources about Tasmania do not mention the exhibition at all. The only secondary source devoted entirely to it is Peter Mercer, "The Tasmanian International Exhibition, 1894–95—An Ephemeral Event or a Lasting Legacy?" *Papers and Proceedings of the Tasmanian Historical Association* (1981). Mercer thoroughly examines the origin and chronology of the exhibition in this well-researched article. He pulls together well the sparse available material. His article is the most useful reference for the reader who needs a detailed account of the events surrounding the exhibition. Additionally, the second appendix in John Allwood's *The Great Exhibitions* (1977) gives useful statistical information, although the exhibition is only mentioned in passing in the main part of the book. Allwood also provides information on Jules Joubert's career.

Sandra Montgomery Keelan

ATLANTA 1895
COTTON STATES AND INTERNATIONAL EXPOSITION

Atlanta boosters hosted large expositions in 1881 and 1887 to advertise the New South to the nation. With the depression of 1893, *Atlanta Constitution* business manager and former mayor W. A. Hemphill called for a new and larger fair to encourage recovery. On December 28, 1893, 300 businessmen met to plan the exposition.

Eight days later, Atlantans filed for a charter to incorporate the Cotton States and International Exposition Company with the objective to exhibit "products and resources of the Cotton States and other States of the United States and of all other countries, and of the appliances, machinery, inventions and devices used in the cultivation, manufacture and use of such products and resources, together with exhibitions or works of art and inventions of all persons who may exhibit." Additionally, organizers hoped to develop trade with Latin American countries while promoting the South to outside investors.

The depression and Atlanta's small population of 100,000 from which to interest subscribers led to financial problems. Citizens subscribed $134,000, the city council appropriated $75,000, Fulton County donated the equivalent of $100,000 in the work of convict laborers, and at a time when the sheriff threatened to lock the gates due to cost overruns, Atlanta banker Samuel M. Inman personally gave $50,000. In all the company expended nearly $1.5 million. Exhibitors and concessionaires shouldered the costs of their specific enterprises, approximately $800,000. The U.S. Congress appropriated $200,000 for a government building. Overall, the exposition cost nearly $2.5 million.

In October 1894, engineer Grant Wilkins began construction on 189 acres in Piedmont Park. Supervising architect Bradford L. Gilbert of New York designed eleven of the thirteen main buildings and achieved an amphitheater effect by arranging the buildings around a 13-acre central lake. Though varied, the dominant architectural style was romanesque. Atlanta architect W. T. Downing designed the Fine Arts Building in Italian Renaissance style. Elsie Mercur of Pittsburgh used a colonial motif for the Women's Building, the fair's most popular exhibit. Wilkins built the Mineral and Forestry Building entirely from native Georgia woods and covered its exterior with bark.

The fair opened on September 18 to great fanfare despite some unfinished buildings, uncleared construction debris, and several wareless exhibitors. From Gray Gables, Massachusetts, President Grover Cleveland pressed a telegraphic key that started the machinery on opening day. The fair's most memorable event was Booker T. Washington's famous Atlanta Compromise speech, which set the tone for black accommodation to discrimination: "In all things that are purely social we can be as separate as the fingers, yet one as the hand in all things essential to mutual progress.'' Visitors crowded into the Negro Building, the first exhibit of its kind in U.S. exposition history.

Fairgoers arriving by streetcar at the main entrance saw the 3,000-seat auditorium and the domed Georgia state building directly in front of them, with a formal plaza and the lake beyond. Walking clockwise through the full circuit of main exhibits, they visited the following buildings: Fine Arts, U.S. Government, Manufactures, Women's, Electricity, Transportation, Georgia Manufactures, Negro, Machinery, Minerals and Forestry, and Agriculture. On the fair's southernmost boundary, visitors could enjoy a midway boasting the world's largest ferris wheel or attend Buffalo Bill's Wild West Show. Other attractions included state buildings representing New York, Pennsylvania—with its Liberty Bell—Alabama, Illinois, Massachusetts, and California, as well as Mexican and Japanese villages and several Central and South American exhibits. Altogether, sightseers viewed 6,000 exhibits from thirty-seven states and thirteen foreign countries.

When the fair closed on December 31, 1895, 779,560 people had paid to attend. Despite losing $25,000, organizers hailed the fair's success and credited it with stimulating capital investment and a construction boom in Atlanta. Whether that was true or just posture, the fair brought more fame to the leading city of the New South.

BIBLIOGRAPHY

The most complete coverage of this exposition is Walter G. Cooper, *The Cotton States and International Exposition and the South, Illustrated, Including the Official History of the Exposition* (1896). This is a beautiful, huge (and heavy) book with over 500 pages filled with photographs of exhibits, organizers, notables, and Atlanta scenes. Cooper details dates, awards, exhibitors, and daily attendance and includes approximately 450 biographical sketches. For more information concerning specific items included in every exhibit, see *The Official Catalogue of the Cotton States and International Exposition, Atlanta, Georgia, U.S.A., September 18 to December 31, 1895, Illustrated* (1895). Another excellent source for portraits and biographical sketches of exposition officials is *The Atlanta Exposition and the South Illustrated* (1895), which contains interesting descriptions and photographs of building interiors and Atlanta in the 1890s.

A good contemporary account of the fair is W. Y. Atkinson, ''The Atlanta Exposition,'' *North American Review*, 161 (October 1895): 385–93. The pages of the *Atlanta Constitution*, September 18–December 31, 1895, contain interesting articles and highlights. A useful secondary account is Genevieve Pou, ''Fair Helped World Discover Atlanta,'' *Atlanta Journal*, Magazine Section, September 20, 1970, 21–27. An ''Official Programme of Daily Events of the Exposition'' (1895) for December 23, 1895, is located in the manuscripts collection at the University of Georgia. The Atlanta Historical Society owns the most complete collection of exposition materials. See especially the Atlanta Chronology File for 1895 and the photographic collection of the fair. Especially fine is the large color lithograph, 20″ × 24″, entitled ''Atlanta Exposition 1895.'' A bird's-eye view and fifty-eight photographs of Atlanta and the fair can be found in *Views of Atlanta and the Cotton States Exposition* (1895).

The original charter and company bylaws with a list of the original directors and standing committees is in *Charter and By-Laws of the Cotton States and International Exposition Company, Atlanta, Ga.* (1894). Correspondence and information concerning the U.S. government exhibit can be found in National Archives Record Group 43, Records Relating to the Cotton States and International Exposition at Atlanta, 1895 and Smithsonian Institution Archives, Record Group 70, Series II, The Cotton States and International Exposition. The exposition's most famous event, Booker T. Washington's speech, can be found in his *Up from Slavery* (1901).

Russell Duncan

BRUSSELS 1897
EXPOSITION INTERNATIONALE DE BRUXELLES

Because of its prosperity, Belgium wanted to prove that it could compete in the economic realm among the great powers. Around 1900, France exported one-seventh of its industrial production and England one-fourth, but Belgium surpassed both by exporting one-third. By the volume of its foreign commerce, Belgium ranked fifth among world powers.

Originally there was some concern that this exposition, preceding that of Paris in 1900, might not succeed. Construction was delayed by torrential rains that postponed the projected opening date from April 24 to May 10. During the first few weeks, there was no water in the fountains, and the electrical lighting was not completed. The site of the exposition was the parc du Centenaire; in addition, it incorporated an exhibition of colonial affairs at Tervueren, the museum of African art. The interior decoration there was done by two famous Belgian art nouveau architects, Paul Hanker and Henri Van de Velde.

Although there was little significant architecture at this exposition, a reconstruction of an old quarter of Brussels, called Bruxelles-Kermesse, surrounded by a fourteenth-century wall with a Renaissance entrance gate, attracted a great deal of interest. This project, designed by Paul Saintenoy, was inspired by the city halls of Ghent and Audenarde. The old quarter included the palace of the Grand Conseil in Malines, as well as several private hotels, such as the Nassan and the Ravenstein, flanked by a carillon tower. The belfry (4 meters in diameter and 37 meters high) was perhaps the finest piece of architecture at the exposition. There were also reproductions of the three famous statues of Brussels: Mast's Menneken-Pis, the *Spitter* (le Cracheur), and the *Three Young Virgins* (les Trois Pucelles). At night the electrical lighting provided a clear view of the luminous Fountain of Chimeras by Van der Stapen.

The jewel of the exposition, according to a member of the Belgian government, was the array of exhibits from France that spread over 15,000 square meters. The English exhibits occupied 6,500 square meters. For the first time in an exposition, mathematics and the physical and natural sciences were organized in an autonomous international section. Numerous lectures and demonstrations helped draw visitors to the various exhibits, including a prominent one on the "manual labor of women."

One of the most popular exhibits was that representing the Independent State of the Congo, Belgium's proud possession in Africa. The Congo exhibit featured a model native village, ethnological items, ivory carvings, and a painted panorama of the Congo by Amédée Lynen. Even the noted African explorer Henry M. Stanley was impressed with its artistry and workmanship. Among other exhibits, an Alpine panorama used special technical effects that permitted visitors to experience the sensations of an actual mountain excursion.

Sporting events also found their way into the exposition schedule. On Sunday, May 30, in the velodrome of Tervueren, a major international bicycle race drew 20,000 spectators. It was won by a Frenchman, P. Bourrillon, followed by a Dutch cyclist, Jaap Eden, and a Belgian named Proten.

An interesting attraction of this fair was a competition in which the Belgian government offered 300,000 francs in prize money for answers to 408 questions or problems related to all sections of the exhibits. There were technical problems such as the best design for a bicycle seat to accommodate men and women "hygenically" or a system of frost-free hydrants for public roads. One question with contemporary relevance called for a learning program on the prevention of alcohol abuse to be used in elementary schools, middle schools, and normal schools.

Because of the construction delays, the fair opened on May 10, three weeks late. When it closed on November 8, it had attracted some 6 million visitors, about twice the number who had attended the Antwerp fair three years earlier.

BIBLIOGRAPHY

Several official publications are available for this fair. *Bruxelles Exposition. Organe officiel de l'Exposition internationale de Bruxelles* (1897) and *Catalogue général officiel 1897 Bruxelles*, 2 vols. (1897) contain much descriptive material. *A Travers l'Exposition internationale de Bruxelles (1897)* (1897) is aimed at fair visitors.

Works touching on more specific aspects of this exposition include *Livre des Expositions universelles 1851–1980* (1983), which contains a good description of the impact of the colonial section of the fair, along with an appreciation for the Bruxelles-Kermesse exhibit of Old Bruxelles. The colonial exhibit at Tervueren was to be a permanent exhibit since Leopold II, king of the Belgians, was also sovereign of the Independent State of the Congo. The best source, however, is the *Guide de la Section de l'Etat Independant du Congo à l'Exposition de Bruxelles-Tervueren en 1897* (1897) published under the direction of M. Le Commandant Liebrechts. There are over five hundred pages about the Congo— its people, the climate, the economy, and the flora and fauna. The French section of the exposition was the largest, with over 3,000 exhibitors. One report available on the French exhibit is G. E. Puel de Cobel and E. Lourdelet's report of Committee XXXI, *Section française-Livret souvenir du Comité XXXI-Commerce-Colonies* (1897).

Maurice Gendron

GUATEMALA CITY 1897
EXPOSICIÓN CENTROAMERICANA

The Central American Exposition of 1897 took place within the context of a furious drive to erect a Central American union composed of the five sister republics of Guatemala, Honduras, El Salvador, Nicaragua, and Costa Rica. The push for this latest effort to realize an ideal that had eluded Central American statesmen since the breakup of the original United Provinces of Central America (1823–1838) came from the Nicaraguan Liberal strongman, José Santos Zelaya. Zelaya had evicted British officials from the Mosquito Territory in 1894, legally integrating the region into Nicaragua. A subsequent British blockade of the Pacific port of Corinto in 1895 illustrated the need for a united Central American defense against foreign aggression and gave stimulus to a new union enterprise. In 1895 the states of Nicaragua, El Salvador, and Honduras united as the Greater Republic of Central America (República Mayor), leaving open the possibility that Costa Rica and Guatemala would join.

The Central American Exposition was sponsored by the pro-union Guatemalan government of General José Maria Reyna Barrios. Its principal organizer was the eminent Guatemalan Juan F. Ponciano. The "Gran Certamen" had as its overt purpose the promotion of the union of Central America. It was also designed to exalt the stable and progressive government of Reyna Barrios, nephew of the great reformer and martyr of Central American union, Justo Rufino Barrios. And it was meant to show that Guatemala and its sister republics were in the mainstream of historical progress, to stimulate international respect for Central America (especially the union project), and to expand commercial links and foreign investment. Guatemala had eagerly participated in the most recent international expositions in Paris (1889) and Chicago (1893), taking gold medals for its fine coffee.

The fair ran from March 15 to June 30. The fairgrounds occupied some 800 acres on the outskirts of Guatemala City. Three main buildings spread over 20 acres housed the competing exhibits, composed primarily of the flora, fauna, and agrarian produce of the isthmus and the latest manufactures of Europe and the United States. Ironically the main edifice was constructed by a French firm from Bordeaux. To attract international participation, the usual tariffs on many goods were greatly reduced or eliminated during the course of the fair. All goods to be exhibited entered the country duty free. The Guatemalan fair attracted participants from England, Germany, France, Italy, Belgium, the United States, and Chile, as well as from each of the states of Central America. Some $200,000 was allotted for prize money, to be divided evenly among the native and foreign sections. Literary and musical contests accompanied the fair. Attendance for the opening ceremonies was estimated at 7,000 visitors.

The fair placed an enormous burden on the Guatemalan government. The total cost of the fair probably exceeded $2 million. The Guatemalan budget of 1897 alone allotted some $600,000 toward the fair, almost a third of the national budget. Subsequently the Reyna Barrios government experienced great difficulty in meeting its obligations and was chronically unable to pay the salaries of governmental employees. In May 1897 Reyna Barrios relieved all Guatemalan banks from obligations to redeem their notes or other obligations in specie and made bank notes legal tender until January 1, 1898. Notably, in June Reyna Barrios assumed dictatorial powers. Later the same month a juridical congress composed of delegates from Guatemala, Costa Rica, and the Greater Republic signed a provisional treaty of union. But civil strife throughout the isthmus and the insolvency of the Guatemalan government, due largely to the exposition, led the respective congresses of Costa Rica and Guatemala to reject the convention, ending yet another unification attempt. The Central American Exposition thus failed in its primary purpose.

BIBLIOGRAPHY

The principal source for the study of this exposition is "Guatemala en 1897," a collection of articles appearing in the quasi-official newspaper, *El Progreso Nacional*, in 1897, including an informative preface, photographs, and the official *Guia de la Exposición*. This material is available in the Biblioteca Cesar Brañas of the University of San Carlos in Guatemala City. Additional contemporary information on the fair may be found in the New Orleans *Times-Picayune* for March 16, 1897, and in the diplomatic correspondence of the U.S. Legation to Guatemala and Honduras for 1897, available on microfilm in the Latin American Library at Tulane University and at other repositories as well.

Three secondary sources provide useful information on the historical context in which the exposition was held: see Alberto Herrarte, *La Unión de Centro América* (1964); Thomas Karnes, *The Failure of Union* (1961); and Ralph Lee Woodward, *Central America: A Nation Divided* (1985).

Richmond F. Brown

NASHVILLE 1897

TENNESSEE CENTENNIAL AND INTERNATIONAL EXPOSITION

The 1897 Tennessee Centennial and International Exposition was an ambitious, promotional affair that celebrated, among other things, Confederate pride and Union patriotism, modern technology, and frontier life. The exposition's Negro and Women's buildings reflected the liberal progressive spirit of the period. And military pride, which would be transformed into the jingoistic policies that culminated in the Spanish-American War just a year later, was evident in the displays of the War and Navy departments in the U.S. government building.

The centennial was the second in less than two decades for Nashville, which held its centennial in 1880, the city being nearly twenty years older than the state. The exposition, which ran for six months from May 1 to October 31, 1897, was located on 200 acres about 2 miles from downtown Nashville. The architectural centerpiece of the event was the Parthenon building, which housed fine arts exhibits and was a replica of its namesake. The Parthenon was the inspiration of the president of the event, John W. Thomas, Nashville, Chattanooga and St. Louis Railway board chairman, who wanted the structure in order to revitalize the notion that Nashville was the Athens of the South. Other major structures were built around either the Parthenon or Lake Watauga. A replica of the Venetian Rialto building was erected over the lake. The names of many of the buildings reflected dedication to commerce and technology: Commerce, Machinery, Agriculture, Transportation, Minerals and Forestry. However, the currents of cultural changes were evident, too, with the Negro Building in particular being cited as perhaps the most attractive structure at the site and its stated purpose being to show the progress of blacks in the United States.

The styles of the buildings tended to be classical, such as the Ionic influence in the Commerce Building and the Auditorium, which was the largest exposition building at more 150,000 square feet with a two-story central pavilion, the Renaissance style of the Agriculture Building, and the Roman-Doric architectural style of the Minerals and Forestry Building.

The centennial was actually held a year late because it proved impossible to complete the grandiose buildings in 1896. Nearly every state in the union participated in some fashion, and five states—New York, Illinois, Alabama, Texas, and Arkansas—erected their own buildings. The cities of Cincinnati, Louisville, Memphis, and Knoxville also erected buildings at the site. A number of foreign countries participated in the exposition, including Great Britain, France, Germany, Austria, Russia, Italy, Switzerland, Norway, Sweden, Denmark, Belgium, China, Canada, Mexico, and Chile. The different nations highlighted the

NASHVILLE 1897. Trying for some level of ideological purity, fair planners constructed a replica of the Parthenon. (Courtesy Peter M. Warner)

cultural diversity of the event by setting up villages, some of them quite detailed, such as the Cuban village with its two theaters.

The highlight of the centennial and exposition was a two-day visit in June by President William McKinley. The incongruity of celebrating southern tradition and Union pride was apparent when a detail of Confederate veterans escorted the president's coach during the parade. McKinley, a Union veteran, gave a soldier's salute to a crowd that greeted him with a rebel yell. And a military band from the president's home state, Ohio, played "Dixie" to greet him. Apparently earlier concerns about an unenthusiastic or unfriendly reception for the president turned out to be unwarranted. He spoke to a capacity crowd in the 6,000-seat Auditorium, with some news accounts estimating the attendance as high as 8,000.

The mixture of southern pride and national patriotism may have reflected practical concerns. Nashville, as the Athens of the South, was promoting its uniqueness. And the U.S. government had a strong presence, with its own building containing exhibits from at least ten different departments, including War, Treasury, Justice, Post Office, and the Smithsonian Institution. The centennial flagpole perhaps best symbolized the two cultural-political threads of the centennial and exposition. The flagpole was built of southern pine and held together by northern steel, "rendering it not unlike our Union," in the words of an exposition board publication.

In addition to the technological and military exhibits, the eclectic range of exhibits included stuffed animals in the Children's Building, a brewery exhibit in the Commerce Building, a giant seesaw on the fairgrounds, and even a 5-ton block of Tennessee phosphate.

The exposition and centennial attracted nearly 1.2 million paid admissions over a six-month period and had a final cash balance on the books of $39.44. This probably meant a successful event in consideration of its promotional purpose and the business it generated for Nashville.

BIBLIOGRAPHY

One of the most valuable sources for information about the Tennessee Centennial and Exposition of 1897 is the *Report on the United States Government Exhibit at the Tennessee Centennial Exposition, Nashville, 1897* (1901). In spite of the name, though, it is more than a report on the U.S. government exhibits. It contains the detailed auditor's report, attendance figures, a list of special days and events at the exposition, and numerous illustrations of the buildings and layout of the fairgrounds. It is available in the Special Collections department of the library at the University of Tennessee, Knoxville. Also available there are two excellent pictorial works on the centennial and exposition. *Official Views of the United States Government Exhibits with Principal Buildings at the Tennessee Centennial Exposition, Nashville, Tennessee, 1897* (n.d.) is a collection of pictures of the government's exhibits. The other item is a booklet, *Tennessee Centennial and International Exposition* (n.d.), apparently commissioned by the exposition board, which contains color lithographs and detailed descriptions of the exposition buildings.

Two good secondary sources contain limited but interesting information about the exposition and help place the event into the context of Nashville history: Jesse C. Burt, *Nashville: Its Life and Times* (1959), and Henry McRaven, *Nashville: Athens of the South* (1949).

Edward Caudill

STOCKHOLM 1897
ALL MÄNNA KONST-OCH
INDUSTRIUTSTÄLLNINGEN

After fifteen years of proposals by manufacturers and artisans, an official government decree of June 7, 1895, created the central committee for the planning and operation of Stockholm's Great Art and Industrial Exhibition of 1897. The fourth in a thirty-year tradition of Scandinavian exhibitions, the Great Art and Industrial Exhibition was originally intended to be an exclusively Scandinavian exhibition; however, it grew to include Russian-Finnish industry and art as a testimony of good faith toward the Russians and the Finns.

Construction of the site for the exhibition began in July 1895. The site included an area of 208,000 square acres on a narrow slip of land bounded on the east by the river Djurgårdsbrunnsviken, on the south by Skansen, on the west by the Stockholm harbor, and on the north by the city of Stockholm. The site was divided into three main components: the main exhibition grounds, Skansen, and Old Stockholm.

The exhibition opened on May 1, 1897, and its exhibits, located primarily within the main exhibition grounds, were divided between two categories: the art department and the industrial exhibit. Five groups comprised the exhibits of the art department: paintings and drawings, sculpture, architecture, etchings and engravings, and decorative objects. The art department was open to all Scandinavian exhibitors, as well as foreign exhibitors by special invitation. The industrial exhibit, which was open to Scandinavian and Russian-Finnish exhibitors, contained displays on education, domestic handiwork, engineering, industry and handicraft, machines, navigation and fishing, electricity, the military, and sports.

Major structures within the exhibition grounds included the Industrial and Machinery halls. The Industrial Hall was the focal point of the exhibition. Designed by G. F. Boberg and Fredrik Lilljekvist, its area measured more than 15,000 square meters. The cupola of the hall rose to a height of 97 meters, including the flag staff. Constructed of 2,000 standards of wood, it was the largest wooden building in the world. Around the base of the cupola was a frieze representing the different branches of industry, art, and handicraft. At the top was a giant sun with the emblem of the exhibition in its center. The cupola was surrounded by four minarets, which held a viewing platform offering a view of the entire exhibition grounds, as well as the city of Stockholm.

The Machinery Hall, although smaller than the Industrial Hall, was no less grand. Constructed of iron and glass and covered with wood, its single room occupied an area of 10,000 square meters. Designed by G. F. Boberg, it was situated at the southeast corner of the exhibition grounds, its pastel green and blue colors contrasting with the whitewash of the other exhibition structures.

The most exciting features of the exhibition were Skansen and Old Stockholm. Developed on 200,000 square acres of a wood-covered mountain area just outside the main exhibition grounds, Skansen was an open-air museum dedicated to recreating the country life of Sweden's past. Skansen, designed by Doctor Arthur Hazelius, showed living examples of Swedish homesteads and farms.

Along the shore of Djurgårdsbrunnsviken could be found Gamal Stockholm (Old Stockholm). The work of architect Fredrik Lilljekvist, Old Stockholm was designed to represent sixteenth-century Stockholm during the reign of King John III. Built in the medieval style, Old Stockholm included Helgenad House (the lepers' hospital) and the Royal Castle, as well as representations of coppersmiths, goldsmiths, breweries, residences, and fortified gates. During the exhibition, there were parades and performances depicting daily life in sixteenth-century Stockholm.

The exhibition closed its gates October 3, 1897. Its success could be measured in the fact that all Scandinavian countries were fairly and equally represented and that Russian and Finnish exhibitors were extended the opportunity to show their handiwork.

BIBLIOGRAPHY

Major sources in Swedish include the following: *Allmänna konst-och industriutställningen: Officiel berattelse ... under red. af L. Loostrom* (1899–1900); *Allmänna konst-och industriutställningen: Officiel katalog* (1897); A. Hasselgren, *Utstäkkningen i Stockholm 1897* (1897); and a more recent description, E. Cornell, *De stora utstållningarna* (1952).

Very few English-language descriptions of the Stockholm fair exist. A translation of the official guide to the exhibition provides the most comprehensive look at the fair: Thore Blanch, ed., *Official Guide to Stockholm and the Great Art and Industrial Exhibition of 1897* (n.d.). A few articles in volume 72 of the *Builder* described the construction of the fair buildings; these may be found in the issues of February 20, May 15, and May 29, 1897. W. S. Harwood, "The World's Fair in Stockholm," *Outlook*, July 24, 1897, provides a tourist's view of the fair, and J. Douglas, "The Scandinavian Exhibition at Stockholm," *Nation*, November 4, 1897, deals with the exhibits.

Linda Bastyr

OMAHA 1898
TRANS-MISSISSIPPI EXPOSITION

After the Civil War, the government's intention to populate the prairie states of Nebraska, Kansas, and the Dakotas under the Homestead Act of 1862 ended in disaster when the impossibility of turning grazing land into farming land became apparent. The pioneers who had made their way west in search of fortune and a better life were forced to return to central cities such as Omaha looking for rescue.

News of the tragic farming experiment labeled the prairie states places of failure. Nebraska and its neighbors did not have a chance to prove their worth to the rest of the country until 1895, when Edward Rosewater, Nebraska state representative and founder of the *Daily Bee*, proposed Omaha as the site for an international exposition. Rosewater saw the fair as a vehicle for proclaiming the recovery of the trans-Mississippi region and its potential for greatness. The ingenuity and culture that the pioneers initially brought to the plains through their Yankee optimism finally found a spotlight.

The Trans-Mississippi Exposition of 1898 was a success emotionally and financially. To avoid comparison with the Chicago world's fair of 1893, which had ignored the western states with its emphasis on the industries of the East, the architects in chief, C. Howard Walker and Thomas R. Kimball, carefully designed buildings and exhibits to celebrate the accomplishments of the trans-Mississippians. To the classic structures and ivory color popularized at Chicago's fair, they added colorful friezes, elaborate sculpture, a Grand Court with a Venetian lagoon, and a Greek colonnade, interlacing fine art with the expansive breadth of the western landscape and dispelling the belief of many that the trans-Mississippians lacked refinement and learning. Beside the Fine Arts Building were the Manufacturing and Machinery buildings and the Mining and Agriculture buildings, containing inventions, such as a western double-sulky corn planter, and discoveries, such as alfalfa, the positive by-products of the failed "farming experiment" under the homestead law. The Arch of States at the exposition's southern entrance displayed the coats of arms of twenty-three trans-Mississippi states, forming "a gleaming belt of emblems, in which the stars of empire, rivers, mountains, and plains, the wheat and corn, the plow and locomotive" symbolized the "enterprise of the pioneers" (Walker, p. 519).

There were three cattle exhibits glorifying the third largest meat-packing capital of the world and a conference on education in June, supporting the region's commitment to its numerous agricultural colleges. The Midway, with its varied attractions, was especially popular. A cabaret of exotic villages and restaurants, the Midway included an Afro-American village, a Chinese village, and a Philippine village, as well as a Wild West show. High standards were set for all attractions on the Midway, which helped its popularity; however, occasionally, questionable entertainment needed guidance. Kenneth Alfers notes that one exhibit featuring "a group of girls performing at a concession known as the 'Streets of Cairo' was questioned, and Abraham L. Reed, head of the concessions department, took action which forced the girls to moderate their dancing" (Alfers, pp. 325–26).

Perhaps the most unusual and timely exhibit at the exposition was a huge teepee containing an ethnological museum and surrounded by an authentic Indian encampment. Twenty-three tribes came to participate and found themselves a curiosity and a symbol of conquered territory. This "validated Indian Congress" was overseen by James Mooney, a member of the Bureau of American Ethnology at the Smithsonian Institution, who worked to guarantee its authenticity and to separate it from the more theatrical Wild West shows of the Midway. Its leading feature, however, was sham battles between whites and Indians that bordered on the theatrical and caused some concern about the verisimilitude of the exhibit. Mooney eventually tried to dissociate himself and the institute from the Indian exhibit, but it nevertheless remained a huge success to the end of the fair. In fact, President William McKinley's visit in October 1898 during the successful Peace Jubilee Week celebrating the end of the Spanish-American War was highlighted by an elaborate battle between the Indians from different tribes. The production, says Rydell, "depicted both the 'degeneracy' of Native Americans and the paternal role of government." McKinley and the nearly 100,000 people who attended the fair on the day of his visit were impressed (Rydell, p. 121).

Despite the approach of the Spanish-American War in February 1898 and other incidents—such as one involving a Lieutenant Dorothy Mauer of the Salvation Army, her trusty axe, and a mutilated nude statue days before the exposition opened—the fair was operating in the black by August. Rosewater, it would seem, was correct about his expectations for the fair. As Alfers notes, "The Trans-Mississippi and International Exposition was at first planned as a symbol of progress achieved in only one area of the country. But so vast and so rich was the region that the Fair's first flush of success was also heralded as a triumph for the entire country" (Alfers, p. 323).

BIBLIOGRAPHY

The records of the Trans-Mississippi and International Exposition are housed at the Nebraska State Historical Society in Lincoln. Also at this repository are the papers of William V. Allen, a Nebraska senator who was especially interested in an Indian exhibit at the fair, and Charles Wooster, a populist state legislator who opposed the appropriation of state funds for the event. In addition, the scrapbooks of John A. Wakefield, the general manager of the exposition, are at the Omaha Public Library, with microfilm copies at the historical society.

James B. Haynes, *History of the Trans-Mississippi and International Exposition of 1898* (1910), is the official history of the fair, authorized by the board of directors. Other contemporary sources include Charles Howard Walker, "Great Exposition at Omaha,"

Century Magazine 55 (February 1898): 518–21, which voices the anticipation of the fair and the pride in the Midwest that must have been felt by all those in the area at that time, and Albert Shaw, "The Trans-Mississippians and Their Fair at Omaha," *Century Magazine* 56 (October 1898): 836–52, which puts the fair into clear historical perspective and includes a detailed description of its buildings, exhibits, and events. A pictorial view of the exposition may be found in *Snap Shots of the Trans-Mississippi Exposition at Omaha, Nebraska* (1898), which features black and white photographs of the most prominent buildings, the Midway, the Grand Court, and a number of Indians who participated in the Indian congress.

Among modern sources, Robert Rydell, *All the World's a Fair* (1984), is the most complete and detailed account of the exposition. The chapter on the Omaha fair, "Concomitant to Empire," takes the reader from early 1897, when the state legislature debated the exposition appropriation bill, to the last days of the fair. Kenneth Alfers, "Triumph of the West: The Trans-Mississippi Exposition," *Nebraska History* 53, no. 3 (Fall 1972): 313–29, looks closely at the political debate and scandal that accompanied the fair, as well as the rivalry between the two local papers, the *Omaha Bee*, edited by Edward Rosewater, and the *World-Herald*, edited by Gilbert Hitchcock. In "Omaha Unites a Nation," *World's Fair* 3, no. 3 (Summer 1983): 1–5, William Kahrl presents a contrasting view of Rosewater and his role in the fair.

Toni Oplt

PARIS 1900

EXPOSITION UNIVERSELLE

On July 13, 1892, not quite three years after the close of the successful 1889 exposition, the French Third Republic announced an Exposition universelle for 1900. Jules Roche, the minister of commerce, noted the symbolic importance of this year, the end as well as the beginning of centuries of astonishing achievement, adding: "The Exposition of 1900 will synthesize the nineteenth century and ascertain its philosophy." No doubt—but rumors circulating in June that Kaiser Wilhelm II planned a world's fair for Berlin in 1900 supplied a more immediate stimulus. Mixed motives aside, the French mounted in 1900 the largest of the world exhibitions to date, and it celebrated, more by recapitulating the expiring century than by anticipating the nascent one, the ideals, values, and accumulated industrial triumphs of European civilization at its height, all within a comparative historical framework. It also allowed exhibiting nations to boast peacefully about their wealth and power, while providing both an architectural fantasia and an entertaining miscellany of attractions and diversions, not to mention a surfeit of consumer products. The exposition accordingly mirrored fin-de-siècle Europe while revealing harbingers of the coming century.

Formal planning began on September 9, 1893, when a decree named Alfred Picard head of the Governing Commission. An official at the 1889 exposition as well as author of its report, an engineer by training and a civil servant by profession, Picard received almost complete autonomy in preparing the 1900 exposition. Within a month, he announced as its site the esplanade des Invalides, the Champ de Mars, the Trocadéro, and the neighboring quays. And by November 1895, he had sketched its themes, projected attendance figures of 60 million, and suggested financing schemes. Of the fifty-three foreign powers invited, over forty had accepted, including all the great powers; for the first time, the German empire was to attend a Paris exposition. Noisy opposition in the legislature and the press notwithstanding, the authorization bill passed easily, becoming law on June 13, 1896. Approved was an expenditure of 105 million francs, to be raised from subventions of 20 million francs each from the French state and the city of Paris and the sale of 65 million francs of coupons redeemable for admission tickets.

While Picard and his commission supervised the preparation of the site, the construction of exhibition buildings, and the organization of the exhibits, matters beyond their control affected attitudes toward the fair, the content and reception of certain exhibits, and attendance figures. Deep-seated uncertainties, economic and social as well as political and international, prevailed in France during the exposition's planning, and advocates hoped it would not only stimulate the economy but renew domestic accord. Naturalism, positivism, and scientism, the reigning ideas of those who, like the planners of the exposition, retained faith in reason, progress, and human potential, were contested by metaphysical idealists and by a mood of intellectual and social decadence. And both long-term political and social divisions and their more immediate manifestations during the 1890s were aggravated by the Dreyfus affair, which split Paris until the presidential pardon of September 19, 1899, issued, some argue, because foreign supporters of Dreyfus threatened to boycott the exposition.

French international anxieties, the legacy of the German victory of 1870–1871, and the subsequent diplomatic isolation were lessened by the Russian alliance of 1894. Meanwhile, imperialistic ambitions led to clashes like that between the Marchand expedition and British troops at Fashoda (1898), the humiliating withdrawal poisoning relations with England, as did French support for the Afrikaners in the Boer War. Such events, together with eruptions of momentary concern like the Boxer Rebellion in China, made their presence felt at an exposition that was far from ready when the inaugural ceremonies took place on April 14, 1900.

Visitors to this *bilan du siècle* found its classification and layout bewildering, its size dismaying, and its transportation inadequate. Within the main grounds, most walked, the moving sidewalk and the electric train having left large areas bereft of transportation. Worse, the arrangement of the exhibits begot confusion rather than the intended comprehension of industrial processes. According to official figures, exhibits totaled 83,047—38,253 by France and 44,794 by some forty foreign nations, over half European. Largest of the foreign exhibitors, the United States dispatched 7,610 exhibits, filling some 337,000 square feet of space. Picard organized these displays by the traditional method, classifying them not by nation of origin but by 18 subject groups, subdivided further into a total of 121 classes, and ranked hierarchically from education and the fine arts to colonization and the military. More complexity resulted from the inclusion within each group of a historical exhibit illustrating advances since 1800. Outside this formal taxonomy were the official foreign pavilions, divers exhibits, and attractions.

The 1900 exposition occupied a site larger than any previous Paris exposition, with its main grounds in Paris (279 acres) and an annex at the bois de Vincennes (274 acres). The former consisted of five sections arranged along three axes, the whole forming an immense letter A laid across the topography of central Paris. Arrayed along one axis were the fine arts exhibits (Group II) in the Grand and Petit Palais and displays of decorations and furnishings (Group XII) and miscellaneous industries (Group XV) in two rectangular buildings facing each other on the esplanade des Invalides.

The principal exhibition area extended from the Ecole Militaire to the Trocadéro. Parallel to the Ecole Militaire, the Galerie des Machines housed displays of agriculture (Group VII) and food and drink (Group X), separated by the Salle des Fêtes, site of both the opening and the awards ceremonies. Following exhibits of mechanics (Group IV) and electricity (Group V), the exhibition palaces bifurcated, reaching in parallel rectangles along the Champ de Mars toward the Seine and enclosing a garden with the Chateau d'Eau at one end and the Eiffel Tower at the other. To the left were chemical industries (Group XIV), civil engineering and transportation (Group VI), education and teaching (Group I) and letters, sciences, and arts (Group III), while opposite were mechanics again, threads, cloth, and clothing (Group XIII) and mines and metallurgy (Group XI). At the base of the Eiffel Tower clustered restaurants and a potpourri of unclassified attractions, including the Panorama du Tour du monde and displays by motoring and climbing clubs. Across the pont d'Iéna and beneath the Palais de Trocadéro, built for the Exposition universelle of 1878 and demolished for that of 1937, sprawled the colonial exhibits (Group XVII), the exotic harvest of European imperialism.

Linking these axes were the displays that lined the quays of the Seine from the pont d'Iéna to the pont Alexandre III. Here were forestry, hunting, fishing, and gathering (Group IX), military displays (Group XVIII), social economy, sanitation, and public assistance (Group XVI), and horticulture (Group VIII). Also flanking the Seine were the foreign pavilions of the rue des Nations, halls for scholarly conferences, and assorted unclassified exhibits and attractions. Overall the exposition grounds in Paris created an unforgettable visual impression, one oriented around celebrated monuments and replete with splendid vistas.

Relegated to the Vincennes annex around Lake Daumesnil and little visited even after the Métro opened were exhibits, attractions, and competitions unsuitable for central Paris. Yet more agricultural exhibits, automobiles, and a Hall of Railways joined displays of heavy farm equipment, such as that sent by the McCormick Harvester Company. In addition to the second modern Olympic Games, competitive events ranged from equestrian to ballooning, from tennis and croquet to motorcycle and automobile racing.

Exposition exhibits created a mosaic of European civilization at its summit of power and influence. Most displays, especially those in the national pavilions, celebrated national pride as well. Appreciation of these achievements, however, eluded many, since the exposition lacked a self-evident theme, and the classification system not only separated exhibits that belonged together but also placed them in unexpected locations. Perfumes appeared with the chemical displays, while visitors interested in planned worker housing had to visit the Palais des Congrès, the German pavilion, and the Vincennes annex. And because the retrospective exhibits were segregated by classification group, it was all but impossible to gain a historical overview. Perhaps the exposition offered the promised synthesis of the nineteenth century, but if so, even the learned Henry Adams failed to ascertain it.

Exposition architecture incorporated existing buildings, permanent new structures, and temporary exhibition palaces. The Palais du Trocadéro remained from the 1878 exposition, while the Galérie des Machines and the Eiffel Tower survived from 1889, the latter two making evident that the architecture of 1900 would be less innovative than these austere structures of iron and glass.

The single enduring transformation of urban space occasioned by the exposition affected a site enclosed by the Seine and the Champs Elysées, the former avenue d'Antin and the place de la Concorde and then occupied by the Palais de l'industrie, erected for the 1855 exposition. Picard won approval for its replacement with an aesthetically unified complex, the Grand Palais, the Petit Palais, and the pont Alexandre III, which would restore the vista from the Champs Elysées to the facade of the Invalides. Construction began when Félix Faure, then president of the Third Republic, and Czar Nicholas II of Russia laid the cornerstone of the pont Alexandre III on October 7, 1896. Modern in design yet traditional in ornamentation, it realized a long-contemplated project for a Seine bridge and celebrated in both name and decoration the Franco-Russian Alliance of 1894.

Built to face each other across the new avenue Nicolas II, the Grand Palais, designed by Henri Deglane, Louis-Albert Louvet, and Albert Thomas, and the Petit Palais, the work of the Prix de Rome winner Charles-Louis Girault, remain as representatives of late beaux-arts splendor. Since affiliates of the Ecole des Beaux-Arts dominated the selection of exposition architects, the design of these permanent buildings, as well as of the temporary exhibition palaces, derived from this school's concept of public architecture. Behind neobaroque or neo-rococo stone facades, historically eclectic in style as well as allegorical and ennobling in decoration, these architects concealed innovative uses of iron and glass.

The temporary exhibition palaces inspired the American publisher of a photographic album and most visitors to proclaim the exposition a dream city. Yet critics disparaged these buildings as chaotic and bizarre, likening them to the extravagant productions of a demented pastry chef or an opium smoker. With a few exceptions, the exhibition pavilions adhered to the same beaux-arts principles as the Grand and the Petit Palais, although they were more mannered in design and embellishment. With iron or steel frameworks covered by light-colored plaster facades, they featured massive ornate porticoes, long colonnaded galleries, sweeping staircases, and semicircular arcades of rounded arches. Seeking novelty in decoration rather than originality of design, architects covered exterior surfaces with freestanding statues and didactic sculpted groups, colored frescoes and friezes, while rooflines were broken by yet more sculpture and a jumble of domes, towers, pinnacles, and urns.

The panorama created by the twenty-two foreign pavilions along the Seine invited praise, and critics no less than visitors admired the "rue de Venise" of the exposition. However arresting, this picturesque ensemble of juxtaposed façades, towers, and cupolas offered neither original nor significant architecture but rather, as recommended by exposition officials, examples of each contributing nation's historical or indigenous style. Most preferred complete historical recreations, as did the British and the Germans, or pastiches of celebrated details, as did Hungary, Italy, and Spain. With its wooden pavilion by Eliel Saarinen,

Finland honored native traditions. Incongruous was Charles A. Coolidge's neoclassical American pavilion.

A miscellany of structures completed the exposition's architecture. The poly-
chromed porte Binet, René Binet's monumental entrance on the place de la
Concorde, could pass 60,000 visitors an hour beneath a dome flanked by two
minarets, the ensemble topped by a controversial figure representing the city of
Paris and illuminated by thousands of multicolored lights. Besides the art nouveau
buildings, only Charles Gautier's horticultural pavilions of iron and glass appeared modern. To accommodate railway traffic for the exposition, Victor Laloux
designed the Gare d'Orsay, reopened in 1986 as the Musée d'Orsay.

Within the exhibition buildings, cluttered and often pedantic displays awaited
visitors. Some scrutinized model classrooms, while others marveled at the lin-
otype composing machine, the new motion picture machines, or the operation
of X-rays. The few still drawn by the machinery of the nineteenth century admired
steam engines, a selection of railway equipment, hot-air balloons, and experimental flying machines. Still others ambled among horticultural, agriculture,
and foodstuff displays. And in each foreign pavilion exhibits celebrated national
character: Bosnia's artisans working in precious metals and cloth; historical
traditions, such as Hungary's Hall of the Hussars; scenic panoramas, like Sweden's dioramas; and the fine arts, such as Germany's re-creation of the library
and three rooms from Sans-Souci.

But by 1900 such displays no longer thrilled the imagination. What did was
that "fairy electricity." Visitors crowded the Palace of Electricity to watch steam-
driven dynamos power the exposition's machinery and the thousands of lights
that transformed the Trocadéro, the Seine panorama, and even the porte Binet
into a nocturnal fantasy. Visitors marveled at the newly invented automobile
and viewed—some with pride, others with misgivings—the military might of
the great powers. With extensive colonial displays, the French not only celebrated
their acquisitions but also educated the public with displays of native life, like
the Dahomey village, and re-creations, such as the newly discovered temples at
Angkor Wat. The Boer and the Chinese pavilions received special attention
owing to contemporary events.

Much applauded were the fine arts displays at the Grand Palais and the Petit
Palais, the latter housing a historical survey of French arts from provincial
libraries, museums, and churches. The Grand Palais sheltered both the "Centennale," a retrospective exhibit of nineteenth-century French paintings, and the
"Décennale," an international exhibition of fine arts from the previous decade.
In the French portion of the Décennale beaux-arts painters predominated, exhibiting their customary portraits, landscapes and seascapes, religious and genre
scenes, nudes, and sentimental historical tableaux, often with Napoleonic associations. Notably absent were the impressionists and the postimpressionists.
Bolder foreign exhibitors showed works by James Ensor, Gustav Klimt, and
Ferdinand Hodler. The sculpture displays were also conservative, and Auguste

PARIS 1900. The Palace of Electricity, seen through an arch of the Eiffel Tower, the great symbol of the Paris exposition of 1889. (Courtesy Peter M. Warner)

Rodin showed the *Gates of Hell* in a separate pavilion. For the Centennale, Roger Marx selected works by the impressionists for display alongside recognized masterpieces by Jacques-Louis David and Gustave Courbet. Connoisseurs and artists in search of more modern art had to quit the exposition grounds for the Parisian galleries.

Art nouveau enjoyed a special prominence at the exposition, notably in the decorative arts and the architecture of smaller buildings, but the frequent assertion that the 1900 exposition saw its triumph remains controversial. Examples of this fin-de-siècle style, with its emphasis on the long and sinuous line and its cele-bration of the fanciful, the bizarre, and the exotic, may be found in the grand staircase of the Grand Palais, the iron gates of the Petit Palais, the Métro stations of Hector Guimard, the Pavillon Bleu, and the dance pavilion designed for the American Loïe Fuller by Henri Sauvage and Pierre Roche. Art nouveau rooms, featured in the German and Austrian exhibits, filled the pavilions of the art dealer Samuel Bing and the Union Centrale des Arts Décoratifs; a room from the latter, designed by Georges Hoentschel and containing jewelry by René Lalique and glassware by Emile Gallé, survives in the Musée des Arts Décoratifs in Paris.

Entertainments included commercial attractions, festival days with themes, special banquets, music, theatricals, dance, and sports. Of the admission-charg-ing entertainments clustered beneath the Eiffel Tower and along the rue de Paris on the right bank of the Seine, some were superficially educational, offering vicarious travel in space or time. At the Tour du monde, plaster re-creations and dioramas of exotic scenes in Europe, North Africa, the Middle East, and the Far East predominated, and the Celestial Globe promised an imaginary journey into space. For the less adventurous, the Swiss village provided, with its Alpine landscape, farms, and a village inhabited by costumed peasants, a bucolic and historical respite. The more historically minded could stroll the streets of Albert Robida's Vieux Paris, a picturesque evocation of medieval and Renaissance Paris, or view the historical tableaux at the Palais du Costume.

Seekers of thrills rather than edification favored the giant ferris wheel or the Manoir à l'Envers ("inverted house"). Exposition festivals, in addition to the opening and closing ceremonies and the inauguration of a statue of Lafayette by the United States on July 4, celebrated flowers, wine, automobiles, and military music. At the famous Banquet of Mayors of September 22, 20,777 dined si-multaneously. And along the rue de Paris were grouped small theaters and cabarets like the Maison du Rire. Scattered pavilions, such as the Palais Lu-mineux, a sort of oriental-rococo fantasy of colored glass illuminated by thou-sands of electric lights, captivated evening visitors. Even within serious displays entertainments lurked. At the Russian pavilion, visitors sat in a mock coach of the trans-Siberian Railway and ate Slavic foods while painted scenery rolled by, creating the illusion of a journey from Moscow to Peking.

Total attendance for the Exposition universelle (April 15–November 12) was 50,860,801 (48,368,504 in Paris and 2,492,297 at Vincennes). Festivals orga-nized by worried officials bolstered attendance, which lagged behind predictions until August. September saw the most visitors (9,555,059) and the midpoint for total paid attendance. On October 7, the greatest single day for attendance, 652,082 visited the exposition. Foreign visitors came chiefly from Germany; the English stayed home, a result of French sympathy for the Boers and anti-British sentiments in Parisian newspapers. Also reducing attendance from the projected 60 million were the tardy completion of the exposition grounds, summer heat, international resentment engendered by the Dreyfus affair, and the absence of visiting monarchs, many of whom viewed Paris as home to anarchist assassins. Despite disappointment that attendance did not exceed official estimates, the figures established a long-standing record for a one-season fair.

Drawing up a financial balance sheet for the Exposition universelle proves difficult, though few would dispute that the French economy benefited, directly or indirectly. Operators of the admission-charging attractions, like the Tour du monde (cost: 2 million francs; receipts: 691,245 francs), however, experienced losses, as did restaurateurs and other concession holders. Reports of profits or losses for the exposition itself vary, often depending on the accounting procedure. Picard's initial estimates (January 1901) set the loss at 2 million francs, less than 2 percent of expenditures. Figures of April 30, 1903 (expenses: 119,225,707 francs; receipts: 126,318,169 francs) indicate profits of 7 million francs, while others suggest profits as high as 9½ million. Even the loss figures are insignificant when juxtaposed with the additional revenues taken in by the state, the city of Paris, the railroads, and the Bank of France, not to mention the increased income enjoyed by Parisian hotels, restaurants, stores, and theaters. The exposition must be reckoned a financial success.

The Exposition universelle of 1900 was the last, as well as the greatest, of a cycle of five Parisian expositions that began in 1855. With respect to attendance figures or impressions carried home, most contemporaries regarded it a success but not the astonishing success anticipated. Among Frenchmen who believed expositions provided an opportunity for France to show its best face, some concluded that it revealed instead a second-rate power, a nation overshadowed by the Germans, the Americans, and even the Japanese. Both foreign commentators and their French counterparts wrote of the exposition with an ambiguous mixture of optimism and fin-de-siècle pessimism. Among the favorable, Patrick Geddes decried beneath a glittering surface its retrospective character as a "literal museum of the present" and an "incipient museum of the History of Civilization," though he found overwhelming the exposition's size and diversity. And while some lamented the absence of revolutionary advances in technology, Henry Adams contemplated the gigantic dynamos and saw a world of power he could not understand. Those sharing Adams's pessimism perceived, as Richard Mandell has suggested, the dim outlines of the twentieth century, where material progress would race ahead of humanity's ability to deal with it, where things and knowledge would so accumulate that people could neither adequately classify nor fully comprehend them, and where simple faith in science, reason, and progress was about to be shattered. The exposition accordingly mirrored Europe of the belle époque, a brilliant, if often arrogant and naively optimistic, civilization that all too rarely examined itself with discernment.

BIBLIOGRAPHY

Study of the 1900 exposition begins with the annotated bibliography in Richard D. Mandell, *Paris 1900: The Great World's Fair* (1967). Listed are specialized bibliographies, official documents, guidebooks, contemporary newspapers and journals, and secondary accounts. Because this book is readily available, only the more important sources will be listed here, together with works omitted by Mandell or published since 1967. Of the two works by Alfred Picard, general commissioner of the exposition, the *Rapport général administratif et technique*, 8 vols. (1902–1903) is essential; also see his *Le Bilan d'un siècle* (1801–1900), 6 vols. (1906). Of much interest are the *Catalogue général officiel*, 20 vols. (1900), the commercial guidebooks (especially the Hachette guide, which is available in English), as well as the separate guides for each exhibit and for each nation's displays. For U.S. participation, see the *Report of the Commissioner-General for the United States to the International Universal Exposition, Paris, 1900*, 6 vols. (1901), published as Senate Document No. 232, 56th Congress, 2d session, vols. 27–32. At the National Archives are the records of the U.S. Commission; see the inventory for Record Group 43. A short and relatively accessible preview of U.S. participation is Ferdinand Peck, "The United States at the Paris Exposition in 1900," *North American Review* 168 (January 1899): 24–33.

Contemporary opinion concerning the exposition may be found in the periodical literature of the exhibiting nations, beginning in the mid-1890s. For France, see especially: *L'Illustration* (for maps and pictures), *Revue des deux mondes*, *Revue de Paris*, and *Gazette des beaux arts*. A collection of translated excerpts relating to art and architecture is in Elizabeth Gilmore Holt, ed., *The Expanding World of Art, 1874–1902*, vol. 1: *Universal Expositions and State-Sponsored Fine Arts Exhibitions* (1988). For visual impressions of the exposition, consult the many illustrated albums, such as José de Olivares, *The Parisian Dream City: A Portfolio of Photographic Views of the World Exposition at Paris* (1900), and James Penny Boyd, *The Paris Exposition of 1900: A Vivid Descriptive View . . .* (1900). For architectural views, see A. Raguenet, *Les Principaux Palais de l'Exposition universelle de Paris* (1900), and *L'Architecture et la sculpture: Exposition de 1900* (1900?). Verbal descriptions are legion; among the available are Paul Morand, *1900 A.D.*, trans. Mrs. Romilly Fedden (1931) and vol. 9 of William Walton, *Paris from the Earliest Period to the Present Day*, 10 vols. (1899–1902). For the reflections of Henry Adams, see *The Education of Henry Adams. An Autobiography* (1918) and *Letters of Henry Adams* (1892–1918) (1938). Delightful as an antidote to the usual ponderous accounts is Gaston Bergeret, *Journal d'un nègre à l'Exposition de 1900* (1901).

Secondary works include: Adolphe Démy, *Essai historique sur les Expositions universelles de Paris* (1907), 438–688; Philippe Jullian, *The Triumph of Art Nouveau, Paris Exhibition 1900*, trans. Stephen Hardman (1974); John Allwood, *The Great Exhibitions* (1977); and Pascal Ory, *Les Expositions universelles de Paris* (1982). Useful for the mood of fin-de-siècle France are: Jacques Chastenet, *La République triomphante, 1893–1906* (1955), vol. 3 of his *Histoire de la Troisième république*, 6 vols. (1952–1963); Charles Rearick, *Pleasures of the Belle Epoque: Entertainment and Festivity in Turn-of-*

the-Century France (1985); Eugen Weber, *France Fin de Siècle* (1986); and Theodore Zeldin, *France, 1848–1945*, 2 vols. (1973–1977). Of considerable interest is Rosalind H. Williams, *Dream Worlds: Mass Consumption in Late Nineteenth-Century France* (1982); she views the exposition as a ''scale model of the consumer revolution.'' Art nouveau can be studied in Jean-Paul Bouillon, *Art Nouveau, 1870–1914* (1985), and in Franco Borsi and Ezio Godol, *Paris 1900*, trans. J. C. Palmes (1977). Beaux-arts architecture and the Petit Palais are discussed in Derrick Worsdale, ''The Petit Palais des Champs-Elysées: Architecture and Decoration,'' *Apollo* 107 (March 1978): 207–11; superb notes make this article a guide for further work. And also of interest are: Emmanuelle Toulet, ''Le Cinéma à l'Exposition universelle de 1900,'' *Revue d'histoire moderne et contemporaine* 33 (April-June 1986): 179–209: William H. Schneider, ''Colonies at the 1900 World Fair,'' *History Today* 31 (May 1981): 31–36; and Arthur Chandler, ''Culmination: The Paris Exposition Universelle of 1900,'' *World's Fair* 7, no. 3 (Summer 1987): 8–14.

Robert W. Brown

BUFFALO 1901
PAN-AMERICAN EXPOSITION

On May 1, 1901, the *Buffalo* (N.Y.) *News* announced the opening of the Pan-American Exposition in excited terms: "The promise that the Pan-American would be the electrical marvel of the opening century has been kept." The exposition that began with such praise ended six months later under the shadow of the assassination of President William McKinley in the Temple of Music on September 6, 1901, and the financial failures that marked the fair's closing weeks. Organizers reported a deficit of more than $3 million, and a newspaper editor sadly concluded, "The whole exposition business has been heavily overdone."

The promoters of the Pan-American had hoped to bring the spirit of world's fairs and expositions to northern New York in a manner that would stimulate the economy of Buffalo and increase popular awareness of the region. Although the exposition won applause for its electrical lighting, color scheme, and hemispheric theme, the fair itself experienced both bad luck and policy mistakes that contributed to its general disappointment in 1901. The Pan-American lacked a clear vision of what it hoped to achieve, opened late with much unfinished, and then had the disaster of a presidential assassination at a time when it might otherwise have expected to attract the most visitors.

The idea for an exposition in Buffalo originated in 1895 when businessmen from the city, attending the Cotton States and International Exposition in Atlanta, contemplated putting on a comparable event in their own locality. The arrival of low-cost electric power from Niagara Falls in November 1896 caused spokesmen for Buffalo's future to announce their intention to hold an exposition "in celebration of that event." The Pan-American Exposition Company was formed, and preliminary planning went ahead in 1897, including the selection of a site, the issuance of bonds, and the filing of requests for aid from New York State and the federal government. The stated aim of the organizers had now evolved into "promoting and conducting an exposition to illustrate the material progress of the New World during the nineteenth century." The proposal envisioned better relations with the peoples of Latin America and the encouragement of U.S. trade with that region. The aims were ambitious and somewhat diffuse, but the planners had optimism and confidence on their side.

The rising tension between the United States and Spain over the fate of Cuba in early 1898, culminating in war in April, made it necessary to postpone the exposition past the 1899 target date. Since the Paris exposition would occur in 1900, the Buffalo planners chose the period May to November 1901 for their project. Congress appropriated the money for a U.S. government building, and New York State put up $300,000 for its exhibit. Popular subscriptions, primarily in the Buffalo area, brought in $1.5 million. The exposition leaders hoped to have an abundance of exhibitions from Latin American nations. In fact, both the degree of local support in Buffalo and the participation from South America were overestimated during the preparation phase.

To direct the construction and operation of the exposition, the organizers chose William I. Buchanan, an American diplomat who had been involved with the Columbian Exposition of 1893. Buchanan was named director general of the Pan-American in late 1899. He brought energy and managerial ability to his assignment, but he soon discovered that the exposition had numerous weaknesses. The city of Buffalo was not excited about the project. "It's high time to put some Chicago into Buffalo," warned the official newspaper of the exposition. More important, the venture was not securely financed, and the city was not prepared for the flood of visitors it would receive. The anticipated role of the Latin American nations would be much more limited than the planners had originally projected.

Buchanan sought to surmount these problems with an extensive advertising campaign that spread the attractions of the exposition across the nation. A representative brochure called the fair "the most beautiful and instructive exposition ever held." Despite the success of Buchanan's promotional activity, circumstances worked against the Pan-American in early 1901. Bad weather in late 1900 and into the new year delayed construction, but the board of directors remained firm that the gates would open on May 1, 1901. The elements of an exposition were all in Buffalo as that date approached. So too were April snows that held back important concluding details. The fair was still scheduled to begin on May 1, but the official opening ceremonies were set three weeks later on May 20, Dedication Day. This staggered start hurt the Pan-American from the outset. "Early visitors went away with a grievance, to vent their disappointment at home," said a Cleveland newspaper, "and they did much to keep people away from Buffalo all through the season."

Dedication Day itself was successful. Over 100,000 people came to see Vice-President Theodore Roosevelt and other dignitaries, including the exposition's president, John G. Milburn of Buffalo. President McKinley was traveling on the West Coast, but he planned to be in Buffalo later in the year. For now, McKinley sent his greetings by telegram: "I earnestly hope that this great exhibition may prove a blessing to every country of this hemisphere." Despite this auspicious start, the exposition remained an ill-fated affair. The initial reactions of visitors ranged from tepid to hostile, and heavy rains fell in May and June. Worse, Buffalo had the coolest June weather in three decades. The daily attendance hovered around 10,000 paying customers, and it seemed likely that the Pan-American would be an expensive flop.

If the Pan-American lost at the turnstiles, it achieved much more positive reviews from the critics and journalists who visited the grounds in the summer of 1901. After surveying the exposition, Mary Bronson Hartt said that it was "industrially too significant, educationally too important, and aesthetically too superb to be passed by.'' The feature of the fair that drew the most attention was the artificial lighting that the closeness to Niagara Falls and its power made possible. The Electric Tower, 375 feet high, became "the high C of the entire architectural symphony.'' Niagara power generally "blossoms in a whole firmament of electric stars which make up the glory of the Pan-American illumination.'' Another enthusiastic writer observed that when the lights went on each night the first-time visitor understood "something of the ecstasy of the sun-worshipper when the red disk appears above the Persian hills.''

The general plan of the exposition was the work of John M. Carrère, and it featured "a logical arrangement and significance in the groupings of buildings.'' As visitors approached the grounds from Delaware Park, they crossed a bridge that led into the Esplanade. On their right was the building of the U.S. government. Ahead, the Temple of Music and the Ethnology Building were on either side of the court of the fountains, beyond which were the Machinery and Transportation Building and the Manufactures and Liberal Arts Building. Farther along stood the Electric Tower, the Electricity Building, the Agriculture Building, and finally the delights and temptations of the Midway. "Felicity of arrangement and fantasy in construction are the Exposition's cardinal merits,'' concluded one art critic. As a modern historian has noted, the fair also embodied "a carefully crafted allegory of America's rise to the apex of civilization.''

This didactic purpose was followed out in the buildings themselves, the sculpture that filled the grounds, and the overall color scheme of the Pan-American. The structures were done in Spanish Renaissance style, chosen to suggest "the historical continuity of life in the Americas.'' The color scheme of the exposition and the organization of the sculpture came from the collaboration of Karl Bitter, who supervised the sculpture, and Charles Y. Turner, who was in charge of color for the fair. The two men decided to make their particular areas assert the larger themes of the exposition. "If Mr. Turner in his color scheme has tried to depict the struggle of man to overcome the elements, Mr. Bitter has attempted in his scenario to give a complete allegory of man and his development.''

Bitter arranged the sculpture to have "a clear, distinct, and well-defined meaning.'' In front of the building of horticulture, for example, the artworks exemplified "the apotheosis of nature's bounty.'' The sculptures located near the government buildings represented the "glorification of human institutions.'' Although one critic remarked that "the psychology of this is about as subtle as that of the sign post,'' another contended that it constituted "one of the most novel and impressive features of the Exposition.''

Turner's color scheme for the fair elicited even more positive reactions. "The Buffalo Exposition,'' wrote Hamilton Wright Mabie, "adds to the charm of order and grace the beauty of color.'' Turner used color to draw visitors along the pathway of civilization from its beginnings, represented by harsh primary colors at the perimeters of the exposition grounds, to the height of modern civilization, symbolized by the Electric Tower at the center of the site, decorated in subtle, harmonious pastel shades. "An ethical significance is aimed at,'' said a promotional pamphlet, "in the chromatic arrangement as in the architectural plan; the whole symbolizing progression from a less civilized stage to a higher. Thus the strongest, crudest colors are nearest the entrances." It required a great deal of skill and planning to achieve Turner's desired effect; the comments of observers indicated that he succeeded. "Nowhere else in the world, I think, has exterior wall tinting been attempted upon so heroic a scale," argued Mary Hartt. Hamilton Mabie told his readers that "the general effect is rich and striking, and the eye which loves color finds delight in the warm tones modulated over a great space with a harmonious set of values."

Within the exposition itself, the allegorical purposes were embodied in exhibitions that instructed Americans regarding the peoples over which they now exercised an imperial sway. The organizers wanted to feature the Philippines among the newly acquired possessions. A government ethnologist, Frank F. Hilder, became the driving force behind the effort to have a Philippine exhibit. Although Hilder died before the display opened in the government building, the collection of Filipino cultural artifacts and photographs that he assembled became one of the most popular aspects of the federal exhibit. There was also a Filipino village on the midway, "one of the most thoroughly native things on the Street of Streets." The *New York Times* said that it was "almost as good as a trip to the islands."

The keynote of the exposition was the linkage between the United States and the other nations of the Western Hemisphere. The implementation of the theme, however, was less successful than the sponsors of the Pan-American had hoped. There were separate buildings for Canada, Chile, Cuba, the Dominican Republic, Ecuador, Guatemala, Honduras, and Mexico, but the other Latin American nations had displays within exhibition halls or sent only a commissioner to the fair. "The Latin Americas, inconspicuous or wanting in other buildings," wrote Mary Hartt, "come out strong in agriculture. Some of them, like Argentina and Nicaragua, have preferred to mass their products here rather than scatter them through other departments." Despite the rather spotty participation of the countries at which the exposition was aimed, observers of the Pan-American believed that the fair had achieved its goal. "The word American has never received, however," said Hamilton Mabie, "a broader or deeper interpretation; and the thoughtful visitor will find in the beautiful unity of the Exposition a parable which Americans of English descent will do well to study."

As the summer of 1901 continued, the financial prospects for the Pan-American improved. Daily attendance in July was higher than in May and June, and by August more than 40,000 visitors paid their way into the fair each day. With good weather in September and October, the Pan-American might limit the losses that its promoters would have to absorb. The visit of President William McKinley in early September would bring great crowds to Buffalo as the chief executive took part in what he termed "my Exposition." There would be a major presidential speech on September 5, extensive tours of the grounds, and a public reception at the Temple of Music on September 6.

The original date for the president's visit was June 13, 1901. It was to have been the concluding event of a six-week tour of the nation that would take McKinley to the West Coast and back. Toward the end of the journey, Mrs. McKinley became ill, and the presidential party hurried back to Washington. The scheduled stop at Buffalo was postponed as the McKinleys spent a quiet summer at their home in Canton, Ohio. A delegation of Buffalonians visited the president in the first days of August, and the date of September 5 was agreed on for the observance of President's Day at the Pan-American Exposition. McKinley intended to use the event to endorse the administration's policy of tariff reciprocity and to push for the ratification of trade treaties then stalled in the Senate. The Pan-American setting would be an ideal opportunity to advance a central purpose of the president's second term.

McKinley's stay at the exposition began well. The day was warm and sunny, and the public came out in large numbers. More than 116,000 persons attended the fair to see the president. Before a crowd estimated at 50,000 in the Esplanade, McKinley paid a tribute to the fair. Expositions were, he said, the "timekeepers of progress" that stimulated "the energy, enterprise, and intellect of the people and quicken human genius." The speech, which argued forcefully for reciprocity, was received with enthusiastic cheers. Throughout the day the crowds were friendly, and in the evening the electric lights came on. Then fireworks formed a portrait of the president and spelled out the greeting: "Welcome to McKinley, Chief of Our Nation."

For the second day of his visit, the president went sightseeing at Niagara Falls before his afternoon reception at the Temple of Music. At the turn of the century, it was expected that on ceremonial occasions presidents would receive their fellow citizens and shake their hands. The Secret Service men, the managers of the exposition, and the aides of the president were all conscious of security problems, but a combination of carelessness and human accidents enabled a lone assassin, Leon Czolgosz, to be in the receiving line with a revolver concealed in a handkerchief. At 4:07 he fired two shots that mortally wounded the president.

McKinley was taken to the home of the exposition's president, John G. Milburn, and a vigil began that lasted eight days. William I. Buchanan coordinated press coverage of the president and made plans for the fair to continue once the crisis had passed. As McKinley's condition worsened, the Pan-American Exposition was closed for the weekend of September 14–15. On Saturday morning, September 14, the president died.

The exposition reopened and went on until its scheduled closing date of November 2, 1901. Attendance in September was only down a little from the August totals, and the closing month of October brought in a surge of customers. Merchants at the Pan-American did a brisk business in McKinley memorabilia that associated the Temple of Music with the fallen president. The connection between McKinley's death and the future of the nation became a favored theme of the orators who appeared in Buffalo during the final days of the Pan-American.

The official end of the exposition was almost anticlimatic. The directors had been winding down performances and exhibitions, and Buchanan had already left the country to represent the United States at a conference of the American nations in Mexico City. In March 1902 the director general submitted his report on his stewardship of the fair. He said that the exposition had spurred "commercial well being and good understanding among the American republics and dependencies." For Buffalo it had brought new jobs and fresh opportunities. As one Philadelphia newspaper put it, "The city has been advertised, a new life infused into all its channels, and several million dollars have been left there by visitors." To the Pan-American had come more than 8 million people, which fell midway between the 2.7 million who attended the Trans-Mississippi and International Exposition in Omaha in 1898 and the more than 19 million visitors to the Louisiana Purchase Exposition in St. Louis in 1904.

The promoters of the Pan-American probably did not share the optimistic conclusions of their director general. On closing day the deficit in the Pan-American's accounts was in excess of $3 million. Those who held the $2.5 million of stock in the exposition lost their investment. Many of the bonds that had been issued were also defaulted. Lawsuits against the Exposition Company proliferated. "White cities and Rainbow cities are well enough once a decade," said a West Coast editor, "but there is no demand for a steady succession of them."

The Pan-American Exposition of 1901 did not do for Buffalo what its promoters had hoped, and some historians of the city see the fair as part of a general failure to be more than a respectable urban center in upstate New York. Any impact that the exposition had on Latin American relations was probably slight at best. To the degree that it taught Americans that they should fulfill proudly the duties of imperialism, modern scholars regard the Pan-American as an expression of cultural chauvinism and racial hegemony that represents all they find dubious about the United States of William McKinley.

The most lasting historical association of the Pan-American Exposition is with the shooting of the president. Because Theodore Roosevelt succeeded McKinley in the century's first year, there is something symbolic in the way that an accident of history took McKinley off the stage and made room for a dynamic young executive to face the challenges of modern America. When thoughts of the Pan-American Exposition occur, then, they are not of the electric lights that are no longer a technological novelty. Nor do they recall the painted buildings, the Electric Tower, or the hemispheric theme of trade and friendship. At the Pan-American Exposition as a historic event, it is always 4:07 on Friday, September 6, 1901, and President McKinley reaches forward to shake another hand. As he does so, he and the Pan-American Exposition pass into history.

BIBLIOGRAPHY

The most important primary source for the Pan-American Exposition is the William I. Buchanan Collection at the Buffalo and Erie County Historical Society. The collection contains Buchanan's correspondence as director general, along with other reports and documents relating to the exposition. The Archives of the Smithsonian Institution, Record Group 70, Series 14, covers the participation of the institution at Buffalo. There is also an extensive file of clippings about the exposition at the society. The William McKinley Papers, Manuscript Division, Library of Congress, detail the arrangements for the president's visit; see also William I. Buchanan, *Pan-American Exposition, Report of William I. Buchanan, Director General* (1902).

Harold F. Peterson, *Diplomat of the Americas: A Biography of William I. Buchanan* (1977) is very helpful on the organization of the Pan-American, and Robert Rydell's chapter on Buffalo in *All the World's a Fair* (1984) discusses the cultural implications of the event. Joann Marie Thompson, "The Art and Architecture of the Pan-American Exposition, Buffalo, New York, 1901" (Ph.D. diss., Rutgers University, 1980), looks at the artistic aspects of the exposition. "Pan-American Exposition," *Senate Report No. 2204* (1901) is informative on the organization of the fair.

The most fruitful sources for contemporary views of the Pan-American are the periodical articles that appeared in 1901. See, for example, Mary Bronson Hartt, "How to See the Pan-American Exposition," *Everybody's Magazine* 5 (October 1901): 488–491; Charles Edward Lloyd, "The Pan-American Exposition as an Educational Force," *Chautauquan* 33 (July 1901): 333–36; Hamilton Wright Mabie, "The Spirit of the New World as Interpreted by the Pan-American Exposition," *Outlook*, July 10, 1901, 529–547. William I. Buchanan, "The Organization of an Exposition," *Cosmopolitan* 31 (September 1901): 517–21, provides the perspective of the director general. Also helpful are: "Opening of the Pan-American Exposition at Buffalo," *Literary Digest*, May 11, 1901, 564–566; "Art at the Pan-American Exposition at Buffalo," *Literary Digest*, June 22, 1901, 753–54, and "The Pan-American Three Million Dollar Deficit," *Literary Digest*, November 9, 1901, 561–562. For President McKinley's visit, see Margaret Leech, *In the Days of McKinley* (1959).

Lewis L. Gould

GLASGOW 1901
GLASGOW INTERNATIONAL EXHIBITION

Riding the crest of the successful 1888 exhibition, which had filled the city's coffers sufficiently to fund the erection of a new art museum, Glasgow produced another, yet grander, exhibition in 1901 to celebrate its new museum and to commemorate the fiftieth anniversary of London's Great Exhibition of 1851. Staged during an economic boom, the exhibition extolled Britain's world supremacy, a claim substantiated by technological virtuosity and colonial domination.

The "New Country Exhibition," as some called it, was officially opened by the duke and duchess of Fife on May 2. By its close on November 9, over 11½ million visitors—twice as many as had attended the 1851 exhibition—had descended upon Kelvingrove Park to witness the display of industrial products, resources, and machinery and to view in retrospect nineteenth-century industrial, scientific, and artistic accomplishment.

The 75-acre site in Kelvingrove Park—virtually the same site upon which the 1888 exhibition had been constructed—was transformed into a sort of fin-de-siècle Disneyland. Design of the buildings was entrusted to James Miller, an architect whose prefabricated white wood-and-plaster panel pavilions in the Spanish Renaissance style provided a setting of sufficient grandeur and picturesqueness. Curiously and conspicuously absent was design representative of Glasgow's own art-nouveau style, formalized by Charles Rennie Mackintosh and his coterie.

At the corner of Sandyford and Gray streets the 200,000-square-foot Industrial Hall, outlined in electric lights and crowned with a golden dome, accounted for the lion's portion of the exhibition space. The Grand Avenue, 1,000 feet long and 75 feet wide, ran out of the Industrial Hall, along Sandyford Street, and bridged Dumbarton Road, providing direct access to the 160,000-square-foot Machinery Hall, which contained exhibits of machines in motion and the concert hall in the park grounds, which boasted its own pipe organ and could seat an audience of 4,000. These formed the nucleus of the temporary buildings. In addition, Canada, Ireland, Japan, and Russia constructed national pavilions, and there were restaurants and kiosks scattered about the park. The architectural centerpiece of the exhibition was surely the new City Museum and Art Galleries, built of red sandstone and highly ornamented, from the designs of Simpson and Allen of London.

Exhibits were arranged in eight classes covering raw materials, industrial manufactures, machinery and power, transportation, marine engineering, lighting and heating, science and music, and sport. In addition, there were the Women's Section, highlighting the products of women's labor; an Education Section; a

Photographic Section; and a Scottish History and Archaeology Section; as well as the highly regarded Fine Art Section.

On any given day, outside attractions might include an Indian theater featuring jugglers, athletes, and snake charmers; a model farm, with displays of the latest agricultural technology, buildings, and a working dairy; a water slide, gondolas, and electric launches on the River Kelvin; band concerts and organ recitals, shooting galleries, a switchback railway, a miniature railway, and at dusk the illumination of the grounds.

When the books were tallied at the close of the exhibition, a substantial surplus was recorded—more than £35,000—proving once again that Glasgow was flourishing.

BIBLIOGRAPHY

A large collection of primary sources is available in the Glasgow Room of the Mitchell Library in Glasgow. Among the holdings are the various catalogs, guides, and souvenir-printed ephemera, some of them publications of the Exhibition Committee and some commercial publications. These include *Glasgow International Exhibition, 1901: The Official Catalogue* (1901); *The Exhibition Illustrated: A Pictorial Souvenir of the Glasgow International Exhibition, 1901* (1901); *Glasgow International Exhibition Viewbook* (1901); *Photographic Souvenir of Glasgow International Exhibition 1901* (1901); and *White's Pictorial Souvenir and Guide to International Exhibition Glasgow 1901* (1901).

The Glasgow Room at the Mitchell Library also holds some personal souvenirs of the fair. Of particular interest is an anonymous but annotated photo album of the exhibition, full of personal snapshots but without attribution.

A contemporary journal, the *Builder*, ran a series of articles on the exhibition between April 1901 and March 1902 that dealt not only with matters of building, design, and aesthetics but also with details of the exhibits. Consult the issues of April 6, June 8, 22, and 29, July 20, August 17, 24, and 31, and September 14, 1901, and March 15, 1902.

Two secondary sources that contain both summaries and interpretations of the various Glasgow exhibitions are Alastair L. Goldsmith, "The Glasgow International Exhibitions, 1888–1938" (M.Lett. thesis, University of Strathclyde, 1985), and Perilla Kinchin and Juliet Kinchin, *Glasgow's Great Exhibitions, 1888, 1901, 1911, 1938, 1988* (1988). The Glasgow exhibition is also mentioned briefly in John Allwood, *The Great Exhibitions* (1977).

Ken Carls

CHARLESTON 1901–1902

THE SOUTH CAROLINA, INTER-STATE AND WEST INDIAN EXPOSITION

Following hard on the heels of the Pan-American Exposition in Buffalo, the South Carolina, Inter-State and West Indian Exposition was designed to promote both the port of Charleston and the surrounding agricultural area it served and the prospect of increased trade with the major West Indian islands, especially Cuba and Puerto Rico, recently acquired in the Spanish-American War. In particular, promoters were anxious to boost sales of Sea Island cotton, reputed to be the world's finest, as well as rice, silk, and tea.

A site of some 160 acres, located along the Ashley River about 2½ miles from the central business district, was chosen. It incorporated the old Lowndes plantation, owned by the fair board's president, F. W. Wagener, and the plantation mansion became the Women's Building and the social center for the fair. There were fourteen exposition buildings; those in the so-called Natural Section, near the Lowndes mansion, were low buildings in a Mexican mission style; those farther to the south, in a more open setting, were of a Spanish Renaissance style and grouped around a large plaza featuring a sunken garden. The most imposing structure, as might be expected, was the Cotton Palace, 360 feet long, topped by a 130-foot-high dome 100 feet in diameter. Other buildings included an auditorium, seating 4,000, the Machinery and Transportation Building, and the Negro Building. Visitors could also enjoy the Midway, a half-mile race track, and a livestock exhibit that covered 15 acres.

The exhibits emphasized the economic attributes of the region. An extensive cotton exhibit coordinated by D. A. Tompkins, of Charlotte, North Carolina, filled the Cotton Palace with products and machinery contributed or lent by sixty different mills. In the Women's Building, an exhibit of silkworms, cocoons, and silk garments from colonial days demonstrated the viability of a long-neglected silk culture, and local hostesses served tea brewed from leaves grown in South Carolina. An art exhibit, featuring works of colonial and early national artists borrowed from local estates, brought to public view some early masterpieces seldom seen before. Five statuary groups of families, representing Huguenots, Aztecs, Indians, Negroes, and a generic mother and child, were located in the plaza area.

The high festive point of the fair was President's Day, in April 1902, when President Theodore Roosevelt and his wife paid a well-received visit. Later in the season there was a somber note when the death of local Confederate hero Wade Hampton was memorialized.

Open from December 1, 1901, to June 1, 1902, the West Indian exposition, as it was commonly known, attracted visitors and earned a small profit. Frequently (and favorably) compared with the Buffalo fair of the previous year, the exposition had a relaxed ambience about it, and the spacious grounds prevented the crowding that sometimes marked fairs located in more urban settings. While it did not make much of an impact on the southern economy, it appears, by all accounts, to have been a pleasant and memorable experience for its visitors.

BIBLIOGRAPHY

Basic information about the South Carolina, Inter-State and West Indian Exposition can be found in the 100-page *Official Guide to the South Carolina, Inter-State and West Indian Exposition* (1901), as well as a number of other privately produced contemporary guidebooks. These include Alexander D. Anderson, *Charleston and Its Exposition* (1901); *Charleston, S.C. and Vicinity Illustrated: South Carolina, Inter-State and West Indian Exposition* (1901); and *Charleston and the South Carolina Inter-State and West Indian Exposition and of Historic Places and Prominent Features of the City* (1902), a guide that was reprinted by the West Charleston Sertoma Club in 1958. In addition, the fair was covered in the *Charleston News and Courier*.

  Three nationally circulating journals published favorable descriptive articles on the exposition as well. Most useful is T. Cuyler Smith, "The Charleston Exposition," *Independent*, January 16, 1902, 142–51, which contains several illustrations; other details and impressions can be gleaned from Lillian W. Betts, "Sunny Days at the Exposition," *Outlook*, May 10, 1902, 120–24, and "Charleston and Her 'West Indian Exposition,' " *American Monthly Review of Reviews* 25 (January 1902): 58–61, also illustrated.

John E. Findling

HANOI 1902–1903

EXPOSITION FRANÇAIS ET INTERNATIONALE

The idea of holding an international exhibition in Tonkin (now Hanoi) originated in the 1890s and received additional impetus at the 1900 Paris Universal Exposition when French colonial authorities and the French Committee on Foreign Expositions determined to organize a fair in French-controlled Southeast Asia to highlight the economic resources of the region and the possibilities of trade with colonies of other nations and to underscore French colonial prowess.

Under the direction of Paul Bourgeois, secretary of the French Committee on Foreign Expositions, an exposition complex operated between November 16, 1902, and February 15, 1903, on 41 acres of land near the railroad station in Hanoi. The exposition buildings were designed in the beaux-arts style, and included pavilions devoted to displays from the Philippines, Malaya, Siam, Japan, China, Formosa, and Korea. In addition to these national and colonial exhibition halls, the fair included galleries of machines and agriculture, as well as a pavilion devoted to the beaux-arts movement. The latter building, designed by Roger Marx, housed artistic displays assembled by nearly 200 French artists.

Exposition planners grouped exhibits from over 4,000 exhibitors into three general categories: fine arts and sciences, natural resources, and machinery. Exhibits ranged from musical instruments and theatrical art to forest products and perfumes to electrical generators and early airplanes. In addition, the fair boasted cabarets, ethnological parades of indigenous people, and a Philippine village organized by the French vice-consul in Manila with the approval of the U.S. government.

It is difficult to measure the impact of the fair. The published official history does not provide attendance figures, but reports indicate that, after opening day, despite free admission to the fair, attendance sharply declined. Most of the exhibition buildings and galleries were demolished after the close of the fair, with the notable exception of the Grand Palace, which was intended as a permanent structure to house a colonial museum. Perhaps the most important aspect of the fair was that it represented one more link in the chain of colonial fairs that Western imperial powers stretched across the Third World. It provided lessons in imperial hubris and, if reports of limited attendance are any indication, of colonial resistance.

BIBLIOGRAPHY

Sources from the Hanoi fair are limited. Some manuscript materials are available in the Archives nationales in Paris and Archives d'outre mer in Aix-en-Provençe. The most complete record of the fair is found in Paul Bourgeois and G.-Roger Sandoz, *Exposition d'Hanoi, 1902–1903; Rapport général* (1904). Also consult the critical report issued [by M. le capitaine Ducarré], *Mission à l'Exposition de Hanoi et en Extrême-Orient, Rapport général* (1903). Other accounts are scattered in such journals as the *Bulletin de la société de géographie commerciale du Bordeaux* and the *British North Borneo Herald*. For a quick summary of the purposes of the fair, consult the 1901 *Consular Reports* on file in the Larson Collection, Department of Special Collections, California State University, Fresno. A good assessment of the imperial context in which the colonial fairs took place can be found in William H. Schneider, "The Image of West Africa in Popular French Culture" (Ph.D. diss., University of Pennsylvania, 1976), and Thomas G. August, "Colonial Policy and Propaganda: The Popularization of the Idée Coloniale in France, 1919–1939" (Ph.D. diss., University of Wisconsin, 1978).

Robert W. Rydell

ST. LOUIS 1904
LOUISIANA PURCHASE INTERNATIONAL EXPOSITION

The 1904 St. Louis world's fair, officially known as the Louisiana Purchase International Exposition, commemorated the centennial of the 1803 land purchase that brought Missouri into the United States along with all of the land from the Mississippi River to the Rocky Mountains and from Canada to the Gulf of Mexico, excluding Spanish Texas. Originally planned for 1903, the St. Louis fair was delayed in order to accommodate the foreign exhibitors and states. David R. Francis, president of the World's Fair Commission, and his agents visited European capitals early in 1903 to encourage foreign participation. Other fair representatives traveled to Asia, Latin America, and North Africa with an invitation to bring people and exhibits to St. Louis. They did such a spectacular selling job that latecomers found that they needed more time to assemble and transport their exhibits. Some states delayed in making appropriations for the fair and thus were unable to meet the 1903 deadline.

St. Louis civic leaders had discussed an official Louisiana Purchase commemoration as early as 1889. Then Governor David R. Francis led a delegation from Missouri to Washington, D.C., in 1890 to secure the Columbian Exposition for St. Louis. The rival city of Chicago secured the prize, to Francis's chagrin. He determined that St. Louis should hold a bigger and better celebration for the Louisiana Purchase centennial.

The fair promotion movement coasted until 1896 when Richard Bartholdt, a German-born congressman representing the St. Louis district, proposed a Louisiana Purchase celebration to bolster a stagnant economy resulting from the depression which began in 1893.

Francis, still smarting from the loss of the Columbian Exposition to Chicago, joined forces with Bartholdt, Pierre Chouteau, heir to the creole tradition, and others to become the driving force behind the fair project. Francis mobilized the Businessmen's League, and at the kickoff fund-raising rally in 1899 league members pledged nearly $5 million in a single evening. Within a year, the fair promoters had successfully solicited support for a special city bond issue of $5 million and a federal loan subsidy for the same amount—the latter in part as a result of persuasive lobbying by Richard Bartholdt. The federal government subsequently doubled the original amount when construction proved more costly than anticipated.

By May 1901 the Louisiana Purchase Exposition Company had been organized with Francis elected president and ninety-three directors made up of business and civic leaders. Civic boosterism motivated Francis and the directors who sought to dispel St. Louis's tarnished image resulting from a violent turn-of-the-century transit workers' strike. The strike pointed up the city's poor municipal services and corrupt cronyism among political and business leaders who ran a Boodle ring. (Boodle referred to businessmen bribing city officials to win special privileges.) Although both major political parties engaged in this corruption, Republican municipal assemblymen dominated the Boodle ring. In 1900, Democrats ran Rolla Wells, a civic leader and successful industrialist, as reform mayor. Wells and fellow Democrats supported a world's fair along with improved streets and services and other progressive reforms under the banner of the "New St. Louis." Reformers hoped that the coming exposition would draw the citizens together in a great cooperative enterprise.

Imperialism was another theme of the 1904 fair. As a result of the Spanish-American War, the United States had acquired possessions and established protectorates in the Caribbean and the Pacific. The 1904 world's fair presented an opportunity to show the benefits bestowed by civilization on recently conquered countries. Anthropological exhibits such as the Philippine village showed the world a living exhibition of natives at their daily activities and provided the United States with a rationale for its emergence as a world power. Francis stated that fair planners were promoting universal peace by bringing diverse people together from remote areas in a spirit of mutual respect.

The progressive era reformers devoutly believed in the advantages of technology, which would work for the ultimate good of humanity. The St. Louis world's fair emphasized the latest technological developments in all exhibits.

Selecting a site for the fair was the first order of business. After considering a number of possibilities, fair officials chose the western half of Forest Park. Located toward the western end of St. Louis at a central point between north and south away from unsightly slums and factories, the park seemed an ideal spot for the fair. The park, which derived its name from the vast acres covered by virgin forests, was a 40-minute carriage ride from downtown St. Louis and in close proximity to homes of fair officials.

When it soon became apparent that buildings and exhibits would overflow the park boundaries, fair officials negotiated with the trustees of Washington University for use of its recently completed but not yet opened buildings and campus. Even this newly leased land proved inadequate, so the exposition company leased additional ground west and north of the park and campus sites. The entire fairgrounds covered 1,272 acres—1.75 by 1.05 miles. In developing Forest Park for the fair, workmen cut down trees, drained the extended lake, and reshaped it into a grand basin. They cleared trees from the wilderness area by burning some and cutting down others, then blasting out stumps with dynamite and gunpowder. Some trees were carefully dug and uprooted, then replanted elsewhere on the fair grounds. Steam shovels removed a hill at the western end of the park to make way for construction. The flood-prone River Des Peres, which cut a crooked path through Forest Park, was rerouted, reduced to half its length, and partially covered. Park employees traced Forest Park spring to its source and piped it to a new source, repaired a bandstand, pruned shrubs, resurfaced drives, built new walkways and flower beds, and enlarged roads. Workmen paved West End Streets leading to the park, and construction accelerated in private places north of Forest Park.

Determined to show its best face for the fair, the city joined with private corporations to improve the appearance and services of St. Louis. The transit company added 450 new cars equipped with air brakes. Railroads built a belt line to the fairgrounds and freight terminals to facilitate the moving of equipment and, later, passengers to the fair. Trains ran to the fair every 15 minutes. An intramural railroad was built to transport people in and around the fairgrounds. Mayor Wells had workmen install machinery to filter and purify the murky St. Louis water.

The Civic Improvement League, made up of St. Louis business and professional men and club women, started a grass-roots campaign to promote neighborhood improvements and succeeded in getting new playgrounds built on vacant lots, refurbishing tenements, cleaning up yards, and fighting crime.

Mayor Wells directed the rebuilding of over 70 miles of streets and the construction of 30 miles of new streets, thereby reducing the amount of airborne dust and solid matter by the opening of the fair. The Chief Smoke Inspector's Office fined steamboats, barge companies, and firms spewing out large amounts of smoke. This reduced smoke by 70 percent. Enterprising entrepreneurs built new hotels to house fair visitors. Rolla Wells's vision of a "New St. Louis" was at least partially realized.

Site preparations laid the groundwork for world's fair construction. Prior to the start of construction, a commission of architects and landscape engineers from all parts of the country met in St. Louis to design the "main picture." According to their plan, the main exhibit palaces should fan out from the central Festival Hall, which occupied a commanding site atop Art Hill in Forest Park. The fair should have broad, curved boulevards, spacious plazas with lagoons, sunken gardens, and landscaped, tree-shaded open spaces between the exhibit palaces. General construction rules called for buildings no higher than 65 feet above average grade, windows that would open, and entrances on all sides.

Main exhibit palaces and most of the other structures were built of ivory-colored staff with towers and decorative trim of every hue. Staff is a mixture of plaster of paris reinforced with Manila fiber; it could be poured, molded, and carved. This nearly fireproof and weatherproof material covered the wooden framework of fair buildings.

Although most of the main exhibit palaces radiated below Art Hill, the huge Palace of Agriculture, which covered nearly 24 acres, as well as the Horticulture and Forestry palaces, were located to the west of Forest Park.

The Plateau of States with most of the state pavilions rose to the southeast in Forest Park. The large U.S. Government Pavilion was to the north of them. The Washington University campus contained foreign pavilions, the athletic field, and the stadium (site of the Olympic Games). There was also the Aeronautic Concourse staging area for balloon, airship, and kite-flying contests.

The Philippine village, populated by more than 1,000 natives, covered a large area around Arrow Head Lake to the southwest of Forest Park.

The enormous Inside Inn, the hotel just inside the fairgrounds, housed visitors at its location at the southeast corner of the Park. The Statler Hotel chain had its origins with the Inside Inn.

The amusement and concession area, the Pike, extended 1½ miles from the main fair entrance on Lindell Boulevard west to the end of Forest Park and then turned sharply at Skinker Road and continued to the west.

Fair organizers appointed St. Louis architect Isaac Taylor as director of works, charged with choosing the other architects, and Emmanuel L. Masqueray as his chief design assistant. The architectural commission included other St. Louis firms and firms from the Midwest, West, and East.

Masqueray, working with the commission, developed the fan-shaped plan for the exhibit palaces. He also designed the colonnades and pavilion restaurants, as well as structures on the Pike. New York architect Cass Gilbert designed the highly ornate Festival Hall, with its huge concert auditorium and 145-foot-diameter dome. Gilbert's permanent structure, the Fine Arts Building with its smooth, blank walls and facade of unfluted column shafts, occupied the area behind Festival Hall. Gilbert, a dominant figure among the 1904 fair architects, had won a gold medal for his structures at the Paris exposition. He also designed the Minnesota state capitol, the U.S. Custom House in New York, and in 1913, the Woolworth Tower in the same city. Gilbert won a gold medal for his designs at the St. Louis world's fair.

The main palaces of the 1904 fair featured the Renaissance revival style in the tradition of the beaux-arts school, emphasizing symmetry, large-scale planning, and elaborate ornamentation.

Theodore Link, notable as the architect of the 1894 St. Louis Union Station, designed the Palace of Mines and Metallurgy, a composite of Egyptian, Greek, and Byzantine styles.

Many of the states and foreign nations erected derivative structures based on indigenous historic buildings. The Austrian and Swedish pavilions furnished at least two exceptions to this trend. The graceful Austrian pavilion gave fairgoers a glimpse of art nouveau—the only foreign nation to feature this style. Sweden presented a typical country home with simple lines and unpretentious decor as its architectural contribution to the fair. The fair thus featured an urban ensemble architectural scheme rather than one spectacular single structure dominating lesser structures, as was the case at earlier London and Paris expositions.

Education characterized by life and motion was to be the keynote of the fair. Director of exhibits F.J.V. Skiff set the stage for this education theme by planning exhibits showing man and his works. There were twelve major classifications of "man and his works," and they were housed in the main exhibit, Palaces. Education exemplifying the means through which humans enter social life came first. Next, art showed the conditions of culture and its development. Liberal arts and applied sciences were placed third to show the results of education and

ST. LOUIS 1904. The Palace of Transportation was typical of the neoclassical architecture of this fair, which capitalized on the success of the World's Columbian Exposition architecture eleven years before. (Courtesy Peter M. Warner)

culture by exhibits illustrating tastes, inventive genius, scientific attainment, and artistic expression. Then came agriculture, horticulture, mining, and forestry, representing human use and conservation of the forces of nature; these were followed by manufactures showing what use people had made of nature and machinery, pointing up the tools developed for that use. Transportation showed how people had overcome distances; electricity exemplified the forces they had discovered and utilized. Anthropology focused on the ways in which people study other people; social economy showed the development of the human race and the stages of civilization. The exhibits concluded with physical culture, stressing a strong body as essential to a keen intellect.

As trains brought exhibits directly to the exposition grounds and main palaces, exhibits' director Skiff carried out a previously agreed-upon plan of juxtaposing products with processes. Accordingly, fair visitors viewed an operating exhibit of diamond cutting along with precious stone displays in the Liberal Arts Palace. In other exhibit palaces, visitors saw the printer, the rope maker, the farmer, and the engineer actually at work and the end result of this labor.

Unlike some other fairs, the St. Louis exposition featured exhibits from different countries in the same exhibit palace so that visitors could compare one country's products with those of another. They could see an array of agricultural implements from around the world or study the methods used in schools all over the world without having to run from one building to another.

After viewing the great technological advances on the main section of the fairgrounds, visitors then observed the "least civilized and advanced people," such as the Filipinos on their reservation at the far western end of the grounds. The exhibits at the 1904 fair were designed to demonstrate the progress of humanity from barbarism to the pinnacle of Anglo-Saxon civilization. The historical and anthropological exhibits were arranged to emphasize the superiority of caucasians over peoples with complexions of a darker hue. The American Indian exhibit set a village of reservation-tame redmen in aboriginal costume against their grandchildren learning white ways in a model government Indian school. The Philippine exhibit displayed dog-eating Igorots and stone-age cannibals living side by side with Philippine governor William Howard Taft's well-drilled and smartly garbed native constabulary.

Opening day of the fair, April 30, 1904, drew an estimated crowd of 200,000. From the White House, President Theodore Roosevelt pressed the key of the telegraphic instrument signaling the start. At the signal, a battery of artillery fired a national salute in the direction of Washington. David R. Francis lifted his hands and issued an invitation to "enter herein, ye sons of men" while 10,000 flags unfurled, fountains sprayed into the air, water tumbled down the Cascades, and bands played to signal the start of the fair.

Visitors could choose among some 540 amusements and concessions. The Pike stayed open in the evening when exhibit palaces had closed. Fairgoers visiting the Pike shivered at the satanic sights in the Hereafter, giggled at their grotesque images reflected in the trick mirrors of the Temple of Mirth, and gasped at the amazing antics of Jim Key, the Educated Horse.

The giant ferris wheel, also featured at the 1893 Columbian Exposition, carried visitors smoothly and silently over 260 feet in the air for the best view of the fairgrounds. People rented cars on the giant wheel and partied on board, enjoying evening lights in and around buildings, under arches and cascades, highlighting architectural details not apparent in daylight, while marveling at the technology of the wondrous wheel. Maude Nicholson, repeating a stunt she had performed in 1893 at the Columbian Exposition, made two revolutions standing on top of a car on the observation wheel. Technology was also apparent to visitors who enjoyed the illusion of a submarine ride and an airship trip over Paris in the concession Over and Under the Sea. A trip through the incubator concession of the Pike educated visitors on the most up-to-date medical technology regarding premature infant care.

The Pike also featured the Cliff Dwellers, Zuni, and Moki Indians who had "never been shown before"; it had burros conveying visitors along steep inclines, Mysterious Asia with camel rides along its winding streets, and the Geisha Girls entertaining visitors to Fair Japan. Most Pike attractions ranged in price from ten cents to fifty cents. Not everyone approved of pricing policies on the Pike. One St. Louisan visiting the Pike for the first time noted that the Tyrolean Alps concession charged separate admissions for the passion play and Alpine railroad trip after he had paid to see the mountain and village scene. With a separate admission price for each concession, the Pike proved to be too expensive for some families.

St. Louis hosted the third modern Olympiad in conjunction with the world's fair. Although the International Olympic Committee required that virtually all sports competitions held during the fair be designated as Olympic events, most interest centered on one week—August 29 to September 3—when track and field events took place. Athletes competed as individuals or as members of athletic clubs; national teams did not enter the picture until later years. Competitors equaled or surpassed previous Olympic records. Olympic organizers in 1904 admitted the first black athlete to compete in the modern games, George Poage of Wisconsin.

St. Louis also claimed the distinction of staging the first successful demonstration of wireless telegraphy between the ground and the air in the United States. At heights varying from 1,400 feet to 2 miles, three men received twenty messages from a station at the fairgrounds. St. Louis is credited with mounting the first meteorological balloon experiments in the United States. Small rubber balloons ascended to altitudes of up to 51,000 feet and traveled as far as 280 miles at speeds of 101 miles per hour recording temperatures as low as -76 degrees. The experimental balloons expanded until they burst. They then drifted to earth, their descent slowed by tiny silk parachutes. Aeronautic events also included kite-flying contests, tethered balloon ascensions, and two free sustained flights.

There is an enduring myth that iced tea, hot dogs, and ice cream cones originated at the St. Louis 1904 World's Fair. This tradition has no basis in fact but forms part of fair folklore.

The Louisiana Purchase Exposition drew to a close on December 1, 1904. President Francis gave the closing remarks: "Farewell, a long farewell, to all thy splendor." A band struck up "Auld Lang Syne." Great geysers of fireworks blazed forth ending with the fiery words "Farewell—Goodnight." According to official attendance figures, 19,694,855 people passed through the turnstiles during the seven months of the fair.

The 1904 fair was a financial success. Profits from it were used to build the Jefferson Memorial in Forest Park to house the records of the Exposition Company and the collections of the Missouri Historical Society. The Memorial was the first national monument to Thomas Jefferson and cost nearly $500,000 to build. The fair also generated enough revenue to build a park pavilion, commission a permanent bronze statue of King Louis IX (a replica of the plaster of paris version that had stood at the main entrance to the fair), and pay the exposition's debts.

The 1904 St. Louis world's fair proved significant in a number of respects. St. Louisans had worked together to build a fair that succeeded in realizing David R. Francis's goal of bringing diverse people together from remote areas in a spirit of mutual respect. Francis and the other fair planners had also hoped that this great gathering would promote universal peace. Their hopes were short-lived; less than a decade later, nations became embroiled in a bloody conflagration with the outbreak of World War I.

The fair reinforced unfortunate racial stereotypes in the ordering of exhibits contrasting "civilized" peoples with their "barbaric, hardly human" counterparts and in the Old Plantation exhibit, which cast the antebellum South in a golden glow.

On a local level, the 1904 fair paved the way for reforms instituted by Dwight Davis (who was elected park commissioner in 1911). Forest Park had lost most of its wilderness character as a result of clearing of the land and its landscaping for the fair. Davis established public recreational facilities in these new open spaces.

Certainly civic improvements accelerated prior to the fair. The Art Museum and the Bird Cage of the Zoo (site of the Smithsonian's Aviary exhibit) remain as permanent reminders of the fair. The World's Fair Pavilion, the bronze statue of King Louis IX, and the Jefferson Memorial Building stand as enduring monuments to the Louisiana Purchase Exposition.

BIBLIOGRAPHY

The Missouri Historical Society (MHS), St. Louis, is the major repository of 1904 world's fair papers. The MHS archives contain the papers of David R. Francis, president of the Louisiana Purchase Exposition Company, diaries and letters in which visitors react to and write about their experiences at the fair, and the fully indexed Louisiana Purchase Exposition Collection, 1898–1913, the most important source of information concerning the fair. Anyone interested in the exposition will find a gold mine of information in the Contemporaneous Publications of the Missouri Historical Society's library—official reports of participating nations, exhibit catalogs, bulletins, final reports, and the *Official History of the World's Fair* (1905). The Pictorial History department of the MHS has a photo archives collection illuminating every phase of the 1904 fair, as well as tickets, lantern slides, stereopticons, and other ephemera, and the museum collection contains clothing, souvenirs, furniture from fair pavilions, and ceremonial memorabilia. Many of these pictures and artifacts may be seen in the exhibit, "Palaces in the Park," at the MHS History Museum located in the Jefferson Memorial Building in Forest Park.

Additional official papers of the fair are located in the archives of the Smithsonian Institution, Washington, D.C., Series 16, Louisiana Purchase Exposition (St. Louis, 1904), 1901–1906, pertaining to the Smithsonian's participation in the exposition, and in the National Archives, Washington, D.C., Record Group 43, No. 17, Records Relating to the Louisiana Purchase Exposition at St. Louis, 1904, Numbers 591–603. Researchers should also consult the Smithsonian Archives' Subseries 1, Marcus W. Lyon indexed correspondence, 1901–1906, which concerns the collection, accession, and preparation of the exhibits sent to the fair. Other information may be found in Subseries 3, Subseries 5, and Box 61.

There are a number of secondary sources of importance to researchers studying this fair. One of the most eloquent and thought-provoking accounts is Robert Rydell's long chapter in *All the World's a Fair* (1984), stressing the anthropological exhibits and the Philippine village. *Lion of the Valley* (1981), by James Neal Primm, describes the social, economic, and political conditions at the turn of the century in St. Louis, as well as the civic leaders who spearheaded the fair effort. An article dealing with the same theme is Stephen J. Raiche, "The World's Fair and the New St. Louis, 1896–1904," *Missouri Historical Review* 67, no. 1 (1972): 98–121. For the architecture of the fair, see Montgomery Schuyler, "The Architecture of the St. Louis Fair," *Scribner's Magazine* 35 (April 1904): 385–95, and F. K. Winkler, "The Architecture of the Louisiana Purchase Exposition," *Architectural Record* 15 (April 1904): 336–60. Finally, Dorothy Daniels Birk, *The World Came to St. Louis* (1979), is an informal reminiscence written many years after the fair; it contains much information and nostalgic spirit. Finally, two articles published in the Summer 1988 issue of *Gateway Heritage* reflect the continuing research interest this fair generates among local historians. Robert Mullen, "The First Monument to the President: The World's Fair Comes to an End," 39–43, details the construction of the Jefferson Memorial in St. Louis, paid for with profits from the fair. Karen M. Keefer, "Dirty Water and Clean Toilets: Medical Aspects of the 1904 Louisiana Purchase Exposition," 33–37, discusses the health problems that the large size of the fair brought to the city.

Hollywood's version of the fair is seen in the 1944 film, *Meet Me in St. Louis*, a warm musical comedy starring Judy Garland and Margaret O'Brien, and directed by Vicente Minelli. The film concerns a family in St. Louis during the time of the fair, and the final scenes are set at the fairgrounds.

Yvonne M. Condon

LIÈGE 1905
EXPOSITION UNIVERSELLE ET INTERNATIONALE

The idea of organizing an exposition in Liège had been suggested as early as 1892. Various people in Antwerp and Brussels, however, had already undertaken plans for such events in their cities. In 1895, a businessman from Liège, Florent Pholien, came up with a new proposal, and in June 1897, a provisional committee was formed with the support of Paul de Favereau (minister of foreign affairs) and Albert Nyssens (minister of labor and industry).

The site selected consisted of 52 acres located on the plain of the Vennes (on a peninsula called Ile des Aguesses, at the confluence of the Meuse and the main branch of the Ourthe River, called Fourchu Fossé). It required the rerouting of the Ourthe and the building of a new bridge on the Meuse. Although the exposition was to be inaugurated in 1903, the project could not be completed, and so 1905 was chosen. This date coincided with the seventy-fifth anniversary of Belgian independence. In addition, fair planners wanted to show off scientific and industrial accomplishments from 1830 to 1905.

On July 21, 1903, Prince Albert laid the first stone for the facade of the great exhibit halls and fastened the first rivet for the construction of the bridge (pont de Fragnée). The winner of the competition for the design of the facade was de Braey, an architect from Antwerp. An annex had been erected at the plateau de Cointe to house the colonial, agricultural, and forestry exhibits and to provide various concessions. The main area of the exposition was divided into three parts: an area for the exhibit halls (formerly the hall of the jardin d'Acclimatation and the parc de la Boverie), the plaine des Vennes linked to the exhibit halls and gardens by the Mativa bridge, and beyond the Ourthe, Ole Liège and an amusement zone in the plain behind the Fragnée bridge.

The Hall of Machines contained one section dedicated solely to Belgian scientific achievement in the last seventy-five years. Among the exhibits were marble busts of the most famous Belgian men of science. One of the exhibits, "Ancient Art in the Country of Liège" (the old principality and diocese of Liège), featured brasswork and its practice over eight centuries, especially in the eleventh century. One hall presented the "manual labor of women," and another was dedicated to lace. Of particular interest were exhibits of bicycles, motorcycles, and automobiles.

International participation was broad, with thirty-three countries participating. France, with its 7,950 exhibitors, was by far the largest foreign participant. The highlight of the French exhibit was the chromophone, combining cinema and phonograph to reproduce synchronized sound and movement. An exhibit of the

Paris police department showed the role of fingerprints in criminology. Among other foreign participants, Sweden and Norway, although united, each had separate pavilions. Germany, having participated in Paris (1900) and St. Louis (1904), declined to participate officially at Liège, although German products were displayed under the auspices of private companies. In addition there were impressive colonial exhibits and much praise of the Japanese, who, despite a late decision to participate and involvement in the Russo-Japanese War, nevertheless sent exhibits and won medals.

The fine art exhibit contained much French and American art. American artist John S. Sargent was a winner of the Grand Medal of Honor. According to a tradition inaugurated at Antwerp in 1894, there was a recreation of Old Liège located on 10 acres between the Meuse and the Ourthe tributary. It was a tribute to Walloon architecture.

By closing day, November 6, the exposition at Liège had attracted about 7 million visitors, some of whom came for the many academic and professional conferences held in conjunction with the fair. The exposition made a small profit, and its success was an encouragement to organizers of fairs in Brussels in 1910 and Ghent in 1913.

BIBLIOGRAPHY

The Liège exposition was documented in a number of official publications produced either by the fair managers themselves or by committees representing foreign participants. Two that are available and contain much useful information are Gustave Dreze, *Le Livre d'Or de l'Exposition universelle et internationale de 1905—Histoire complete de l'Exposition de Liège*, 2 vols. (1905), and Comité Français des Exposition à l'Etranger, *Rapport général de la section Française*, 2 vols. (1905). Lewis S. Ware, U.S. commissioner to the Liège exposition, had chosen works of American artists to be exhibited. One of these, John Singer Sargent, won one of the four Grand Prizes, the Grand Medal of Honor, for his full-length portrait of the Comtesse C. A. described as "full of strength of touch and delicacy of treatment." House Document 454 of the U.S. 59th Congress contains the report of the commissioner about U.S. participation in the exposition.

There were a number of events and special publications in celebration of the seventy-fifth anniversary of Belgium. One such publication is *La Nation Bèlge 1830–1905, Conférences jubilaires faites à l'Exposition universelle et internationale de Liège en 1905* (1905). A contemporary article by R. C., "French and American Art in Liège," *Brush and Pencil* 16, no. 3 (September 1905): 98–100, discusses fine art at the exposition and praises the American contribution. In *Memorial de l'exposition universelle et internationale de Liège en 1905* (1905), Charles Piron includes forty-seven plates of photos about the exposition, providing a very good pictorial overview of the event.

Maurice Gendron

PORTLAND 1905

THE LEWIS AND CLARK CENTENNIAL AND AMERICAN PACIFIC EXPOSITION AND ORIENTAL FAIR

Portland entered a new era with the celebration of the Lewis and Clark Exposition. In official rhetoric, the industrial and scientific fair was a "school of progress" to inform and entertain its visitors. For civic leaders in their clubrooms and real estate offices, it was also an international advertisement to attract investors and immigrants. The ostensible purpose was to memorialize the great explorers, but the impetus and organization came from bankers, brokers, and the Board of Trade.

The first serious efforts toward an exposition came from J. M. Long of the Portland Board of Trade, who organized occasional meetings during 1900 to consider a Northwest industrial exposition. The date and the theme came from the Oregon Historical Society. Led by *Oregonian* editor Harvey Scott, the society on December 15, 1900, endorsed the suggestion that a commercial exposition be held in conjunction with the centennial of Lewis and Clark's exploration of the Oregon country. Two months later, the Oregon legislature endorsed the suggestion and pledged state aid once an effort was underway. Organizers filed articles of incorporation on October 12, 1901. The corporate name summed up the dual goals of historic commemoration and regional boosterism: Lewis and Clark Centennial and American Pacific Exposition and Oriental Fair. Banks, railroads, hotels, utilities, department stores, and breweries took the lead in subscribing the initial stock offering of $300,000 within two days. The board of directors for the exposition company reconfirmed business leadership.

A successful fair required participation by the state of Oregon, other western states, and the national government. Oregon's legislature acted early in 1903 to appropriate $450,000 for an exhibition of the state's "arts, industries, manufactures, and products" to be held in Portland in cooperation with the work of the Lewis and Clark Exposition Company. The legislators established the Exposition Commission with four members from Portland, four from downstate, and Jefferson Myers of Salem as chair. The corporation was to organize, promote, and manage the exposition. The state commission was to pay for many of the buildings, obtain state and county exhibits, and keep an eye on the businessmen who were running the show in Portland. In addition to Oregon, sixteen other states sent exhibits to the fair. Ten of these constructed special buildings, the largest by Missouri, Massachusetts, New York, California, and Washington.

Federal participation was obtained in 1904. As the authorization bill moved through Congress, an original appropriation of more than $2 million shrank to

$475,000 as congressmen worried about the cost of the 1904 exposition in St. Louis and a pending request for the planned Jamestown exposition in 1907. According to the official account, Harvey Scott's influence with Theodore Roosevelt played a decisive role in securing a federal building and exhibit.

The corporation had picked the site in 1902. The 400-acre tract at Guild's Lake was located just beyond the settled section of the city to the northwest of the central business district. It included a low bluff, market gardens, pasture, and marshes that were periodically inundated by high water from the Willamette River. John Olmsted, of Olmsted and Sons Landscape Architects, received $5,000 for a site plan in 1903. Careful dredging plus water pumped from the Willamette turned the marshes into a shallow lake that formed the center of the site. Visitors entered from the southeast corner through a gate flanked by Ionic columns and crossed the Pacific Court to a sunken garden between the Agriculture and European exhibit buildings. Beyond the balustraded garden was Lakeview Terrace, with a view of Mount St. Helens on clear days, and a grand staircase down the bluff to the bandstand, boat landing, and waterfront esplanade. The federal building lay on a peninsula on the far side of the lake. It was reached by a causeway lined for part of its distance with the amusements of "The Trail," built on pilings over the lake.

The buildings as well as the formal design expressed the aesthetic of the City Beautiful era. With one exception, they followed the agreed style of Spanish Renaissance with domes, cupolas, arched doorways, and roofs covered with red tile or red paint. Because the Exposition Company had leased its land with promises to return it in its original condition, the exhibition structures were constructed with relatively light wood frames covered with lath, plaster, stucco, and white paint. Most were designed by local Portland architects such as Edgar Lazarus or Ion Lewis, of the prominent local firm of Whidden and Lewis. The federal building, a cross between a railroad terminal and a Mexican cathedral, was by James Knox Taylor.

The only truly distinctive building at the Lewis and Clark Fair was the Forestry Building, with pine cone decorations, samples of lumber, and dioramas of elk and panthers. The building was an immense log cabin, stretching 105 by 209 feet, fronted by a portico of tree trunks with the bark intact. The interior was modeled on the nave of a cathedral, with colonnades of tree trunks supporting a high ceiling and setting off side galleries and balconies. The largest foundation logs weighed 32 tons and measured 5 feet across.

From opening day on June 1 through closing on October 15, the fair attracted 1,588,000 paid admissions—540,000 from Portland, 640,000 from elsewhere in Oregon and Washington, 250,000 from California and the Rocky Mountain states, and 160,000 from east of the Rockies. They found a fair that was heavy on exhibits relating to western resources. In addition to the forestry exhibits and the farm produce in the Oregon and Washington buildings, the U.S. building included working models of the Salt River and Palouse (Washington) irrigation projects, Haida and Tlinget totem poles from Alaska, and an aquarium and hatchery from the Fish Commission. Foreign exhibits were weighted toward Asia. The nine European nations represented in the Foreign Exhibits Building were balanced by the equally large Oriental Exhibits Building, where Japan had the most extensive display.

The exposition was a practical success, opening on time and operating without major hitches. National newspapers and magazines were generally complimentary. Walter Hines Page summarized the consensus when he told readers of the *World's Work* that "the enterprise has from the beginning been managed with modesty, good sense, and good taste." It made an operating profit and returned 21 percent of the capital to the original investors (over the protest of the state commission, which argued that the operating profits should go to the state of Oregon).

The fair had a substantial impact on the economic development of Portland. It coincided with the substantial expansion of railroads, farming, and stock raising in Portland's natural hinterland of eastern Oregon and eastern Washington. The years from 1905 to 1912 were flush times in the Northwest, with Portland gaining substantially in commerce and manufacturing. Local businessmen identified the summer of 1905 as the start of a sustained real estate boom and gave the fair credit for attracting new investment.

Impacts on the physical form of Portland, however, were minimal. The neo-Mediterranean buildings of the disposable kingdom were soon dismantled, with only the Forestry Building remaining until a spectacular fire in the early 1960s. John Olmsted had suggested that the site of the fair could be incorporated into a citywide park system; however, delays in the purchase of parklands and the attractions of land speculation combined to end the idea of a riverfront park in northwest Portland. Guild's Lake itself disappeared under a deluge of silt in the 1910s, when land developers used high-pressure hoses and sluices to cut building lots and streets out of the hills behind it. Dredge spoils from the Willamette were added to the fill. The majority of the site remained unoccupied for another generation while the mud settled. Guild's Lake and the adjacent lowlands are now a warehouse and industrial district. The site of the Forestry Building is new upscale housing.

BIBLIOGRAPHY

The starting point for information on the exposition is Henry E. Reed, "Official History of the Lewis and Clark Centennial Exposition" (1908), available in the Reed Collection at the Oregon Historical Society in Portland. Other sources of documents are: the official report of the State Commission; the central office correspondence of the Exposition Company and the photographic collections at the Oregon Historical Society; mayor's office correspondence at the Portland City Archives; records dealing with construction and with the St. Louis Fair of 1904 at the Oregon Division of Archives, Salem; and records relating to the fair at the Multnomah County Public Library, Portland.

The contemporary public view of the fair and its city can be found in the locally edited *Pacific Monthly* and the *Lewis and Clark Journal* (the official bulletin of the fair) and in the daily *Portland Telegram* and *Oregonian*. The role of the federal government can be followed in the record of hearings before the House of Representatives Committee on Industrial Arts and Expositions and in the correspondence of the State Department representative on the Government Board of Management relating to the transportation of federal exhibits (National Archives, Record Group 43).

Comprehensive analyses of the Lewis and Clark Exposition can be found in Carl Abbott, *The Great Extravaganza: Portland's Lewis and Clark Exposition* (1981), and in Holly J. Pruett, "A Sense of Place . . . Pride . . . Identity: Portland's 1905 Lewis and Clark Fair" (bachelor's thesis, Reed College, 1985). The architecture of the fair is treated in George McMath, "The Lewis and Clark Fair," in Thomas Vaughan and Virginia Ferriday, eds., *Space, Style, and Structure: Building in Northwest America* (1974). The exposition in relation to the development of urban planning is covered in Carl Abbott, *Portland: Planning, Politics, and Growth in a Twentieth Century City* (1983). A chapter in Robert Rydell, *All the World's a Fair* (1984), discusses the Portland fair (in conjunction with the Seattle fair of 1909) with emphasis on the anthropological aspects of many of the exhibits.

Carl Abbott

MILAN 1906
L'ESPOSIZIONE INTERNAZIONALE DEL SEMPIONE

The international exposition at Milan in 1906 was planned as a celebration of the completion of the Simplon tunnel, a 12.3-mile railroad tunnel through the Italian Alps that was an engineering achievement comparable in some ways to the Panama Canal. With the support of the government and King Victor Emmanuel III, some 12 million lire was subscribed to finance the fair, and building commenced at two sites in Milan, located 2 miles apart but connected by a specially constructed electric railway.

In the Parco Real, an existing municipal park, buildings housing fine arts exhibits and cultural events were located, while in the Piazza D'Armi, formerly an open space, a more formal site plan included foreign pavilions and buildings housing industrial and engineering exhibits. The planners' notion of separating art from engineering at the two sites was blunted somewhat by the fact that many of the foreign pavilions were highlighted by fine arts displays.

Although the architecture of this fair was not highly rated by contemporary critics, there were a few significant structures, including the Galleria del Sempione, which featured a tunnellike entrance and contained a replica of the actual tunnel, the concert hall, an incredibly ornate building in a combination of baroque and rococo styles, termed ''barocco'' by one critic, and the Marine Transport Building with its 200-foot lighthouse tower, which afforded the best view of the fairgrounds. There were two quite distinctive pavilions from a topical standpoint: one dedicated to hygiene, containing medical exhibits ranging from Red Cross uniforms to surgical instruments, and the Motor Car building, probably the first at a world's fair.

Amid great ceremony, King Victor Emmanuel opened the fair on April 28 in the Parco Real; a second ceremony two days later provided the king's blessing to the exhibits at the Piazza D'Armi. In addition to the pavilions already noted, visitors enjoyed the aeronautic section, a large enclosure from which tethered balloon ascents were made, and the many exhibits featuring railway engineering. Next to the engineering displays, Italian and Hungarian art exhibits attracted the most attention. The fine arts pavilion was entirely given over to Italian national art, and a concerted effort was made to feature the works of younger artists, sculptors, and designers. The Hungarian exhibit in an adjacent building received much praise for its lack of commercialism and the interesting Byzantine motifs seen in many pieces. Tragically, both the Italian and the Hungarian art exhibits were destroyed in a fire on August 2.

Foreign nations participating included most of the countries of Western Europe, Japan, China, Turkey, and Canada. Several South American nations had a combined pavilion, and the United States participated but only in a minor way. Special displays and events included Pope Pius IX's railway car, given to him by Louis-Napoleon in 1848, Buffalo Bill's Wild West Show, and a Streets of Cairo village with exotic attractions and performances.

By the time the fair closed on October 31, about 5.5 million visitors had attended. Contemporary observers labeled the fair a success in its demonstration of Italian industrial and engineering progress and as a showplace for artists and designers beginning to reflect the influence of modern art.

BIBLIOGRAPHY

The principal source for the Milan 1906 exposition is E. A. Marescotti and E. Ximenes, *Milano e l'Esposizione Internazionale del Sempione 1906* (1906), an illustrated chronicle of the fair in forty-two parts (652 pages), with lavish illustrations and articles on all aspects of the fair. For German readers, *Die erste italienische Weltausstellung ihr Schauplatz und ihre Vorgeschichte* (1907), by Alfons Leon, provides a general description of the exposition and its background, with additional information on the Simplon tunnel and rail travel into northern Italy. The official report of the French section at the Milan fair is *Exposition Internationale de Milan 1906* (1906?), by Paul Dreyfus-Bing and G.-Roger Sandoz. In English, the most general description is "The Milan Exposition," by Dexter G. Whittinghill, in *World To-Day* 12 (January 1907): 69–75. The fair's architecture is described by Robert W. Carden in "The Milan International Exposition," *Architectural Record* 20 (September 1906): 353–68, and Alfredo Milani discusses Italian and Hungarian art at the fair in "Italian Art at the Milan Exhibition," and "Hungarian Art at the Milan Exhibition," *International Studio* 29 (August and October 1906): 147–56, 300–9.

John E. Findling

CHRISTCHURCH 1906–1907

THE NEW ZEALAND INTERNATIONAL EXHIBITION OF ARTS AND INDUSTRIES

Numerous expositions, small and large, were hosted by New Zealand throughout the nineteenth and early twentieth centuries. The New Zealand International Exhibition of Arts and Industries, held during the 1906 summer in Christchurch, however, surpassed all past efforts in size and in grandeur. In 1903 New Zealand's premier, Richard Seddon, had proposed that the colony host an international exhibition. On December 18, 1905, Seddon laid the foundation stone in Hagley Park, Christchurch, but he died before the exhibition opened. Industrial development had been progressing throughout the colony, and the forthcoming exhibition was seen as an ideal opportunity to show this progress to the rest of the world. To help ensure a national, as opposed to provincial, character for the exhibition, the government provided the necessary funds.

On November 1, 1906, the exhibition opened with 1,321 exhibits, of which 384 were from overseas. Fronted by the Avon River, the exhibition buildings were spectacular. On either side of the main building were towers 160 feet high, which dominated the city's skyline. They also provided an excellent view of the city, compliments of Christchurch's first electric lift. The buildings covered nearly 14 acres and featured the use of stuccoline, which gave them a brilliant white coloring. In total the exhibition buildings cost nearly £90,000, an impressive sum of money for temporary buildings. Of the total floor space (476,500 square feet), the British, Canadian, Fijian, and New South Wales governments had generous allocations for their exhibits.

The Maori greeting—"Haere Mai"—written in lights above the main entrance welcomed all to the exhibition. The centerpiece in the Great Hall was a group of plaster Maori figures. Maori names had been given to all the passages, corridors, and avenues, enhancing the cultural identity of this New Zealand exhibition. Major attractions included the Fernery, housing about eighty species of ferns; the Machinery Hall, home to the wonders of mechanical engineering; the Art Gallery, containing a magnificent collection valued at over £150,000; and the Concert Hall with its own orchestra, which entertained and educated thousands of visitors with the finest orchestral music ever heard in Australasia. The overseas exhibits represented various agricultural products and manufactured articles. Although the British art collection and educational exhibits were very impressive, the New Zealand courts dominated the exhibition. The various districts of the colony proudly exhibited products and features unique to their areas. Many government departments also had excellent displays. The Aviary, Aquarium, and model of Rotorua, with spouting geyser and bubbling mud lakes, were popular attractions, as was the Maori Pa, a replica of a fortified village featuring traditional dance and song.

The exhibits constituted a fascinating representation of New Zealand's developments in agriculture, industry, and the arts; however, there can be no doubt about the popularity of the amusements and sideshows. One of the favorites was the water chute that plunged boats and passengers into a lake especially dug for the occasion, which remains as a haven to Christchurch ducks. "Wonderland," the helter-skelter (a spiral slide around a tower), the haunted castle, and the penny arcade were just a few of the other attractions.

By the time the exhibition closed on April 15, 1907, nearly 2 million visitors had attended. In a country whose population was only 1 million, the success of the exhibition was obvious. Although the exhibition did not show a financial profit, the city of Christchurch flourished, and the exhibition was a success in all other ways, bringing education, interest, and enjoyment to all its visitors.

BIBLIOGRAPHY

The most useful source for research on this exhibition is the *Official Catalogue and Souvenir of the New Zealand International Exhibition, 1906–1907* (1906). Other primary sources are *Official Record of the New Zealand International Exhibition of Arts and Industries Held at Christchurch, 1906–7: A Descriptive and Historical Account* by J. Cowan (1910) and *British Government Exhibit: Official Catalogue (1906)* and *Fine Art Section: Official Catalogue* (1906). These sources are held in the New Zealand Collection of the Canterbury Public Library, as is microfilm of the *Christchurch Press*, which has detailed coverage of the exhibition, as well as an excellent editorial after the official closing. Photographs can also be found in the *Canterbury Times* and *Weekly Press*, also available at the Canterbury Public Library.

There has not been much secondary work done on this exhibition. It is, however, mentioned in *A History of Canterbury Vol. 3: 1876–1950* (1965), edited by W. J. Gardner. The most interesting secondary source is the display of photographs, with commentary, in Hagley Park, Christchurch, where the exhibition was held.

Felicity Caird

DUBLIN 1907
IRISH INTERNATIONAL EXHIBITION

This 1907 exhibition was wholly inspired by domestic sociopolitical considerations—in particular, Irish economic nationalism and the desire to curb emigration and promote industrial development. The Irish Industrial Conference,
attended by a wide spectrum of economic and political interests from both north
and south, was held in April 1903, and this established two committees, one of
them charged with organizing an international exhibition in Dublin. The idea of
holding an exhibition was undoubtedly inspired by the success of the Cork
exhibition in 1902–1903. The organizers rapidly raised subscriptions and guarantees in the amount of £157,000 from major businesses; the London construction
firm of Humphreys of Knightsbridge, which had erected many exhibition halls
throughout the British empire, was charged with the building work. The main
building consisted of a central palace in Florentine Renaissance style with four
wings radiating from it, representing the four provinces of Ireland. The overall
impression was reminiscent of highly ceremonial imperial buildings favored by
the empire in India; the smaller buildings throughout the grounds tended to favor
a Tudor style.

Initially it was hoped to locate the exhibition to the west of the city, in Phoenix
Park; when this failed, the earl of Pembroke offered a 52-acre site in the elite
suburban Pembroke township to the southeast of the city.

A division emerged among the organizers between those anxious to promote
the international aspect and others more concerned with establishing a national
identity. Ultimately the latter group was victorious. Unlike previous international
exhibitions, British and Irish exhibits were segregated, with Irish products con-
stituting over 50 percent of total displays. Twelve other countries also contributed, with the French exhibit exceeding Great Britain's. It was decided to avoid
the monotony of previous exhibitions by organizing displays in a less systematic
manner.

Monotony was also relieved by the wide array of exotic entertainments. The
fair attracted a substantial number of side attractions: live theatre; Indian jugglers,
conjurers, and fakirs; a water chute; shooting ranges; a concert hall; organ recitals;
fire brigade displays; a cinematograph hall; and a Somali village complete with
native huts and native children in a schoolhouse. Other innovations included an
increased interest in health and urban planning; the Women's National Health
Association provided an educational display on tuberculosis, and the exhibition
grounds displayed a model village hall and hospital and model artisan and laborers' cottages.

A record 2.75 million people visited the fair, among them King Edward VII
and Queen Alexandra, but expenditures of £340,000 exceeded income by almost

DUBLIN 1907. This flume ride, shown on a contemporary postcard, represents the increasing attention given to entertainment at world's fairs by this time.

£100,000, which was contributed by the fair's guarantors. The main buildings were demolished, but some of the smaller neo-Tudor buildings survive. Part of the site was turned into a public park, and the rest now contains housing, including a substantial area of working-class housing built shortly afterward conforming to the wishes of those who saw the fair as a stimulus to Irish industrial nationalism.

BIBLIOGRAPHY

All material available on the 1907 Dublin exhibition is highly factual, and most publications contain similar material. *Record of the Dublin International Exhibition 1907* (1907) is useful on the background to the exhibition and on its financial details. It also contains detailed descriptions of the exhibition buildings. *Irish International Exhibition: Dublin 1907. Handbook and Guide* (1907) describes the exhibits and the buildings. The official catalog, *Irish International Exhibition Dublin 1907. Official Catalogue* (1907), can be supplemented with special catalogs for the Irish Historical Loan Collection, the Home Industries Section, and the Fine Arts Exhibit. There were occasional articles on the exhibition in the *Times* of London. See especially the issue for April 1, 1907. Dublin newspapers doubtless provided coverage on practically a daily basis.

Mary E. Daly

JAMESTOWN 1907

JAMESTOWN TERCENTENNIAL EXPOSITION

The idea for a fair to celebrate the three hundredth anniversary of the founding of the first permanent English settlement originated around 1900. Several individuals, including the president of William and Mary College, Dr. Lyon G. Tyler, suggested the idea, which rapidly gained currency. The Association for the Preservation of Antiquities, an organization founded in 1889 to save the colonial church town in Jamestown, endorsed the idea and gave it wide publicity. Other groups followed, including Williamsburg's Businessmen's Association, which pressed the Virginia legislature to pass a resolution supporting the idea of a national tercentennial to be held in 1907. By early 1901, the state senate and house of delegates had done so.

Although the location initially settled on was Richmond, the energetic efforts of James D. Thomson, editor of the *Norfolk Dispatch*, and a committee from the Common and Select Councils of the city resulted in the selection of a Hampton Roads site. The Jamestown Exposition Committee found a 5,000-acre, mile-long frontage at Sewell's Point and began to raise the $1 million required by the state legislature in 1904 in order to retain their charter. The committee conceived of the fair as a moneymaking enterprise and as a way to advertise the state.

The person first selected to raise money and promote the fair was Fitzhugh Lee, a nephew of Robert E. Lee and a major general in both the Civil and Spanish-American wars. (He barely succeeded in raising the requisite million but was less successful in lobbying Congress, which he asked for $3 million.) Congress complied but added the proviso that the exhibition be a celebration of the navy, army, and marines. Lee also visited state legislatures to encourage them to contribute funds for buildings. He died in 1905 before plans for the fair were complete and was replaced by a former congressman and law school dean, Henry St. George, who continued the fund raising and did manage to coax more money from federal and state sources.

The site for the fair was flat and undeveloped, and it had severe drainage problems. Because of these and because of the lack of funds, the fair was always behind schedule. The builders had to clear the land, install drainage, and construct piers and a boat basin for the naval display before building the permanent facilities. They planned twenty major exhibit buildings but were able to complete only about half of them before the fair opened, and they never did finish two. The layout of the grounds was based on a grid as the developers planned to build houses following the fair. The architecture of the fair was, in keeping with the Virginia locale, Greek revival, of brick construction with Corinthian pillars and Roman domes. Perhaps the most forward-looking structure at the fair was the Larkin Building, a privately built exhibit hall, designed by Frank Lloyd Wright in his prairie style.

While originally designed to emphasize Virginia's history, the fair moved in other, more commercial, directions. There were, however, state-sponsored exhibits in history, the economy, and education. These, like others, were plagued by a lack of money and failed to fill the space provided, though private donors helped close some of the gaps. The two educational exhibits that attracted the most attention and critical acclaim were the Negro exhibit organized by Giles B. Jackson of Richmond and the exhibit of mineral and timber resources of the state. The Virginia General Assembly financed the former with a $100,000 grant. Blacks planned and executed the display, which featured their achievements in industry, education, and art. President Theodore Roosevelt visited the exhibit and was impressed enough to stop in Richmond to congratulate Jackson. The latter exhibit, housed in the Mines and Metallurgy Building, promoted exploitation of the state's resources and resulted in a book, *Mineral Resources of Virginia*, published at the same time by the Jamestown Exposition Committee.

The fair opened officially on April 26, 1907, with the triumphal entry of President Roosevelt, who came by yacht and reviewed the North Atlantic fleet prior to making his address. Crowds attracted to opening day were disappointed by the unfinished exhibits; this caused considerable adverse publicity in the nation's press and earned the fair the sobriquet the "Jamestown Imposition."

The fair improved as time passed but never was a complete success. The major attractions were military; naval units from Great Britain, France, Germany, Austria, Brazil, and the Netherlands participated. The fair abounded in encampments, drills, and parades, the largest of which involved 14,000 men who marched through the grounds on June 10, Georgia Day. President Roosevelt returned that day to speak again. His speech echoed the military theme, as did the amusement area built along a street called the Warpath.

While the fair attracted numerous luminaries, including Woodrow Wilson and Charles Evans Hughes, and tried to attract various occupational groups on special days, it never became very popular, although attendance improved as buildings were completed and filled with exhibits. The total attendance was 2,850,735 visitors, only half of whom paid admission. The reasons for the poor showing were the small population of the region, the adverse publicity at the fair's opening, and the relative inaccessibility of Norfolk. The American Automobile Association, for example, advised its members that the roads to the fair were quite poor.

When the Jamestown Tercentennial closed on November 30, it had lost approximately $2.5 million. Less than a week after closing, the company was in receivership. Ten years later the site became part of the Norfolk Naval Base. Although the fair was a financial failure, it was deemed a success because of its promotion of the state. In a larger, symbolic sense, it exemplified in its military emphasis the jingoism of the American nation at the time.

BIBLIOGRAPHY

Most information about the Jamestown Tercentennial Exposition of 1907 must be gleaned from the newspapers and journals of the time. For the U.S. government role, however, see U.S. Senate, 60th Cong., 2d sess., no. 735 (Vol. 16), *Final Report of the Jamestown Ter-Centennial Commission* (1909), which emphasizes the government's exhibits but also includes a lengthy chapter on the Negro exhibit. Locally produced guides and histories include Charles Russell Kiehy, *The Official Blue Book of the Jamestown Ter-Centennial Exposition* (1909), which contains much information about the fair, and J. E. Davis, *Round about Jamestown* (1907), which is more informative on Jamestown and its early history than on the fair.

Articles on the fair's origins and operations on a day-to-day basis appeared in the *Richmond Times-Dispatch*, the *Norfolk Dispatch*, and the *Virginian-Pilot*. For a critical account of the fair's opening, see William Inglis, "Troubles at Jamestown," *Harper's Weekly*, June 8, 1907, 834–37. A more favorable contemporary account of the fair is Plummer F. Jones, "The Jamestown Tercentenary Exposition," *Review of Reviews* 35 (1907): 305–18. This article is illustrated and contains a map of the fairgrounds but must be discounted because it was written prior to the fair's opening. Another less critical account is Charles F. Stansbury, "Jamestown Expositions," *World's Work* 14 (1907): 8931–40. William H. Ward, "Race Exhibition," *Independent*, November 14, 1907, 1168–72, gives a good account of the black exhibit at the fair. The best modern account of the exposition is Robert Taylor, "The Jamestown Tercentennial Exposition, 1907," *Virginia Magazine of History and Biography* 65 (1957): 167–208. Finally, Virginius Dabney, *Virginia: The New Dominion* (1971) provides useful historical background for the exposition.

Dwight W. Hoover

LONDON 1908

THE FRANCO-BRITISH EXHIBITION

The Franco-British Exhibition opened on May 14, 1908, and embodied the spirit of the entente cordiale in its spectacular presentation of the industry, commerce, and culture of the French and British empires. Planning had commenced in 1905 when the French Chamber of Commerce and the British Empire League had responded to the ideas of Imre Kiralfy, an established entrepreneur in the exhibition field, and charged his company with creating the exhibition. The year 1908 was chosen so that the exhibition might also provide the site of the London Olympics. An area of agricultural land in Shepherd's Bush, West London, part of which Kiralfy owned, was developed to provide a 140-acre site close to good transportation facilities.

The exhibition was laid out in a basic cross shape comprising distinct areas for "The Arts," "Progress," entertainments, the sports stadium, the prestigious Court of Honour, and the central gardens. Waterways were a prominent feature, and the prevailing style featured white buildings, designed by a number of architects under the supervision of John Belcher and Marius Toudoire. From this came the nickname the White City. Principal buildings were the Palace of Decorative Arts, the Palace of British Applied Arts, the Palace of French Applied Arts, the Palace of Music, the Palace of Women's Work, the Royal Pavilion, the Machinery Halls, the Court of Honour, the Education Buildings, and the two main entrances. Other pavilions represented countries within the two empires, and a further series of halls linked the main site with a nearby railway station.

Exhibits covered a wide range, combining trade fair with cultural exposition. Heavy industry was represented by displays on mining, iron and steelwork, armaments manufacture, shipbuilding, pumping and motive power machinery, electricity generation, and textile and printing machinery. Light industries and crafts included leather, dying, furnishing, and textiles. The Palace of Women's Work brought together historical and contemporary exhibits ranging from tapestry to photography and inventions by women. One hall was devoted to British education and another to British social economy, which drew heavily on the work of cooperative and trading societies. A major display of French fine arts was assembled from museum and gallery collections.

The entertainments section, Merryland, was substantial. It was dominated by the Flip Flap, a counterpoised metal structure whose arms could lift a viewing carriage to 200 feet. Further entertainment was provided in July by the Olympic Games. Over 2,000 competitors from twenty-two nations took part in twenty sports, the event as a whole being dominated by the U.S. and British teams.

Palace of Women's Work,
Franco-British Exhibition, London.

LONDON 1908. The Palace of Women's Work, shown here, is typical of pavilions dedicated to women that were a feature at most fairs between 1876 and World War I.

Apart from the marathon, all events took place in the exhibition stadium so as to maximize the benefits for both ventures in capturing an audience.

The exhibition closed on October 31. Total attendance came to 8.4 million, with receipts of over £420,000 ensuring its financial success. Contemporary opinion concluded that the event was an outstanding success, a demonstration of Anglo-French cooperation, and a personal triumph for Kiralfy. The site continued successfully to be used for international exhibitions until World War I and thereafter fell into disuse, although the stadium remained in use until 1984.

BIBLIOGRAPHY

The most important source of primary research material on this topic is the Imre Kiralfy Collection at the Museum of London, which includes manuscript and printed material, a photograph album showing the construction of the White City, and another of the Franco-British Exhibition itself. Hammersmith and Fulham Archives, Shepherds Bush Library, London, also holds in the Hammersmith Local History Collection printed and photographic material concerning the exhibition, including programs, postcards and tickets. More material, including recorded oral interviews, is being collected by the White City Community Project, which may be contacted through Hammersmith and Fulham Archives.

Contemporary printed items include the *Official Guide* (1908), which ran to several editions, and an official souvenir, *The Franco-British Exhibition: Official Souvenir* (1908). A program of events, *Daily Programme* (1908), was published each day. Other guidebooks published that year also referred to the exhibition, such as *Pictorial and Descriptive Guide to London and the Franco-British Exhibition, 1908* (1908). There are numerous contemporary newspaper accounts, particularly in the national dailies such as the *Times* and the *Daily Mail*. The local paper, the *West London Observer*, covered the event, and there was an exhibition paper, the *White City Herald*. A few days before the exhibition closed, a banquet was given, and an account was published as a *Report of Proceedings at the Complimentary Banquet at the Garden Club of the Franco-British Exhibition in Honour of Mr. Imre Kiralfy, the Commissioner General, Wednesday 28th October 1908*. Material concerning the 1908 Olympic Games includes the program, *Programme [of the] Olympic Games of London 1908, IV International Olympiad* (1908), and the official report, *The Fourth Olympiad, Being the Official Report of the Olympic Games of 1908 Celebrated in London . . . and Issued under the Authority of the British Olympic Council* (1908).

After the exhibition closed, a detailed account was published, edited by F. G. Dumas, *The Franco-British Exhibition: Illustrated Review, 1908* (1908). In 1910 a film was made showing the exhibition ground and the buildings: *Farmer Jenkin's Visit to the White City* (1910). A short book was published to coincide with the seventieth anniversary of the first exhibition: Donald Knight, *The Exhibitions: Great White City, Shepherds Bush, London* (1978), and a thesis has also been researched that includes consideration of the Franco-British Exhibition: Brendan Gregory, "The Spectacle Plays and Exhibitions of Imre Kiralfy, 1882–1914" (thesis, University of Manchester, 1988).

Christopher Jeens

SEATTLE 1909

THE ALASKA-YUKON-PACIFIC EXPOSITION

The aim of the Alaska-Yukon-Pacific Exposition (AYP) was to draw attention to the beginning of a new era of commercial and industrial growth in the Northwest and particularly in Seattle, which advertised itself as a new gateway to the Pacific and to Alaska. This aim was symbolized in the design of the official seal of the exposition: three women, representing Japan, Alaska, and the Pacific Northwest, cradled, respectively, a steamship, a gold nugget, and a railway locomotive. In his opening day address, James J. Hill, builder of the Northern Pacific Railroad, proclaimed that visitors would "carry away with them along with recollections of new possibilities of wealth, new methods, new markets and new trading peoples, a fund of new ideas and old ones recast in a larger mold."

Planning for the exposition got started in familiar fashion with the formation, in the spring of 1906, of an association and an executive committee made up of local businessmen charged with raising money. The head of this group was John E. Chilberg, a banker. Ira A. Nadeau, a former general agent of the Northern Pacific Railroad, was named director general of the exposition. A 250-acre site on the campus of the University of Washington was selected, and the Olmsted Brothers of Boston, a famous landscape design firm, were commissioned to lay out the grounds. John Langley Howard, architect of the campus of the University of California at Berkeley, was appointed to design the exposition buildings. Opening day was set for June 1, 1909, and closing was to be October 16.

The AYP was advertised as the "World's Most Beautiful Exposition." The Olmsted-designed main axis site opened toward a view of Mount Rainier. Secondary axes bisected the Rainier axis at 45-degree angles and offered views of Lake Union and Lake Washington. John C. Olmsted's plans to cut down all the native fir trees and to create buildings in a Russian-inspired style were rejected, however. Most of the buildings Howard designed were of beaux-arts derivation, reminiscent of the classical style of seventeenth-century French court architecture. The Forestry Building, however, was constructed from massive timbers logged in Snohomish County. It apparently contained few practical architectural features, though, and failed to inspire a school of Northwest architecture. Besides the Forestry Building and an administration building, other important buildings were contributed by California, Oregon, Idaho, Utah, New York, and the state of Washington. The federal government contributed four buildings housing exhibits from Alaska, the Philippines, and Hawaii. The Smithsonian Institution sent a portrait gallery of distinguished Americans and an exhibit devoted to the peoples of the Pacific Coast and "our island possessions." After the fair, some of these buildings were to be occupied by the university. Japan contributed an exhibit, the only Asian country to do so. Additionally, a group of Japanese civic and business leaders toured the fair and later the country as guests of the U.S. government and the Associated Chambers of Commerce of the Pacific Coast.

The amusement section was called "Pay Streak" and included, as must any self-respecting exposition after Chicago's World's Columbian Exposition, a ferris wheel. The architecture of the Pay Streak was a curious melding of totem poles and Japanese lanterns, dubbed "Jap-Alaskan." Besides an Igorot village from the Philippines, there were an Eskimo village, Japanese and Chinese villages, and a Streets of Cairo exhibit. The Igorot village, inhabited by Filipinos hired by a touring exhibition company, proved to be one of the most popular exhibits of the exposition. Seattle schoolchildren by the thousands were taken to see the villagers moving about in their artificial environment. University of Washington administrators also brought out Alfred C. Haddon, a Cambridge University anthropologist, to teach a summer school course, "The Growth of Cultural Evolution around the Pacific."

The AYP was on a closely monitored budget, and consequently the large commemorative and allegorical fountains characteristic of some previous fairs were absent, as were extensive plantings. Total paid attendance at the AYP was 3,740,551, a figure greater than that for the Portland exposition of 1905, but far fewer than that for Chicago, St. Louis, or Philadelphia.

BIBLIOGRAPHY

Archival records of the Alaska-Yukon-Pacific Exposition are housed in the Manuscripts Division of the Suzzallo Library at the University of Washington under the name Miscellaneous Records of the Alaska-Yukon-Pacific Exposition. The papers of the Olmsted brothers relating to the AYP are also held here. The library also maintains a Pacific Northwest Collection; here may be found a variety of published guidebooks and other souvenirs from the fair, including the principal one, *Alaska-Yukon-Pacific Exposition: Official Guide* (n.d.). Another quite comprehensive locally produced guide is *Seattle and the Pacific Northwest* (1909), published by the curiously named Division of Exploitation in Seattle and containing a series of articles on the fair, its architecture, its amusements, its special days and events, and Seattle and the Pacific Northwest as well. Local newspapers and magazines, especially the *Seattle Post-Intelligencer*, *Pacific Northwest Commerce*, and a special promotional publication begun in 1906, the *Alaska-Yukon Magazine*, contain numerous articles on the fair. Also of use is a pre-fair article by exposition committee president J. E. Chilberg, "The Alaska-Yukon-Pacific Exposition," *The Coast* 12 (1906): 289–92.

A good deal of factual information on the planning for the AYP can be found in the *Hearing before the Committee on Industrial Arts and Expositions, U.S. House of Representatives: Alaska-Yukon Exposition, January 27, 1908* (1908). The record of U.S. government participation is detailed in U.S. Senate, 61st Cong., 3d sess., No. 671 (vol. 29), *Report on Alaska-Yukon-Pacific Exposition* (1911), and the displays mounted by the Smithsonian are described in *The Exhibits of the Smithsonian Institution and the United States National Museum at the Alaska-Yukon-Pacific International Exposition* (1909).

George Frykman, "The Alaska-Yukon-Pacific International Exposition," *Pacific Northwest Quarterly* 53, no. 3 (July 1962): 89–99, is a good modern survey of the fair. Robert W. Rydell, *All the World's a Fair* (1984), stresses the racial and anthropological aspects of the AYP.

Raymond L. Wilson

BRUSSELS 1910
EXPOSITION UNIVERSELLE ET INTERNATIONALE

This exposition confirmed Belgium's role as a major host of international events. Staged only thirteen years after the previous Brussels exposition and a year after an imperial international exhibition in London in which Belgium had a very large pavilion, the 1910 fair revealed the heavy commitment of the Belgian government to international display. The major part of the organization was carried out by the Ministry of Finance and Public Works, with the Ministry of War providing administrative support for the military and imperial elements. M. le Comte de Smet de Naeyer, minister of finance and public works, was the controlling figure within the organizational structure. Above him, King Albert carried the symbolic role of *Haute protecteur de l'exposition*. The major participants were France, Holland, Britain (including Ireland), Russia, Germany, Brazil, Spain, and Italy. A pavilion for all other nations was erected, in which several dozen countries put up stands. The number of nations committing themselves to a major investment was therefore less here than at any other Belgian event.

About halfway through its run, the exposition was marred by an event that might have been, but for good fortune, a tragedy. Shortly before nine on the evening of Sunday, August 14, after most of the day's crowd had left, a fire broke out near the central gallery and quickly spread to the British section, the city of Paris pavilion, and a French restaurant. After several hours, the fire was brought under control, the rest of the site saved; no lives were lost. What remained of the British industrial exhibit was then moved to the Salles des Fêtes. The incident greatly increased the publicity surrounding the fair.

The site was southwest of the parc de Solbosch and northwest of the bois de la Cambre. Its most striking feature was a series of lavish ornamental gardens, which led up to the jardin de la Ville de Paris and the jardin Hollandais at the core. The popular literature surrounding the event made repeated claims that this was the most beautiful site ever used for an international exposition, a dubious assertion but nevertheless one that served to highlight the unusually green site and the pleasant atmosphere. The site architecture was almost exclusively historicist—that is, verbose and superficial copies of earlier styles. A heavy neobaroque, evident in Paris in 1900 and London in 1908, dominated the skyline. Perhaps the only structure of note among the official sections was the vast Machine Hall, which had a greater total floor space than the legendary Galeries des Machines of the Paris expositions of 1889 and 1900.

The exhibits were not divided in the traditional manner of raw materials, manufactures, machinery, and fine arts but were classified into twenty-two

BRUSSELS 1910. A major fire on August 14 destroyed the principal gallery and several other buildings at this fair.

groups, each with its controlling executive and judges. The most significant groups were Education, Works of Art, Appliances relating to Literature, Science and Art, Engineering, Electricity, Agriculture, Mining, Decorative Arts, Textiles, Chemical Industries, Social Economy, Woman's Labor, the Army and Navy, and Colonies. There was also a Congress Hall, in which numerous commercial and academic conferences and conventions were held.

Perhaps the two most popular areas, not for the last time at a Belgian exposition, were the colonies and the fine arts. In the former, it was the French who put on the most dramatic display, with stunning pavilions for Indochina, West Africa, Algeria, and Tunisia. The latter two attracted the most attention; they were built in indigenous North African styles, surrounded by gardens with exotic plants and with large numbers of Algerians and Tunisians in traditional costumes servicing the buildings. The interiors of these pavilions contained serious and quite dry displays of the economic prosperity France had brought. This was unusual; the French normally preferred an exotic splash of decorative splendor to serve as imperial propaganda. There was also a general colonial pavilion for smaller French dependencies and a building for the colonial press. The pavilions dedicated to the Belgian Congo were impressive but outdone by the French display. The British expended little energy on the colonial area, unusual for them.

The fine arts were divided into old and new art, the former of which was enhanced by a Maison de Rubens. Without any doubt, the show of Flemish art was the key attraction here, with masterpieces gathered from the best public and private collections in Belgium. The modern section was chiefly of interest for the fine collection sent by the French, a surprisingly liberal selection in relation to the normal French contribution to official expositions. The usual *grands pompiers* were all present, notably Leon Bonnat (three works), Jean Beraud (one work), and Albert Besnard (one work), but apart from these, Claude Monet (three works), Auguste Renoir (three works), and Auguste Rodin (three works) gave a different view of the older generation. More surprisingly, Edouard Vuillard (two works), Pierre Bonnard (two works), Maurice Denis (one work), Paul Signac (one work), and Henri Matisse (two works) were allowed to represent their country. This was most unusual and must be put down to the enlightenment of chief commissioner for the fine arts, André Saglio.

BIBLIOGRAPHY

The general features of the Brussels exposition, including its organization and exhibits are found in these official reports and catalogs: *Brussels Exhibition 1910: Official Catalogue of the British Section* (1910); *Catalogue general, Exposition universelle et internationale, Bruxelles 1910* (1910); *Catalogue special officiel de la section français* (1910); *Livre d'or de l'exposition universelle et internationale de Bruxelles 1910* (1910). The fair's organizers published a journal of fair-related news, beginning in November 1907 and continuing through December 1910. Published monthly before the fair's opening and more frequently during the run of the fair, *Moniteur de l'exposition universelle et internationale Bruxelles 1910* contained both general interest articles and articles on specific features of the exposition. Both the *New York Times* and the *Times* of London carried occasional articles about the exposition, especially about the mid-August fire.

Modern works that mention this fair include A. Cockx and J. Lemmens, *Les expositions universelles et internationales en Belgique de 1885 à 1958* (1958), which devotes a brief chapter to it, and John Allwood, *The Great Exhibitions* (1977).

Paul Greenhalgh

NANKING 1910

NAN-YANG CH'UAN-YEN HUI
(NANKING SOUTH SEAS EXHIBITION)

On December 15, 1908, Governor-General Tuan Fang of the Liang-kiang provinces proposed that China hold an international exhibition to promote the country's national products and to advance the modernization of its economy. Tuan believed that an international exposition would increase the growth of the Nanking area, stimulate national industry, inspire necessary educational and social reforms, and encourage the provinces to participate in "healthy competition." The last resulted in small exhibits and trade shows, with each province or region displaying its most distinctive wares months before they were to be shown at the international exhibition. This helped to promote interest and excitement among the people, and fair officials hoped that it would affect the attendance figure. It did not.

After numerous delays, the exposition finally opened on June 5, 1910, with Viceroy Chang Jen-chun and Adjudicator-General Yang Shih-chi leading the opening ceremonies. By then, numerous news articles describing the political turbulence and antiforeign sentiment in China had been released, and this adverse publicity most likely accounted for the lower than estimated attendance figures. But despite the fear of outbursts and antiforeign violence, the opening ceremonies were quite peaceful.

The site selected in Nanking seemed to be a perfect place to stage an exposition. Located on the Yangtze River and near the Nanking railway station, the land available for such an endeavor was also adjacent to a popular and scenic park, containing approximately fifty lakes and various bamboo patches.

Ground was broken in July 1909, and construction immediately began. Stagnant and disease-infested lakes were transformed into beautiful lagoons, and many of the natural features, such as the bamboo patches, were incorporated into the overall landscaping scheme. Flowers, shrubbery, shady walks, and beautiful water fountains were added, creating a relaxing atmosphere and enhancing the overall scenery.

The grounds covered an area of 90 to 100 acres, and the exposition was dubbed the "White City." All (except for one red-brick Georgian house) of the site's twenty-six buildings and pavilions, designed by the Shanghai-based architectural firm of Messrs. Atkinson & Dallas, were white. China's fair officials wanted to recreate well-known Western expositions of Europe and the United States, so most of the buildings were modernistic in design, although they contained distinctive Chinese ornamental features. Although some exposition buildings were unfinished at the beginning of the fair and some were not scheduled for completion until September, when the fair was half over, what was there was said to be a credit to the promoters.

There were two main gateways to the exhibition grounds. The main entrance, facing south, was decorated in an ornate traditional palace style and was intended for public entry. The other gate, done in a European style, was intended as an exit, and it faced west. Large buildings, such as the Industry, Education, Machinery, Public Health, and Transportation buildings were all one story and lined a broad avenue that passed through the fairgrounds. The Fine Arts building was the only two-story structure on the grounds and was considered impressive.

China's first world's fair attracted fourteen other nations and seventy-eight private companies or agencies. In addition fifteen Chinese provinces participated, erecting pavilions as well. The spirit of competition had caught on, and so displays, most of which were exhibited in a Western style, were spectacular. Each province, not wanting to be outdone by a neighbor, displayed its best commodities. Exhibits included Chinese and foreign products, manufactures and machinery, model schools and factories, traditional handcrafted items, textiles, agricultural products such as tea, grains, and liquors, and modern armaments. There were foreign restaurants, a race track, a botanical garden, and a zoo located on the grounds. The site featured a brick clock and observation tower.

Although this exposition did not make a profit or attract as many tourists as was hoped, it should not be considered a failure in all regards. Visitors who did go to the fair had a grand time, and despite the political uneasiness, participants felt a certain camaraderie toward each other. Tuan's vision of a "healthy competition" between the provinces was realized, and his reasoning "that progress in one country or area could inspire another" was correct. That is precisely what world's fairs and expositions are all about. It is nations and people putting aside their petty differences and coming together in friendship, proudly showing off their most prized possessions and inventions and bringing with them the potential for technological advancement that ultimately benefits all humanity. And that is exactly what China's first world's fair accomplished. It was a brilliant endeavor by a country facing political unrest.

BIBLIOGRAPHY

Primary sources are limited for this fair; however, researchers will find a well-written article by Michael R. Godley, 'China's World's Fair of 1910,'' in *Modern Asian Studies* 12 (1978): 503–22, to be a very helpful and resourceful piece. The article is informative in regard to the historical aspects of the fair and in depicting the political turbulence of the time. "China's First World's Fair," *American Review of Reviews* (June 1910): 691–93, although brief, provides some good background information, and also includes photographs of pavilions under construction. Selected articles in the London *Times* provide information on the opening ceremonies, the exhibition grounds, and the site's architecture. See especially, the issues dated June 6 and July 1, 1910.

Kimberly Pelle

LONDON 1911
FESTIVAL OF EMPIRE

To celebrate the coronation of King George V and to reassert imperial solidarity on the eve of World War I, the British held an international exhibition, the Festival of Empire, in and around the Crystal Palace at Sydenham, outside London. Although the Crystal Palace had been used almost continuously as a large entertainment hall and convention center since its removal to Sydenham in 1854, the Festival of Empire was the largest event held there since the Great Exhibition of 1851.

This fair was divided into three distinct parts. One, called the All-Red Route because of the small trains that carried visitors through it, was an imperial exhibit. Its main feature was a series of replicated dominion parliament buildings, constructed on a scale of two-thirds their actual size. Other colonies were represented by big game exhibits or historical tableaux. South Africa displayed $2 million worth of diamonds lent by the DeBeers Company, and the exhibits from Canada included a miniature wheat field, a fruit display, pictures executed in grains, and sculptures of butter. Of all the parliament buildings, Canada's was the most popular, and it was left to stand a second year at the site after the rest of the fair was demolished.

The second part of the Festival of Empire was the All-British Exhibit, held in the Crystal Palace. The palace, redecorated for the event, contained a comprehensive display of British arts and industry, including a Fair of Fashion, featuring live models.

The third part of the exhibition was an outdoor theatrical spectacle, the Pageant of London. This extravaganza, involving 10,000 actors, covered the history of London and the British empire from prehistoric times until the proclamation of Queen Victoria as the empress of India in 1876. A scenic amphitheater seating 10,000 was constructed for this event.

In addition, various kinds of entertainment and special events accompanied the Festival of Empire. There was, for example, an interempire wrestling tournament, a Boy Scout rally, and a special lecture on New Zealand theater within a typical week. Periodically, grand military tattoos, with as many as nine bands and 500 torchbearers, delighted the crowds. More fun-loving visitors could see Mr. Bostock's Menagerie, a 200-animal zoo, or ride on the Topsy-Turvy or the Maxim Flying Machine.

A total of 144,234 attended the fair on opening day, May 12, hoping to catch a glimpse of the royal family, there to participate in the elaborate opening ceremonies. Large crowds continued to flock to Sydenham throughout the summer, despite the competition offered by the smaller Coronation Exhibition at Shepherd's Bush, a permanent park and amusement area located elsewhere in greater London. Notwithstanding the large crowds, the Crystal Palace Company, which owned and operated the Crystal Palace and bore most of the financial burden for the Festival of Empire, fell into bankruptcy after the fair. By 1913, the Crystal Palace was owned by the government, which renovated it during the 1920s and held various entertainments there until its final destruction by fire on November 30, 1936.

BIBLIOGRAPHY

Although Patrick Beaver asserts that the Festival of Empire was the largest event ever staged at the Sydenham Crystal Palace, historians have not paid it much attention. There is some material available at the Bromley Local Studies Library, located not far from the Sydenham site, and more information may be obtained from the Crystal Palace Foundation in London. Beaver's book, *The Crystal Palace* (1970), is a comprehensive and well-illustrated history of the building, but it devotes little space to the Festival of Empire. It does, however, contain a number of photographs of the fair. Probably the best and most accessible source of information for the fair is the *Times* of London, which published a substantial number of quite detailed articles on the fair over a span of several months in 1911. See, in particular, the issues of February 6, May 5 and 13, June 5, July 5, and August 7, 1911.

John E. Findling

GHENT 1913

EXPOSITION UNIVERSELLE ET INDUSTRIELLE

This star-crossed exposition was the largest and most elegant of the several fairs Belgium hosted before World War I, and it was the last European fair before the outbreak of that war. Ghent, located halfway between Brussels and the coast, is a textile and garden center, and these two elements played a central role in the planning and execution of the fair and its exhibits. A site of 309 acres, developed around a city park, served as a backdrop for the pavilions and was laden with banks of flowers in nearly every conceivable location. Belgium, France, and Great Britain dominated the exposition; each of the four largest Belgian cities had its own pavilion, and France and Britain constructed large buildings flanking the Court of Honor. Other nations, including the United States, Canada, the Netherlands, Germany, Persia, and the Belgian Congo, also participated.

King Albert of Belgium opened the exposition on April 26, initiating seven and a half months of intense activity based on the theme of "Peace, Industry, and Art." The fair hosted over sixty international congresses on topics as diverse as agriculture and the sport of fencing. There was the usual panoply of fine arts attractions, including artworks in the fine art pavilion thought to be so scandalous that Cardinal François Joseph Mercier forbade priests, school principals, and parents to visit it. More generally acceptable were special performances of the Russian ballet, featuring the renowned Nijinsky.

The most distinctive pavilion was that of the Belgian Congo, a circular structure 50 feet high and 500 feet in circumference, which featured an immense panorama of the Congo, created by Belgian artists Paul Matthieu and Alfred Bastien. A good deal of emphasis was placed on showing both Belgian imperialists and the Belgian empire in a favorable light; King Albert, in a speech opening the Belgian section on May 15, exhorted his parliament to adjust its relations with the Congo to give the natives more autonomy and work to improve their standard of living in order to benefit the empire. After seeing the Congo pavilion, visitors could amuse themselves at the highest water chute in the world, a 3-mile scenic railway ride around the fairgrounds, a rapid "joy-wheel" of "improved design," or Mr. Bostock's Menagerie, which had also been popular at the recent Festival of Empire in London.

This, however, was an exposition plagued with more than its share of disaster. At least six fires struck the fair, destroying, among other things, the Indochina pavilion, a German restaurant, and much of Old Flanders, an area built in the style of a medieval city. On July 28, a gold ingot valued at $20,000 was stolen from the Belgian colonial pavilion; only later was it discovered that what had been stolen was merely an imitation worth just $200. In the Filipino village, an anthropological exhibit doubtless modeled after those in recent U.S. fairs, the natives were reported to be starving, and nine of the fifty-five had died from exposure by early November. The Filipinos complained they had received no wages for eight months, since the agency that had brought them to Ghent had gone bankrupt. A U.S. congressman pleaded with the Belgians to send them back home lest they all starve or be jailed as vagabonds.

By the time the fair closed in early December, some 11 million visitors had been counted. Negative publicity from the fires and the plight of the Filipinos probably contributed to keeping the attendance 2 million below that of the Brussels fair of 1910, but the extensive flower beds and the impressive textile machinery exhibits received high praise from contemporary observers. Within a year, however, Belgium would be overrun by German armies, and not until 1930 would its tradition of international fairs be resumed.

BIBLIOGRAPHY

As with most of the earlier Belgian fairs, material on the Ghent 1913 exposition is hard to find. A. Cockx and J. Lemmens, *Les Expositions universelles et internationales en Belgique de 1885 à 1958* (1958), is a general work on Belgian fairs and contains information of value on this one. An official report was published by the Ministère de l'industrie et du travail, *Exposition universelle et internationale de Gand* (1913), and the exposition committee published a journal of fair-related news, *Organe officiel de l'Exposition universelle et internationale de Gand*. From March 1911 until the opening of the fair, this was published monthly; during the run of the fair, it appeared more frequently. Although contemporary magazines in Great Britain and the United States generally ignored the fair, the *New York Times* and the *Times* of London ran occasional articles on it, and French and Belgian papers doubtless gave even more space to it.

John E. Findling

SAN FRANCISCO 1915
PANAMA PACIFIC INTERNATIONAL EXPOSITION

In 1915, just nine years after a devastating earthquake and fire and one year into a world war, San Francisco put on a highly successful world's fair in which twenty-eight foreign nations and thirty-two states and territories participated. A virtual city, 2½ miles long by ½ mile wide, was constructed. There were more than 18 million paid admissions in the ten months that it was open.

As early as 1904, the San Francisco Chamber of Commerce had proposed a world's fair to advertise the city's growing commercial potential. Such advertisement became urgent after the earthquake and fire of 1906. Businessmen and politicians wanted to show the rest of the world that San Francisco had recovered from this disaster. A postcard of the period, labeled "Undaunted," shows a wounded California bear rising from the ashes with an idealized exposition at its feet.

From the beginning, an exposition had been planned to celebrate the completion of the Panama Canal, which occurred in 1914. But San Francisco was not the only city wanting such a fair. Southern California was also interested in self-promotion, and San Diego, strongly backed by the Los Angeles business community, made a bid for the exposition. Taking advantage of this rivalry, New Orleans announced its intention to hold the Panama Canal exposition. The Californians, realizing that their continued squabbling might lose them the fair altogether, worked out a compromise whereby San Francisco would receive full state support for its exposition in return for support of a more limited exposition for San Diego. The latter became the Panama California Exposition of 1915–1916. New Orleans mounted a strident campaign in which it claimed to be the logical point for the fair because it was more centrally located. It also lined up an impressive number of congressmen on its side. San Francisco countered with a blizzard of postcards (at one point the West Coast ran out of cardboard) urging people to write their congressmen to support a San Francisco fair. In the end, California won largely because, unlike New Orleans, it was willing to accept federal recognition without federal funds.

The exposition was financed by the merchants of San Francisco. Charles Moore, owner of an engineering firm, became president of the exposition, and directors included leading bankers, publishers, department store owners, shipping magnates, and executives of the utilities and railroads. On April 28, 1910, the businessmen held a public meeting at which they raised over $4 million in two hours. Municipal and state bond issues of $5 million each guaranteed adequate financing of the exposition.

Federal recognition enabled the exposition's organizers to solicit foreign participation, but the whole enterprise was put in jeopardy by the outbreak of World War I. Germany and Britain mutually agreed not to participate, but France stayed on and constructed a replica of the Palace of the Legion of Honor, which it shared with Belgium, overrun by the Germans before the exposition opened.

The contest now shifted to the choice of a site in San Francisco for the fair. Developers, businessmen, and politicians fought over proposed sites. For a time Golden Gate Park (site of the 1894 California Midwinter Exposition) was favored, and President William Howard Taft actually broke ground there in 1911. But eventually an undeveloped site on San Francisco Bay was chosen, and it was here and in the neighboring Presidio that the 635-acre fair was built.

Early plans for the exposition had envisaged a totally remodeled San Francisco with wide boulevards and chains of parks. Daniel Burnham, director of the World's Columbian Exposition in Chicago in 1893, drew up plans, but by 1912 they had been abandoned as too expensive and too impractical. The fair did stimulate the rebuilding of the Civic Center with an Exposition (now Civic) Auditorium and a new City Hall, but none of the buildings of the exposition itself survived except for the Palace of Fine Arts, which had to be almost entirely rebuilt in the 1960s and which now houses a popular science museum. The site itself was developed in the 1920s to become the Marina District facing a yacht harbor and park on the waterfront.

The Panama Pacific International Exposition (or PPIE, as it was commonly called) opened, as scheduled, on February 20, 1915. San Franciscans were awakened at 6:00 A.M. by whistles, steam sirens, horns, and fifteen marching bands. A procession 2½ miles long wound its way toward the exposition, and by 10:00 A.M. more than 100,000 people packed the grounds. In Washington, President Woodrow Wilson touched a key that started the Fountain of Energy. The fair was open.

The design and layout of the fair were innovative. Instead of great avenues of imposing beaux-arts palaces, the PPIE was laid out in courtyards, each designed by a different architect. The exhibition buildings formed the walls of these courtyards and at the same time protected fairgoers from the winds of the Pacific. They also made the exposition compact and thus easier on the feet. The layout was the inspiration of Ernest Coxhead. There were three major courts: in the center, the Court of the Universe designed by the firm of McKim, Mead and White and enclosed by the Palaces of Transportation, Manufactures, Liberal Arts, and Agriculture; to the east of this, the Court of Ages (later renamed the Court of Abundance), designed by Louis Christian Mullgardt and enclosed by the Palaces of Transportation, Mines and Metallurgy, Varied Industries, and Manufactures; and to the west, the Court of the Four Seasons, designed by Henry Bacon and enclosed by the Palaces of Agriculture, Food Products, Education and Social Economy, and Liberal Arts.

Each exhibition palace was surmounted by a central dome, with smaller domes and half-domes at the corners of each building. But the "City of Domes," as the fair was often called, was not limited to these. South of the courts rose the

Palace of Horticulture, an immense glass dome bigger than that of St. Paul's Cathedral in London, and the Festival Hall, another vast domed building that was the exposition concert hall. To the east was the huge Palace of Machinery, in which Lincoln Beachey flew an airplane, a publicity stunt billed as the world's first indoor flight—an occupation with a limited future. To the west, separated from the courts by a lagoon, rose Bernard Maybeck's Palace of Fine Arts, a colonnade partially surrounding a domed rotunda. The most visible feature of the PPIE was the 432-foot Tower of Jewels. Its arches were larger than the Arc de triomphe, and it dripped with allegorical statues and murals depicting the triumph of the West. It was covered with more than 100,000 faceted glass jewels, each backed by a tiny mirror.

The tight harmonious layout of the fair unraveled at the edges with national and state pavilions in a myriad of styles fanning out west of the Palace of Fine Arts. Beyond these were livestock buildings, athletic grounds, and a race track. To the east was the visual jumble of the amusement area, dubbed the Joy Zone.

The older nations constructed their pavilions in traditional architectural style: a Renaissance palace for Italy, teahouses for Japan, a bit of the castle of Kronberg at Elsinore for Denmark, a Norwegian chieftain's medieval castle, a Siamese palace. Newer nations—Australia, New Zealand, and those of Latin America—tended to build in classical or beaux-arts style. States followed a similar pattern. Those that had notable buildings—the State House in Massachusetts, Independence Hall in Pennsylvania—reproduced them in reduced versions at the fair. Those that did not tried something else to impress visitors. Oregon constructed a reproduction of the Parthenon with forty-eight columns of douglas fir with the bark left on. The California pavilion was in the form of a huge mission—far larger than any actual mission in the state. Within were elaborate agricultural displays from various counties and a ballroom in which dances and the principal exposition social functions were held. It also housed the administration and was the headquarters of the Women's Board, which was in charge of reception and entertainment.

The PPIE was the first world's fair to make extensive use of indirect lighting. Previous fairs had been lit almost entirely by outlining buildings in light bulbs, as was the common practice on theater marquees. The PPIE relied on more than 370 searchlights and 500 projectors on roofs and at other vantage points. These lights reflected the texture and color of the buildings and highlighted statuary and planting. The dome of the Palace of Horticulture glowed like an opal, and lights played on the Tower of Jewels each night producing dazzling and incandescent effects. A squad of U.S. Marines changed colored filters on a battery of forty-eight searchlights located on a pier in the bay. On foggy nights, the mist took on various hues as it drifted across the exposition grounds, and on clear nights, a stationary locomotive produced clouds of steam to give a similar effect.

Plaster and lath had been the standard building materials for most other world's fairs, producing glaring white structures. The PPIE used artificial travertine, a

SAN FRANCISCO 1915. Although most fairs after 1901 had spectacular nighttime vistas, that of the Panama-Pacific Exposition may have been the most impressive. (Courtesy Special Collections, Madden Library, California State University, Fresno)

material developed by McKim, Mead and White for the Pennsylvania Station in New York. Not only did this material look like the real travertine marble of Rome, but also it could be tinted. Jules Guerin, who was known for his theatrical designs and watercolors, coordinated the color scheme of the exposition. His inspiration was the California landscape. The buildings were in pastel shades of green, blue, pink, lemon, and ochre. Even the plantings were color coordinated to complement the buildings.

John McLaren, who had been largely responsible for creating Golden Gate Park, was in charge of the landscaping. Hundreds of full-grown cypresses, palms, and orange trees were transplanted. A living green wall 1,150 feet long formed the southern boundary of the exposition. It was made by planting cuttings in boxes measuring 2 by 6 feet but only 2 inches deep. Chicken wire was nailed over the top to retain the plants, and the boxes were upended to form the wall. It took 8,700 of them to complete the wall.

The grounds and courts abounded with sculpture. In charge was A. Stirling Calder (the father of Alexander Calder). His giant sculptural groups, *Nations of the East* featuring an elephant and *Nations of the West* featuring, rather chauvinistically, a covered wagon, surmounted the immense triumphal arches in the Court of the Universe. His massive Fountain of Energy epitomized the thrust of progress in the west. Mullgardt's Court of Ages was devoted to social Darwinism, with bas-reliefs depicting creatures from invertebrates to humans creeping up the walls. In the center was Robert Aiken's Fountain of the Earth surrounded by friezes with such titles as "Survival of the Fittest" and culminating with "Intellectual Attraction." The most famous sculpture of the exposition was James Earle Frazier's *End of the Trail*, which depicted an exhausted Indian on an exhausted horse, sentimentally epitomizing what was thought to be the fate of native Americans. When the fair closed, *End of the Trail* was sold to Tulare County and was erected in Mooney Grove Park, Visalia. There it remained, gently decaying, and was lost track of, though reproductions of it were to be found all over the United States. Even Frazier (who was also the designer of the buffalo nickel) did not know where it was. In 1968 a group of wealthy westerners located it and wanted to buy it for the National Cowboy Hall of Fame in Oklahoma City. The citizens of Visalia would agree only if the purchasers would give them a full-sized reproduction of the statue in bronze. The original plaster version is now in the museum in Oklahoma City, and a bronze *End of the Trail* graces Mooney Grove Park.

The Palace of Fine Arts housed the first major international contemporary art exhibition to be held on the West Coast. There were more than 11,400 works of art, all of which were supposed to have been produced within the previous ten years. Two-thirds of the works came from the United States and included such artists as Childe Hassam, Arthur F. Matthews, John Singer Sargent, James McNeil Whistler, Gertrude Vanderbilt Whitney, and N. C. Wyeth. There was a room devoted to Edvard Munch from Norway, and the Italian futurists were shown for the first time in the United States.

Over 2,200 concerts were given at the exposition. Fritz Kreisler, Ignace Paderewski, Victor Herbert, Mme. Schumann-Heink, and the Boston Symphony performed. The aged Camille Saint-Saëns composed "Hail California" in honor of the exposition and gave three concerts in the Festival Hall. Bands, of which the most famous was John Philip Sousa's, played every day, and there were daily recitals on the giant festival organ (now in the Civic Auditorium).

Classification of exhibits at the PPIE reflected the general theme of uplift, which was so characteristic of the fair. Art headed the list, followed by Education. Third came Social Economy, which included agencies for social betterment, eugenics, hygiene, labor, cooperatives, banks, and charities. Next came Liberal Arts, which covered everything from printing to medicine, architecture, and musical instruments. It was followed by Manufactures and Varied Industries, Machinery, Transportation, Agriculture, Live Stock, Horticulture, and Mines and Metallurgy. Each had a separate exhibition building except for the livestock, which were in pens and outbuildings at the western end of the fairgrounds.

A popular exhibit was the Ford assembly line in the Palace of Transportation, which turned out eighteen Model-Ts a day. Henry Ford toured the fair with his friend, Thomas Edison, and on one occasion took a place on the assembly line. Another wonder was the first transcontinental telephone line, which had been completed on January 25, 1915. Visitors could hear readings of headlines from the New York papers and the pounding of the waves of the Atlantic Ocean. Aeroplanes (as the word was then spelled), a great attraction, made daily flights over the fairgrounds. At night flares were attached to the wings and tail of Art Smith's fragile plane as he looped the loop over the bay. Moving pictures were utilized by exhibitors at the PPIE probably to a greater extent than at any previous exposition. It is estimated that over a million feet of film was shown in sixty cinemas. Eastman Kodak displayed two-color Kodachrome photographs, and General Electric showed "The Home Electrical" with built-in vacuum cleaner outlets in each room and an electric piano. The Underwood Typewriter Company attracted attention with a working typewriter 15 feet high, 21 feet long, and weighing 14 tons. There was a full-sized coal mine that "blew up" at 2:00 P.M. each day, bringing a full rescue apparatus into play. A two-story color press was capable of producing 1,728,000 newspaper pages an hour.

The railroads played a crucial role at the PPIE. They not only brought the goods but also the people to the fair, vying with each other in providing bargain fares from the East. In the end it was the railroads and not the Panama Canal that brought prosperity to the West Coast. In addition to their extensive exhibits in the Palace of Transportation, several railroad companies build separate pavilions. Union Pacific produced a miniature Yellowstone Park with working geysers, and Santa Fe reproduced the Grand Canyon with a full-sized Hopi village, with living inhabitants.

Nearly every day witnessed special events. There were days for nations, states, and counties, for learned and not so learned associations, for Theodore Roosevelt, Luther Burbank, and Thomas Edison. The American Association for the Advancement of Science held its first Pacific Coast meetings at the fair. There were sports events such as horse racing, motor racing for the Vanderbilt cup, a golf tournament, and a dog show. Perhaps the greatest publicity stunt of the fair was the progress of the Liberty Bell from Philadelphia across the nation to San Francisco. It was greeted by bands and local dignitaries at every stop. People kissed it, threw flowers, and burst into tears. Nearly 115,000 people greeted it in the exposition grounds on July 17, 1915, when they heard Champ Clark, Speaker of the House of Representatives proclaim that he was not a jingo but that peace at any price was demoralizing and degrading. Though the United States had not yet entered the war, the military was in evidence at the fair. The army and marines paraded daily, and warships rode at anchor in front of the exposition.

The garish colors and strings of naked lights of the Joy Zone contrasted with the harmonious pastels and indirect lighting of the main fair. Dominating the zone was an effigy of a suffragette and two tin soldiers about 90 feet high. A 120-foot gilded Buddha marked the entrance of "Japan Beautiful" (which had been seen at other fairs) with its shops and tea stalls. There were an ostrich farm and an alligator farm and the usual rides. A novelty was the Aeroscope, a long metal arm terminating in a two-storied house and capable of lifting 120 people 265 feet in the air. Ethnic exhibits included villages of living Samoans, Hawaiians, Mexicans, Maoris, Egyptians, Filipinos, Japanese, and native Americans.

The most important exhibit in the zone was a working model of the Panama Canal, which covered nearly 5 acres. A moving platform of seats transported spectators around the exhibit while they held telephone receivers to their ears to hear recorded lectures on what they were seeing. The mechanism foreshadowed the famous General Motors "Futurama" at the 1939 New York World's Fair.

When the Panama Pacific International Exposition closed on December 4, 1915, there had been 18,876,438 admissions. This figure does not represent separate individuals; most people came more than once. In one way, the war had helped the exposition. Easterners who were in the habit of visiting Europe each year came to the West Coast instead. Unlike most other world's fairs, the PPIE made a profit. By August 30, 1915, two-thirds through the season, it had made enough money to pay off its mortgage. Ex-president Taft burned it publicly on a toasting fork at the exposition grounds. The exposition profits amounted to $2,401,931.

The 1915 exposition did more than just commemorate the completion of the Panama Canal. It celebrated the rebuilding of San Francisco; it asserted the importance of California and the American West; it turned American attention toward the Pacific and South America. It epitomized a whole view of American society, a view conceived in optimism and carried through despite the outbreak of World War I. It was, perhaps, the last collective outburst of this sort of naive optimism.

BIBLIOGRAPHY

The most extensive archival collection on the Panama-Pacific International Exposition is in the Bancroft Library of the University of California at Berkeley. Other important collections may be found in the History Room of the San Francisco Public Library and in the libraries of the California Historical Society and the Society of California Pioneers, both in San Francisco. These collections also contain a wealth of ephemera on the fair. A videotape, with original footage, *1915 Panama Pacific Fair*, by Burton Benedict, is available from the educational television department at the University of California at Berkeley.

The most comprehensive printed source for the PPIE is Frank Morton Todd, *The Story of the Exposition*, 5 vols. (1921), characterized by a highly readable writing style. Two short guides are Ben Macomber, *The Jewel City* (1915), and John D. Barry, *The City of Domes* (1915). Barry's book, written as a dialogue between author and reader after an introduction on the fair's background, is particularly good for the architecture of the PPIE. A contemporary tribute to the fair is Louis John Stellman, *That Was a Dream Worth Building* (1916), with a poetic text and attractive color plates of fair scenes. A more comprehensive pictorial record is *The Blue Book of the Panama Pacific International Exposition at San Francisco* (1915).

Recent analyses may be found in the essays in *The Anthropology of World's Fairs* (1983), by Burton Benedict et al. See especially the essay by George Starr, "Truth Unveiled: The Panama Pacific International Exposition and Its Interpreters." Robert W. Rydell, *All the World's a Fair* (1984), contains a chapter on the anthropological exhibits at the PPIE. For art at the exposition, see Eugen Neuhaus, *The Art of the Exposition* (1915), Rose V. S. Berry, *The Dream City: Its Art in Story and Symbolism* (1915), Juliet James, *Palaces and Courts of the Exposition* (1915), and Stella G. S. Perry, *The Sculpture and Murals of the Panama Pacific International Exposition* (1915). All of these offer critical interpretations of the works. More objective is the two-volume *Catalogue of the Department of Fine Arts* (1915), edited by John E. D. Trask and J. Nilsen Laurvik, which lists the works displayed in the Palace of Fine Arts.

Burton Benedict

SAN DIEGO 1915–1916

THE PANAMA CALIFORNIA EXPOSITION

The Panama California Exposition, presented by the little town of San Diego in 1915 and 1916, was a jewel of a fair that had a profound impact on the host community. The idea was first suggested on July 9, 1909, by banker G. Aubrey Davidson, who proposed an exposition tied to the opening of the Panama Canal. Such a fair would call to the attention of the world the fact that San Diego was the first American port of call for vessels coming through the canal.

Planning began immediately. Private contributors pledged over $1 million, and voters approved a city bond issue of an equal sum. Transportation facilities were built, and leading citizens organized the Order of the Panama to promote the fair and related matters. The town renamed City Park (where the fair would be located) Balboa Park. One complication was that San Francisco had also planned an international exposition at the opening of the canal. As a result, San Diego encountered difficulty in obtaining certification and government aid, but in time Congress did grant recognition, and a compromise was worked out whereby San Francisco would host a major world's fair and San Diego would present a more modest regional one.

Before opening day, many decisions had to be made. The first was the choice of the site for the fair within the 1,400-acre Balboa Park. Previous plans for the park had emphasized the picturesque concept of park planning with an emphasis on landscaping and few buildings. Accordingly the planning firm, the Olmsted Brothers, proposed tucking the exposition into a corner of the park. Some local business interests, however, wanted the fair located on Viscaino Mesa, a high point in the middle of the park. That would necessitate running a tram to the middle of the park to bring visitors to the exposition, and after the fair was over, it would be easy to convince the public to extend that line to serve the growing suburbs north of Balboa Park. The main real estate and railroad figures involved were acting director Joseph Sefton, Colonel D. C. Collier, a prominent local realtor, and John D. Spreckels, the most powerful businessman in San Diego and owner of the local rail system. By withholding pledges, they drove the exposition into near-bankruptcy, so the site was changed to Viscaino Mesa. The Olmsted firm resigned in protest over this move, which they believed would destroy a major natural area in the park.

Another question to be decided was the architectural style of the fair. Early planners had assumed the exposition would be in the relatively simple mission revival style, an appropriate statement for this city with its Spanish mission roots. But the nation's most prominent exponent of Spanish colonial architecture, Bertram G. Goodhue, wanted the opportunity to design an exposition in high baroque style, which he thought appropriate to the evocative Mediterranean-like atmosphere of southern California. With a clever campaign of letters and support from sympathetic architects, Goodhue won the commission, and San Diego was set to build in a high baroque Spanish-Mexican colonial style. The core of the fair was to be laid out along an avenue (called the Prado) with a central plaza, all to create the mood of a Spanish city. The other attractions were located behind the exhibit buildings to the north and south. A major part of the concept involved extensive landscaping to create a garden atmosphere. Over 2 million plants were put in before the fair opened. The overall impact of the buildings and the landscaping created a Mediterranean atmosphere, which is exactly the point San Diego wanted to make about itself.

When the city gathered just before January 1, 1915, to open the Panama California Exposition, they had before them a tightly conceived little fair in which every aspect was clearly thought out in advance, and each part related tightly to every other part. Although it can be argued that the success of the exposition was more in its buildings than in its exhibits, the exhibits were notable. The theme of the fair was the progress and the possibilities of the human race, and the starting point for presenting that was a permanent building with extensive exhibits on human evolution. The exhibits were done with considerable assistance from the Smithsonian Institution; they were the core of the exposition. Most of the other exhibits focused on matters of concern to the region. Since this was not a certified international fair, foreign governments did not have pavilions. There were, however, many foreign exhibits sponsored by private organizations and firms. Most of the exhibits showed the possibilities of the region. They included mining and flour milling, the uses of electricity, and a model farm. There were displays of many products, manufactured and agricultural. There was entertainment—Barney Oldfield raced, and there were airshows, films, music, and lectures. There was also the ubiquitous midway. At this exposition it was called the Isthmus, and it, too, followed anthropological themes. Visitors dressed in native costumes and danced the "Indian rag" or viewed a fictitious Aztec village or exhibits showing humanity in various stages: Japanese in a garden, Chinese in an underground Chinatown, Afro-Americans on a southern plantation, and Singhalese working on a tea plantation. One of the most effective exhibits, the Painted Desert, showed Southwest Indian cultures. The compact fair put a great stress on comfort, so there were various hospitality centers, ease of getting about, and a firm policy forbidding "keep off the grass" signs, so visitors would feel free to enjoy the garden atmosphere.

The exposition was successful enough the first year to keep it open through 1916. For the second year, Los Angeles provided a cash subsidy, and San Francisco sent a number of exhibits from its 1915 exposition. The exposition closed on December 31, 1916. It had been financed by private subscription, a bond issue, government grants, and exhibitor fees. Since apparently no final official report was issued, it is hard to know exactly how the fair did financially. It probably cost about $5 million to put on, and it is clear the exposition ended with a profit, although how much is not known. It was attended by 3,747,916 people.

The significance of the Panama California Exposition was extraordinary; it became one of the major factors shaping the identity of San Diego. Obviously the fair promoted the city; it brought in millions of visitors, and the publicity generated reached millions more. The exposition provided stimulation to the local economy by creating many new jobs in the construction, tourist, and related industries. The impact may have been considerable; between 1910 and 1920 San Diego doubled in population, and the world's fair must have been one factor causing that growth.

The exposition left a permanent mark on Balboa Park. Most of the baroque Spanish colonial buildings were preserved (over the objections of architect Goodhue, who saw them as mere "stage props") and are the core of Balboa Park today. A number of local institutions emerged from the fair—the San Diego Zoo and the Museum of Man, for instance. Of even greater significance was the way in which the Spanish colonial architecture fixed San Diego's hispanic past in the community. Prior to 1915 there were virtually no buildings in the town in a Hispanic or Mediterranean style. From the exposition on, hispanic architecture began to predominate. It was used in the Santa Fe Depot, the Serra Museum, Navy Hospital, Marine Corps Recruit Depot, San Diego State University, and in private structures large and small. As Oscar Cotton put it, the exposition "gave San Diego an entirely new look." Some architectural historians have suggested that Goodhue's San Diego buildings did much to popularize Spanish colonial architecture on a national basis.

This fair also affected San Diego in another way: it brought to the community many distinguished visitors, and out of the resulting contacts, the city laid the foundations for many of the features that still shape the community. To cite one example, the contacts with U.S. Marine Corps officers Joseph H. Pendleton and George Barnett, and with Assistant Secretary of the Navy Franklin Delano Roosevelt, led to the establishment of many of the navy and marine corps facilities in San Diego.

San Diego's Panama California Exposition was an unqualified success in an artistic and economic sense; it left its host city changed forever.

BIBLIOGRAPHY

Although no official report was published by the Panama California Exposition, there is a vast quantity of official material extant. The San Diego Public Library California Room holds the official architectural drawings and maps of the buildings and grounds. It also has several boxes and two open shelves of ledgers and manuscripts, including daily reports, gate receipts, maintenance, payroll, pledge cards, salvage sales, vouchers, contracts, correspondence, and even the records of the pigeon feed account. The Public Library has a clipping file and a large number of published items on the fair. The San

Diego Historical Society has three box files of published and manuscript materials, including such items as incorporation papers and bylaws, correspondence and a variety of legal papers. The society holds a number of scrapbooks, clipping files, related collections of individuals involved, oral history interviews, biographical files that contain pertinent information and a superb photograph collection. Researchers should also consult the National Anthropology Archives of the Smithsonian Institution (especially the Aleš Hrdlička Papers), and the Charles F. Lummis Papers in the Southwest Museum in Los Angeles. Scattered information can be found in published autobiographical sources by a number of San Diegans, including Oscar Cotton, *The Good Old Days* (1962); "Autobiography of Julius Wangenheim," *California Historical Society Quarterly* 36 (March 1957): 66–71; and Mary Marston, *George White Marston: A Family Chronicle*, 2 vols. (1956). There is also considerable information in the San Diego newspapers—the *Union*, *Evening Tribune*, *Daily Transcript*, and the *Sun*. A number of contemporary magazines such as *Sunset*, *Overland Monthly Magazine*, *Kingdom of the Sun*, and *West Coast Magazine* covered the exposition.

A number of secondary sources are helpful. Richard Pourade, *Gold in the Sun*, vol. 5 of *The History of San Diego* (1965), gives the general story as it unfolded, but the book is most important for its photo essay comparing the San Diego exposition buildings with the Spanish and Mexican structures upon which they were modeled. One of the best-researched articles is Gregory Montes, "Balboa Park, 1909–1911: The Rise and Fall of the Olmsted Plan," *Journal of San Diego History* 28 (Winter 1982): 46–57, which traces in detail the skullduggery that shaped many decisions about the fair. Two contemporary books are important: Carlton M. Winslow, *The Architecture and the Gardens of the San Diego Exposition* (1916), includes an introduction by exposition architect Bertram Grosvenor Goodhue and is one of the best sources for the objectives of the architect; Eugen Neuhaus, *The San Diego Garden Fair* (1916), tells about the gardens and plants. Lynn Adkins has an excellent article on one of the more distinctive exhibits, "Jesse L. Nusbaum and the Painted Desert in San Diego," *Journal of San Diego History* 29 (Spring 1983): 86–95; and Lucille Du Vall covered the local congressman's role in securing federal help in "William Kettner: San Diego's Dynamic Congressman," *Journal of San Diego History* 25 (Summer 1979): 191–207. *The Romance of Balboa Park*, 4th ed. rev. (1985) by Florence Christman is most useful for detailed descriptions of exposition buildings and features which still remain in Balboa Park. Elizabeth MacPhail, "The Order of the Panama," in San Diego Westerners' *Brand Book Number Six* (1979), explains the general concern in the community over its Hispanic past, a major theme of the Panama California Exposition. In *All The World's a Fair: Visions of Empire at American International Expositions 1876–1916* (1984), Robert W. Rydell devotes part of a chapter to the San Diego exposition. Those consulting Rydell's book on the San Diego fair should keep in mind that it was not the author's purpose to provide a balanced overview of the exposition but rather to explore racist and anthropological aspects in order to support his thesis that the world fairs of the era did not merely reflect but indeed purposely tried to shape America's racist culture. If that is kept in mind, Rydell's chapter can provide some useful insights, although it does contain some factual errors. In conclusion three helpful master's theses should be noted: Carleton M. Winslow, "The Architecture of the Panama-California Exposition, 1909–1915" (University of San Diego, 1976); Dana A. Basney, "The Role of Spreckels' Business Interests in the Development of San Diego" (San Diego State University, 1975); and Grace L. Miller, "The San Diego Progressive Movement, 1900–1920," (University of California, Santa Barbara, 1976).

Raymond Starr

NEW YORK 1918

BRONX INTERNATIONAL EXPOSITION

New York City had to wait two-thirds of a century after its Crystal Palace Exhibition for its second world's fair. Very few expositions had realized a profit approaching that of London's Crystal Palace, prompting the creator of Coney Island's Luna Park to observe in 1908 that although in essence the fairs were only shows, almost never had they been run by a showman. The Bronx International Exposition, capping a decade-long effort to create the first permanent exposition in the United States, opened in 1918, with showman Harry F. McGarvie at the helm. The "exhibition doctor" had often been summoned to tend to ailing world's fairs, as at St. Louis, where he originated the system of special events—later much copied—and achieved a complete fiscal turnaround.

Each Bronx exposition season, planned to last five months, was to feature the arts and industries of a different foreign country. The most specific models for the fair were London's ongoing Earl's Court and Shepherd's Bush, which, except for one at Lyons, France, had been the only other permanent world's fairs. The site, leased from William Waldorf Astor, was at the borough's geographic center, served by excellent mass transit, and was in the path of a huge population wave. Although backers expected gain from a financial ripple effect, as with all prior international fairs, the chief motivation was the sale of goods, particularly those of exhibitors at the recent expositions at San Francisco and San Diego, many of whom were unable to return to their native lands due to World War I.

It was envisioned that the devastated European nations would turn to the United States for postwar rebuilding—primarily to New York City, its greatest port—and that Latin American trade would grow. South American countries indeed indicated considerable interest in the Bronx exposition. Following a tradition dating back to 1867 of using fairs for international public relations, Brazil and Japan requested entire buildings. The unity of Kenneth M. Murchison's Spanish colonial design echoed a trend initiated at San Francisco and San Diego, and an American practice of close collaboration between architects and sculptors emanating from the Buffalo fair was carried forward. Paintings and formally exhibited sculpture at the exposition were shown to great advantage in small galleries, countering a trend toward increasingly poor art displays at U.S. world's fairs. Due to the war's limitation on cultural exchange, art from other countries, a tradition since the Paris Universal Exposition of 1855, was not displayed. The Holland No. 9, one of the first practical submarines, whose inventor John P. Holland was hailed nationwide as the outstanding mechanical genius of his age, was a popular exhibit located near the main entrance.

The key element influencing exposition attractions was the global conflict, which the United States entered two months before the originally scheduled opening day. Energies required for the war effort caused the fair's start to be delayed a full year and brought about the cancellation of the vast majority of national and international exposition plans. Many major exhibits, such as the U.S. navy cyclorama and a reproduction of a European battlefield, were military related.

Ten major exhibition halls were planned, but only one was completed, diminishing the serious nature of the exposition. Bicycle races were symbolic of the ventures' overwhelmingly recreational character even before the fighting ceased.

Phenomena such as immigration restriction, the red scare, and the death of the fair's bid for congressional backing showed the period to be not remotely as internationalist in outlook as in the very recent past. Given the financial strain, the wariness with which many viewed foreign competition, and the envy many felt about potential New York gain, financial support collapsed, and the exhibition component was not revived after the hostilities ended. Speaking to the American people's deferred needs for a more pleasurable existence and guided by men with midway experience of enormous depth, the amusement component prospered, as had exposition midways since their inception a quarter-century before. Thus, the venture lived on as the Bronx's largest amusement park, Starlight Park, a survivor of grand plans and turbulent times.

Although capture of trade opened up by global conflict had been a prime reason for the Bronx International Exposition's creation, the same conflict was ultimately the prime reason for its demise.

BIBLIOGRAPHY

The complete story of the Bronx International Exposition is recounted in Ronald O. Roth, *Starlight in the Bronx: A Forgotten World's Fair and a Mirror of Urban Recreation, 1918–1946* (sponsored by The Bronx Historical Society; forthcoming).

Congress heard testimony on the Bronx fair in early 1918, and the hearings contain a good deal of factual information on the fair organizers, the international situation in which the fair tried to exist, and the economic and geographic rationales for the fair. See U.S. House of Representatives, Committee on Industrial Arts and Expositions, "Hearings on Bronx International Exposition, January 25, 1918" (1918). Articles regarding early planning for a permanent fair in New York City may be found in the *New York Times*, March 18, 1907, October 28, 1910. More specific planning for the Bronx fair is described in *Billboard*, July 29, 1916, May 19 and December 22, 1917; *Interborough Bulletin* 8 (April 1918): 5; and *New York American*, May 12, 1918.

The one-year delay in the fair's opening is discussed in *Interborough Bulletin* 7 (July 1917): 33; *Billboard*, May 19, 1917; and *New York Sun*, May 27, 1917. The attractions at the fair are recounted in *Nation*, October 5, 1918, 380–81. On the scaling down of exposition attractions and the increased recreational character, see *North Side News*, August 4, 1918.

Ronald O. Roth

RIO DE JANEIRO 1922–1923
EXPOSIÇAO INTERNACIONAL DO CENTENARIO DO BRASIL

One of the very few international expositions to have been held in South America, the Brazilian Centennial Exposition was a celebration of that country's independence, following a theme of other expositions, most notably the Centennial Exposition in Philadelphia in 1876. On September 7, 1822, the prince regent, soon to be Dom Pedro I, emperor of Brazil, proclaimed the independence of the country. In honor of this occasion, the Brazilian congress on November 11, 1921, authorized a national exhibition that would celebrate the one hundredth anniversary of Brazilian independence. Soon, however, plans changed; as the official guide noted, "The Government was compelled by the interests of several friendly nations to transform the simple national celebration into a great international affair."

The exposition was held in Rio de Janeiro at a 62-acre site along the bay shore. Commissioner General Carlos Sampaio did the site planning, dividing the grounds into two sections, national and foreign.

In the national section were the halls that exhibited the many products of Brazil. The largest of these was the Palace of Industries, in what had been an old arsenal. The structure was completely renovated according to plans drawn up by A. Memoria and F. Cuchet. Several buildings, constructed expressly for the fair, featured the Brazilian colonial baroque style; these included the Crystal Restaurant and the Agriculture and Transportation Palace, both designed by Morales de los Rios Filho. Other buildings in the national section were the Pavilion of Hunting and Fishing, the Palace of Minor Industries, the Administration Building, the Pavilion of Statistics, the Pavilion of States, and the Festival Palace.

The foreign pavilions were located along the Avenue of Nations. Participating nations included Argentina, the United States, Japan, France, Great Britain, Italy, Denmark, Mexico, Czechoslovakia, Norway, Belgium, Sweden, and Portugal.

The U.S. Congress appropriated $1 million for its building and exhibits. Designed by Frank L. Packard, the pavilion did not open until December 23, 1922, more than three months late, due to construction delays. Various government departments sent displays. The War Department showed off military uniforms, weapons, and models of ships. The Department of Agriculture exhibited crop samples and models of farms. Following the fair, the pavilion was transformed into a new U.S. embassy.

Japan, as it had in past expositions, built its pavilion in the style of an ancient pagoda. Inside were fine exhibits of silk, porcelain, and handcrafted objects.

The French pavilion was a replica of the Petit Trianon of Versailles. After the fair, it was donated to the Brazilian Academy of Letters, and it still stands today. The Argentine pavilion, which opened over two months late, featured exhibits related to cattle raising, agriculture, petroleum, and manufactured products.

The exposition opened September 7, 1922, with a ceremony at the Festival Palace attended by President João Pessoa and other Brazilian officials, foreign dignitaries, and the press. Although the fair was originally scheduled to last only a month, its size and international component dictated a longer duration, and it did not close until July 31, 1923. Over the eleven months, some 3,626,402 visitors attended. Contemporary legacies of the exposition include the Palace of Industries, which has become the National Historic Museum, the Palace of Hunting and Fishing, now the Captainship of Ports, and the Pavilion of States, currently the Image and Sound Museum.

BIBLIOGRAPHY

The records of the U.S. commission to the Brazilian Centennial Exposition are housed in the National Archives, Record Group 43. These include general records, administrative correspondence, records of the director of exhibits, and the final report of the commissioner general. The exposition was well covered in the *New York Times* (see issues of August 21 and 27, September 24, and December 25, 1922, and March 25 and August 13, 1923) and the *Times* of London (see issues of July 29, August 26, and September 2, 5–9, 1922, and April 11, June 25, and November 10, 1923). Annie S. Peck, "The International Exposition of Brazil," *Current History Magazine [New York Times]* 17 (March 1923): 1043–49, provides a comprehensive view of the fair, while J. P. Curtis, "Notes on the Brazilian Centenary Exposition," *Hispanic American Historical Review* 5 (August 1922): 503–15, and several articles in the May 1922 issue of the *Bulletin of the Pan American Union* are useful, and relatively accessible, sources. One source in Italian is F. Blanco, "La celebrazione del centenario brasiliano," *Nuova Antologia*, August 16, 1922, 348–56. For the architecture of the exposition, see J. P. Curtis, "Architecture of the Brazil Centennial Exposition," *Art and Architecture* 16 (September 1923): 94–104.

Michael L. Gregory

WEMBLEY 1924–1925
BRITISH EMPIRE EXHIBITION

The idea of a British Empire Exhibition had first been mooted by the British Empire League in 1902. In the late nineteenth century, the British concentrated on empire as the principal theme of their exhibitions, starting with the Colonial and Indian Exhibition of 1886. In the 1890s and the Edwardian period, a series of imperial and "diplomatic" exhibitions was mounted on a private enterprise basis by Imre Kiralfy at Olympia and later at the White City in London. These included the Empire of India (1895), Greater Britain (1899), Franco-British (1908), Japan-British (1910), and the Coronation (1911). In 1911, a rival Festival of Empire exhibition at the Crystal Palace also stressed the imperial theme. In 1913, the Canadian high commissioner, Lord Strathcona, who had been associated with Kiralfy's projects, revived the idea of an officially sanctioned empire exhibition.

The scheme was held up by World War I, but in 1919 it was resurrected at a meeting of the British Empire Club. The prince of Wales (later Edward VIII) became president of the general committee, and the government of David Lloyd George gave the project official recognition. It had now developed a new significance: to restore national and imperial confidence after the war and to proclaim the economic importance of empire in what was to be a period of recurrent crisis in the international economy. This was emphasized by the fact that only territories of the British empire were invited to participate. By 1921, the financial guarantees (totaling £2.2 million, roughly half from the British government) were in place, and a site had been chosen at Wembley in North London. The Metropolitan Railway had reached Wembley in the 1880s, and a developer, Sir Edward Watkin, had planned a great pleasure park and tower there. Only the base of the tower was constructed, however, and it was subsequently dismantled. The Wembley Urban District Council wanted to turn the area into a peaceful garden suburb of high quality. They therefore opposed the siting of the exhibition, but in 1921, a 216-acre site was purchased at a cost of £100,000. In the same year, the prince of Wales announced to dominion prime ministers attending an imperial conference in London that a "great national sports ground" was to be constructed on the exhibition site and would open with the Football Association Cup Final in 1923. Thus Britain's national sport with the widest working-class following would draw the public's attention to Wembley and its exhibition.

The exhibition had been planned to open in 1923, but more time was needed, and it was not completed until 1924. The architects were Sir John W. Simpson and Maxwell Ayrton, the consulting engineer was Sir E. O. Williams, and the contractors were Robert McAlpine and Sons. The buildings at Kiralfy's exhibitions had often been orientalist in style and of a temporary construction. The buildings at Wembley, on the other hand, were generally classical, except for those that merited a more localized style (like the pavilions of Burma and Ceylon) and were built of ferro-concrete on a framework of steel. Wembley thus marked the transfer on a grand scale of ferro-concrete techniques from the United States to Britain. Even lampposts, flagpoles, drinking fountains, bridges, entrances, and the lion symbols were in concrete.

The plan of the site was pyramidal in shape. A garden was placed at its apex to the north, with the largest buildings, including the Palaces of Industries, Engineering, and Arts, together with a mock-up of a coal mine, below. Lakes and gardens separated these from the southern half of the site. The most important territories of the empire—Australia, Canada, New Zealand, and India—had pavilions facing these lakes, with Malaya and Burma occupying adjacent sites. The stadium and the pavilions of smaller colonies occupied the base of the pyramid. These included Bermuda, Gold Coast, Sierra Leone, Nigeria, Palestine and Cyprus, East Africa, Malta, Ceylon, Hong Kong, West Indies, British Guiana, and on the fringe (symbolically as subsequent history was to prove), South Africa. The British government building, together with those of New-foundland and Fiji, occupied an eastern area adjacent to a large bandstand and the horticultural exhibits, with the amusement park behind them.

The exhibition was opened on April 23, St. George's Day, by King George V and remained open until November 1. During this period, there were 17,403,267 visitors. The exhibition reopened between May 9 and October 31, 1925, and received 9,699,231 visitors, for a total of 27,102,498 over the two years. In addition to the exhibition buildings, which stressed the industrial might of Britain and its dependence on the markets and raw materials of the empire, visitors enjoyed a wide range of rides and other features at the 40-acre amusement park. Bands from all over the empire performed at five different bandstands, one of which could accommodate 10,000 people. There were elaborate celebrations of Empire Day on May 24, a rodeo in the stadium during June and July, and in late July and August a massive Pageant of Empire illustrating its historical origins and development, involving 15,000 human performers and many animals. Audiences of 50,000 to 60,000 enjoyed this spectacle. There was a scout jamboree, a colonial boxing tournament, and a Searchlight Tattoo that was so popular its run was extended.

Like many of the other British exhibitions, Wembley had little significance for the development of design and the fine arts. It introduced concrete as a building form, but many would now see this as a baleful influence. The fair was perhaps more important in the history of advertising. Joseph Emberton designed a series of more than thirty kiosks that were described as "three-dimensional posters," intended to convey an impression of the products they advertised. The splendors of the empire and the economic, cultural, and ethnic messages of Wembley were conveyed to a wider public through an intense publicity campaign. There were enormous sales of ephemera, novelties, souvenirs, sheet music, and records, as well as stamps and other philatelic items.

A few famous names were involved. Rudyard Kipling named all the roads at the exhibition. The architect of New Delhi, Sir Edwin Luytens, designed the Queen's Doll House, which featured the miniaturized work of sculptors, artists, decorators, and craftsmen. Other notable features included a replica of the recently discovered tomb of the Egyptian king Tutankhamen. The opening ceremony, including the king's speech, was broadcast by the BBC, marking the first time the monarch's voice was heard on the radio.

The exhibition's financial loss over the two years amounted to £1,581,905. Some of this sum was covered by public donations. Many of the buildings were sold and moved to other sites, and others were demolished. Large quantities of concrete were converted into hard core for road construction, and thousands of tons of steel were salvaged. A few of the buildings remain, but only the stadium continues to be used for its original purpose.

The exhibition served to renew and perpetuate the importance of empire to the British in the interwar years. The empire continued to be seen as a panacea for economic ills, and the message of the imperial preference system, or zollverein, which was a prime ideological objective of Wembley, was developed through the Empire Marketing Board (1926–1933) and the Ottawa agreements of 1932 and resurfaced at the Glasgow Empire Exhibition of 1938.

BIBLIOGRAPHY

The most convenient route into the study of the Wembley exhibition, as with many other exhibitions, is through its ephemera. In addition to the extensive official guide, a large number of programs and guides were issued for many of its features and displays. Collections are found in the Library of the Royal Commonwealth Society and the Grange Museum in North London. The former also contains many of the special issues of newspapers (for example, there were exhibition supplements to the *Times* on April 23, May 24, July 29, and September 30), while the latter has sheet music, novelties, and commemorative items. Large quantities of newsreel and other film footage have been deposited in the National Film Archive, London.

The organization of the exhibition involved a great deal of intergovernmental communication, and files relating to these negotiations can be found in the records of the Colonial Office, the Dominions department (after 1925, the Dominions Office), and the India Office deposited in the Public Record Office and the Indian Office Library and Records in London. Various studies of empire were associated with Wembley and were published in Hugh Gunn, ed., *The British Empire*, 12 vols. (1924), and E. C. Martin, *The Place of Imperial Studies in Education* (1924).

Among secondary sources, John Allwood, *The Great Exhibitions* (1977), offers a useful starting point. Donald Knight, *The Lion Roars at Wembley* (1984), is a valuable compendium of facts and figures gleaned from guides and contemporary unofficial sources. John M. MacKenzie, *Propaganda and Empire* (1984), examines the propagandistic and ethnic significance of Wembley, and Paul Greenhalgh, *Ephemeral Vistas* (1988), is especially concerned with its cultural and artistic importance. F. A. Fletcher and A. D. Brooks, *British Exhibitions and Their Postcards*, pt. II (1979), is useful for ephemera. Kenneth Walthew, "The British Empire Exhibition," *History Today* 31 (August 1981):

34–39 offers a summary of the history of the exhibition but lacks any pretense at interpretation or recognition that the exhibition continued in 1925. Local publications include
Geoffrey Hewlett, *A History of Wembley* (1979), and *The British Empire Exhibition*
(1974). For the economic and popular cultural context, see, respectively, Stephen Con-
stantine, *The Making of British Colonial Development Policy, 1914–40* (1984), and John
M. MacKenzie, ed., *Imperialism and Popular Culture* (1986).

John M. MacKenzie

PARIS 1925

EXPOSITION INTERNATIONALE DES ARTS DECORATIFS ET INDUSTRIELS MODERNES

At the 1925 Paris Exposition internationale des arts decoratifs et industriels modernes, art deco emerged as a popular international mode. The movement had begun some twenty years before as an exclusive avant-garde style. In the 1920s, largely due to its exposure at the 1925 Paris fair, art deco developed into a broad, comprehensive trend encompassing not only the decorative arts but fine art and fashion as well. It had become a veritable life-style.

At the heart of the 1925 Exposition internationale was the goal of promoting understanding and harmony between art and industry. Although this suggests a unity of spirit between artist and craftsperson, in reality there were few joint ventures. The government originally planned to hold the fair in 1914; however, various delays and World War I brought several postponements, and it was not until 1921 that funds were voted for the exhibition.

The planners of the fair intended to reestablish France's position as the premier arbiter of taste and style in the industrial and decorative arts in the aftermath of the war. Excluded from display were all reproductions and copies. Articles and exhibits were to display originality, fulfill a practical need, and be expressive of modern inspiration.

Despite this intent, the fair was more a celebration of fine, traditional craftsmanship. Two structures, Le Corbusier's Pavillon de l'esprit nouveau and Konstantin Melnikov's Russian pavilion, were the only signals of the emerging modernist movement, and Le Corbusier's modernist work was so scorned that the fair managers hid it behind a 20-foot fence. Objects of practicality, function, and logic basic to that style were largely absent. Most of the displays at the exposition were demonstrative of bravura and virtuosity in decoration and manufacture.

Although broadly interpreted by individual designers, art deco was a unifying thread among the work of many of France's decorative artists during the interwar years. The style seems to have had two stages. Initially, floral and neoclassical motifs, perhaps influenced by art nouveau, were characteristic. These motifs became increasingly geometric, angular, and streamlined, borrowing from cubism, French colonial art, and Egyptian culture. (Tutankhamen's tomb was discovered in 1923.) It has been said that the best of French art deco was always expensive, making use of exotic woods and expensive materials.

There was another type of French art deco, however, and this catered to the average consumer. The availability of quality design using affordable material was a concern of the established French department stores, such as the Galeries LaFayette, Bon Marche, and the Printemps. Interior designers, often employed by these stores, created the syntax of art deco. They had considerable influence with society's new rich, who emerged after the war and sought a distinctive style to show off their wealth.

The Société des artistes decorateurs was instrumental in promoting and setting up the exhibition. Lucien Dior, minister of commerce, persuaded the city of Paris to donate 3 million francs and 72 acres of land to the exposition. The site was located in the center of the city and utilized some existing buildings, including the Grand Palais and the Petit Palais, structures bequeathed to the city by the 1900 exposition. Other temporary structures and pavilions lined both the Right and Left Banks of the Seine, and rows of shops were built across the pont Alexander III forming a Venetian-like archway. The exhibition continued along the esplanade des Invalides, finally spreading out beneath the army hospital and church built by Louis XIV.

The chief architect for the fair was Charles Plumet, who was charged with creating a temporary fairyland. Louis Bonnier was in charge of landscaping. Because of the central site, no permanent buildings could be erected, and architects were able to give free rein to their creative fancies. Everything was designed to dazzle the viewer. Historian and designer Marjorie Townley has commented that "the exhibition stood within the heart of Paris when Paris was the heart of the world." Indeed, this central location proved to be an advantage for the fair in that it was accessible from all over the city. From the time the exposition was opened to the general public on April 30 until its gates were closed on October 15, some 14 million visitors had attended.

The grand gate of honor (porte d'Honneur), designed to receive distinguished guests, was one of fifteen entrance sites. Designed by André Ventre and Henri Favier, it was located between the Grand and Petit Palais, just north of the pont Alexander III. Neon-lit crystal caps crowning four pairs of fluted cast-metal columns were intended to represent stylized fountains. Each pair of columns was staggered back and connected to the next gate by an open decorative grille designed by Edgar Brandt and continuing the fountain motif. These staggered entrances meant that six separate lines of access were available at all times so as to eliminate unnecessary queueing. The porte de la Concorde, designed by Louis Patout, took the form of large, circular concrete pylons. Inside was a single statue, *Paris*, created by the sculptor Dejean, making a gesture of welcome. When seen by floodlight, this entrance was highly dramatic in its impact.

For many visitors, however, the most striking entrance was the porte d'Orsay, designed by Louis-Hippolyte Boileau. This art deco steel form acted as a large frame for a mural. This was semiabstract in conception and consisted of figures and objects labeled "The Book," "Furniture," "Ceramics," "Sculpture," "Architecture," and, most prominent, "Fashion." This was a highly symbolic panel, portraying the implied unity of fine and applied arts at the 1925 exposition.

The Grand Palais was the official center of ceremonies and receptions. It housed various displays of French and foreign industrial arts—ground level for the former and upper level for the latter. Different areas of the building were assigned to designers and architects to create a variety of appropriate settings, under the overall control of Charles Letrosne. The regulations of the fair prohibited the display of raw materials; however, section designers were ingenious in devising methods to bring these into their exhibits. Every aspect of design and material was showcased, from metal, glass, and ceramics to textiles, hairdressing, embroidery, lacquerwork, leatherwork, and printing.

The foreign pavilions, located along the cours la Reime on the Right Bank, were demonstrative of great cultural diversity. Just past the handsome Pavillon du Tourism, a multifaceted information center, were four sites flanking the central road between the porte d'Honneur and the pont Alexander III. These sites were assigned to Italy, Great Britain, Belgium, and Japan. Interestingly, the choice Japanese location was originally intended for the United States. This country did not respond to France's invitation on the unusual pretext that no modern art had been produced and therefore there was nothing original to exhibit. One might remember that the modern American skyscraper had been influencing world architecture for more than a decade.

In view of this, the absence of participation on the part of the United States seems strange indeed. The Italian pavilion combined ancient Roman and modern architecture in a style intended to glorify the new spirit of fascism. The Swiss edifice reflected a traditional style with its projecting tile roof. The pavilion from Holland fused elements of that flat country, its seafaring people, and its foggy climate in a highly creative manner. Scandinavian mythology and the eventful history of Denmark were suggested in a square edifice of gray and red brick. The red and gold Czechoslovakian structure bore an athletic statue at its entrance representative of a culture full of vitality. Other participating countries were Poland, Austria, Greece, Turkey, China, Luxembourg, Latvia, Finland, and Yugoslavia. Germany was not invited to participate.

The pavilions representing French cities and provinces were familiar in style in that they tended to perpetuate local architecture. The French sections were located along the esplanade des Invalides on the Left Bank of the Seine. This area was the cours des Métiers ("Avenue of Trades"). In addition to domestic pavilions from such regions as Brittany, Alsace, and Normandy, there were kiosks and displays representing many manufactories such as Sèvres and Copenhagen porcelain, creative glass design by René Lalique, Fauguez and the Baccarat glass works, jewelry and metal work by the Orfeveries, and Gobelin tapestries and silk from the Lyons manufacturers. Much excitement was elicited by Madagascar laces and Indochinese tapestries. Along the Esplanade were four lofty towers that served as centers for gastronomic treats and wines representing various parts of France and illustrating their importance in everyday French life.

Included along the cours des Métiers were fairgrounds, a stained glass pavilion, a toy village built to entertain children, crafts shops and galleries, a theater, a library, Sue et Mare's Museum of Contemporary Arts, the diamond dealer's pavilion, and several pavilions representing the work of individual artists, such as that of the sculptor Joseph Bernard.

A number of these pavilions were highly demonstrative of the luxury and finesse of French art deco. Jacque-Emile Ruhlmann designed a remarkable Grand Salon for the Pavillon d'un Collectionneur. In this lofty circular room lit by a grand chandelier with cascading glass beads were furniture and decoration epitomizing art deco and affordable by only the very rich. Similarly, André Groualt's sumptuous and sensual "Lady's Bedroom," designed for the Pavillon d'un Ambassadeur, was without peer as an influence in the development of art deco as a luxury style.

With the sum of a million francs, promised by Paul Leon, director of the beaux-arts and assistant commissioner general for the exhibition, the Société des artistes decorateurs furnished and decorated the exhibition rooms around the Crafts Courtyard into a prototype for a French embassy. This structure was located at the end of the cours des Métiers at the place des Invalides. Artists and decorators were invited to submit projects for the twenty-four rooms, vestibules, and passageways. Each designer was able to choose collaborators to supply items of decoration necessary to complete each environment, such as wallpapers, rugs, sculpture or pottery, fabrics, and light fixtures. One wing was devoted to the official side of the embassy, the other to the private side with bedrooms, a bathroom, a gymnasium, and a music room. A list of the architects, artists, and craftspeople participating in this project was practically a complete roster of art deco designers working in Paris at this time.

The influence of this exhibition and the art deco style was enormous, not just in Paris but throughout the rest of the world as well. Its impact was felt in the United States for the next twenty years as architects and designers adhered to its particular idiosyncrasies. If one aim of the organizers of the exposition was to show that a modern decorative style could be formed without relying on the traditions of the past, then they achieved their goal, and modern decorative design was launched.

BIBLIOGRAPHY

The most comprehensive printed source on this exposition is *Encyclopédie des arts décoratifs et industriels modernes au XXeme siecle en douze volumes* (1928), also published as *Exposition internationale des arts décoratifs et industriels modernes, 1925. Rapport général: section artistique et technique.* This is a spectacular and detailed coverage of all aspects of art and architecture at the Paris 1925 fair, in twelve volumes, with hundreds of heliotype and color plates and ample description. Another primary source is a publication of the Editorial Committee of the Department of Overseas Trade of Great Britain, *Reports on the Present Position and Tendencies of the Industrial Arts . . .* (1927), which relates the exhibits at the Paris fair to the present position, tendencies, and influences of similar art forms in the major countries of the world.

A number of contemporary visitors' accounts exist. William Scheifley and A. E.

DuGord, "Paris Exposition of Decorative Arts," *Current History* 23 (December 1925): 354–62, and Elbert Francis Baldwin, "The Paris Decorative Arts Exhibition," *Outlook*, July 29, 1925, 454–56, provide valuable background information on the fair and colorful descriptions of the foreign and domestic pavilions, while W. Francklyn Paris, "The International Exposition of Modern Industrial and Decorative Art in Paris," *Architectural Record* 58 (September and October 1925): 265–77, 365–85, contains detailed descriptions of the displays and structures, as well as many fine photographs. Frank Scarlett and Marjorie Townley, *Arts Décoratifs 1925: A Personal Recollection of the Paris Exhibition* (1975), written to commemorate the fair's fiftieth anniversary, contains information on the background of the fair, the British antecedents of art deco, the French, British, and other foreign sections of the fair, and Le Corbusier's "Le Pavillon de l'Esprit Nouveau," as well as the aftermath of the art deco movement.

For the development of the art deco movement, see Dan Klein and Margaret Bishop, *Decorative Art, 1880–1980* (1986), and Stephen Bayley et al., *Twentieth Century Style and Design* (1980). Both books also focus on the work of individual artists whose creative design figured prominently in Paris in 1925.

Two recent works reflect continuing scholarly interest in this fair. Victor Arwas's chapter on the Paris fair in his *Art Deco* (1980) provides a comprehensive overview of the fair, replete with illustrations and a site plan. Arthur Chandler, "Where Art Deco Was Born," *World's Fair* 9, no. 1 (January–March 1989): 1–7, surveys the exhibition and draws some interesting contrasts between the Left Bank and Right Bank neighborhoods in the vicinity of the fair.

Susan M. Matthias

DUNEDIN 1925–1926

NEW ZEALAND AND SOUTH SEAS INTERNATIONAL EXHIBITION

When, in 1923, Edward Anscombe suggested staging an exhibition "which would eclipse anything previously held in New Zealand, and which would be a symbol of New Zealand's spirit," he found a receptive audience in Dunedin's business and civic leaders. New Zealand had emerged from World War I with a strong sense of pride and patriotism. In the southern province of Otago (of which Dunedin was the capital), this was tempered by concern at the region's loss of population to the rapidly expanding northern cities. Dunedin remained the manufacturing center of the dominion, and its leaders hoped that an exhibition would refocus attention on the south.

By mid–1923 an exhibition company had been formed. After some debate, the committee agreed to drain Lake Logan, a tidal estuary only 2 miles from the city center. This provided the exhibition a sheltered 65-acre site and created land for future development in the Dunedin foreshore reclamation program. The site was ready for development in December 1924.

Anscombe drew up the plans for seven wooden pavilions, an Art Gallery, Amusement Avenue, and several smaller structures. Construction was completed in July 1925. The centerpiece of the layout was the Festival Hall, with its eye-catching domed roof rising to a height of 100 feet.

The exhibition opened before a crowd of over 45,000 on November 17, 1925. Twenty-six nations were represented, the largest exhibitors aside from the hosts being Great Britain, the United States, and Canada. The exhibits ranged from ancient coins and relics to the latest in aircraft, cars, and locomotives.

The arrangement of the displays reflected New Zealand's position as a proud member of the British empire. British exhibits received pride of place, with other sections set aside for Otago, other New Zealand provinces, British colonial nations, the New Zealand government, New Zealand secondary industries, motor vehicles, education, and general exhibits.

Two focuses of public interest throughout the six-month exhibition were the Amusement Arcade and the Argyll and Sutherland Highlanders' Band. Brought especially from Scotland, the band was welcomed enthusiastically by a city proud of its dominant Scottish heritage. Equally well supported, the Amusement Arcade featured seven large imported devices together with sixty-three private sideshows. Over 2 million tickets were sold for rides on the main attractions. Other popular features included a cabaret and a radio station.

Crowds from throughout New Zealand flocked to the exhibition, generating prosperity and prestige for the city of Dunedin. The growing northern cities of Auckland, Wellington, and Christchurch looked on with envy. Overall attendance was 3,200,498—a remarkable figure for a city of 85,000 in a geographically isolated country of fewer than 1.5 million. The highest daily attendance of just over 83,000 was recorded at the closing ceremony on May 1, 1926.

Financially the exhibition was a success, with a dividend being paid to original shareholders. Business in Dunedin flourished during the exhibition. Otago hoteliers reported record bookings. Profits from a tram service to the exhibition paid for a new town hall.

With the exception of the Art Gallery, the exhibition buildings were temporary. After their demolition, the site was developed as a sports ground.

The 1925–1926 exhibition was the largest and most successful ever staged in New Zealand, but if observers had seriously believed it would reverse Dunedin's decline, they were disappointed. The revival was brief, and population drift north continued, particularly with the onset of the Great Depression in the 1930s.

BIBLIOGRAPHY

Records of the exhibition company along with other relevant archival material are housed in the Hocken Library of the University of Otago, Dunedin. Official publications include G. E. Thompson, *Official Record of the New Zealand and South Seas International Exhibition* (1926), and Leo Fanning, *The Pictorial History of the New Zealand and South Seas International Exhibition* (1929).

The exhibition was covered in all major New Zealand newspapers, but the most comprehensive articles are found in the *Otago Daily Times* and *Evening Star*. Both the Hocken Library and the Dunedin Public Library contain files of these newspapers, and the Hocken Library additionally has three books of clippings on the fair and a file containing "exhibition special" newspapers.

Among secondary works, the most useful is Miriam Smith's thesis, "The History of New Zealand Exhibitions with Particular Reference to the New Zealand and South Seas International Exhibition, 1925–1926" (Auckland University, 1974), available at the Hocken and the Auckland University libraries. Another work of interest is *The Inside History of the Exhibition* (1929), in which Edward Anscombe, the author and exhibition architect, reveals the shortcomings of the organizers.

David Thomson

PHILADELPHIA 1926
SESQUI-CENTENNIAL INTERNATIONAL EXPOSITION

Philadelphia's Sesqui-centennial International Exposition of 1926 was widely regarded as a flop, especially when compared with the city's dazzling Centennial Exposition a half-century earlier. Planning got off to a late start; most of its buildings remained incomplete until well after opening day; the Philadelphia city government spent millions of dollars to bail out the bankrupt Sesqui-centennial Exhibition Association after the exposition closed its gates, and it rained 107 of the 184 days the exposition was open. Critics of proposed international expositions in Chicago and New York City in the 1930s cited the Philadelphia experience as proof that the day of the giant world's fair had ended.

Yet another look at the Sesqui-centennial International Exposition reveals many innovations—the use of talking motion pictures, public address systems, colored lighting, radio advertising—that contributed to the success of subsequent world's fairs. And while the exposition did little to influence the nation's concept of its future in the manner of the international expositions in Chicago in 1933–1934 and New York City in 1939–1940, it did much to shape the nation's concept of its past.

The shadow of the 1876 Centennial fell on the Sesqui-centennial Exposition from its inception in 1916, when John Wanamaker, a member of the Finance Committee in 1876, proposed that the city stage an international exposition to commemorate the 150th anniversary of the signing of the Declaration of Independence. Serious planning did not get underway until 1921, with the formation of the Sesqui-centennial Exposition (later Exhibition) Association. The association's appeals to the federal government for $20 million and to the Pennsylvania state government for $2.5 million were ignored, despite President Warren G. Harding's message to Congress in 1922 endorsing the exposition idea. In the end, the state and federal government provided approximately $1 million and $2 million, respectively, barely enough to cover the cost of their own buildings at the exposition.

Most of the money for the exposition came from the city government. In 1924, Mayor W. Freeland Kendrick assumed the presidency of the Exposition Association, and the following year the Philadelphia City Council voted to back the exposition with a $5 million guarantee fund. Few expected that the exposition would use it all, but by the time the Sesqui-centennial Exhibition Association closed its books in 1929, the city had made seven appropriations to the exposition totaling nearly twice that amount—$9.7 million—much of it used to reimburse the association's numerous creditors.

The city also provided an estimated $5 million worth of services to the exposition, the bulk of it from the Department of Public Works, which prepared the exposition grounds for visitors. The association considered fourteen different sites for the exposition, including the site of the 1876 Centennial in Fairmount Park, before deciding on 1,000 acres adjacent to the League Avenue Navy Yard in South Philadelphia. This site had the advantage of already being largely owned by the city—but the disadvantage of being swampland. Transforming the South Philadelphia marsh into level fairgrounds required dumping several million cubic yards of fill, in places 20 feet deep. The spongy soil conditions also dictated that the foundations of the exposition buildings be placed on pilings sunk deep into the ground.

Because of the late start, the enormous task of site preparation, and the exposition's uncertain funding, businesses and state and foreign governments were slow to purchase exhibit space, and consequently buildings were slow to rise on the fairgrounds. The exposition's first director general, David Collier, a veteran of the 1915 Panama California Exposition in San Diego, quit seven months before opening day when it became clear that his elaborate plans for the fair could not be realized. His successors reduced the number of exhibit halls from five to three, combining categories that had been displayed in separate buildings at other fairs. The three principal exhibit halls were the Palace of Liberal Arts and Manufactures, Palace of Agriculture and Foreign Exhibits, and Palace of U.S. Government, Machinery, and Transportation, the last not completed until July 20, nearly two months after the exposition opened to the public. Several smaller buildings, the Palace of Education and Social Economy and Palace of Fine Arts, also opened well after the rest of the exposition. Only seven buildings came from foreign nations, while six came from states. Other exposition structures included an auditorium, in which the American Kennel Club organized the first dog show in its history; administration buildings; amusement concessions in the Glad Zone; and a gaudy 80-foot high, 80-ton Liberty Bell outlined in 26,000 electric lights. A 100,000-seat Municipal Stadium built for the exposition hosted extravaganzas such as the $1.7 million heavyweight championship fight in which Gene Tunney dethroned Jack Dempsey. Renamed John F. Kennedy Stadium, it has remained in use for special events such as the Live Aid benefit concert for African famine relief in 1985.

Exposition planners declared that the multicolored stucco and rounded edges of the fair's official buildings struck a contemporary look, suggesting neither a particular historical style, such as beaux arts, nor the ultramodern. But the most influential architectural style at the exposition was a historical one, that of colonial revival. New York State reproduced two colonial buildings on the fairgrounds— replicas of Washington's headquarters in Newburgh and of Federal Hall in New York City where Washington was sworn in as president. Ohio erected a replica of William Henry Harrison's home and the National Society of Colonial Dames of America a replica of Sulgrave Manor, ancestral home of the Washington family in England. The Philadelphia YWCA built a replica of Mount Vernon on the exposition grounds as headquarters for its visitor services. Even the Jell-

O Company dispensed samples of its quivering product in a replica colonial cottage within the Palace of Agriculture and Foreign Exhibits.

Far and away the most extensive exercise in colonial revival architecture at the exposition was High Street, a collection of twenty homes along a replicated colonial Philadelphia street. Organized by the Women's Committee with a grant of $200,000 from the Exhibition Association, the exteriors were built in collaboration with the Philadelphia chapter of the American Institute of Architects and architectural historian Fiske Kimball, the new director of the Pennsylvania Museum (renamed the Philadelphia Museum of Art). Responsibility for furnishing the interior of each building went to a different women's organization, such as the National League of Women Voters and the Daughters of the American Revolution. Sponsoring organizations also staffed their houses with members in period costume. A replica of Indian Queen Inn served meals, in the tradition of the "New England Kitchen" restaurants at earlier world's fairs. *Good Housekeeping* magazine sponsored a replica of the home of colonial physician Thomas Shippen, installing the latest in modern kitchen, bathroom, and laundry fixtures behind the replica eighteenth-century facade to "demonstrate that one can possess one's ancestral home and be modernly at home in it." The popularity of High Street set the stage for the opening of outdoor museum villages such as Greenfield Village and Colonial Williamsburg in the 1930s, as well as offering a boost to the fledgling historic preservation movement.

While High Street's version of the world of the colonial urban gentry demonstrated the Anglocentrism of American elite culture in the 1920s, other parts of the Sesqui-centennial International Exposition displayed the cultural pluralism of the modern city. A Roman Catholic Mass celebrated by Cardinal Dougherty packed even more visitors into the new Municipal Stadium than the Dempsey-Tunney fight. The exposition remained open on Sundays, flaunting Pennsylvania's blue laws. If the official exposition historical pageants, "America" and "Freedom," slighted the role of Afro-Americans in the nation's past, two other pageants at the fair were explicitly devoted to black history. One, "Loyalty's Gift," featured a 500-voice chorus with young soloist Marian Anderson. It appears, however, that public facilities at the exposition remained segregated. The Women's Committee constructed a separate "hostess house" for blacks, with a cafeteria and emergency health station, not far from the High Street it erected for white visitors.

The Sesqui-centennial International Exposition embodied many of the contradictions of its decade. In years known for economic boom and ballyhoo, the fair was a financial and public relations disaster. In a decade in which the automobile transformed American life, the fair's most striking exhibit was a replica of the walking city of the eighteenth century. Like the Shippen House on colonial High Street, the fair employed the latest in modern technology—to drain the swamps, advertise on radio, automate exhibits through moving pictures—but wrapped inside a facade playing homage to the world of the founding fathers. Many Americans felt more at home in this world, constructed on the exposition grounds in accordance with their idealized image of the past, than in their own.

BIBLIOGRAPHY

The principal work on the Sesqui-centennial International Exposition is the official history written by E. L. Austin and Odell Hauser, *The Sesqui-centennial International Exposition: A Record Based on Official Data and Departmental Reports* (1929). To get behind this history, researchers should consult the extensive records of the Sesquicentennial Exhibition Association (Record Group 232) in the Philadelphia City Archives. These records include the names of subscribers to the association; minutes of the board of directors; files of the officers of the exposition and of the directors of the various divisions and departments; official publications, such as press releases, guidebooks, and daily programs; approximately 4,000 photographs; and eighteen volumes of newspaper clippings and miscellaneous memorabilia.

Other Philadelphia repositories with materials concerning the exposition include the Manuscripts Department of the Historical Society of Pennsylvania, which houses the papers of Elizabeth F. L. Walker, and of Albert M. Greenfield, chairman of the Finance Committee; the Free Library of Philadelphia, which has several volumes of photographs and site plans; and Temple University Urban Archives, which contains records documenting the participation of many local groups, including blacks, in the fair's activities. The Atwater Kent Museum has a collection of paintings of the twenty houses on High Street by Arrah Lee Gaul, official artist of the Women's Committee.

Outside Philadelphia, materials pertaining to the exposition are in the National Archives (Record Group 43, files 607–18), which document the preparation and construction of federal government exhibits; and in the Library of Congress, in the papers of Frank Lamson Scribner who prepared exhibits for the U.S. Department of Agriculture at Philadelphia, as well as Rio de Janeiro (1922–1923) and Chicago (1933–1934).

There is little in the secondary literature that adds to an understanding of the exposition, but a sympathetic contemporary work is Sarah D. Lowrie and Mabel Stewart Ludlum, *The Sesqui-centennial High Street* (1926). A check of the standard indexes will lead to contemporary journal and newspaper articles on the fair. Modern works include Alan Axelrod, ed., *The Colonial Revival in America* (1985).

David Glassberg

LONG BEACH 1928
PACIFIC SOUTHWEST EXPOSITION

Late in 1927 leaders of the Long Beach, California, Chamber of Commerce decided to organize an international exposition to promote trade through the city's improved harbor. By the time it opened, the Pacific Southwest Exposition had become the biggest international fair in the West since those held in San Francisco and San Diego in 1915.

Long Beach was a prosperous seaside resort and commercial city of 145,000 people. Near its center was the Signal Hill Oil Field, where oil had been discovered in 1921, and on its western boundary was Los Angeles Harbor. Adjacent to that older harbor, Long Beach was building its newer harbor, financed by a $5 million bond issue approved by voters in 1924. In May 1928 while the exposition was being planned, voters sustained the local mood of optimism and approved $2 million in additional bonds to complete the harbor work.

To emphasize the significance of harbor development, the 63-acre site chosen for the exposition was at the end of a peninsula between two newly dredged channels in the inner harbor. The site had a dock, so visitors could arrive by boat, and a regatta was one of the exposition's featured events. Promoters arranged free use of the previously undeveloped land for the duration of the exposition.

Exposition promoters chose Tunisia as their architectural theme, they explained, because it was a coastal land of traders with a climate similar to that of Long Beach. Local architect Hugh R. Davies designed exposition buildings with white walls and low, flat roofs topped by domes and pinnacles. Davies's buildings were made of plasterboard with an outer covering of stucco and roofed with stretched canvas, almost like movie sets, in response to the need to keep the cost of the buildings low, build them quickly (Davies was commissioned just ten and a half weeks before the exposition opened), and return the site to its owners at the end of the exposition. Inside the exposition's walls, landscaping transformed the harbor sand, which promoters said looked like the Sahara Desert, into an oasis.

There were three main groups of buildings at the exposition. The first was the Palaces of Exhibition, headed by the largest building, the General Exhibit Palace. There were also Palaces of Education, Fine Arts, and Aeronautics and Transportation. Second came the the Street of Nations. The buildings grouped along it celebrated the products and culture of the nations of Europe, Asia, and the west coast of Latin America. Third was the Amusement Zone. There was also an outdoor stadium and a bandstand surrounded by a reflecting pool where the municipal band played twice daily. A pageant performed daily represented the history of the Southwest from the time of the Indians to the present.

Official attendance was 1.1 million, stimulated by a series of special days dedicated to cities, clubs, businesses, and special interest groups of every imaginable type. Officials set the cost of the exposition, which was "self-sustaining," at $650,000.

On the last day of the exposition, the tower atop the Palace of Fine Arts collapsed, perhaps reflecting its insubstantial construction. Like the tower, which stood long enough that its collapse was of minor significance, the Pacific Southwest Exposition celebrated the boom of the 1920s in Long Beach at a time when reports that the boom might not go on forever seemed insubstantial and of minor significance.

BIBLIOGRAPHY

When the exposition was over, one of its organizers, John W. Ryckman, compiled and edited *Story of an Epochal Event in the History of California: The Pacific Southwest Exposition . . . 1928* (1929). It includes reprints of Bruce Mason, "The Pacific Southwest Exposition at Long Beach California," *American Architect*, October 5, 1928, 431–34 and William L. Woollett, "Architecture of the Pacific Southwest Exposition, Long Beach, California," *Architect and Engineer* 94 (August 1928): 57–59. Woollett, an architect, praises the exposition's buildings while noting their insubstantial construction and the small scale of the event. Mason, a Long Beach city attorney and the architect's brother-in-law, also praises the exposition and its buildings.

Long Beach Public Library became holder of the official books of clippings and ephemeral materials from the exposition. Four volumes of these materials have been microfilmed. They contain copies of most of the large number of articles published in local and out-of-town newspapers about the exposition. (One notable exception is "Woman Injured by Tower Crash: Structure at Long Beach Exposition Falls," *Los Angeles Times*, September 4, 1928.) There are also exposition publications such as its preliminary announcement, "Long Beach Invites the World, July 27 to August 13," "Official Souvenir Guide," and "Catalogue of Invited Works by Painters, Sculptors and Craftsmen."

Kaye Briegel

BARCELONA 1929–1930
EXPOSICIÓN INTERNACIONAL DE BARCELONA

The second major international exposition in Barcelona in less than a half-century electrified Spain's eastern seaboard for almost nine months. With its lavishly illuminated palaces, avenues, fountains, and waterfalls, the International Exposition of Barcelona was a celebration of light.

More than a mere crowd pleaser, the lights-and-water spectacles symbolized the economic transformation of the Catalonia region of Spain. The city, which had staged a successful exposition in 1888, began planning a second fair in 1913 to mark its recent electrification and industrialization. Construction halted with the outbreak of World War I, but interest revived in the early 1920s as Europe recovered.

Although the fair was financed by the city of Barcelona, the Spanish government enthusiastically backed the exposition for diplomatic reasons. General Miguel Primo de Rivera, the military dictator who came to power in 1923, hoped the exposition would win him favor among his European neighbors.

The exposition covered an area of almost 300 acres atop a hill named Montjuich. Strategically perched above the Mediterranean, Montjuich formerly had served as a fortress, prison, and site of executions. The exposition transformed the area into a permanent city park with the construction of landscaped avenues, palatial museums, water gardens, and a 60,000-seat sports stadium. Pedro Domenech headed a team of regional architects in planning the site.

The Plaza de España, a circular plaza where the major avenues of the exposition converged, marked the main entrance. Permanent pavilions, or palaces, which housed the principal exhibits, flanked the Avenida de la Reina María Cristina, leading to the Palacio Nacional, the fair's primary pavilion.

The scene was particularly stunning at night, when colored lights illuminated the monumental fountain at the center of the plaza and the cascades of water descending from Montjuich. Art deco–styled pedestals lighted both sides of the avenue, and enormous light beams burst into the sky behind the Palacio Nacional.

Although only fourteen nations, all European, were officially represented at the fair, participants from Japan, the United States, and other countries were among the scores of private exhibitors. Although this was officially an exposition of industry, Spanish art, and sport, the spotlight shone brightest on industry. Eleven separate pavilions housed exhibits of Spanish and foreign industrial achievements in textiles, chemicals, electricity, agriculture, city planning, and other areas.

Despite the industrial emphasis, however, the Barcelona exposition is remembered more for its cultural achievements. The neoclassical-style Palacio Nacional housed the Arte de España, a chronicle of art on the Spanish peninsula from the

BARCELONA 1929-1930. The art deco lighting that surrounded the Palacio Nacional, around which this exposition was staged, was striking.

cave paintings of Altamira to the early seventeenth century. The exhibit featured 15,000 objets d'art gathered from museums, cathedrals, and private collections throughout Spain.

The Pueblo Español, or Spanish village, was a living tribute to the traditional rural architecture and artisanry of Spain. The village—the product of ten years of research, site surveys, and architectural drawing—featured precise replicas of 320 homes, churches, plazas, and other architectural specimens from every region of the country. Swordmakers, silversmiths, leather workers, and other artisans lived and worked in the village during the exposition.

Germany sponsored the most famous foreign pavilion. Designed by Bauhaus architect Ludwig Mies van der Rohe, the one-story structure would influence modern architecture for decades following its appearance in Barcelona. The pavilion itself, built of Roman travertine, green Tinian marble, onyx, and other precious materials, was the chief attraction. The pavilion housed a tiny collection of objects selected by the architect, including his own barcelona chairs. Although the pavilion was removed after the exposition, numerous models based on the original plans have been constructed for exhibition and study. In the 1980s, a replica of the pavilion was constructed on the site of the original.

The International Exposition of Barcelona ran concurrently with the Ibero-American Exposition in Seville. Together the fairs were called the General Exposition of Spain.

BIBLIOGRAPHY

The archives of the International Exposition of Barcelona are housed in the Instituto Municipal de Historia and the Archivo Administrativo Municipal, both in Barcelona. The exposition published several guides with photos of key pavilions and maps of the grounds, including Catálogo oficial; Guía oficial; and Exposición Internacional, Barcelona: Su significación y alcance (all 1929). A description of the Arte de España exhibit, illustrated with thousands of plates, appears in the two-volume Catálogo Histórico y Bibliográfico de la Exposición Internacional de Barcelona, 1929–30 (1931, 1933).

General descriptions of the architecture and attractions of the Barcelona and Seville expositions are contained in "Spain and Her Two Great Expositions," Living Age 336 (April 1929): 136; and Arthur Stanley Riggs, "The Spanish Expositions," Art and Archaeology 27 (April 1929): 147. In the same issue of Art and Archaeology, Joseph Pijoan's "The Spanish Village" provides a detailed architectural discussion of this exhibit.

Timothy Palmer

SEVILLE 1929-1930
EXPOSICIÓN IBERO-AMERICANA
(IBERO-AMERICAN EXPOSITION)

The idea of a Spanish-American fair took hold in Seville in 1905, with national pride still sore from the Spanish-American War and the loss of Spain's only remaining American colonies. The exposition that finally took place almost a quarter-century later was an attempt to win the colonies back—culturally, if not politically.

In 1908 Seville hosted a national fair, Spain in Seville, commemorating the centennial of Spain's liberation from Napoleon. In 1910 the city created a commission to stage an international exposition in 1914. With the outbreak of world war, however, planning and construction stagnated.

In 1924, the year of the British colonial exposition at Wembley, Spain's new military dictatorship recognized the diplomatic potential of a fair of its own. An exposition celebrating the cultural history between Spain and its former colonies promised to advance the idea of "hispano-americanismo," a political strategy aimed at restoring Spanish influence in international affairs by creating a Spanish-American bloc.

The exposition was labeled Ibero-American when fair planners broadened its scope slightly to include Portugal and Brazil. The question of U.S. participation generated considerable protest from Spaniards angered by alleged U.S. imperialism in Central and South America. The Spanish government ended the dispute by inviting the North Americans to take part.

Although the government proposed moving the exposition to Madrid, King Alfonso XIII favored Seville because of the city's role in the history of Spanish exploration. (Columbus sailed from Seville on his first voyage to the New World.) In 1926 the government named José Cruz Conde to replace the current director of the exposition; Cruz Conde managed to complete planning and construction within three years.

The exposition lay on an expanse of parkland along the Guadalquivir River south of Seville, encompassing one of the city's most famous parks, the Parque de Maria Luisa. The main entrance to the exposition, the Plaza de España, lay opposite another city landmark, the tobacco factory depicted in Bizet's opera *Carmen*.

The Plaza de España was designed by the exposition's chief architect, Vicente Traver. The plaza and the principal exhibition buildings blended Renaissance and Mudéjar styles to reflect Seville's Christian and Moorish heritage. Under construction for fourteen years, the plaza featured a series of exhibition buildings connected by a sweeping, semicircular corridor. Along the inner arc of the corridor, a series of tile works depicted historic scenes from every province of

Spain. Similar works, all made of glazed "sevillano" tiles, decorated benches, fountains, bridges, and pools throughout the exposition grounds.

The Ibero-American focus limited the exposition's commercial potential for Spain. Like Spain, most of the participating countries were agrarian and more in need of U.S. and European technology than of Spanish agricultural products. Fair officials decided to emphasize the fine arts and Spain's cultural ties to its former colonies, leaving commerce and industry to the Barcelona exposition.

Among the cultural attractions were the Exposición del Libro, which examined the historic role of printing and publishing as a method of exporting Spanish culture; the Exposición Nacional de Bellas Artes, which Seville shared with Barcelona; and the Historia de Sevilla, featuring rare artifacts from the Roman, Visigoth, Moorish, Christian, and romantic eras of the city's history.

Seville also emphasized its role in the discovery of the New World. The Historia de América exhibit displayed authentic maps, documents, and other treasures from the city's famed Archivos de los Indios. A replica of Columbus's ship, the *Santa María*, complete with fifteenth-century nautical instruments and other details of the period, was docked on the river.

The exposition was a catalyst for growth and modernization in Seville. The extensive parkland acquired for the fair site stretched the city limits southward. In addition to the construction of the exposition buildings, which later housed permanent museums and the Hispano-American University, Seville modernized its system of public works and dredged a canal from the river to the Atlantic, enabling modern steamships to transport tourists directly to the city.

Construction also spurred an in-migration of skilled artisans, whose craft shops boosted the city's appeal to tourists. A number of new hotels and hostelries were built to accommodate this tourist influx, including the luxurious Alfonso XIII, which stands just outside the exposition site. Many hostelries were converted into public housing following the fair, alleviating a shortage in the city.

The Ibero-American Exposition ran concurrently with the International Exposition of Barcelona. Together the two fairs were named the General Exposition of Spain.

BIBLIOGRAPHY

The archives of the Ibero-American Exposition are housed in the Hemeroteca Municipal in Seville. The *Libro de Oro Iberoamericano* (1929) is the first of a proposed two-volume official guide to the exposition. Volume 2 was never published. Renewed interest in Seville and the 1929 exposition, spurred no doubt by the exposition planned for 1992, has resulted in a number of recent studies. Two detailed sources regarding the fair's lengthy political history are Eduardo Rodriguez Bernal, *La Exposición Ibero-Americana en la prensa local* (1981), covering the period from 1905 to 1914, and Encarnación Lemus López, *La Exposición Ibero-Americana a través de la prensa* (1987), which treats 1923 to 1929.

General descriptions of the architecture and attractions of the Barcelona and Seville expositions are contained in "Spain and Her Two Great Expositions," *Living Age* 336

(April 1929): 136; and Arthur Stanley Riggs, "The Spanish Expositions," *Art and Archaeology* 27 (April 1929): 147.

The architecture of the fair is featured in Alberto Villar Movellán, *Arquitectura del regionalismo en Sevilla, 1900–1935* (1979). A series of thirty-two articles on the exposition appeared in the newspaper *ABC de Sevilla* between August 30 and October 12, 1961. A description of the U.S. pavilions appears in Frances Parkinson Keyes, "A Little Window into Seville," *Good Housekeeping* 89 (September 1929): 34.

Timothy Palmer

ANTWERP 1930 and LIÈGE 1930

EXPOSITION INTERNATIONALE COLONIALE, MARITIME ET D'ART FLAMMAND EXPOSITION INTERNATIONALE DE LA GRANDE INDUSTRIE, SCIENCE ET APPLICATION ART WALLON

It would be a mistake to assume from the title of this entry that there were two international exhibitions in Belgium in 1930. Rather there was one held on two sites. Antwerp was by far the bigger and more lavish venue, with the subtitle Coloniale, maritime et d'art Flamand, while Liège had the sciences, industry, social economy, agriculture, and music. The split was due to the discord and rivalry caused during the deliberations as to which city should be chosen as focus for the celebrations of Belgium's centenary of independence from Spain. Brussels had staged the most impressive earlier expositions, and Antwerp and Liège decided it was their turn. Ultimately Brussels built the Heysel Stadium to mark the anniversary, and Antwerp and Liège agreed to split the exposition between them.

Antwerp proved by far the more successful site, for two reasons. The display of Flemish art from the previous five centuries proved a tremendous attraction throughout Europe, and the colonial sections, as at all other expositions in the early twentieth century, were staggeringly impressive. It was these latter sections that dominated the official literature and set the atmosphere for the exposition.

Belgium had profited handsomely out of the scramble for Africa at the close of the nineteenth century, and the government had taken care to exhibit its empire at all expositions from 1900. Antwerp staged the most lavish display of empire ever held on Belgian soil, partly due to the city fathers' zeal and partly to the willingness of other empires to display their gains. Great Britain, France, Holland, Italy, and Portugal built substantial pavilions along the avenue de la Colonie, with pride of place going, naturally enough, to the Belgian effort, the Palais du Congo. With various colonial villages, filled with peoples from various conquered nations, dotted around the area, the whole was a spectacular, exotic expression of European imperialism, surpassed in Europe only by British and French efforts, revealing the extent to which empire had come to grip the economy and imagination of Belgian government and population.

The Flemish art exhibition was the most complete and impressive since the Brussels exposition of 1897 and included examples from many European collections. This showing was complemented, in terms of atmosphere at least, by the attraction Vieille Belgique, a reconstructed medieval city, which had by 1930 become an absolute standard in Belgian fairs. The period feeling of Renaissance

Flanders was enhanced by various sideshows and entertainment features around the site.

In contrast, there were impressive examples of modern architecture, notably the Finnish, Norwegian, Dutch, and Italian pavilions (architects unknown) and the Pavillon des Villes Hanséatiques. This last piece, sponsored mainly by Bremen and Hamburg, has in hindsight an air of tragedy about it, as its international style would soon become proscribed in the midst of the National Socialist pogroms. By the same token, the Italian pavilion was one of the last pieces of modernism to come out of Italy with government approval. By 1937, at Paris, Mussolini had firmly harnessed classicism to the cause of Italian fascism. Marcel Schmitz, an architect and writer chosen by the central committee to report on the architecture of the site, felt positive about the prospective effects of the exposition: "Taken as a whole, one can see a marked advance on previous manifestations, and one is able to say that there has been a clear benefit for the evolution of modern architecture in our country." Apart from the buildings already mentioned, Schmitz pointed to various edifices put up by the Belgians themselves, including the Decorative Arts Palace, the Pavilion of the City of Antwerp, and the Electricity Pavilion. Indeed, photographic evidence indicates that these were full-blooded examples of international-style modernism. These were steel-framed buildings sheathed in concrete, with an emphasis on fenestration, the manipulation of space, and abstraction. Decoration was wholly absent, roofs were flat, and walls were white. It was quite progressive for a government to allow itself to be represented by architecture much more modern than, say, that of the French in the 1925 Paris art deco show. Indeed, the architecture at Antwerp can be compared with that shown by Mies van der Rohe, Le Corbusier, J.J.P. Oud, and others in Stuttgart at the 1927 Weissenhof housing exhibition, which drew much attention to the most forward looking concepts in architecture, construction techniques, and even furniture design.

By comparison the Liège exposition had more of the air of a trade fair or conference about it, having been stripped of those features normally thought to be most colorful at these events. Nonetheless, in terms of international participation and the trade it created, it remains a significant event in the recent history of the city.

The size of the attendance is not contained within the official reports. Everything indicates, however, that the two sites had good attandance throughout and that the events were officially considered successful. The large amounts of money the British, French, Italians, and Portuguese spent on their contributions confirms that they considered them events of the first class with massive audience potential.

BIBLIOGRAPHY

For the Antwerp exposition, see *Exposition internationale, coloniale, maritime, et d'art Flamand: Rapport général* (1931) for the factual aspects. The Liège fair is similarly treated in Leon Michel, *L'exposition internationale de Liège 1930* (1929). The *Times* of

London published several articles of interest dealing with this joint exposition; see, especially, the issues of March 4, 24, April 26, 28, May 9, July 18–19, 23, and October 9, 1930.

Among modern works, Paul Greenhalgh, *Ephemeral Vista* (1988) discusses Antwerp/ Liège in the context of their imperial displays, while John Allwood, *The Great Exhibitions* (1977), briefly mentions the Antwerp fair and provides some statistical data on the fair at both sites.

Paul Greenhalgh

PARIS 1931

EXPOSITION COLONIALE INTERNATIONALE

The French empire had an important place in national and international expositions from the beginning of the Third Republic. Great expositions such as those held in Paris in 1889 and again in 1900, and even lesser ones such as the 1906 Marseilles fair, exposed millions of visitors to the economic, political, social, and cultural dimensions of colonial imperialism. The promotion of empire, and with it the idea of a "greater France," reached its zenith with the International Colonial Exposition of Paris in 1931.

For the French colonialists, whose multiple political and cultural associations and powerful economic organizations made up the colonial party, national and international expositions were a privileged moment in the promotion of empire. Indeed, members of the colonial party were extremely involved in the conception and organization of the 1931 exposition. In every way the International Colonial Exposition (ICE) of 1931 corresponded to the objectives pursued by the French colonial party: to show what France had accomplished in its colonies and what the colonies had contributed to France—in other words, to provide a justification for empire and give the French an imperial consciousness. In particular, the colonialists wanted to convince French public opinion of the economic potential represented by the empire in an era of economic crisis. Thus the exposition became a propitious event to present the underexploited wealth of the various colonies as a fertile ground for the development of agricultural, commercial, and industrial enterprise.

When the inauguration of the International Colonial Exposition finally took place in May 1931 after five years of intensive preparations, the entire colonial world could be proud of the achievement. All of the colonial empires were present on the impressive Vincennes site in the east end of Paris. But the British and German governments had pleaded financial constraints in order to justify their limited participation in the exposition. The other European colonial powers (Denmark, Belgium, Italy, the Netherlands, Portugal) and the United States each had its own national pavilion.

The French empire took up most of the 148 acres of the Vincennes site. At the entrance of the exposition, visitors were welcomed by an imposing information center that housed all the data on the exposition and offered a number of activities, including permanent showings in a 1,500-seat auditorium (80 kilometers of film had been produced just on the French colonies for the occasion). Moreover, businessmen could obtain practical information on the colonies and the various agencies dealing with colonial matters.

Visitors could view many different facets of the French empire in the exposition's museum. In order to inform and educate public opinion, a major objective

Exposition Coloniale Internationale de Paris 1931.

2236. Angkor-Vat, la nuit.

Blanche arch tes

PARIS 1931. Colonial expositions often showed a wide variety of architectural styles reflecting the far-flung imperial outposts of the mother country. Shown here at this French colonial exposition is the Indo-China pavilion.

of the exposition, the museum offered a full retrospective on French colonial history since the Crusades. It also showed the colonial influence on French literature, art, and music. The museum's prominent themes included the educational effort made by various establishments, such as the Ecole colonial in Paris, the provincial colonial institutes, and the technical and professional schools in the colonies. Under the influence of Marshal Hubert Lyautey, the general commissioner of the exposition, the military and the religious missions also found a noticeable place in the museum. Moreover, the army, the navy, and Catholic and Protestant missions had pavilions in order to emphasize their role in the colonization process. Today, the museum, which is the work of the architects Leon Jaussely and Albert Laprade, remains a symbol of the 1931 exposition.

Beyond the information pavilion and the museum, the new and fabulous world of the colonies unfolded before the eyes of the visitor. Among the numerous themes at the exposition, the most pervasive and constant clearly was the economic dimensions of empire. Thus there appeared, in a variety of forms, the multiple colonial economic activities.

Aside from the colonial business groups, the metropolitan business community played a significant part; not only did it make a major contribution to the organization of the exposition, but various enterprises also had their own impressive expositions, including a number of pavilions. At the Palace of Industrial Groups, the latest products of the electrical, metallurgical, mechanical, automotive, and chemical industries—along with many more—found a prominent place. The luxury trades were also present. In fact, a special pavilion had been built to house beauty products, jewelry, fashion, and other consumer products. The textile industry had a large window on the Vincennes site, exhibiting numerous items dear to colonial trade, such as clothes, threads, and fabrics.

Exhibits of colonial industrial and agricultural products stressed the commercial relations between France and its colonies. Each colony naturally wanted to demonstrate its particular value to the metropolis and thus attract investments. The various exploitable primary products, the progress of public works (along with graphics of rail and road networks, maquettes of harbors, and the like), and data on the state of the local economy and the development of trade since the beginning of the century were displayed in every colonial pavilion.

Beyond this wealth of information offered by the colonial governments, industrial, public works, financial, and commercial enterprises held their own exhibitions. The pavilion for Algeria contained about 400 exhibits by local enterprises; Morocco had 224 and Tunisia 220. Even for the French colonies south of the Sahara, where business was less active, seventy-two enterprises had a stand in the French West Africa pavilion and thirty-three in the French Equatorial Africa pavilion.

In general, the colonial pavilions were colorful and demonstrated artistic imagination. Such was the case with the Indochinese temples designed by the firm of Charles and Gabriel Blanche, under the general supervision of Albert Tournaire, chief architect for the exposition. At the heart of the Indochinese complex, which took up a tenth of the Vincennes site, stood a replica of the Cambodian Angkor Wat temple. The massive central building with its five life-sized towers, symbolized not only the prestige and wealth of Indochina among the colonies but also French imperial power. At the center of the temple, visitors could admire the opulence and economic potential of Indochina through the elaborate exhibits of its products and the presence of its enterprises.

The exposition featured numerous special attractions. For the purpose of authenticity, ritual processions and religious ceremonies were organized on a regular basis. Frequent concerts brought music from all parts of the empire to the exposition, and African and Vietnamese dances were regularly presented. Another sort of special attraction were the native villages constructed for the occasion. The zoological garden, a living museum of exotic animals, attracted much attention.

Conservatively estimating at least 8 million visitors, most contemporaries considered the exposition a tremendous success. Indeed, the ordinary citizen could not help but be impressed by the exposition as well as informed on the empire. The exposition had an even wider impact through the simultaneous proceedings of numerous congresses and symposiums, including the congress of the International Institute of African Languages and Civilisations, the one on intercolonial transportation, and the National Congress on Cotton and Natural Fibers, among others. These events allowed the exchange of ideas and information among all those interested in the future of the empire and allowed debate on colonial policy as well as on the multiple problems facing the empire in those years of economic and political crisis.

The International Colonial Exposition of 1931 demonstrated the economic and political success of French colonial imperialism: the empire had a world dimension second only to the British, and trade, production, and even investments had experienced continuous, even if often modest, growth. Moreover, the numerous reports and recommendations resulting from the national and international congresses and symposiums argued that the future development of the empire depended on France's capacity to invest and to build. Finally, the exposition stimulated the imagination of ordinary citizens and offered a vision of Empire capable of educating public opinion.

BIBLIOGRAPHY

The principal archival sources for the International Colonial Exposition of Paris are located in the Section Outre-Mer of the French National Archives in Paris. These records contain reports on all aspects of the exposition, as well as detailed information on the preparations for each colonial section, the pavilions, the exhibits, and other attractions. They are catalogued under Agence de la France Outre-Mer (FOM). See, notably, FOM, box numbers 527–28, 530, 538–39, 544, 824, 829, 832, 873, 892, 948. The Section Outre-Mer also holds the papers of the Service de Liaison avec les originaires des territoires d'outre-mer (SLOTFOM). In these records may be found much information on anticolonial groups and activities, along with numerous reports concerning natives from the French colonies at the time of the exposition. See SLOTFOM, série III, especially box 5. The U.S. National Archives contains primary sources concerning U.S. participation in the exposition. These include the records of the Commission Representing the United States at the International Colonial Exposition at Paris, 1931. In particular, consult the General Correspondence files for 1930–1932, especially the correspondence of C. Bascom Slemp, the commissioner general, and the Record of Disposition or Shipment of Exhibits, 1931–1932 (see Record Group 43).

A basic published primary source on the exposition is the *Rapport général*, by Governor General Marcel Olivier, titled *Exposition colonial internationale de Paris*, 5 vols. (1933). This monumental work contains a complete catalog and description of the exposition, its organization, historical background, and objectives, along with a detailed description of each section.

Among secondary sources, Charles-Robert Ageron, *France coloniale ou parti colonial?* (1978), contains an insightful analysis of the colonial exposition's impact, notably on public opinion, and provides an overview of colonial France. Ageron also discusses the mythic nature of the fair in "L'exposition coloniale de 1931: mythe republicain ou mythe imperial?" in Pierre Nora, ed., *Les Lieux de memoire*, vol. 1: *La Republique* (1982). *L'Impérialisme á la française, 1914–1960* (1986), by Jean Bouvier, René Girault, and Jacques Thobie, is a lucid discussion of the nature of French colonialism and offers a conceptual and historical framework for understanding an event such as the colonial exposition. Raoul Girardet also mentions the exposition in his analysis of French colonialism, *L'Idée coloniale en France, 1871–1962* (1972). On the occasion of the fiftieth anniversary of the fair, Jean-Pierre Gomane briefly surveyed the French colonial experience in "L'Héritage colonial: souvenirs d'une exposition," *Etudes* (June 1981), while Thomas August dwelt on the same theme in "The Colonial Exposition in France (1931): Education or Reinforcement?" *Proceedings of the 6th and 7th Annual Meetings of the French Colonial Historical Society* (1980–1982). Another descriptive article is Catherine Hodier, "Une Journée à l'exposition coloniale, Paris 1931," *L'Histoire* 69 (1984), and the most recent study of the exposition is Arthur Chandler, "The Exposition Coloniale Internationale de Paris 1931," *World's Fair* 8, no. 4 (Fall 1988): 15–20. For a contemporary portrait of Marshal Lyautey, see Roger Homo, "Lyautey et L'Exposition coloniale internationale de 1931," *Compte rendu des séances de l'Académie des sciences outremer* 21, no. 4 (1961). Finally, Du Vivier de Streel, *Les Enseignements généraux de l'exposition coloniale* (1932), contains an analysis of the educational and ideological dimensions of the exposition, written by a major figure in the French colonial party.

Marc Lagana

CHICAGO 1933–1934

A CENTURY OF PROGRESS EXPOSITION

The idea for an international exposition to celebrate the centennial of the founding of Chicago was suggested by various civic leaders in the mid–1920s, and on April 8, 1926, Mayor William E. Dever called a meeting to create a planning body. Mayor William H. Thompson, who replaced Dever in 1927, initially rejected the idea of a fair but was persuaded to change his mind, and planning resumed in December 1927. In January 1928, a board of directors was formed, with Rufus G. Dawes, an oilman and brother of former vice-president Charles G. Dawes, as chairman. The board then chose Lenox R. Lohr, a retired army officer, as general manager of the fair.

While the official name of the fair, A Century of Progress, was not formally adopted until June 1929, the notion of using as a theme the scientific and industrial progress over the century since Chicago's founding dated from at least 1927, for that year, Dawes held the first of a series of meetings with representatives of the National Research Council, a little-known organization created in 1916 to facilitate cooperation among science, industry, and the military. After World War I, the council had become an agency to coordinate scientific research in industry and academia and, in general, to promote the benefits of science to humanity and the corporate state. Clearly, to focus a major world's fair on this theme would suit the council's objectives. During the planning process, the Science Advisory Committee, created by the National Research Council and funded by the fair corporation, provided a great deal of input on what should be exhibited in the areas of pure and applied science. The idea of having co-operative industrial exhibitions arranged along thematic lines was dropped in favor of letting larger industries prepare exhibits and, in some cases, entire pavilions, on their own; industrial giants such as General Motors and Sears, Roebuck and Company were willing to pay to have their own pavilions because of the highly favorable publicity that would be generated. By the time the fair opened in 1933, the trauma of the Great Depression made the positive, upbeat theme of scientific progress even more popular among visitors.

Early on, fair planners decided to finance the exposition independent of government subsidization. Instead, an array of innovative schemes was used to raise funds. Beginning in April 1928, the public was invited to purchase for five dollars a certificate of membership in the Chicago World's Fair Legion, good for ten admissions to the fair; $634,000 was raised in this manner, as well as a great deal of free publicity, significant because the board of directors had decided to avoid paid advertising, and let the news-worthiness of their activities publicize the exposition.

A much more important source of funds was a $10 million bond issue, secured by 40 percent of the gate receipts, that ironically was announced one day before the stock market crash in October 1929. Despite the unfortunate timing, about $7.74 million of bonds had been subscribed by June 1932, and about $6.11 million actually paid in, providing sufficient funds to pay for the construction of the Hall of Science, the Travel and Transport building, and the Electric Group. Exhibit space in these buildings was offered to industry, which paid nearly $2 million. In addition, some $3 million in concession contracts came from fifteen food, transportation, and entertainment providers. The federal government appropriated $1 million for the erection of a pavilion and an official government exhibit, and eighteen participating states paid out another million dollars for their exhibits. Virtually every observer commented favorably on the careful financial planning done for the Century of Progress exposition.

From the beginning, the board was determined to site the fair on parkland along Lake Michigan and land reclaimed from the lake just south of Chicago's Loop. The state legislature gave its approval in June 1929, and the fair was built on a 427-acre strip of land, seldom wider than a quarter of a mile, that stretched 3 miles from Twelfth Street down to Thirty-ninth Street. Included in the site were two large lagoons that occupied about 86 acres.

Rufus Dawes and the fair board appointed the Architectural Commission to design the buildings for the fair. Not since Chicago's previous fair in 1893 had a world's fair enjoyed the services of so many of the nation's most distinguished architects. Daniel H. Burnham, son of the man responsible for the architecture of the 1893 fair, was the commission secretary, and the other members included Edward H. Bennett, Arthur Brown, Jr., Hubert Burnham, Harvey Wiley Corbett, Paul Philippe Cret, John A. Holabird, Raymond Hood, and Ralph T. Walker. Joseph Urban, a well-known stage set designer, was named director of color, and Louis Skidmore and Nathaniel Owings, later to become two-thirds of the noted architectural firm of Skidmore, Owings, and Merrill, were in charge of exhibit design and concessions, respectively.

Given that the theme of the fair was scientific progress and that the members of the commission had been identified with the beginnings of modern architecture in the United States, it is not surprising that the decision was made to avoid a derivative classical style of architecture and build instead on the precedents of the Bauhaus and the successful modernism seen in the Paris 1925, Barcelona 1929, and Paris 1931 fairs. Not only did such unornamented and generally functional architecture seem to suit the times and the theme of the exhibition well, but also it was economical to build. The fifteen cent a cubic foot cost was less than the cost of some buildings for the World's Columbian Exposition in 1893.

Fair buildings were constructed very simply by using ½-inch wallboard over a steel framework and, for the most part, shunning the use of windows. The lack of windows freed exhibitors from worrying about the vagaries of daylight illumination, provided more interior space for exhibits, and saved money. In place of applied ornamentation, the commission decided to use color and illumination to provide the desired decorative effect, and Urban's color scheme consisted of twenty-three intensely bright colors, usually three or four to a building, with black, white, blue, and orange predominating. The color scheme also utilized a zoning principle, with the same color scheme used for related groups of buildings or exhibits in order to help visitors find their way around. Exterior lighting was handled cooperatively by Westinghouse and General Electric and consisted of a variety of functionally designed fixtures that provided white light at ground level and colored light coordinated with the buildings at higher levels.

Most of the fair buildings had some kind of distinctive architectural feature, often a tower or pylons. The Federal Building, for example, had three such pylons, rising 150 feet into the air and representing the three branches of the federal government. The General Motors Building, designed by Albert Kahn, boasted a 177-foot tower, and the Electrical Building had two 100-foot pylons framing a water gate through which visitors could enter by boat from across the lagoon. The most distinctive building from a design and engineering standpoint was the Travel and Transport Building, which featured a domed roof suspended 125 feet high by cables attached to twelve steel towers around the exterior perimeter of the building. This provided an interior exhibition space of over 200 feet, uncluttered by columns or interior load-bearing walls. The dome was also made with expansion joints, which allowed it to rise or fall by as much as 18 inches, depending on the weather.

The commission was pleased with its work. Harvey Wiley Corbett remarked, "The fair stands as a symbol of the architecture of the future—the icons of the past cast aside, the ingenuity of the designers of the present thrown on their own resources to meet the problems of the day." But many other architects scorned the Century of Progress design. Frank Lloyd Wright, whose checkered past had denied him a place on the commission, said, "There is nothing in the fair except wholesale imitation, hit or miss," and Ralph Adams Cram, the dean of neo-Gothic architecture, termed the fair architecture "a casual association of the gasometer, the freight-yard, and the grain elevator." Clearly there were some design problems. The irregular site, with its lagoons, made it all but impossible for the architects to plan a coherent layout comparable to that employed at most previous fairs. The fair buildings, while colorful and built according to the same construction scheme, often did not relate well with their neighbors. And the entire scale of the fair and its buildings was badly damaged by the looming presence of the Sky-Ride, with its 628-foot-high steel towers, bisecting the site and destroying its sense of proportion.

Louis Skidmore and the exhibits committee emphasized their desire to show processes in action rather than static machines. It was also decided to encourage innovation by eliminating any competition for blue ribbons. Exhibits, especially those in basic science and medicine, were understandable even by the uneducated, while applied science exhibits leaned heavily toward miniaturized or replicated processes. Visitors could see an operating oil refinery, an automobile assembly

CHICAGO 1933-1934. The futuristic architecture that was the hallmark of the Century of Progress Exposition was nowhere more evident than in the Travel and Transport Building. (Courtesy Peter M. Warner)

line, a radio-controlled tractor, and a toothpaste tube–packing demonstration. Other exhibitors employed film, talking dioramas, and pageants using actors.

There were a number of exhibits of special significance. "The World a Million Years Ago" featured six dioramas and lifelike dinosaurs and other prehistoric animals. The Golden Temple of Jehol, the summer residence of Manchurian emperors, was reproduced in 28,000 pieces in China and sent to Chicago for assembly. Chicago's history was reflected in reconstructions of Fort Dearborn and the cabin of Jean Baptiste Point du Sable, the first person to settle in the Chicago area, whose black ancestry provided a focal point for some mild protests against racial discrimination.

Foreign participation in the Century of Progress was originally encouraged by a delegation of fair officials who toured Europe in the fall of 1930 and established an office in London run by Sir Henry Cole, a veteran fair organizer who had played a major role in Britain's Wembley fair of 1924–1925. In January 1931, the International Convention on Expositions gave its consent for members to participate in the Century of Progress, but problems arose with respect to America's high tariff rates and European resistance to the fair board's suggestion that foreign exhibits be designed to attract American tourists rather than display scientific progress or industrial products. Eventually Congress allowed foreign merchandise for display to enter duty free but demanded that customs duties be paid on items sold. Meanwhile, Belgium built a model village as a means of attracting tourists; it was so successful in 1933 that several other nations did the same for the 1934 season. Among foreign participants, China, Czechoslovakia, Italy, Japan, Sweden, and the Ukraine had their own pavilions, while other nations exhibited in a Hall of Nations located in the Travel and Transport Building.

In addition to the domestic and foreign exhibits, the Century of Progress offered art lovers an expansive show held at the Art Institute on Michigan Avenue, a few blocks north of the fairgrounds. An agreement was made in June 1932 by which the Art Institute would provide and conduct an art exhibit connected with the fair and have control over the selection and display of works exhibited. In return, the fair board agreed to give the Art Institute 20 percent of any surplus remaining at the end of the fair. This arrangement spared the board from having to build a fireproof, secure structure for an art show without which it could not have obtained loans of important works of art.

The art exhibit theme for 1933 was "A Century of Progress in American Collecting," which brought together an assemblage of works, all but one borrowed from private collectors in the United States. In 1934, the theme was simply "American Art," seen in the context of world art. The exhibit showed masterpieces borrowed from Europe, including many works of the French impressionists, which set off a survey of American art from the Revolutionary era to the twentieth century. Special attention was paid to James McNeill Whistler, whose centenary was being celebrated, and to Thomas Eakins and Winslow Homer, considered among the most important of all American artists. Just under

3 million visitors paid a twenty-five cent fee to see the art exhibits in 1933 and 1934.

Special attractions of an entertainment nature were a staple at the Century of Progress. The Sky-Ride, with its giant towers, transported visitors 1,850 feet across the fairgrounds in "rocket cars" 200 feet above the ground. The Enchanted Island was a 5-acre playground for children that also functioned as a day-care center for parents who wanted to see the fair free from requests to buy cotton candy or find the bathroom. The Midway included such attractions as Spoor's Spectaculars, with giant movie screens and 64-mm films; the Odditorium, with exhibits from Ripley's "Believe It or Not"; Bring 'Em Back Alive, the well-known Frank Buck wild animal show; and Midget Village, where sixty midgets lived in tiny houses and put on plays and other entertainment.

Among the entertainment at the fair, the most controversial was Sally Rand and her fan dance, a revealing act that tested the moral scruples of midwestern fair officials and visitors from all parts of the nation. Rand, who was born Helen Gould Beck in Hickory County, Missouri, was a former Kansas City model, silent movie actress, and vaudevillian before entering the world of burlesque in the early 1930s, where she found steady work and plenty of notoriety. For the fan dance, she completely covered her nude body with white "cosmetic white-wash" and powder and then danced behind two large feathery fans. At the end of her performance, she raised her fans high, revealing her entire body, which, with the whitewash and powder, made her look much like an alabaster statue. Although she began dancing at the fair and at downtown clubs in late May, she was not arrested until August 4, at which time she was fined $25 and told to wear clothes beneath her fans. Arrested again on September 23, she was fined $200 and sentenced to a year in jail, but the case was dismissed on appeal, and her popularity was enhanced by virtue of the publicity. At the beginning of the 1934 season, fair directors announced their intention of raising the cultural level of the entertainment presented, but by July, Sally Rand was back again, this time in a "bubble dance" with a 5-foot semitransparent bubble.

The Century of Progress Exposition did not shy from lending its name or association with a large number of special events and special days, both on and off the fairgrounds. The first major league baseball all-star game was played at nearby Comiskey Park, the home of the Chicago White Sox, on July 6, 1933. Five college football games were played at Soldier Field, adjacent to the fair-grounds, in the fall of 1933, and a national boys' marbles championship was held there as well. The National Roque League staged the annual tournament of this croquet-like sport in early August as a collateral event to the fair. The Chicago Symphony, under the direction of Frederick A. Stock, presented a series of concerts for fairgoers, and public school bands and choruses seemingly never ceased performing.

At the fair, most states and many ethnic groups had their own special days, and fair officials designated still other days as special for one reason or another. To commemorate the end of prohibition, the fair provided free beer and sandwiches on November 8. Fifty thousand visitors showed up, drank 1,000 barrels of beer, and ate almost 200,000 sandwiches on that day, dubbed Personal Responsibility Day. On November 10, all people on relief rolls were admitted free upon presentation of their identity card.

Between May 27, when Postmaster General James A. Farley officially opened the fair, and November 12, when the 1933 season closed, a total of 22,320,456 visitors attended; another 245,403 tickets were sold but not used, making the grand total of ticket sales 22,565,859. In October 1933, the fair board decided to open the exposition for a second season. Although all agreed that the fair had been a success and that it would be a shame not to take advantage of the expertise gained during the first season, the principal reason for reopening was to enable the bondholders to be paid off in full; receipts for 1933 had fallen short of that goal. Support came from state and city governments, and most of the industrial exhibitors renewed their contracts for 1934, while new ones, including the Ford Motor Company, were added.

In most respects, the 1934 version of the Century of Progress was similar to the 1933 one. Physically, some changes were made to the entryways, the lagoons, and the lighting. Joseph Urban had died, and his successor, Otto Teegen, adopted a new, simpler exterior color scheme but one still based on bright, intense colors. The success of the Belgian village led other nations to construct their own model villages featuring typical food, drink, and entertainment. In general, exhibitors relied more on dramatized entertainment or live demonstrations then they had in 1933. Chrysler used its quarter-mile track for stock car races, and Standard Oil Company replaced its film on the oil industry with a free wild animal act, called "Cage of Fury." Hupmobile placed would-be drivers in front of a film that reacted to their driving skills, and the Safety Glass demonstration invited visitors to throw a rock at a window. Armour meatpacking used "auburn-haired beauties" in a bacon slicing and wrapping exhibit, and even Petrolagar, a laxative, enjoyed popularity with a diorama showing a doctor treating a critically ill child.

The most significant addition to the 1934 Century of Progress was the Ford Motor Company pavilion, a 900-foot long building with a rotunda in the center displaying a 20-foot globe indicating Ford's international operations. On the walls of the rotunda was a mural by Walter Dorman Teague, a noted industrial designer, showing an automobile assembly plant. The pavilion contained the Industrial Hall, showing Ford's latest technological innovations, and the Industrial Barn, containing farm machinery and a replica of Henry Ford's father's barn as it was in 1863, the year of Ford's birth. The Detroit Symphony played daily in a bandshell located in a garden setting in front of the pavilion; the garden was inside a 2,000-foot oval with twenty-one sections representing different historic highways. The Ford exhibit occupied 11 acres, cost a reported $5 million to produce, and received the personal attention of Henry Ford in most of its detail. It paid off, however; 70 percent of the daily visitors toured the pavilion, making it the most popular of the 1934 season.

On the last day of the fair, October 31, 1934, nearly 375,000 visitors came, as the mayor declared a half-holiday for city workers, and many businesses and schools were closed. That day, the fair received its sixteen millionth visitor of the year, a Chicago grandmother making her fiftieth visit to the Century of Progress, and bestowed a truckload of gifts upon her, including 5 acres of land and a monkey. Late in the evening, a near riot ensued as visitors, sensing the finality of the fair, spontaneously began disassembling and taking with them fair fixtures and anything else portable that seemed a likely souvenir. Police were called in, and many people were forced to leave their prizes behind, but only one arrest was made—a man had wrapped a toilet seat in an American flag and was charged with desecration of the flag. Since most of what the fairgoers had tried to take was scheduled for demolition anyway, the actual damage amounted to only about $5,000. Altogether, the 1934 season saw ticket sales of 16,486,377, with actual attendance of slightly over 16 million. The city council, recognizing the continuing popularity of the fair, passed a resolution authorizing the formation of a committee to explore ways in which the Century of Progress could be maintained as a permanent attraction for tourists. The committee was also assigned the task of raising $2.5 million to reopen the fair on a sound financial footing. The fair board, however, discouraged such plans, asserting that "the orange has been squeezed dry," and nothing ever came of the council's resolution.

The Century of Progress Exposition ended its two-year run with a surplus of $688,165, out of which demolition, future claims, and corporate dissolution expenses had to be paid. Most of the buildings were torn down, although the fair's administration building served the same function for Chicago's parks for a number of years. The final profit amounted to $160,000, with the South Park Corporation and the Museum of Science and Industry each receiving 25 percent, the Art Institute 20 percent, and the Adler Planetarium 10 percent. The remaining 20 percent was divided among a number of other participating groups.

By most standards, the Century of Progress Exposition was a success. It was carefully financed and turned a profit, even during a period of national economic crisis. Although many contemporary architects had serious reservations about the style of the fair's buildings, the bold and colorful architecture sustained the modernist movement and showed its influence in the streamline style of industrial design in the 1930s and in the architecture of the New York World's Fair of 1939–1940. Finally, the fairyland architecture and futuristic exhibits based on the theme of scientific progress were, for most visitors, a vehicle that transported them for a day out of the real world of unemployment, bread lines, and human misery. It was, almost literally, a dream world on the shores of Lake Michigan.

BIBLIOGRAPHY

The official records of the Century of Progress Exposition are housed in the Special Collections Department of the library at the University of Illinois at Chicago. These records include correspondence, reports, minutes of meetings, legal and financial records, press releases, clippings, photographs, blueprints, and other material relevant to all phases of the fair. There is an unpublished guide to these records available at the library.

The *Chicago Tribune* and other Chicago newspapers covered the fair on a daily basis and are a source for detailed information on special days and events. The official guide to the fair was called *Book of the Fair*; nearly 200 pages in length, it provided a comprehensive overview for visitors. Contemporary magazines published an abundance of articles on all aspects of the fair, and some are quite useful. For the architecture of the fair, see E. H. Klaber, "World's Fair Architecture," *American Magazine of Art* 26 (June 1933): 292–98; Arthur F. Woltersdorf, "Carnival Architecture," *American Architect* 143 (July 1933): 10–20; and "Branding the Buildings at the Chicago Fair," *Literary Digest*, August 12, 1933, 14. "Science at the Century of Progress Exposition in 1934," *Scientific Monthly* 39 (November 1934): 475–78, is a useful summary, and J. Parker Van Zandt and L. Rohe Walter, "King Customer at a Century of Progress," *Review of Reviews* 90 (September 1934): 22–27, present some interesting insights on the changes made for the 1934 season. Finally, Rufus G. Dawes, in his *Report of the President of a Century of Progress to the Board of Trustees* (1936), and Lenox R. Lohr, the general manager of the fair, in *Fair Management: A Guide for Future Fairs* (1952), present detailed accounts of their roles in the planning and execution of the Century of Progress.

There has been relatively little historical research done on the Century of Progress. Most recent histories of Chicago give passing mention to the fair, and John Allwood, *The Great Exhibitions* (1977), also surveys it. Robert W. Rydell, in "The Fan Dance of Science: American World's Fairs in the Great Depression," *Isis* 76 (December 1985): 525–42, explains the important role of the National Research Council in establishing and carrying out the theme of scientific progress. The relationship of black Chicagoans to the fair is described in "Negro Protest at the Chicago's World's Fair," *Journal of the Illinois State Historical Society* 59 (Summer 1966): 161–71, by August Meier and Elliott M. Rudwick. And, finally, in "The Lost City of the Depression," *Chicago History* 4 (Winter 1976–1977): 233–42, Cathy Cahan and Richard Cahan provide a retrospective view of the fair through the reminiscences of Martha McGrew, Lenox Lohr's assistant.

Two collateral works may also be of interest. The eminent historian Charles Beard was commissioned to edit a book outlining the advances of industry and applied science during the past century; the result was *A Century of Progress* (1933). David Mamet's play, *The Water Engine*, which is set in Chicago during the Century of Progress, was first produced in 1977.

John E. Findling

BRUSSELS 1935
EXPOSITION UNIVERSELLE ET INTERNATIONALE

This was the largest exposition so far held in Belgium, covering a 250-acre site adjacent to the public park at Laeken. The other boundaries of the site were along the chausée Romaine, the avenue de Meysse, and the avenue Rouba Destrooper. Interestingly, the holding of an exposition in Belgium in 1935 appeared to violate the agreement made at the Convention Relating to International Exhibitions held in Paris in 1928, which stipulated that two universal expositions—the largest type—could not be held in the same country within a decade. The Antwerp–Liège event of 1930 should have meant that Belgium would not hold another one until 1942, but the intense sense of rivalry among the Belgian cities led to Brussels' applying for permission to hold an exposition in 1935. The Bureau of International Exhibitions, based in Paris, bent to the pressure, and Brussels was allowed "a general exhibition of the first class." It was probably these events that led to the general collapse of the agreement less than a decade after it was made. Soon after 1935, other nations swept it aside.

A major publicity and selling point—more than with any other Belgian fair—was the monarchy. King Albert, "King of the Belgians," was high patron, and his blessing, speeches, and insignia were ubiquitous. In addition, the history of Belgium was in high profile, more so even than at Antwerp in 1930, when the centenary of independence had been celebrated.

There were nine main categories for exhibits at the exposition: (1) instruments of all kinds relating to science and arts: (2) products of the soil and subsoil; (3) transformation industries; (4) energy; (5) civil engineering; (6) public buildings and housing; (7) clothing and accessories; (8) economics; and (9) tourism and sport. The principal foreign participants were Austria, Denmark, France, Great Britain, Hungary, Italy, Luxembourg, the Netherlands, Poland, Sweden, Switzerland, Czechoslovakia, and the United States.

The site boasted some striking features, including the Monumental Palace, which contained the bulk of the Belgian exhibits, and the Palace of Art. Both were constructed from permanent materials. A stadium capable of holding 75,000 people was built to host sporting events planned in conjunction with the exhibition. Luxurious parks, gardens, luminous fountains, and an artificial lake were created especially for the exposition. The total architectural effect of the site was eclectic and historicist rather than modern. A definite art deco atmosphere prevailed everywhere, a superficial but stylish compromise between the contemporary and the old. If a particular phrase had to be applied to the site architecture, it would be "deco-classicism." The influence of the 1925 Paris show was everywhere, with the work of Pierre Patout showing itself significantly. Almost compulsory at Belgian fairs by 1935, an "Old Brussels" was constructed on the edge of the site. This was a medieval city, peopled by costumed inhabitants going about their business.

The Palace of Art followed lines that were standard in Belgium and most other nations. Half of the space was given over to old art, half to contemporary. A stunning display of works from all nations, called "Five Centuries of Art, 1400–1900," proved a massively successful crowd puller. Perhaps the most impressive section was that of contemporary art, especially due to the contribution sent by France. The French section included, among many others, works by Pierre Bonnard, Georges Braque, Marc Chagall, André Derain, Raoul Dufy, André Lhote, Henri Matisse, Francis Picabia, Pablo Picasso, Suzanne Valadon, Kies Van Dongen, Maurice de Vlaminck, Edouard Vuillard, Georges Rouault, Jacques Lipchitz, Auguste Maillol, and Ossip Zadkine. Such a showing had distinct political importance in 1935, as the Germans had recently declared their ideological opposition to modernism by closing the Bauhaus. By 1935, the French had finally and completely embraced modernism even in the highest official circles and were readily promoting it as a distinctly French phenomenon. Two years later, at the Paris Exposition universelle, this new love of the contemporary spirit made itself fully evident, but the first full-blooded sign of it was the selection of art sent to Brussels in 1935. Great Britain's selection was also surprisingly liberal, including works by Ivon Hitchens, Paul Nash, Stanley Spencer, Mark Gertler, and Matthew Smith as representatives of progressive practice.

Despite the lavishness of the site, there was a peculiarly hollow ring to the exposition, probably due to the generally confused state of Belgian design and architecture. After the decline of Belgian art nouveau and the switching of Victor Horta from art nouveau back to a form of classicism, the struggle to create an appropriate national style and school entered a chaotic phase. The exposition revealed this and offered few pointers as to the direction of Belgian visual culture. Two years later at the Paris Exposition universelle, Henri Van Der Velde was given virtual control of the Belgian contingent in what appeared to be an attempt by bemused authorities to rescue Belgian design. Perhaps it would be fair to say that it was not until 1958 before a genuine design ethic gained currency in Belgian architecture, design, and industry.

BIBLIOGRAPHY

The most complete primary source generally available for this fair is the *Catalogue officiel Exposition universelle et internationale bruxelles 1935* (1935). The official guidebook to the fair, published in French and English, is titled *Official Guide and Plan of the Brussels International Exhibition* 1935 (1935). Charles Pergameni, *Exposition universelle et international 1935* (1935), is an anecdotal guide to the exposition, with good illustrations. Other contemporary information may be found in major Brussels, Paris, London, and New York newspapers.

Two secondary works touch significantly on the fair. Paul Greenhalgh, *Ephemeral Vistas: Expositions Universelles, Great Exhibitions and World's Fairs, 1851–1939*

(1988), contains information on this and most of the other major Belgian fairs, with some emphasis on their imperial aspect. A Cockx and J. Lemmens, *Les Expositions universelles et internationales en Belgique de 1885 à 1958* (1958), is an informative general reference on Belgian fairs.

Paul Greenhalgh

SAN DIEGO 1935–1936

CALIFORNIA PACIFIC INTERNATIONAL EXPOSITION

In 1934 San Diego decided to dispel the depression doldrums by staging an international fair similar to the one that had been so successfully presented in 1915. On May 29, 1935, after less than a year of preparation, the California Pacific International Exposition opened.

The exposition was built with money from advance ticket sales, exhibitor fees, government appropriations, and a local subscription in which 3,275 individuals pledged $700,647. One reason the fair could be organized so swiftly was that Balboa Park, the site of the 1915 fair, was again used. The previous exposition buildings were incorporated into the new scheme but were lighted with the newest technology out of the Hollywood movie industry. This became one of the distinctive features of the new exposition. Some remaining old exhibits were used, and the permanent residents of Balboa Park—the zoo, Natural History Museum, and Fine Arts Gallery—were absorbed into the plan. Several new gardens were built, as were some new structures, such as the Spanish village of shops and cafés, the Old Globe Theatre, and the House of Pacific Relations, where foreign exhibitors' consuls held forth. A single major new area was built—a mall surrounded by several exhibition buildings and an amphitheater located to the southwest of the old area.

The 1915 buildings had been designed in an elaborate baroque Spanish colonial style. The 1935 architect, Richard Requa, tried to expand on that by presenting examples of the evolution of styles in the New World. Thus he designed buildings in the Pueblo, Aztec, and Mayan styles, culminating with an example of contemporary industrial architecture. Although Requa's buildings were effective exposition structures, they did not have the dramatic appearance or the long-range impact of the 1915 structures.

On its compact 185-acre site, the California Pacific International Exposition offered over 400 exhibits drawn from twenty-three countries, several governments, and many corporations. The exhibits were not particularly distinctive. As one local writer has observed, the exhibits were "generally true to their descriptive titles." They included Palaces of Natural History, Food and Beverages, Better Housing, Fine Arts, Science, Electricity and Varied Industries, Education, and Water and Transportation. The only unique exhibits were those by Ford Motor Company and a miniature village behind the Palace of Better Housing. The Ford exhibit let people see how automobiles and various by-products were manufactured. At the end of the exhibit, one could ride a new Ford motor car over a replica of a world-famous road. In the home exhibit, there were blocks of tiny, modern homes, showing all the latest and best aspects of

1930s housing, which periodically turned over to show examples of the Victorian gingerbread houses they were designed to replace. Beyond these two notable examples, visitors found most interest and entertainment beyond the formal exhibits. There was an outdoor auditorium, the Ford Bowl, where people could listen to major orchestras and musical groups, which the Columbia Broadcasting System frequently broadcast over its radio network. There was a $1.5 million midway with "only the high class shows," a gold gulch mining town (sometimes with illegal gambling), nude exhibitionists at the Zoro gardens, a midget town and farm, restaurants, and religious centers. In keeping with the international aspect of the exposition (which was better honored in name than in fact), there was a collection of fifteen cottages, collectively called the House of Pacific Relations, which were manned by representatives of foreign countries. Of both immediate and long-range impact was the replica of Shakespeare's Old Globe Theatre, which showed abbreviated versions of the Bard's plays in 1935 and 1936 and later evolved into one of the nation's major regional theaters. Subsuming all else were elaborate gardens designed especially for the fair and professional lighting at night.

At the end of the first year, 4,748,811 people had attended, and there was a cash surplus of $400,000. After much local squabbling, the directors opened the exposition for a second year in 1936. In that sequel, the fair drew only 2,004,000 visitors, and the surplus dwindled to a mere $44,000.

Although not meeting the promotors' expectations, the 1935–1936 California Pacific International Exposition did bring much to San Diego. The entertaining of visiting dignitaries brought cheer into the otherwise dour depression-era social life. The fair brought millions of dollars into San Diego from exhibitors, governmental funds, and visitors. It created thousands of jobs and was undoubtedly at least one of the reasons San Diego climbed out of the Great Depression sooner than most of the rest of the nation. In addition, the fair left more permanent buildings in Balboa Park and laid the foundations for more local institutions, such as the Old Globe Theatre and the Starlite Theatre. The California Pacific International Exposition of 1935 and 1936 was a success.

BIBLIOGRAPHY

There are two major collections of primary sources on the 1935 California Pacific International Exposition. The San Diego Historical Society contains a variety of material. In one box file is a miscellany of printed materials (guidebooks, maps, brochures, etc.) plus a number of folders of manuscripts (letters, committee reports, cash flow summaries, auditors' reports, etc.). Unfortunately, most of the manuscript material consists of bits and pieces, and virtually none of the files is complete. The society also has a large number of excellent scrapbooks, which contain a wealth of materials, several oral history interviews with pertinent information, and a large photograph collection with many images of the fair. At the San Diego Public Library's California Room, researchers will find a large number of printed items, a clipping and miscellany file, working drawings and maps of the buildings and grounds, plus a thirty-three-box collection of official records. These boxes contain minutes, insurance papers, office files, loan subscription papers, contracts, correspondence, invoices, journals, press releases, and related materials. These materials should be supplemented by local newspapers, which can be found at a variety of sites, including the Historical Society, the San Diego Public Library, and San Diego State University. The San Diego State University Archives on San Diego History also has a variety of published items on the 1935 exposition in its memorabilia and ephemera files.

The most comprehensive secondary source is the account by the exposition architect, Richard Requa. In *Inside Lights on the Building of San Diego's Exposition, 1935* (1937), he describes the origins, organization, architecture, landscaping, illumination, and music of the fair. Richard Amero, "San Diego Invites the World to Balboa Park for a Second Time," *Journal of San Diego History* 31 (Fall 1985): 261–79, is an overview of the fair based almost entirely upon newspaper accounts. An insider's view can be found in Oscar W. Cotton, *The Good Old Days* (1962); Cotton was in charge of the subscription campaign. In *The Rising Tide*, vol. 6 of *The History of San Diego* (1967), Richard Pourade intersperses the story of the exposition throughout his general history of San Diego in the 1930s. Another brief overview can be found in Florence Christman, *The Romance of Balboa Park*, 4th ed. (1985), which covers the story generally and is most valuable for descriptions of the buildings and features that are still standing in Balboa Park. There have been several magazine articles on the California Pacific International Exposition; probably the best is Sam Ervine, "The 1935 Exposition," *San Diego Magazine* (June 1965): 65–71, 95. He draws somewhat upon his own memories of the fair. In general, however, no thorough history of the California Pacific International Exposition has been written to date.

Raymond Starr

JOHANNESBURG 1936–1937
EMPIRE EXHIBITION

The Johannesburg exhibition was one of a series of celebrations of the British empire conducted in the face of the evident decline of that empire during the twentieth century. A Festival of Empire had been staged in London in 1911, and a larger empire exhibition was held in the London suburb of Wembley in 1924–1925. South Africa had been represented at these earlier fairs, and thus it was fitting that on January 9, 1935, the Grand Council of the Federation of British Industries adopted a resolution supporting a proposal to hold an Empire Exhibition in Johannesburg in 1936 in conjunction with the golden jubilee of that city. Although only fifty years old, Johannesburg had grown spectacularly because of the nearby gold mining industry and was the largest European city in Africa, with a population of about a half-million.

The site chosen for the exhibition was a 100-acre section of Milner Park, about a mile from the city center. Work began in 1935, and on September 15, 1936, Lord Clarendon, the governor-general of South Africa, officially opened the exhibition, or Rykstentoonstelling, as it was called in Afrikaans.

As visitors passed through the main entrance on Empire Road, they found themselves on Prosperity Avenue, the main thoroughfare dividing the grounds east and west. There were five major exhibit halls, the largest of which was the Hall of Industries, covering 5 acres. South of this was a large hall that contained the art gallery, a ballroom, and the first ice rink in Africa. In the far southwest corner of the fairgrounds was the Hall of Light Machinery and Manufactures. The other two major exhibit halls were both dedicated to heavy machinery and featured a 200-foot Tower of Light between them. On the other side of the site were three smaller buildings: the Hall of South African Industries, the Ford Motor Company pavilion, and the Provincial Courts pavilion.

In the center of the grounds, along Prosperity Avenue, was a variety of foreign and corporate pavilions. As visitors entered the grounds, the first building on their left was the Cape House, notable for its wine cellars. Next, on the right, was the Victoria Falls pavilion, containing a model of the famous waterfall over which 2,000 gallons of water poured every minute. Next was a large L-shaped building containing most of the colonial exhibits, including those from New Zealand, Ceylon, Australia, and Canada. Part of the Australian exhibit was an impressive model of Sydney harbor with its newly constructed Harbor Bridge. Canada displayed its wide variety of industrial and agricultural products. Next was the grand pavilion of Great Britain, designed by Howard Robertson. Circular in form and rising to a height of 90 feet, it was a replica of the pavilion constructed for the Brussels exposition the year before.

Across the avenue was the small East African pavilion, representing the colonies of Kenya, Uganda, and Tanganyika. Next to the British pavilion was the largest of the colonial pavilions, that of the host nation. The Pretoria government had appropriated £50,000 for this pavilion, and each government department had its own display. It proved to be one of the showcases of the exhibition, as was the Golden Reef building, celebrating South Africa's gold mining industry. This building contained a large, detailed scale model of the Rand gold mining district. Other colonies represented at the fair included Southern Rhodesia, Trinidad, Nigeria, Seychelles, Swaziland, Bechuanaland, Nyasaland, and Basutoland. In addition, Scotland had a separate exhibit.

The exhibition grounds contained an open-air arena, seating 20,000, which hosted a wide assortment of special events, such as native war dances, pageants of African history, and a rodeo. There was a 10,000-seat open-air theater with a stage set on an artificial lake. One particularly distinctive event associated with this exhibition was a highly publicized air race from England to South Africa, offering $50,000 in prizes.

The Empire Exhibition closed on January 15, 1937. During its run, it attracted about 1.5 million visitors, and it closed its books with an estimated loss of £70,000 against a total cost of £2 million. No international exposition has since been held in South Africa.

The exhibition had been built close to the University of Witwatersrand. During the late 1970s, the growing university incorporated the remaining permanent buildings from the exhibition into the campus. These included the Cape House complex (presumably with its wine cellars intact), the Bien Donne restaurant, the ballroom and ice rink, the two heavy machinery halls and the accompanying Tower of Light, and the South African pavilion.

BIBLIOGRAPHY

Basic factual information about this fair can be found in the *Official Guide to the Empire Exhibition* (1936) and in the coverage given to the fair by the *Times* of London between 1935 and 1937. See especially the issues of July 16, September 16, December 19, 1936, and January 18–19, 1937. There is no significant mention of the exhibition in the *New York Times*, except for a feature article on September 3, 1936.

A number of journal articles deal with specific exhibits and features of the fair, especially those concerned with mining and electricity. See, for example, "Gold and Diamond Mining Exhibits," *Engineering and Mining Journal* 137 (October 1936): 523ff; "Johannesburg Exhibition: Survey of the Electrical Exhibits," *Electrician* (London), October 16, 1936, 457–58; and "Some Impressions of the Lighting at the Empire Exhibition, Johannesburg," *Light & Lighting* (London) 30 (January 1937): 8–10. See also J. Phillips, "Rock Garden at the Empire Exhibition, Johannesburg," *Journal of the Royal Horticultural Society* (London) 61 (August 1936): 333–37. For a more general view, consult "South Africa's Empire Exhibition," *Engineer* (London), October 9, 16, November 13, 1936, 372–73, 406, 511–13.

Michael L. Gregory

PARIS 1937

EXPOSITION INTERNATIONALE DES ARTS ET TECHNIQUES DANS LA VIE MODERNE*

In 1937, the Queen City of Expositions held court for the last time. World War I was scarcely two decades past. The most catastrophic war in the history of the human race loomed less than two years away. The world seemed poised in the eye of a hurricane, between the winds of World War I and World War II. The Exposition internationale would be the final European enactment of the ritual of peace and progress before the deluge.

To their credit, the exposition officials recognized that they were celebrating in a deeply troubled world and did their best to confront the actual and impending disasters within the framework of the exposition itself. The 1937 Exposition internationale faced some of the most important dualisms that divided humanity against itself: the split between Paris and the provinces, between France and its colonies, between art and science, between socialism and capitalism, between fascism and democracy. The official philosophy of the exposition still paid homage to the twin gods peace and progress, as all parties at the great ceremony in Paris intoned the faith: no matter how bleak the world seems to be, the twin gods will see humanity through to a glorious future. "This great lesson in international cooperation will not be forgotten," predicted Fernand Chapsal, the French minister of commerce, in the official public report on the exposition. In less than three years, Paris would belong to the conquering Nazis.

On December 28, 1929, the French Chamber of Deputies passed a resolution calling for an Exposition of Decorative Arts and Modern Industry, in 1936, to be placed under the direction of the minister of commerce. The exposition was first conceived as a follow-up to the Exposition des arts decoratifs modernes of 1925. Although the attendance at the "art deco" fair was only a tenth the number that visited the 1900 Exposition universelle, France congratulated itself on having taken a decisive step in maintaining leadership in cultural affairs. The 1925 exposition, though not as ambitious as the five previous Parisian world's fairs, was pronounced a *succès d'estime* for France. Even if France was losing its place in the first rank of economic and political power, Paris could at least prevail in matters of taste. France planned the new exposition with an eye toward consolidating its claims to cultural authority.

Conceived during the victorious optimism of the 1920s, the Exposition internationale of 1937 (the original opening year was set back) was carried out in the anxious zeitgeist of the 1930s. The Great Depression, unemployment, and

*This article was originally published in *World's Fair* in somewhat altered form and is printed here with the permission of the publisher.

runaway currency inflation forced a change in the government's original plans for a decorative arts exposition. Given the precarious state of the national economy, the decorative arts did not seem a serious enough concern to justify the labor and expense of a major international exposition. Instead, the government announced in the *Livre d'or officiel* that it would integrate the exposition with "the overall plan of economic recovery and the struggle against unemployment."

Although the decorative arts would not be the major focus of the new exposition, the exposition planners believed that the arts themselves should take an active part in the "struggle against unemployment." Because of the Great Depression—and the trend among painters and sculptors toward "unpopular" abstract art—the number of buyers to support the arts had declined sharply. To alleviate the widespread and growing poverty among artists, an embarrassment to the city, which prided itself as the home and center of fine art, the nation of France and the city of Paris commissioned 718 murals and employed over 2,000 artists to decorate the pavilions.

If the decorative arts were not to be the major subject or theme of the great exposition, what would take their place? As time went on, the objectives themselves wavered and shifted in the political storms. Some legislators thought the exposition should celebrate workers' and peasants' lives, in an attempt to heal the split between Paris and the provinces and to give an egalitarian cast to the exposition's theme and purpose. Others wanted to see the artisan exalted in an attempt to involve colonial craftsmen and to fix the status of art as a decorative auxiliary to social concerns.

It was finally decided that the world's fair would take as its theme the division that had grown up between the arts and technology. The very title—International Exposition of Arts and Technics in Modern Life—shows the decisive split from the spirit of the earlier expositions universelles. The fairs of the earlier era and the event of 1937 are all expositions—shows of the products of human ingenuity, under the aegis of peace and progress—but the "universal" is gone from the name and nature of the newest fair. All previous expositions had been international, but national rivalries were supposed to be subordinated to larger, universal concerns: the elevation of taste through the arts and the improvement of everyday life by science through industry. The title of the 1937 exposition breaks down the real meaning inherent in the earlier term *universal* into its component parts: the nationalism inherent in the competition for prestige, the fundamental duality between the arts and technics, and the transforming power of art and science.

The title of the 1937 exposition suggests another change in the thinking of the planners, a change as fundamental as the shift from *universal* to *international*. Now "art" and "science" no longer exist as absolute values. Art becomes artisanship, science becomes technology. The value of art and science derives from its social utility, the exposition planners announced at Paris 1937. Application to daily life is the highest measure of worth.

By 1935, the new exposition had a theme and a name, but as 1936 drew closer, detailed plans for the event had not been drawn up. The opening date was moved up to 1937, and a commission set to work in earnest on the grand schemes and finer details. But the compressed time frame hurried the commission into hasty decisions and improvisational planning.

When the American correspondent for the *Architectural Record* surveyed the exposition, he could compliment the "cheerful magnificence of conception, peculiarly French," while at the same time lamenting that the overall objectives of the exposition were "foiled by a lack of coordination between the idea and the realization." Looking back to the exposition of 1937 half a century later, François Robichon concluded that "the scheme of the whole was undiscoverable, since the placement of the 200 pavilions was made without any overarching plan, with the exception of those in the Trocadéro Esplanade" (*Le livre des expositions universelles, 1851–1989* [1983], p. 237).

As always with Parisian expositions, the work proceeded slowly, and the exposition opening time was pushed back again and again. It was an embarrassment for the French government to watch the Italians, the Germans, the Russians, and many others complete their pavilions while bureaucratic delays and strikes drove the French commissioners to despair. At one point Edmond Labbé, chief commissioner of the exposition, resigned his post with a despairing outburst:

I am a dishonored man, and I herewith tender my resignation. The French pavilion will not be ready in time for the inauguration. The workers pay no attention to me. In spite of all my appeals to their honor and power, they still go on strike.

Workers are not always swayed by the fine words *peace* and *progress*. Parisian laborers in 1937 demanded a pledge from the government that if they helped build the exposition, they would be guaranteed employment thereafter. Labbé was persuaded to continue, and the work proceeded. But would the fair ever open its gates to the public? Just a few weeks before the actual opening date, one of the commissioners approached the director of works and asked him:

"Since you're the builder of all this," the official asked, "can you tell me when the fair will be ready to open?"
"Well," replied the director, "I can't tell you exactly. But I do know that, according to the contract, I have to start demolition on November 2."

The major architectural event of 1937—the official "spike" of the whole exposition—was to be a splendid new modern art museum. There was little public outcry over the proposed demolition of the Trocadéro Palace, the major legacy from the 1878 Exposition universelle. It was leveled in 1934 without ceremony. "The old Trocadéro will be mourned," remarked one French architect, "but only by those who habitually mourn the dead."

The new Chaillot Palace was to be the triumphant vindication of the present age over the past. Unfortunately, as Robichon notes, "The reconstruction of the Trocadéro palace took place in total disorder. After having first decided to demolish the old structure, they opted instead for camouflage." Jacques Carlu,

Louis-Hippolyte Boileau, and Léon Azéma were awarded the commission to rebuild the new Chaillot Palace along the same lines as the colonnade of the old Trocadéro. The idiom of the new building would be modern but not too much so. As deputy commissioner Julien Durand assured the legislature during the budgetary hearings: "The old Trocadéro will be replaced by a monument whose lines, in spite of their modernism, will fit well within the monumental tradition of Mansart, Gabriel, Ledoux, Percier, Fontaine, etc." Both Carlu and Azéma had been winners of the traditionally prestigious Prix de Rome in architecture and could be counted on to design a building not too far out of the mainstream. The radical modernism of Le Corbusier was passed over in favor of a style that mixed traditionalism and the international style.

This return to the past by way of neoclassicism has been seen by some observers as a prime symbol of fascism in architecture. Indeed, Albert Speer, chief architect of the Third Reich, thought so, and his German pavilion at the 1937 exposition was carried out in a spirit quite close to that of the Chaillot Palace. The wide, impersonal sweep of the colonnade conjures up for many a feeling of totalitarianism, a subjection of the individual to the state—in short, an architecture of fascism.

As it turned out, the new Chaillot Palace was not the most exciting architectural event at the exposition. Le Corbusier, whose Pavillon de l'Esprit Nouveau had created such an uproar at the 1925 art deco fair, was excluded from all the design teams of the 1937 exposition. One of his students, Junzo Sakakura, designed the Japanese pavilion. But Le Corbusier himself was too uncompromisingly visionary for the exposition planning commissioners. Undaunted, and following the tradition of refusé painters from earlier expositions (Gustave Courbet in 1855, Edouard Manet in 1867, Henri Matisse in 1889), Le Corbusier and his followers erected a huge tent outside the exposition grounds, just beyond the porte Maillot. Inside they set forth his models and plans for the ideal city of the future. Said the writer for the *Architectural Record*: "It was one of the most exciting, convincing, and most easily remembered exhibits of 1937 Paris."

At the earlier French national fairs held in the first decades of the nineteenth century, the artists refused to lower themselves by appearing in the same expositions as the "lower" mechanical arts. Painters and sculptors displayed their work at their own annual and biennial salons, where patrons and purchasers entered the "higher" world of aesthetic beauty, far from clanking machinery. Since the 1855 exposition, though, artists agreed to compete with each other side by side with the industrialists. But for painters and sculptors, gold medals awarded at world's fairs never had the status comparable to awards from the annual salons. Artists felt that the fine arts were more noble and refined products of the human spirit.

Although art and industry had coexisted at world's fairs, there were never any systematic attempts to integrate the two. Applied ornament might dress up the perceived graceless functionality of the machine, and machinery might serve as a subordinate subject for art (the first painting with a motorcar appeared in the frescoes at the 1900 exposition), but art and science remained separate in the nature and application of their basic values.

The 1937 Exposition internationale was designed in part to effect a unification between these forms of knowledge. In this case, though, the unification meant a subordinate position for art. There was fine art to be seen at the exposition, of course—in the retrospective gallery. And Picasso's *Guernica*, on display in the Spanish pavilion, showed that painters were still capable of making powerful statements about the moral dimension of the contemporary world. But the overall presence of art at the 1937 exposition was as decoration. The term *artisan* is used again and again in the official literature, and the word is used with the kind of respect that indicates the writers felt that artisanship was every bit as worthy as artistry. In the modern view, easel painting was elitist. The muralists and sculptors who adorned the walls of the industrial galleries were the artists truly in phase with the official philosophy of the fair.

The most telling sign that art had declined into servitude was the manner in which artisanship was exalted over art and the condescending admiration bestowed upon the artisans of colonial cultures by their rulers. In 1931, Paris had staged a modest party for the colonies of France, an *exposition coloniale* that presented the natives, in a picturesque encampment out by the Chateau de Vincennes, for scrutiny and appreciation by the citizens of the governing nation. Now the colonials were brought back and placed in isolated splendor on the ile des Cygnes in the Seine. This was the familiar French 1001 Nights dreamland, the exotic Orient and darkest Africa made real by theme pavilions and dusky natives hawking wares in the *quartier d'outre mer*. Here primitive artisanship thrived. Beneath the imported totem poles, between the fronds of the newly planted banana trees, palms, and cactuses, the colonial artisans weaved fabrics and sang their songs on the Parisian island of *outre mer*.

As he surveyed the exhibit of tribal masks from Gabon and the Ivory Coast, the official chronicler of the colonial exhibit, Marc Chadourne, had a vision of the message crying out from these wares: "I am black, but I am beautiful." Chadourne could not see that the *but* was a mountain over which the entire world would one day have to cross.

France had its colonies, Paris its provinces. What the ile des Cygnes was to France, the Regional Center, located in a remote corner of the esplanade des Invalides, was to Paris. Here the French borrowed from the Chicago Columbian Exposition, which had devoted a portion of the fairgrounds to the states of the union. The idea was transferred to Paris, where the provinces seemed to the French as the equivalent of states. But Chicago does not signify to the United States what Paris signifies to France. No one came away from the Columbian exposition with the notion that the other states were provinces of Chicago. At the Regional Center of the 1937 exposition, the fundamental distinctions of prestige and power between Paris and the rest of France were made manifest.

In the Regional Center, picturesquely clad artisans from the provinces displayed their native crafts in pavilions designed as hybrids that wedded French regional traditional styles—the Norman, the Gothic, the Renaissance—with the cool lines of the international style. The visual aspect of these regional pavilions was in effect miniaturized grandeur: reductions of older styles meant for larger buildings. In a spirit of cooperation, even the île de France—the province that includes Paris—participated with a structure that resembled the top part of one tower in the City Hall of Paris.

In the domain of ideas, the 1937 exposition attempted to reconcile, symbolically, art and industry. From the political vantage point, the fair was a vehicle of nationalistic propaganda. The word *propaganda* had not yet acquired connotations of deception, and one saw the word everywhere, in French and foreign pavilions alike. Propaganda continued the tradition of national displays at all previous world's fairs. Each country did its best to show the world the superiority of the political and economic system that had produced the marvels on view in its national pavilions.

Each country stressed the virtues of its home government but added allurements to promote tourism. The French erected a special Pavillon du Tourisme, where the beauties of France could be admired without the distractions of industrial or artistic exhibits. The Italian building showed how lovely Italy had become even lovelier under the benign reign of Il Duce. The Soviet Union mounted the most expensive display of all: a map of mother Russia made entirely of gold studded with rubies, topazes, and other precious stones—a luxurious and luxuriant illustration of the country's industrial growth in recent years.

The most striking feature of the Soviet pavilion was not the exhibits of gold and propaganda; it was the placement of the building face to face with the Nazi pavilion. Nothing in any other international exhibition has ever matched this dramatic architectual confrontation. In the shadow of the Eiffel Tower, the two opponents faced off with self-aggrandizing monuments to their nationalistic spirits. According to his own account, Albert Speer, Hitler's architect in chief and designer of the German building, accidentally stumbled into a room containing a sketch of the Soviet pavilion. This ostensibly innocent accident enabled Germany to dominate its rival on the Esplanade. Facing the heroically posed Russian workingman and peasant woman brandishing hammer and sickle, the German eagle, its talons clutching a wreath encircling a huge swastika, disdainfully turned its head and fanned out its wings. At the ground level, a massively naked Teutonic couple stared at the Russian monument with grim determination.

When the gates to the exposition closed in November 1937, they closed on the final ritual of peace and progress in the queen city of expositions. A total of 16,704 prizes had been distributed to participants. Over 600 congresses had been held on an unprecedented number of topics. Some thirty-one million people had attended the fair, though the final balance sheet showed a loss of 495 million francs. But the officials pointed out that, during the year of the exposition, over 4 million more people attended theatrical and musical performances than in 1936, producing an estimated profit of 40 million francs; admissions to the Louvre and Versailles doubled; the Métro collected 59 million more fares; train travel increased 20 percent; and hotels registered 112 percent more guests. Two new museums—a reconstructed Trocadéro and the new museum on the quai de Tokyo—would bring in money for decades to come. Clearly the monetary goals of the exposition, taken in the larger context of the French economy, had been met.

In spite of these encouraging statistics, most observers counted the exposition as something less than an unqualified success. Fewer than 32 million visitors— half the number of the 1900 exposition—attended this elaborate ceremony of the unification of arts and technics. The mood of the 1937 exposition carried none of the buoyant optimism that had prevailed in 1900. Some enthusiasts talked of continuing the exposition into the next year, but the plan failed to win popular support.

Amid the technological wonders and charming pavilions of artisanship, there lurked an unpleasant feeling of tension, suspicion, and hostility. No one could mistake the brute confrontation between the Russian and German buildings. And there were other tangible evidences of mistrust. Almost none of the major nations distributed information about the materials and processes used in their industrial exhibits. Knowledge was the hoarded property of the nation that discovered and applied it. Guards in every pavilion were posted to stop visitors from photo-graphing the exhibits. Even apparently public displays were to be appreciated, not studied. One architect was making sketches of the nighttime illumination patterns of the French buildings, only to have his drawings confiscated and destroyed by the exposition gendarmes.

The ritual of peace and progress was over. The medals were distributed, and the conquering exhibitors of forty-four nations politely applauded each other during the closing ceremonies on November 2, 1937. Soon the participants departed to their fortified cities and prepared to arm human pride with the tools of technics for the forthcoming tournament of blood. In the City of Light, the lamps were extinguished. The ultimate confrontation was at hand.

BIBLIOGRAPHY

The mammoth *Exposition internationale des arts et techniques, Paris, 1937—Rapport général* (10 vols.) is the most comprehensive document, produced under the imprimatur of the French government from 1938 to 1940. More accessible, and admirably illustrated, is the *Livre d'or officiel de l'Exposition internationale des arts et techniques dans la vie moderne* (1937), especially valuable for information about how the commissioners of each section felt about the moral, social, and aesthetic implications of their part of the exposition. A special edition of *Le Monde*, "Paris 1937 Exposition," was published May 29, 1937, and also contains useful general information.

For the English-speaking student, the best sources for facts and criticism of the 1937 exposition are the essays in the architecture magazines. See T. F. Hamlin, "Paris, 1937: a Critique," *American Architect* (November 1937): 25–34; H. R. Hitchcock, Jr., "Paris 1937: Foreign Pavilions," *Architectural Forum* (September 1937): 158–74; and Elizabeth B. Mock, "Paris Exposition," *Magazine of Art* (May 1937): 266–73. The U.S. and major foreign pavilions are described in detail in two articles in *Architectural Record*:

"1937 International Exhibition," 82 (October 1937): 81–91, and "U.S. Pavilion Carries Skyscraper Motif to Paris," 82 (December 1937): 20–23.

The most comprehensive assessment of the 1937 exposition is Bertrand Lemoine, ed., *Cinquanténaire de l'Exposition internationale des arts et des techniques dans la Vie Moderne*, published in 1987. Its 510 pages are admirably organized and lavishly illustrated (including many color photos), with essays on virtually every aspect of the fair. Also quite good is the substantial and wittily written section on the exposition in Philippe Bouin and Christian-Philippe Chanut, *Histoire Français des foires et des expositions universelles* (1980).

Arthur Chandler

GLASGOW 1938
BRITISH EMPIRE EXHIBITION

The idea for an Empire Exhibition in Glasgow was conceived in 1931 at the height of the depression in a conscious effort to promote employment and to advertise the industries of Scotland. After 1936 it was planned and promoted by the Scottish Development Council, backed by a guarantee fund of £750,000, and cost £10 million to construct. The objects of the exhibition were fivefold: to illustrate the progress of the British empire; to reveal the resources and potentialities of the empire to new generations; to stimulate Scottish work and production and to direct attention to Scotland's historical and scenic attractions; to foster empire trade and closer friendship among the peoples of the Commonwealth of Nations; and to emphasize to the rest of the world the peaceful aspirations of the peoples of the British empire.

The exhibition was built around a hill, 170 feet high, at Bellahouston Park, southwest of the Glasgow city center, and covered 175 acres. The architect was Thomas S. Tait, and the civil engineers were Crouch and Hogg. The exhibition was arranged on three main axes: Scottish Avenue, on which were placed the Scottish pavilions, the concert hall, and the palace of art; Dominions and Colonial avenues, which ran between the pavilions of the imperial territories, together with the palaces of engineering and industries and a range of other buildings devoted to specific industries and companies; and Kingsway, on which stood the pavilions of the U.K. government, the city of Glasgow, and a notable exhibit on the Women of the Empire. Scottish industries like shipbuilding, steel and coal, agriculture, fisheries, and forestry were prominent. There was a Scottish model dairy, an Empire Tea Pavilion, and a Scottish Highland village, An Clachan, which was intended to convey the rugged Scottish spirit that had helped to build the empire. Specific associations (like the Bee-keepers') and companies (like Shell-Mex, ICI and Dunlop) had their own buildings.

Whereas previous British exhibitions had adopted pastiche, eclectic, or antique styles, Glasgow was unashamedly modern. The buildings were in a distinctive thirties style—flat roofed, angular, with smooth surfaces, metal frames, and strongly accented glazing, the vertical elements being provided by pylons, flagpoles, and ribbed frontages. It was a great deal more satisfying than the stolid, almost windowless concrete of Wembley.

The exhibition was open from May 3 to October 29, 1938, and received 12,593,232 visitors (plus another 600,000 who attended events in the stadium, outside the exhibition grounds, and did not visit the exhibition itself). It suffered a loss of £118,691, which was amply covered by sums received from the guarantors.

The exhibition set out to place Scottish industrialism, notably the heavy industries of the Clyde Valley, into the context of the international, though distinctively imperial, economy. But the historic national identity presented was the contrasting one of rural Highland life, which had supposedly formed the Scottish character at home and, through emigration, abroad. The exhibition therefore presented an interesting three-tiered structure: empire, metropole, and Celtic periphery. The Palace of Arts concentrated on Scottish art, and there was a retrospective of the Glasgow school, a significant movement of the late nineteenth and early twentieth centuries.

Although the exhibition was overshadowed by the growing European crisis, attendance was remarkable for a country with a population of little more than 5 million. Ironically, the industries it celebrated were to experience their last great flourishing during the war and the era of reconstruction that followed. Within two or three decades, as the empire also slipped away, Scotland was in search of a new identity. The Glasgow Garden Festival of 1988 and the emergence of the city as a European capital of culture for 1990 represents a wholly new strategy in the late twentieth century.

BIBLIOGRAPHY

Collections of material relating to the Glasgow Empire Exhibition can be found in the Mitchell Library, Glasgow, the University of Glasgow, and the Glasgow Art Galleries and Museums Service. Among these, the report of Sidney Graham to the Administrative Committee (January 11, 1939) is particularly important. The exhibition produced large quantities of ephemera, and there were special supplements to Scottish newspapers like the *Glasgow Herald*. The Imperial Institute in London was the main coordinator of the dominions and colonial exhibits, and the papers relating to these can be found in the institute's records in the Public Record Office (particularly PRO 30/76/161–70).

The most complete account of the exhibition can be found in Alistair Goldsmith, "The Glasgow International Exhibitions, 1888–1938" (M.Litt. thesis, University of Strathclyde, 1986), and Colin McArthur, "The Dialectic of National Identity: The Glasgow Empire Exhibition of 1938," in Tony Bennett et al., eds., *Popular Culture and Social Relations (1986)*, offers an interpretation of the exhibition in terms of the location of Scotland in the cultural and economic periphery. John M. MacKenzie, *Propaganda and Empire* (1984), places the exhibition in its propagandist and ethnic context, while Paul Greenhalgh, *Ephemeral Vistas* (1988) surveys the design, cultural, artistic, national, and gender implications of the exhibits.

John M. MacKenzie

NEW YORK 1939–1940
NEW YORK WORLD'S FAIR

The idea for a world's fair in New York began modestly enough in the home of Joseph Shadgen in Jackson Heights in late 1934. Shadgen's daughter, in response to his question about what she had learned in school that day, said the country was 158 years old. He said that a more accurate date of birth for the country would be Washington's inauguration as president in New York in 1789, which meant the country would not be 150 years old until 1939. Soon after, Shadgen's wife called them to eat, and before dinner was over, the idea for the New York World's Fair was born.

Shadgen took his idea to Edward F. Roosevelt, second cousin of Eleanor Roosevelt, with whom he had had some earlier business dealings, and they in turn went to see George McAneny, a New York banker and strong supporter of New York. After listening to the plans they outlined for him, McAneny said: "My dear Mr. Roosevelt and Mr. Shadgen, a number of us have been sitting around talking off and on for three years trying to figure out what to do about the commercial situation in New York. I think you gentlemen have found the solution."

McAneny, from the start an enthusiastic supporter of the proposed fair, spread the idea around. In addition to talking with financial leaders and businessmen, he met with President Franklin D. Roosevelt, Governor Herbert H. Lehman, and Mayor Fiorello La Guardia. All three expressed interest in the fair and pledged to support the project. By the fall of 1935 the proposal had received enough support that McAneny and others associated with the fair were ready to present the idea to the public, and this they did on September 23, 1935, in articles appearing in New York newspapers.

While it is uncertain what role Chicago's Century of Progress exposition of 1933 and 1934 played in the inception of the 1939–1940 New York World's Fair, the success of the Century of Progress helped create a receptive environment for a New York fair, and the optimism that greeted the announcement of plans for a New York fair was fueled by Chicago's success.

By the time of the announcement in September, plans were well developed. It had been decided that the fair would run for two six-month seasons in 1939 and 1940, would commemorate the inauguration of George Washington, would be held in Queens, and would cover more than 1,000 acres. Most significant was the choice of land: it was familiar to readers of F. Scott Fitzgerald's novel *The Great Gatsby* as the "valley of ashes."

New York's park commissioner, Robert Moses, supported the fair from the start but was not willing to let its promoters build on an existing park site. After investigating other possible tracts of land in New York City, the Queens site was selected because since it was currently an ash dump, it lent itself well to development, first as a fairground and then as a park once the fair closed, and because it provided for access to the fair by water and was close to the geographic center of New York City. There was some question about accessibility of the site, but bridges and parkways were planned to remedy that problem and were completed by the date of the fair's opening.

Robert Moses was the man whose job it was to oversee the reclamation of the dump, and from the start he urged haste. At any time the project would have been a tremendous undertaking; with the fair scheduled to open its gates in slightly more than three and a half years, Moses expressed concern that the work could not be completed in time, and he made it clear that if the opening of the fair were delayed, the fault would not be his.

By the close of 1935, a fair corporation had been formed, plans were being made for a bond issue to finance the project, similar to the way the Century of Progress had been funded, and legislation was being written that would make it possible for the fair corporation to lease the site for the duration of the exposition and allocate funds for government participation. At the same time, the search for a theme for the fair went on.

The decision to design the fair to look to the future rather than to the past was not easily arrived at. Almost from the time of the announcement in September 1935, a variety of opinions were expressed about what the fair should represent and what buildings should be erected there. Most vocal and most influential were the guests, many of them designers and architects, at a dinner party in December 1935 at the New York Civic Club, and a result of the meeting was the formation of a committee to draft a proposal for the "Fair of the Future." The group's plan called for a fair with a unified vision. It should be forward looking, but it should also "stress the vastly increased opportunity and the developed mechanical means which this twentieth century has brought to the masses for better living and accompanying human happiness. Mere mechanical progress is no longer an adequate or practical theme for a world's fair; we must demonstrate that supercivilization that is based on the swift work of machines, not on the arduous toil of men." More specifically, the committee suggested that the fair sponsor a series of focal exhibits, as well as an exhibit to explain the theme of the fair to the public.

This was the plan that the fair followed. The Trylon and Perisphere (a triangular tower 610 feet high and a globe 180 feet in diameter) remains one of the most distinctive theme buildings ever constructed. Because of its size and because it was the only structure at the fair painted white, the Trylon and Perisphere, linked by a ramp called the Helicline, served as a guidepost for visitors.

Inside the Perisphere was the fair's focal exhibit: Democracity. The diorama, created by Henry Dreyfus, one of the leading industrial designers of the 1930s, showed a model of the city of the future and linked the focal exhibits of the various zones into which the fair had been divided. Visitors entered the Perisphere by elevators and exited at the top of the Helicline, 65 feet above the ground.

NEW YORK 1939-1940. The Trylon and Perisphere are the best-known world's fair symbols. (Courtesy Peter M. Warner)

From the Helicline, visitors could best appreciate the plan of the fair. Of the nine zones that made up the fair—Amusement, Communications and Business Systems, Community Interests, Food, Government, Medicine and Public Health, Production and Distribution, Science and Education, and Transportation—two, Amusement and Government, did not have focal exhibits. The divisions were both thematic and geographic, but there were exceptions. Florida's exhibit, for instance, was located in the Amusement zone, and the Masterpieces of Art exhibit appeared in the Communication and Business Systems zone. To help visitors find their way on such a large site, the zones were color coded, each featuring one color—lighter in hue near the theme center and growing darker farther away from the Trylon and Perisphere. The purpose of this planning, according to the official guidebook, was to allow "the visitor to escape, for the first time, much of the mental confusion and the physical exhaustion which have invariably hindered his previous attempts to see and understand a great exposition."

The plan was evidently a success, for while visitors frequently complained about the condition of their feet, they seldom complained about getting lost or being unable to find what they were looking for.

One would expect the architecture of a fair whose motto was "Building the World of Tomorrow" to be modern, and such was the case in New York in 1939, though by no means was it daringly so. One real advantage of constructing temporary structures at a fair is that it allows for experimentation with design that most people would not consider for a permanent structure, and this is reflected in the architecture of the New York World's Fair. The permanent structures (the New York City Building, currently the home of the Queens Museum, and the amphitheater that housed Billy Rose's Aquacade, no longer in use) are rather conservative in design.

Contemporary critics did not respond very favorably to the fair's architecture. It was felt that the fair's modernity did not extend beyond the surface, and some believed that too many of the buildings were more concerned with boosting sales for the company that owned them. In the *Magazine of Art* in 1939, Frederic Gutheim remarked that if the fair created any architectural style, it was "Corporation Style." But if the critics found reason to fault the architecture of the fair, the public responded favorably to it and in particular found the color coding an aid in getting around the grounds.

Visitors to the fair liked what they found inside the exposition buildings. A newspaper article in October 1938 reported that more than a dozen companies were waiting to introduce new products at the fair. Among the most significant of these products was television, featured at the RCA exhibit. Many other large corporations exhibited at the fair, including AT&T, Kodak, Firestone, Heinz, U.S. Steel, Westinghouse, General Electric, National Cash Register, and the three major automobile companies.

In size, the largest exhibit was sponsored by Eastern Railroad's Presidents' Conference and included Railroads at Work, the biggest model railroad ever built, and Railroads on Parade, a stage show that illustrated the development of the streamlined locomotive.

By far the most popular exhibit at the fair was General Motors's Futurama, created by one of the leading industrial designers of the 1930s, Norman Bel Geddes. Approximately 27,500 visitors each day sat in one of 552 moving chairs and looked at Bel Geddes's model of the world of 1960, transformed by a thoughtfully designed highway system. Also among the most popular exhibits, according to a Gallup poll, were Democracity (in the Perisphere) and those presented by AT&T, Ford, the Soviet Union, Great Britain, and the Eastern Railroads.

To a degree not seen in earlier fairs, the New York World's Fair tried to be truly a world's fair. As early as November 16, 1936, President Roosevelt formally invited foreign nations to take part. His request was more than a formal gesture, for it was supported by a prospectus created by the Lord and Thomas ad agency and visits from traveling commissioners representing the fair. Grover Whalen, the fair president, made trips to Europe in an effort to secure foreign participation. He and other fair representatives were successful; by the time the fair opened, fifty-eight nations had agreed to exhibit. Among the most significant of these was the Soviet Union. Whalen, who was justly praised for his ability as a salesman, realized how helpful it would be to the fair if he could sign the Soviet Union to a contract to erect a large pavilion. When his efforts proved fruitful, Whalen invited the press to the signing of the contract. He described the result in his autobiography, *Mr. New York*: "Calls, cables and ambassadors flooded my office the next morning. The log-jam was broken. Some complained that I had, in effect, upset the apple cart, and now every country would have to participate on a large scale. No one was going to allow the Russians to over-shadow them at the Flushing."

The New York World's Fair, despite its lofty aspirations, did not disappoint fairgoers who were there to have fun. As in other respects, the amusement zone was planned carefully. A study was conducted of attractions that had been successful at earlier fairs, and a list was then formulated of the qualities that seemed to result in popular attractions:

1. An appeal to curiosity, which might center in remote places, people, manmade or natural wonders, morbid sights, nudity, or the redepictions of a historical event.

2. Thrill.

3. Exclusive presentation, which involved making sure that no similar spectacle is presented near the visitors' homes.

4. Low price.

5. Short performance.

6. Large capacity, obtained more by a rapid turnover than by a large plant—tabloid doses at tabloid prices.

A partial list of amusement zone concessions indicates how well fair attractions represented these qualities: Strange As It Seems, Seminole Village, Midget Auto Race, Aerial Joy Ride, Sun Worshippers, Parachute Jump, Nature's Mistakes, and Auto Dodgem. The most popular attraction in the amusement zone was Billy Rose's Aquacade, "a musical swimming spectacle," starring Eleanor Holm and Johnny Weissmuller. Staged in the 10,000-seat marine amphitheater, the Aquacade topped $2.7 million in gross receipts in 1939. By comparison, gross receipts for the second most successful concession, the Eastern Railroad's Presidents' Conference, reached only $453,000 in that same year.

The fair corporation was optimistic about the effect the fair would have on the public and the financial success that would naturally follow. Even neutral sources were predicting success. The American Institute of Public Opinion conducted a survey to determine how many people were likely to attend the fair. The results, made public in January 1939, indicated that 13.4 million people were definitely planning to attend, and another 19.6 million hoped to attend. Since these figures did not include those who would attend the fair more than once, it was believed the New York World's Fair had a chance to set an attendance record for expositions held in the United States. The problem, as a 1936 article in *Newsweek* pointed out, was that because of the high cost of building the fair (over $67 million), an attendance of 50 million was needed in order for the fair to make a profit of $1 million. If the fair drew 40 million visitors the first year and 20 million the second, the *Newsweek* reporter continued, the fair would close with a profit of $8 million. The fair never got close to these figures.

The fault cannot be blamed on the publicity department, for the amount of media coverage the fair received was remarkable:

731 radio programs heard on 19,171 stations between April 30 and July 15, 1939.

181 newsreels sent to 16,585 theaters in the United States and Canada.

Approximately 160 special editions of magazines.

12,224,440 column inches in newspapers in the United States.

305,412 photographs distributed to the media.

In addition the fair sponsored a savings club to encourage children to save money for a visit, got Howard Hughes to name the plane he flew around the world in during the month of June 1938 the *New York World's Fair 1939*, sent out a goodwill motorcade to every state, held a preview parade a year before opening day, and held an elaborate New Year's celebration, Dawn of a New Day, on December 31, 1938.

While such efforts were not completely futile, neither did they make the fair the success it was hoped to be. By the time the fair ended its first season, on October 31, 1938, paid attendance was 25,817,265, far below expectations.

Near the end of the first year, the fair had Market Analysts, Inc. conduct an attendance survey. As part of the survey, 449 people were interviewed at Coney Island and Rockaway Beach. Half of those questioned commented that they had heard nothing unfavorable about the fair. Complaints heard by the other half included: "prices in general too high" (64 respondents), "food prices too high" (33 respondents), "too much walking" (21 respondents), and "entrance fee too high" (16 respondents). This would have surprised no one associated with the fair since even before opening day, its promoters were called on to justify an admission price of seventy-five cents when other fairs at this time charged only fifty cents for admission.

On May 11, 1940, the fair opened for its second season, this time under the guidance of a banker, Harvey Gibson. The most significant change was Gibson's decision to downplay the World of Tomorrow theme and make the fair instead a "super country fair." As a result, the amusement zone was given a name— the Great White Way—and concessionaires were treated more kindly.

Another major difference between the 1939 and 1940 versions of the fair was the absence of the Soviet Union, which had withdrawn from participation following the outbreak of World War II in September 1939. In January 1940, the Soviet pavilion was razed and shipped back to Russia at the request of the Soviet commissioners. During the 1940 season, the site was used as an outdoor amphitheater called the American Common, where a variety of musical and theatrical programs were staged. There were other changes in the list of foreign exhibitors. Denmark pulled out, replaced by Iraq; Norway did not participate in 1940, but a group calling itself Friends of Norway kept the exhibit going. This was also the case with Sweden. Argentina's pavilion became the Inter-American House. And the Society of Friends moved in when Siam moved out.

Gibson could not save the fair from bankruptcy, though the fair, under his leadership, did make money, even with the new fifty cent admission. When the fair closed for the year, and for good (there was no serious discussion about keeping it going for a third season, though the possibility was mentioned), the 1940 fair had an income of nearly $13 million and expenses of almost $8 million, for a profit that year of $5 million. Overall, though, the fair registered a deficit of $18,723,222, certainly a disappointment to promoters who had sincerely believed the fair would be a financial success. But as Ed Tyng pointed out in *Making a World's Fair*, there are other forms of success besides financial: "Nearly all world's fairs lose money, but what they lose probably is little to pay for what they accomplish in regard to national development and public consciousness of it, and for what they do by stimulating future public acceptance in their own and other countries of new industrial and scientific developments, and even in widening the sale of commodities and manufactured articles long on the market."

The biggest immediate impact the deficit had was that no money existed to create the park Robert Moses envisioned for the site. Most of the buildings were demolished, and the steel from the Trylon and Perisphere was sold for scrap and used in World War II. The memory of the fair's symbols has survived and continues to appear in such places as the movie *The Natural* and the magazine *National Lampoon*.

But people remember more about the 1939–1940 New York World's Fair than the Trylon and Perisphere. It is one of the most popular fairs of this century because it has come to represent an optimistic world that was destroyed by World War II. For years before the fair opened, there had been talk of another world war, but while the war did not come as a surprise, it also did not stop Westinghouse from burying a time capsule at the fair with instructions that it was not to be opened for 5,000 years. The time capsule remains buried 50 feet below the surface, but the faith in technology and belief in the future that the time capsule represented has been lost, apparently forever.

BIBLIOGRAPHY

The richest source of information is the extensive archives, some thirteen cartons, of the New York World's Fair, located at the New York Public Library in New York City. Additional material can be found in the George McAneny Papers at Princeton University.

Among secondary works that deal at length, or at least in part, with the fair are Ed Tyng, *Making a World's Fair* (1958), based largely on the minutes of the fair directors and executive committee; Helen Harrison, curator, *Dawn of a New Day* (1980), a catalog of an exhibit at the Queen's Museum in New York, with substantial textual material on the fair; Richard Wurts, *The New York World's Fair 1939/1940* (1977), a pictorial record of the fair; and Grover Whalen, *Mr. New York* (1955), the autobiography of the fair's principal executive officer.

Virtually every popular periodical of the day published articles on the New York World's Fair; the *Reader's Guide to Periodical Literature* has two full pages of listings. Of particular interest are Walter Lippmann, "Day at the World's Fair," *Current History* 50 (July 1939): 50–51; S. M. Shalette, "Epitaph for the World's Fair," *Harper's Magazine* 182 (December 1940): 22–31; D. Haskell, "Tomorrow and the World's Fair," *Architectural Record* 88 (August 1940): 65–72; and C. Lazare, "American Art at the Fair," *Nation*, July 1, 1939, 23–24. Coverage in the *New York Times* was extensive and detailed; it is well indexed in the *New York Times* Index.

Two books written in conjunction with the fair's fiftieth anniversary merit mention. Larry Zim, Mel Lerner, and Herbert Rolfes, *The World of Tomorrow: The 1939 New York World's Fair* (1989) is a comprehensive tour of the event, with emphasis on its exhibits and souvenirs. Barbara Cohen, Steven Heller, and Seymour Chwast, *Trylon and Perisphere* (1989) is a coffee table-size pictorial look back at the fair.

A good overview of the fair is *The World of Tomorrow*, a 1984 documentary film produced by Lance Bird and Tom Johnson and available from Media Study/NY, New York City. A videotape version of *The World of Tomorrow* was produced in 1989.

Michael Mullen

SAN FRANCISCO 1939–1940
GOLDEN GATE INTERNATIONAL EXPOSITION

The Golden Gate International Exposition on Treasure Island in San Francisco Bay was the last of the old-style world's fairs. Future expositions would be more commercial and less grandiose.

The Great Depression needed goals and projects. Translated, that meant jobs. Two great bridges, the Golden Gate Bridge and the San Francisco-Oakland Bay Bridge, had already met some of the need for work projects in the 1930s. Celebrations had always been a part of San Francisco history beginning with the California Midwinter Exposition in 1894, followed by the splendid Panama-Pacific International Exposition in 1915. Now it seemed appropriate to celebrate these two monumental engineering feats with a world's fair. It would also provide employment and bring tourist dollars to depression-plagued San Francisco.

Over the decades, open space had disappeared in San Francisco, and so a unique site was selected for the exposition. Treasure Island was created just off Yerba Buena Island in the center of San Francisco Bay. The Bay Bridge went through Yerba Buena Island and provided auto access to the site. Bay ferries could stop as they traversed their routes. The island itself was some 400 acres in size, rectangular in shape and lying low in the Yerba Buena shoals. Because of its location and the changing times, one-fourth of the island was set aside for parking, something not necessary in 1915.

The Golden Gate International Exposition had a Pacific Basin theme incorporating oriental and occidental motifs and ideas. The main entrance to the fair was between two great elephant towers, reminiscent of Angkor Wat, which pierced the solid outer wall of the western side of the exposition's exhibit halls. This wall was designed to ward off the bay breezes as they blew in through the Golden Gate. Baffle entrances between the towers allowed immediate entrance into the Court of Honor, dominated by the 400-foot Tower of the Sun. Art deco in style, with tall arches reaching to spires at three levels, the tower was capped with a golden phoenix.

Extending south from the Tower of the Sun was the Court of the Moon, a long rectangular pool stretching its length. Arches of water crisscrossed the pool and at night became part of an ethereal magic as submerged light turned them into golden phantom arches set off against the deep indigo and rose walls of the court.

East of the Tower of the Sun visitors entered the Court of Reflections. Two long pools reflected the tower from the east, and reflected from the west was the great Arch of the Winds, which separated this court from the Court of Flowers farther east. The Court of Flowers was a square surrounded by arches. In the center was a tiered fountain rising to a statue, *Girl and Rainbow*. Directly east of this court was the Lake of All Nations with two great Towers of the East dominating the outer wall of the Court of Flowers and reflecting off the lake's mirrored surface. Ivory by day, these two towers became orange, orchid, pink, and gold by night with great Thai lanterns illuminating the walkways.

If one turned north from the Tower of the Sun, the whole vista, some 1,000 feet in length, of the Court of the Seven Seas stretched ahead. Great prows of galleys lined the walls honoring the glories of exploration, and ship lights with gay banners brightened the paths. This court terminated in the spacious Court of Pacifica and the Fountain of the Western Waters. *Pacifica*, an 80-foot statue by Ralph Stackpole representing peace, dominated the court. Behind it an oriental prayer curtain tinkled in the breezes; at night it was illuminated in revolving colors as a background for the white-lit *Pacifica*. Before it the Fountain of the Western Waters incorporated figures representing the cultures of the Pacific Basin. The names of the great discoverers lined the walls, honoring those who had opened the Pacific to the Western world.

Across the Lake of All Nations stood the Federal Building with its forty-eight columns representing the individual states. On either side and around the lake were the various state and international exhibits.

On the north side of the Lake of All Nations stood the severely modern and critically acclaimed Pacific House, the theme building for the fair. Inside was an oceanic relief map of the Pacific Basin with spouting dolphins. Six large murals by Miguel Covarrubias displayed the economy and culture of the Pacific theme.

Between the Pacific House and the main parking area at the north end of the island stood the Gayway, a name the fair board would probably not choose today. This was the amusement center. The Diving Bell took passengers to the bottom of a fish tank. A wonderful carousel with hand-carved figures, twin ferris wheels, a roller-coaster, incubator babies, monkey auto races, and Sally Rand's Nude Ranch were some of the attractions that separated visitors from their money.

More upscale than the entertainment in the Gayway was the Calvalcade of the Golden West. Performing behind the Court of Pacifica in an amphitheater with a stage 400 feet wide and 200 feet deep featuring a water curtain 30 feet high, a cast of some 300 actors and 200 animals displayed the history of the West regularly during the run of the exposition.

Billy Rose brought his Aquacade to the fair in 1940. Esther Williams, Johnny Weissmuller, and Gertrude Ederle, along with the Aquabelles and Aquabeaux, not only entertained fairgoers but also made money for Rose.

Treasure Island was a wonderful place to walk. Beautiful gardens, sparkling fountains, and magnificent views across San Francisco Bay gave visitors ever-changing vistas. When walking got to be too much, there were the elephant trains, the swan boats, ricksha rides, and rolling cars. Most spectacular was watching the Pan-American China Clipper take off from Yerba Buena Cove outside the Hall of Air Transporation on its way to the Orient.

Exhibits of all kinds were housed in the various exposition halls. One could see a 1,000-pound cake from Ojai and sample foods in the Food Building. Many people got their first look at television in the Communications Building. Visitors could see what San Francisco was expected to look like in 1999 in the Hall of Mines, Metals and Machinery. General Motors displayed a translucent Pontiac among its exhibits, and Westinghouse introduced a robot, "Willie Vocalite." In 1939, the Palace of Fine and Decorative Arts had a $40 million exhibit of Old Masters, which went back to Europe at the end of the season and was replaced by a show called "Art in Action."

The fact that a rival world's fair was being held in New York at the same time was more cause for concern for New York than San Francisco. There were attempts by New York representatives in the federal government to force San Francisco to postpone its fair, but President Roosevelt continued federal support for the West Coast fair. Eventually even Mayor Fiorello La Guardia came out for dinner.

The Golden Gate International Exposition opened February 18, 1939, and closed September 29, 1940, with a six-month gap in the middle. Leland W. Cutler was exposition president in 1939, and Marshall Dill was the 1940 president. George Creel served as U.S. commissioner for both years. The fair closed with a gross attendance of 17,041,999 for 1939 and 1940. It left a debt of $559,423. Plans to turn the site into an international airport were abandoned as the U.S. Navy took over the island. Dominant features were quickly torn down. *Pacifica*, the personification of peace, had a chain tied around her base and was pulled over on her face, broken into pieces. World War II had already begun.

BIBLIOGRAPHY

While there are literally thousands of sources available for a detailed study of the Golden Gate International Exposition of 1939–1940, four sources are particularly helpful. H. C. Bottoroff, *Closing Report: San Francisco Bay Exposition. Sponsor for the Golden Gate International Exposition* (1942?), is the official history of the fair. Bottoroff, the executive vice-president and general manager, includes a wealth of statistics for the fair, ranging from daily attendance figures to gardening costs. *Treasure Island, the Magic City* (1941), by Jack James and Earle Weller, is a heavily illustrated description of the exposition, with information on activities and special events during the two-season run of the fair and statistical appendixes. There is even a list of all the fair employees during the two years. The art and architecture of the fair is described and explained in Eugen Neuhaus, *The Art of Treasure Island* (1939), while Richard Reinhardt, *Treasure Island: San Francisco's Exposition Years* (1973), is a fascinating and well-illustrated reminiscence by a modern authority on fairs who visited the Golden Gate International Exposition when he was eleven years old. Reinhardt has also written a fiftieth-anniversary retrospective of the fair, "The Other Fair," *American Heritage* 40, no. 4 (May/June 1989): 42–53.

Donald G. Larson

WELLINGTON 1939–1940

NEW ZEALAND CENTENNIAL EXHIBITION

In the summer of 1939–1940 New Zealand celebrated the centennial of its foundation as a British colony in grand style with the Centennial Exhibition. The idea for an international exhibition in Wellington had first been proposed in 1930. By 1938, however, the scope of the centennial exhibition had been determined as imperial, as opposed to international, because of the need for official recognition for an international exhibition. Funds were raised by selling shares in the exhibition company and by government contributions and subsidies. Work progressed quickly on the Rongotai site in central Wellington, which had been chosen for its good transport facilities and for the prospect of minimum engineering difficulties in preparing the site. The playing fields of Rongotai College were also conveniently located for exhibition usage.

On November 8, 1939, the governor-general, Lord Galway, officially opened the New Zealand Centennial Exhibition, despite the fact that World War II had begun two months earlier. The exhibition was thus not only a tribute to the progress of a young nation but also a boost to national morale. Covering an area of 55 acres, the exhibition included 12 miles of pathways around which "Kiwi trains" provided transportation and scenic tours. The buildings, covering 14 acres and costing £50,000, were truly magnificent, though they were only temporary structures. Beautiful gardens, reflective water pools, and a splendid central fountain were major features of the landscaping. The 155-foot tower was a symbolic focal point, which could be seen for miles when illuminated. Lighting on a scale never seen before in the Southern Hemisphere constituted one of the primary devices used to beautify all aspects of the exhibition.

The exhibits and displays at the exhibition were of the highest standard. In spite of the war, the United Kingdom had still sent exhibits for a communications and transport display. The Australian and Fijian pavilions concentrated on resources and travel attractions, and the Canadian court focused on industry and agriculture. But the New Zealand exhibits dominated. Twenty-six departments of state contributed to the outstanding Government Court. The Dominion Court, representing all of the provinces, was a successful alternative to past individual provincial exhibits. The miniature models of cities, farms, industries, and scenery were interesting, educational, and visually stimulating. Other displays focused on manufacturing industries, transportation, and electrical and engineering themes. The Women's Section provided free lectures and demonstrations every day and included the most striking historical display of the exhibition. Two rooms, one from the North Island representing difficult pioneering conditions and the other from the South Island characterizing a later, more prosperous settler's home, were excellent collections of historical artifacts and memorabilia.

Predictably, Playland was one of the most popular sections of the exhibition. A roller coaster, funhouse, miniature race track, magicians, and Chinese acrobats were a few of the attractions.

Overall the New Zealand Centennial Exhibition was a great success. A spectacular tribute was paid to the past, and the future looked bright, which in a time of war was an important achievement. Although an attendance of 4 million had been originally hoped for, the total of 2,641,043 was a success given wartime conditions. While the exhibition did not make a financial profit, there can be no doubt as to its place as one of New Zealand's greatest centennial achievements.

BIBLIOGRAPHY

The best published source for this exhibition is N. B. Palethorpe, *Official History of the New Zealand Centennial Exhibition, Wellington, 1939–1940* (1940). Published by the exhibition company, this volume includes chapters on earlier New Zealand fairs and on the origin, site, buildings, statuary, ceremonies, and general features of this fair. In addition, the *Official Guide to the Government Court, New Zealand Centennial Exhibition, 1939–1940* (1939) is useful. Because of the onset of World War II in September 1939, newspaper coverage of this event in New York and London papers is practically nonexistent; much more information can be found in the Wellington dailies—the *Dominion* and the *Evening Post*.

Felicity Caird

LISBON 1940
EXPOSIÇÃO DO MUNDO PORTUGUÊS

The idea for a Lisbon world's fair came from Antonio Ferro, the national sec-
retariate of propaganda of Portugal, and the fair was organized by Captain
Henrique Galvao, a close friend of dictator Antonio de Oliveira Salazar but later
an opponent of the regime. Its purpose was to glorify the fascist regime of
Salazar, although the official rationale was to "set forth in pageant, dance, and
patriotic community gatherings, the story of eight centuries of Portuguese history." The fair celebrated the anniversaries of the founding of Portugal in 1140
and independence from Spain after sixty years of rule in 1640.

Located in the Belem district near the Hieronymite Monastery in Lisbon where
Vasco da Gama and the poet Luis de Camoes were buried, the fair celebrated
three eras of history. The first cycle, which took place in the spring of 1940,
had medieval history as its theme. The events included town meetings on opening
day, June 2, a speech by Salazar, an exhibit of primitive art in the Museum of
Ancient Art, and a Navy Day festival with a reception aboard a replica of a
fifteenth-century caravel, a naval procession on the River Tagus complete with
a scheduled landing of a Pan-Am Clipper, a review of international fleets, and
an exhibit of the exploits of the first navigators on the Rock of Sagres.

The second cycle's theme, which took place during the summer months, was
imperial history. It featured an exhibit of arts and crafts, a garden containing
colonial designs from Africa, China, and India, a pageant of twenty-one imperial
provinces, a festival for Camoes, and an Olympic week in a stadium newly built
for the fair.

The final phase commemorated the Brigantine Epoch, from 1640 on, and took
place in the fall. It featured gala performances in the reconstructed opera house
and tours of the restored seventeenth-century quarter of Lisbon.

The fair's opening on June 2 coincided with the British evacuation of Dunkirk,
which almost completely crowded it out of the newspapers. Because of World
War II, the fair had much less foreign participation than had been planned. In
particular, the review of international fleets suffered because of the war and
tensions among those countries still neutral. At the opening, Salazar and the
colonial patriarch attended services at the Lisbon Cathedral while the town
council and the National Assembly had ceremonial meetings. On June 30, the
British, anxious to keep Portugal neutral, commissioned the duke of Kent, brother
to King George VI, to award Salazar the Grand Cross of the Most Distinguished
Order of St. Michael and St. George, an award usually reserved for a Briton.
The fair, overshadowed by the war, attracted nowhere near the attention given
to the competing New York World's Fair. When it closed on December 2, there
were rumors that the director of colonial fairs and exhibitions and national

broadcasting had profited from the fair. Salazar dismissed the charges as communist inspired and declared his satisfaction with a fair O. H. de Oliveira Marques described as "a typical Fascist display in its manner of interpreting the past and abusing it to herald the present."

BIBLIOGRAPHY

There is very little information on the Lisbon World's Fair in English either in books or newspapers. There is some mention of the fair in the *New York Times* and the London *Times*, but the former was more occupied with the New York World's Fair and the latter with World War II and England's precarious situation. Nor does it rate more than a passing note in most histories of Portugal and is often omitted from histories of world's fairs.

The best source of information on the fair, once the propagandistic element is discounted, is the *Portuguese Bulletin of Political, Economic and Cultural Information*, no. 30/31, which is completely devoted to the Exhibition of the Portuguese World. Two books in Portuguese contain much information about the fair. The first is Gustaro do Matos Sequeira, *Mundo Português—Images de uma Exposição Historica 1940* (1956). As the title suggests, this book is an illustrated retrospective of the fair that provides a sense of the design of the exposition. The other work is by Augusto de Castro, the general commissioner of the fair. Entitled *A Exposição do Mundo Português* (1940), it traces the history of Lisbon and the Portuguese empire, and discusses the preexhibition planning.

Finally, two general histories provide the necessary political and social context for the exposition. O. H. de Oliveria Marques, *History of Portugal*, vol. II (1972) is a broad treatment, while Antonio de Fegueiredo, *Portugal: Fifty Years of Dictatorship* (1976) concentrates on the mid-twentieth century era of Salazar rule.

Dwight W. Hoover

PORT-AU-PRINCE 1949–1950

EXPOSITION INTERNATIONALE DU BICENTENAIRE DE PORT-AU-PRINCE

The international exposition in Haiti in 1949 was planned to celebrate the bicentennial of the founding of Port-au-Prince, but the main idea behind what came to be known as the "little world's fair" was to attract tourists and stimulate the economy.

Plans for the exposition arose in 1948 while Haiti, with the help of some international financial aid, was undergoing a period of modernization. President Dumarsais Estime wanted to show off the "new Haiti" and its culture and hoped that a world's fair would entice tourists and pleasure seekers. Estime committed approximately $1 million, close to three-fourths of Haiti's entire annual budget, to the bicentennial.

In the latter part of 1948, the Haitian government reclaimed 60 acres of waterfront land on La Gonave Bay, relocated some 20,000 people who lived in this impoverished area, and began converting the land into a scenic wonderland surrounded by lush gardens, beautiful parks, and an abundance of tall coconut palm trees. The site curved 2 miles along the bay and was divided by a boulevard named in honor of President Harry S Truman.

August Ferdinand Schmiedigen, an architect from New York, whose experience included the Paris 1937 and New York 1939–1940 world's fairs, oversaw the construction of the exposition. Modernistic white and gray buildings were erected along the boulevard, their exteriors boasting colorful murals of Haitian life. All of the buildings were permanent structures designed to be used as government offices after the exposition. Although Schmiedigen had time constraints to worry about and unskilled native labor to direct, he ensured that every detail was just right. The Haitian section of the fair, however, was designed by architect Albert Mangones and was said to have had a "pleasing disregard for straight lines."

Throughout the site's strategically placed gardens and parks were an array of statues and sculptures. In the central garden a "super-electric-musical-luminous" fountain was installed. Westinghouse experts said it was one of the most impressive fountains they had ever seen, surpassing even the New York World's Fair fountain for special effects. According to most visitors, the transformation of the swampy slum was breathtaking, and this gave the Haitian citizens feelings of pride and enthusiasm for the upcoming events.

The exposition opened in two sections. On December 8, 1949, the national section, including the agricultural, fine arts, and folklore pavilions, and the amusement area opened along with the government-sponsored National Casino of Haiti. At the opening ceremony, a telegram from President Harry S Truman to President Estime was read, followed by a parade of U.S. soldiers and marines.

During the parade a squadron of nine U.S. Air Force B–29s flew over the line of march.

Ceremonies dedicating the international section were held on February 12, 1950. On the following day, the U.S. pavilion opened along with other official and foreign pavilions. President Estime and his wife, after presiding over the opening ceremonies, took a guided tour of the U.S. exhibit. Other pavilions displayed the exhibits of Cuba, France, Venezuela, Guatemala, Italy, Mexico, Argentina, and other participating nations, as well as the Pan American Union and the United Nations. The Vatican contributed a small, permanent chapel to grace the exposition grounds.

Visitors could walk through the scenic exposition grounds and enjoy native exhibits, consisting of works of art, handcrafted articles of mahogany, needle-work, pottery, silver, historical documents, furniture, and agricultural products. The principal attraction for most visitors was the Haitian folklore troupe, which presented a program of folk dancing several times a month that portrayed the customs and yearnings of the Haitian people. Programs involved voodoo rituals and beliefs, accompanied by drum beating and songs that told stories of primitive religions. These shows were held in an open-air theater, also known as the "voodoo amphitheater."

Other points of interest included a cockfight stadium, a botanical garden, an aquarium of tropical fish, a model banana and sisal plantation, and a burlesque show imported from the United States. The midway, named Les Palmistes be-cause it was built in the heart of a palm tree forest, was also a crowd pleaser. The park was operated by Ross Manning Shows, an amusement company from the United States, and featured carousels, carnival pitchmen, and a variety of thrilling rides and sideshows.

The theme of the exposition, Peace and Progress, was only partially appro-priate. Although Haiti's program of modernization was closely linked to the idea of progress, the country's political conflict with neighboring Dominican Republic was a constant threat to peace. The small attendance figure was attributed to Haiti's political problems. It is estimated that approximately 250,000 people attended the bicentennial celebration before it closed on June 8, 1950.

Haiti's exposition failed to attract as large a number of tourists from the United States as hoped; most of those attending were Haitians. But despite the political unrest and low attendance figures, the exposition was not a complete loss. Haiti, often looked upon as a Third World country, seemed to have a future in the modern world. The exposition created more jobs, new businesses, better roads, beautiful parks, and much-needed government office buildings. Most important, the bicentennial exposition lifted the spirit and morale of the Haitian people.

BIBLIOGRAPHY

Primary sources regarding Haiti's bicentennial exposition are few. For an in-depth study of U.S. participation in this fair, refer to U.S. Senate, Foreign Relations Committee,

81st Cong., 2d sess., *Port-au-Prince Bicentennial Exposition* (1950). For those who are able to read French, Augustin Mathurin, *Bicentenaire de la fondation de Port-au-Prince, 1749–1949* (1975), is an interesting book on the historical aspects of the fair, written in memory of President Dumarsais Estime. Selected articles in the *New York Times* provide good background information. See especially the issues dated October 4, 16, 23, 25, 1949. Additional information can be found in George S. Schuyler, "Haiti Looks Ahead," *Americas*, 1 (December 1949): 6–8; and "Unparalleled Fair," *Time*, 54 (October 17, 1949): 40.

Kimberly Pelle

BRUSSELS 1958

EXPOSITION UNIVERSELLE ET INTERNATIONALE DE BRUXELLES (EXPO '58)

Between April 17 and October 19, 1958, nearly 42 million visitors toured the Brussels Universal and International Exposition, the first major world's fair held in the postwar years and the first since the 1939–1940 New York World's Fair. Like earlier Belgian fairs, the 1958 exposition was intended to promote Belgian economic growth and the development of Belgium-controlled Africa. But the 1958 fair rapidly acquired broader significance as tensions of the cold war increased and doubts deepened about the validity of the longstanding Western habit of equating progress with science and technology. By the time the fair opened, the exposition, with its towering Atomium as centerpiece, had become a place for testing and shaping the possibilities of human existence under the shadow of nuclear destruction.

First proposed in 1947 and financed by the Belgian government, including a grant from the colonial lottery, and various corporations, the fair immediately fell victim to the rumblings of the cold war. Promotors of the event, including powerful Belgian metal and mining industries, initially set 1955 for the exposition's opening, but the Korean War disrupted international financial markets and political relations, forcing postponement until 1958. The cold war was equally in evidence once the fair opened as the United States and the Soviet Union built pavilions dedicated to propagandizing their rival political systems. The era's nuclear umbrella also provided cover for other exhibitors bent on defining the socioeconomic contours of the postwar world: scientists and engineers used the fair to promote the uses of nuclear power in energy development; the Belgian government relied on the fair to reaffirm domestic support for its crumbling imperial policies in the Congo; and multinational corporations, following the pattern of corporation-sponsored exhibits at the 1933–1934 Chicago Century of Progress Exposition, saw the fair as a public relations paradise for promoting the purported benefits that would follow from global economic consolidation.

Direction of the fair was set by Baron Georges Moens de Fernig, the exposition's commissioner-general, and Charles Everaerts de Velp of the government's Ministry of Economic Affairs. In addition to securing royal lands to add to Heysel Park for purposes of expanding the 1935 exposition grounds, exposition directors set up an organization that oversaw exhibit development, architectural planning, and the supervision of as many as 15,000 Belgian and foreign construction workers.

The exposition grounds were vast, covering nearly 500 acres of undulating parkland that proved to be one of the most beautiful settings ever developed for a world's fair. Solving the problem of transportation for an exposition covering such an expanse was no small task, and exposition designers devised a number of innovations to facilitate the comfort of tourists. To alleviate the problem of long climbs in and out of valleys that cut through the grounds, exposition planners designed as 1/3-mile-long concrete passenger viaduct that carried visitors from the edge of the park to the center of the grounds and afforded commanding views of the exposition buildings. At the same time, engineers designed an overhead cable car system and arranged for a variety of motorized ground transportation vehicles to ease the plight of tourists overwhelmed by the size of the exposition grounds and the distances from the entrances to the main exhibition buildings.

The exposition layout assumed an odd form. From a bird's-eye perspective, the design of the fair resembled nothing so much as a child's rendering of a large barnyard animal. Forming the head and shoulders of this design were the Foreign Buildings; the main body was devoted to Belgian and Belgian colonial exhibitions; and the hindquarters was given over to scientific and artistic displays housed in buildings that remained from the 1935 fair. Standing at the heart of the fair as well as at the intersection of four major arterial avenues was the exposition's vital center, the Atomium.

The fair's architect-in-chief, Marcel van Goethem, determined that the main exhibit halls would be designed along modernist lines and that no effort would be made to establish a rigid formula similar to the one imposed at earlier fairs, notably the 1893 Chicago World's Columbian Exposition. The result was striking, if not especially significant architecturally. Exhibition halls represented an eclectic range of modernist styles that emphasized the playful possibilities of structures that seemed to defy gravity. "The fair of roofs," was how one critic described the architectural landscape, while another noted the "glass-box-curtain-wall" effect of many of the buildings. Notable designs included Le Corbusier's Philips' Pavilion (complete with "Electronic Poem," composed by Edgard Varese), often likened to a "collapsed aluminum tent" or to a "serious airline accident"; Egon Eiermann's West German Pavilion, a "necklace" of small two- and three-story exhibition halls; Edward Stone's U.S. Pavilion, "a merry-go-round of latticed plastic"; Alexander Boretski's Soviet Pavilion, which bore an uncanny resemblance to a refrigerator; Guillaume Gillet's steel-roofed French Pavilion; and J. van Dooselaere's beaklike Belgian Civil Engineering Building.

While it is easy to trivialize the architecture of the fair, it would be a mistake to overlook the ideological scaffolding that gave it form. Few critics missed the importance of the Soviet pavilion—the first Soviet structure at any world's fair to break away from the heavy-handed socialist realist style that had guided the design of Soviet exhibition structures at fairs held in Paris (1937) and New York (1939). For the first time, heroic statues of workers and party founders were located inside the building and not joined to the structure's exterior. While Russians were relying on a new architectural design to improve the image of the Soviet Union, Americans were engaged in similar public relations activities.

Located diagonally across from the "closed-in" Soviet pavilion, the American pavilion, according to Western critics, placed a premium on "light, strength, and freedom." Not surprisingly, representatives of other nations watched nervously to determine if the transformation of the fair into an architectural rutting ground between the superpowers carried implications for international relations and noted the irony of locating the smaller pavilions of Middle Eastern countries between those of the United States and the Soviet Union.

In addition to making a spectacle of cold war politics, the fair also permitted politicians in countries like Germany, Japan, and Italy, losers in the war, to refurbish their national images and soothe memories of battle wounds among the victors. The small and unimposing German pavilion, often referred to as a jewel, contrasted sharply to Albert Speer's monument to Nazism at the 1937 Paris exposition. Instead of presenting an exhibition of German power, German exhibits stressed "a Germany striving for a life which is cheerful, friendly and free, unhampered by anxious reference to danger in the world at large." Japan followed suit and seemed bent on exhibiting a new openness through the timber and glass construction of its pavilion, while the modesty and economy of scale of the Italian pavilion seemed light-years away from anything proposed by Mussolini in his plans for a fascist world's fair in the early 1940s.

Architecture was not alone in reflecting broader political configurations. Exhibits within the pavilions often became sources of controversy that reflected the anxieties about the cold war. The U.S. government divided bitterly over the fair. President Dwight Eisenhower felt so strongly about the need for the United States to make a strong showing there that he included a special request for funds in his budget message to Congress, only to encounter strong opposition in the House of Representatives. The House actually reduced the overall budget for U.S. participation to $13 million, a sum that paled beside the reported $50 million that the Soviets had committed to their building and exhibits. One reason for continued congressional opposition to increasing the fair appropriation was that a portion of the U.S. exhibit, entitled "Unfinished Business," concentrated on the unsolved social problems that beset the United States in the 1950s. Of particular concern to southern congressmen, who termed the display a "gross insult to the South," was an exhibition label condemning segregation in the South. Funding cutbacks seriously affected the U.S. displays. When budget cuts forced the reduction of U.S. scientific exhibits in the International Hall of Science and the Soviet Union immediately took over the space previously occupied by the Americans, American anxieties about competing with the Russians worsened. Other aspects of the American exhibit also proved troublesome. The U.S. exposition commission, headed by Howard Cullman, determined to emphasize American life-styles and the supposed freedom that mass consumption had brought to ordinary Americans. But the effort to provide authentic experiences for fairgoers sometimes proved a costly proposition. For instance, the hot dog concessionaire was forced to fly in American buns after American visitors complained about the strange shape and taste of the hot dogs they were served. And

BRUSSELS 1958. The U.S. pavilion, shown here amid an array of state and territorial flags, earned criticism for its poor showing in the cold-war propaganda contest with the U.S.S.R. pavilion.

American officials had to maintain straight faces when polling machines were set up in the U.S. pavilion to record votes for the most popular American personalities—an exercise intended to give foreign visitors a chance to experience the freedom of choice exercised by American citizens. (Final tallies revealed that motion picture actress Kim Novak was more popular than Marilyn Monroe, that Abraham Lincoln was America's greatest statesman, that Louis Armstrong was America's finest musician, and that Albert Einstein was the most important immigrant to the United States.) Of all the displays in the pavilion, the most popular was the Circarama, a large exhibition hall with a 360-degree screen that enveloped visitors with a Walt Disney motion picture tour of the United States.

The Soviet Union treated the propaganda opportunity provided by the fair as seriously as did the Americans. Devoted to the "unseen blooming in Soviet science and culture," exhibits in the pavilion told the story of forty years of Russian technological and scientific progress since the revolution and were explicitly intended to counter efforts by the West to smear the Soviet Union. At the core of the exhibit were models of Sputnik, surrounded by displays intended to convince fairgoers that the Soviet Union would shortly surpass the United States in the production of material goods. Equally important to the Soviet display was an emphasis on the peaceful uses of atomic energy, which the exhibit catalog contrasted to the American use of nuclear power "for the undoing of mankind." In addition to its emphasis on technological and scientific advances, Soviet exhibition planners also underscored Russian cultural prowess. Never before had the Soviet Union so saturated a world's fair and its host city with ballet performances, musical recitals, and exhibitions of Russian art and sculpture. Not everyone was pleased with the Russian success. On at least one occasion, several U.S. servicemen expressed a wider sense of American frustration over their country's showing in Belgium by attempting to climb the flagpoles outside the Soviet pavilion.

While the Brussels World's Fair shed light on—and, at times, basked in the light of—cold war political struggles between the superpowers, it also unshuttered another development of the postwar years: decolonization. The end of the British and French colonial empires was already in sight in 1958. Indeed, the absence of expansive British and French colonial exhibits at the Brussels fair that had characterized those nations' participation at earlier world's fairs made the Belgian colonial exhibits seem all the more impressive—and anachronistic. Intended to demonstrate the "civilizing mission" of Belgian colonial rule in the Congo (now Zaire) and Rwanda-Urundi (now the separate nations of Rwanda and Burundi), the colonial show covered 19 acres of tropical gardens and consisted of seven pavilions dedicated to colonial government, energy and transportation, Catholic missions, agriculture, natural history, mining, and commerce. As a display of imperial aims, the exhibit was a success, but as a display of colonial realities, it masked more than it revealed, as Belgians and the rest of the world would discover two years later when the Congo erupted in a bloody struggle for independence.

Other exhibitors proved similarly adept at re-presenting realities. In the face of a spiraling arms race and profound skepticism about the contributions of science to human progress, exposition planners, with the cooperation of scientific organizations in fifteen nations, set aside one of the permanent palaces from the 1935 exposition for a Hall of International Science dedicated to demonstrating the service of science to humanity. Divided into four compartments devoted to nuclear physics, solid-state physics, general chemistry, and biology, the exhibits stressed the unity of science, the "march of science," and the importance of theoretical research and held out the possibility of new scientific "miracles" that would contribute to a resurgence of humanism.

Underscoring the importance of science to this fair was the exposition's towering, permanent monument to the atom. The idea for the Atomium was first proposed by André Waterkeyn, an engineer with the Belgian metals consortium FABRIMETAL. Waterkeyn never lost sight of promoting the metal industry in the course of designing his representation of a crystal molecule of iron—a design construction that immediately captured the fancy of exposition managers. Waterkeyn's plan for a 334-foot-high structure with nine 59-foot-diameter spheres large enough for scientific exhibits and restaurants and connected by escalator tubes symbolizing binding molecular forces was compelling. His Atomium concept was perfectly attuned to the exposition's twin goals of building public support for the rapid development of nuclear energy facilities and of promoting the idea that human beings were in control of their own destiny. As visitors entered the reception hall in the sphere at the base of the Atomium, they encountered an exhibit arranged by the Belgian Congo Nuclear Group bent on promoting the development of nuclear power plants in Belgium's colonies. From that moment on, messages about the nonmilitary uses of atomic power bombarded Atomium visitors. As they made their way to other spheres, conveyed by some of Europe's longest escalators, they came across national and corporate exhibits that promoted the rapid development of nuclear power plants. When they finally reached the top sphere, fairgoers were treated to spectacular views of the exposition grounds and the surrounding city of Brussels, as if to emphasize that atomic power could have enjoyable consequences. At once instructive and awesome, the Atomium crystallized concerns about the atomic threat while suggesting that the future of atomic energy could be left to the control of scientists and engineers who had the good of humanity uppermost in their minds. At the same time, the Atomium reinforced claims by the burgeoning nuclear power industry that nuclear power was safe—despite the fact that plans to power the exposition with a nuclear generator had to be abandoned because of health concerns.

The role of the fair in promoting nuclear energy development cannot be underestimated. In the Electrical Energy pavilion, a consortium of Belgian industries displayed models of reactors scheduled to begin operation in 1960. Meanwhile, planners of various national pavilions vied with one another to demonstrate the rapid progress of nuclear energy development. Photographs and models of nuclear reactors under development were prominently displayed in the U.S. pavilion. Not to be outdone, the French government unfolded plans to use nuclear power to meet at least one-fourth of France's energy needs by 1967. The British pavilion even included a hall devoted to British nuclear industries, and the Soviet Union proudly displayed its nuclear reactor models as well.

To find relief from the anxieties of the atomic age, fairgoers could turn to midway areas located in various parts of the exposition. In the area of the fair given over to Gay Belgium, a reconstruction of a typical Belgian village circa 1900, visitors could retreat into nostalgia for the past while enjoying a variety of cabaret and nightclub entertainments. Or fairgoers could escape to the future in various midway attractions like the Interplanetary Rocket that supposedly had the capacity to transport visitors to Mars. Flying cars, a centrifugal force machine, plus a variety of other technological amusements located in the Jardin des Attractions translated fear of atomic age technology into pleasurable experiences associated with leisure and mass consumption.

Promoters of the Brussels Universal Exposition tried to provide a "balance sheet of the modern world," constantly emphasizing the possibilities for human beings under the threat of nuclear annihilation to direct menacing scientific and technological discoveries toward human-centered goals. The dominant note of the fair was optimistic and upbeat, but the fair probably stimulated cold war competition as much as it muted conflict. And for all of the rhetoric about the fair's ushering in a new humanism, the exposition probably reinforced pervasive feelings of loneliness and despair as visitors tried to reconcile the exposition's promise of a better future with the evidence that the future would be ever more determined by large-scale industrial and political organizations.

Was the exposition a success? As with all other world's fairs, the answer is more complex than determining whether the ink on the bottom line of exposition ledger books was black. The best estimates available suggest that expenditures for the fair substantially outstripped income, but the indirect economic benefits of the fair were significant. Construction jobs and employment on the fairgrounds provided significant relief from unemployment. In the course of building the fair, Brussels acquired 30 miles of new roads and 5 miles of tunnels. Tourists numbering in the millions spent money for hotels, food, and transportation in Brussels. And once the fair was completed, many of the prefabricated buildings were disassembled and shipped around Belgium and Europe for reconstruction as permanent structures. The city of Liège bought the Transportation Hall for use as a covered market, an Antwerp firm bought the Finnish pavilion, and a Dutch firm purchased the Vatican's exhibit hall. Other exhibition buildings were returned to their countries of origin where they added to urban landscapes around the world. Most visibly, Brussels acquired several hundred additional acres of parkland and a permanent addition to its skyline, the Atomium, as a lasting reminder of an exposition that did as much to shape as it did to reflect the political culture of the atomic age.

BIBLIOGRAPHY

The Brussels Universal Exposition generated and inspired a significant amount of literature. The best starting point for investigating the fair is with the archival records housed in the Department Technique, parc des Expositions, Brussels. The records include manuscript materials on the organization and development of the fair, as well as a significant variety of official exposition publications. Other archives, including the Brussels City Archives and Ministry of Economic Affairs, house published sources but few manuscript materials. The City Archives is especially rich in contemporary newspaper and magazine accounts of the fair.

The most valuable printed source is the eight-volume *Le Memorial officiel de L'Exposition universelle et internationale de bruxelles* (1958–1962), which provides detailed information about the fair's organization and exhibits and includes a volume that bears the ambitious title *Synthèse*. There were numerous official catalogs and guidebooks published in a multiplicity of languages. A good place to begin is with the *Guide officiel: Exposition universelle bruxelles 1958* (1958). Most foreign countries produced their own catalogs and official reports. For the U.S. exhibit, see *This Is America* (1958), along with Marguerite Cullman's autobiographical *Ninety Dozen Glasses* (1960). For the Soviet Union, the best source is the official catalog, *USSR: World's Exposition in Brussels* (1958). Other useful sources of information include general accounts provided in popular magazines like *Time, Newsweek,* and *Reader's Digest* and more detailed coverage in national newspapers like *Le Monde* and the *New York Times*. The best starting point for information about architecture is with articles from the exposition year in *Architectural Forum, Architectural Record,* and *Architectural Review*. For information on the exposition's profits and losses, consult H. de Meyer and P. H. Virenque, *Brussel '58 in Cijfers* (1959).

Secondary source coverage is slim. Other than brief mention in general histories of world's fairs like John Allwood, *The Great Exhibitions* (1977), and Wolfgang Friebe, *Architecktur der Weltausstellungen, 1851–1970* (1983), the best starting point is Fernand Baudhuin's concise account, *Histoire économique de la Belgique: 1957–1968* (1970).

Robert W. Rydell

SEATTLE 1962

SEATTLE WORLD'S FAIR
(CENTURY 21 EXPOSITION)

A few days after the Soviet Union launched its Sputnik satellite in 1957, prominent American scientists associated with the Department of Defense, the National Science Foundation, and the Josiah Macy, Jr., Foundation met in Washington, D.C., to assess the damage to American prestige. The stunning scientific achievements of the previous dozen years suddenly seemed to have been eclipsed by what many had imagined was a bellicose but scientifically backward nation. The scientists proposed that the United States sponsor an international fair to demonstrate that the nation remained a preeminent scientific power.

Across the continent in Seattle, meanwhile, urban developers were seeking support for a Century 21 Exposition, which originally was to have celebrated the fiftieth anniversary of the Alaska-Yukon-Pacific Exposition of 1909. Edward Carlson was the chairman of the Century 21 Corporation, and Ewen Dingwall and James N. Faber were, respectively, director and assistant director. When promoters met scientists and supportive federal officials during a Parliament of Science sponsored by the American Association for the Advancement of Science, the idea for the 1962 Seattle World's Fair was born.

Support for the showcase U.S. science exhibit was predicated on the development of a theme stressing the unity and imagination of science as opposed to a celebration of gadgetry and purely technological achievements. The essence of the nation's ostensible scientific lag seemed to be that the popular American imagination had not yet come to terms with the intellectual vigor of scientific achievement or its special relationship to American life. U.S. scientific exhibits at the Brussels exposition had been overshadowed by Soviet displays. Plans for the U.S. exhibit were integrated into the fair's overall Man in Space theme, which was to be a vision of life in the year 2000.

The fair was projected to run for two years, beginning in 1961, but was postponed for a year, and shortened to six months to help secure the important endorsement of the Bureau internationale des expositions. Without the endorsement, the fair would have been preempted by the much larger New York fair being planned for 1964. Foreign governments initially were reluctant to participate because they apparently expected the U.S. government would provide support. More than forty-nine nations eventually sponsored exhibits or loaned equipment. International exposition historian John Allwood contended that the French exhibit was "the only one which gave any hint that science alone might not answer all man's problems."

The 74-acre downtown site featured the 605-foot-tall Space Needle, a high-speed monorail, an amusement park, and an existing civic center, arena, and stadium. A fountain shot plumes of water 100 feet into the air. Foreign shops, bazaars, and restaurants lined the Boulevards of the World. The exposition was arranged in "worlds" of commerce and industry, art and entertainment, a year 2000 exhibit, and the World of Science, dominated by the U.S. pavilion. Designed by Minoru Yamasaki, the structure took inspiration from the Swedish pavilion at the 1939–1940 New York World's Fair. Five attached units surrounding gardens, pools, and fountains were enhanced by a filagree of Gothic arches. The buildings included theaters, history of science exhibits, a Spacearium, and a children's science laboratory complete with ant farms, gyroscopes, and electric fish.

More than 10 million paid admissions were recorded, and 6,748,000 people passed through the U.S. exhibit, which was constructed and operated with a $9.2 million federal appropriation. One day after the fair ended, the government leased the pavilion for $1 a year to what became the Pacific Science Center, which has since drawn 1 million visitors a year. The entire site became the Seattle Center, comprising museums, theaters, an opera house, shops, restaurants, carnival rides, and arena facilities for professional hockey and basketball teams. The Space Needle houses restaurants and gift shops. Dingwall, who served as director of Seattle Center, reflected on the redevelopment during the twenty-fifth anniversary celebrations: "The concept from the very beginning was that we needed theaters, we needed exposition space. I don't know of any other modern project where this has been done. I think it's sort of a miracle that we had this kind of plan." According to John Allwood, *The Great Exhibitions* (1977) through excellent planning Century 21 "left the city a legacy of outstanding facilities as well as a financial profit," just as the 1909 exposition had done. Nevertheless, Seattle mayor Charles Royer noted in 1987 that the site was "not at its full potential. It's frayed around the edges and taking a lot of our general fund money."

The fair was the first international exposition to be held in the United States in twenty-three years, and the U.S. science exhibit was the first ever staged for the American people. The fair helped generate public support for increased spending for science education. The moon landing at the end of the decade was perhaps a legacy of the U.S. exhibit, which Alistair Cooke called "a single philosophical conception of remarkable majesty."

BIBLIOGRAPHY

The State Archives Regional Center at Western Washington University, a branch of the Washington State Archives system, holds the records of the 1962 Seattle World's Fair and the Century 21 Corporation. This collection consists of corporate, planning, and development materials, as well as fair ephemera. A bibliographic guide to this collection is in preparation.

Among published works, the *Final Report of the United States Science Exhibit at the*

Seattle World's Fair (1962), published by the U.S. Department of Commerce, is primarily concerned with the science exhibit, but it also provides some general background on the fair. James Bently Tayler, *Science on Display: A Study of the United States Science Exhibit, Seattle World's Fair* (1963), is a thorough study of the exhibit conducted by the Institute for Sociological Research at the University of Washington, Seattle.

A general secondary work on the fair is Murray Morgan, *Century 21: The Story of the Seattle World's Fair* (1963), a highly readable account. The *Official Guide to the Pacific Northwest and the Century 21 Exposition* (1961) is aimed toward tourists. Contemporary periodical articles of interest include J. T. Burns, "The Architecture of Century 21," *Progressive Architecture* 45, no. 6 (June 1962): 49–56; and Paul Thery, "A Tour of Century 21," *Architectural Record* 151, no. 7 (June 1962): 141–48, for the architectural aspects of the fair. C. B. Patterson, "Seattle Fair Looks to the 21st Century," *National Geographic* 122, no. 5 (September 1962): 402–72, contains an abundance of illustrations, and Russell Lynes, "Seattle Will Never Be the Same," *Harper's Magazine* 125 (July 1962): 20–25, discusses the impact of the fair on its host city.

Larry Brown looks back on the fair after twenty-five years in "A Silver Science Birthday," *Seattle Times*, October 22, 1987, and Andrew Oppman compares the postfair site development in Seattle and Knoxville in an article in the October 25, 1987, issue of the *Knoxville News-Sentinel*.

A 1963 film, *It Happened at the World's Fair*, starring Elvis Presley and Joan O'Brien, was set in and around the Seattle fair. A romantic musical with a thin plot, the film was directed by Norman Taurog and serves mainly as a vehicle for Presley's singing.

Paul Ashdown

NEW YORK 1964–1965

NEW YORK WORLD'S FAIR

Unprecedented exhibit architecture, rides, and films were created for the New York World's Fair of 1964–1965. The fair, however, did not live up to its potential success of 73 million visitors due to autocratic management (28 million advance ticket sales—triple expectations). The fair suffered from difficult public relations, financial blunders, and the lack of international support.

The idea for a world's fair originated around 1958 by lawyer Robert Kopple while reminiscing about the 1939–1940 fair. This idea was promoted by Charles Preusse, city administrator, and Thomas Deegan, a public relations expert. The fair commemorated the three hundredth anniversary of the founding of New York as an English colony with the theme, Peace Through Understanding.

Robert Moses, chairman of the Triborough Bridge and Transit Authority, was appointed president of the fair. Moses promoted the 1939–1940 and 1964–1965 World's Fairs on the same site to develop the dump at Flushing Meadows into a park. The previous fair cleaned up the dump but did not complete the park. The fair was developed around the park master plan, reusing existing lakes, trees, utilities, and roads. The 1939–1940 fair's financial problems were caused by constructing pavilions it could not pay for through rentals. Exhibitors were rented land to build their own buildings in 1964–1965.

The beaux arts site plan of 1939–1940 was reused in a more formalized manner. New avenues were aligned with loop and radiating avenues to simplify the earlier plan and tie focal points together. Avenues and promenades radiated outward from the center to fountain and pavilion focal points. The fair symbol, the Unisphere, the largest model of the Earth, replaced the Trylon and Perisphere of 1939–1940 at the center. Buildings were not used to create urban spaces or to strengthen the alignment of avenues as in 1939–1940. Avenues were dependent on their alignment, plantings, lighting, and end focal points for organizational strength.

Exhibit zones were simplified and somewhat rearranged. The Transportation and Amusement Zones were located in the same areas. The Amusement Zone was much smaller in the later fair, and some private exhibitors sponsored amusement rides in other zones. The Government Zone, divided into the International and the Federal and State Zones, was relocated around the Unisphere. All other groups except transportation were joined into the Industrial Zone, which was relocated around the Pool of Industry (formerly the Lagoon of Nations).

Except for Spain, the major European countries did not officially participate. Around eighty nations were represented in thirty-seven pavilions, of which about fourteen were privately sponsored. Private European exhibits came from Belgium, Berlin, France, Sweden, and Switzerland, while Austria, Denmark, Greece, Ireland, and Spain had government support. Other privately sponsored exhibits represented Israel, Hong Kong, and multinational pavilions from Polynesia, Africa, the Caribbean, and Central America.

This was the first U.S. fair to have significant participation by developing nations. Asian countries sponsoring pavilions were India, Pakistan, Indonesia, Japan, South Korea, Malaysia, Nationalist China, the Philippines, and Thailand. Others sponsoring pavilions were Guinea, Sierra Leone, Egypt, Jordan, Lebanon, Morocco, Sudan, and Mexico.

The absence of major European countries and the Fair Corporation's abdication of design theme control allowed commercialism to dominate over internationalism. The result was a disorganized image of individual pavilions competing among themselves for attention. Exhibit signs and music conflicted with those of the fair.

Critics of the commercial aspects of the fair were also not very receptive to the architecture. The fair displayed some of the finest commercial exhibit architecture of recent times. National and state exhibits were also well designed. Commercial structures tended to be modern in design, while national buildings were modern or traditional representations of cultural heritage.

Recurring design themes were Andy Warhol–style pop art images, buildings floating above ground, and pavilions set in reflecting pools. Colorful and pulsating night lighting was successfully used to attract attention or highlight buildings, avenues, and other focal points. Pop images of engines, tires, moon surfaces, hats, sand dunes, and umbrellas were everywhere. There were also monumental spherical shapes, entrances, rotundas, domes, colonnades, photo billboards, and corporate logos.

Corporate pavilion design competitiveness replaced a similar rivalry among western nations at the 1958 Brussels exhibition. Most structural frames were hidden inside large image-formed shapes. The Kahn and Jacobs architectural firm designed the Travelers Insurance red umbrella logo to float 23 feet above a fountain. The Bell System's 400-foot-long wing floated 35 feet above the Pool of Industry as designed by the firm of Harrison and Abramovitz. Charles Luckman's U.S. pavilion hovered 18 feet above a plaza. Johnson's Wax architectural firm, Lippincott and Margulies, suspended a saucer-shaped theater 24 feet above ground on six columns. Architect Philip Johnson designed sixteen columns to support a cable roof over a New York State map that constituted the floor. An elevated egg-shaped theater was covered with a repetitive IBM logo pattern by architect Eero Saarinen. The illuminated exposed frame dome of the General Electric pavilion was developed by architect Welton Becket. Architect Javier Carvajal of Madrid designed the Spanish pavilion with national and modern finishes of high quality. The undulating vertical concrete and blue glass block wall of the Hall of Science was designed by Harrison and Abramovitz. For Kodak, Kahn and Jacobs created a moon-scaped canopy with five large photographs displayed around a tower. The Jordanian pavilion featured concrete, blue glass, and gold mosaic domes designed by Victor Bisharat to resemble sand dunes.

Some pavilions used new air-inflated or suspended membranes, glass fiber–reinforced plastic, and silicone sealants to clad and enclose spaces. The raspberry-shaped Brass Rail, dome-shaped Schaefer, and Dancing Waters exhibits had air-inflated roofs. The Festival of Gas, New Jersey, and Berlin buildings had suspended lightweight fabric roofing systems. The American Gas structure used a new suspended plate-glass wall system. The Bell System exterior was clad in lightweight fiberglass panels. The suspended roof of New York State and the U.S. walls were made of colorful plastic panels. The General Electric pavilion was roofed with a liquid silicone rubber.

Traditional ethnic architecture was a delightful contrast and relief from modern corporate constructions. Belgium, the largest national exhibit of 4 acres, was a meticulous reproduction of an 1800s walled village. Other simulated villages included Bourbon Street–New Orleans, Lowenbrau Gardens, Hawaiian, Hollywood, and Rheingold-New York 1904 era street. The China, Thailand, Mormon, and Russian Orthodox pavilions were reproductions of temples and churches.

The most popular exhibit in terms of attendance was General Motors with 29,002,136 visitors. Other popular exhibits were the Vatican, New York State, Chrysler, General Electric, Ford, Florida, Bell System, Federal, and Spain. IBM, Kodak, Du Pont, Johnson's Wax, Illinois, Pepsi, and Coca Cola were also popular.

General Motors, the largest pavilion, previewed the future in a moving chair ride that was an updated version of the 1939–1940 Futurama. Westinghouse provided a new version of the 1939–1940 time capsule. The Vatican displayed the *Pièta*, Michelangelo's 465-year-old marble sculpture masterpiece, the only time it had been shown outside the Vatican. The New York State pavilion had a film, other entertainment, and observation towers. Chrysler's main attractions were a puppet musical comedy by Bil Baird, an assembly line, and a walk-through engine.

The pavilions representing General Electric, Ford, Illinois, and Pepsi served as the proving grounds for audio-animatronics (automated robotic figures) developed by Disney. General Electric's carousel of four auditoriums revolved around stage shows where the history of electricity in the home was told. Visitors also experienced electrical storms in the skydome and witnessed the first large public demonstration of controlled thermonuclear fusion. Ford convertibles transported guests on a "Magic Skyline" to view the fair, prehistoric dinosaurs and cavemen, and a city of the future. The Illinois exhibit featured Lincoln displays and a Lincoln figure that recited excerpts from Lincoln's speeches. Visitors rode around the world at the Pepsi pavilion, where dancing dolls sang "It's a Small World," by Richard and Robert Sherman. Disney audio-animatronics similar to the shows at the fair can still be seen in Disney parks today.

Art at the fair ranged from commercial and pop art, paintings, and sculpture to contemporary, classic, and ancient treasures. Artisan jewelry, sculpture, and handicrafts were displayed and sold by many foreign exhibitors. Ancient treasures from China, India, Sudan, Pakistan, Egypt, Mexico, and South America were exhibited. Eight religious organizations—Vatican, Protestant-Orthodox, Morman, Sermons from Science, Billy Graham, Russian Orthodox, Wycliffe Bible, and Christian Science—exhibited art and films.

After Michelangelo's *Pietà*, Spain had the most significant art display of classic and contemporary paintings by El Greco, Goya, Picasso, Miro, and Dali. New York City exhibited treasures from thirty-four city museums. New York State showed paintings from the Hudson River school and pop art murals by Andy Warhol. A Fine Arts pavilion contained works of 250 living American artists in 1964.

The Unisphere, dinosaurs, and many building exteriors were commercial pop art sculptures. Sinclair's logo, a brontosaurus, was displayed outdoors with eight other life-sized dinosaur sculptures by Louis Paul Jonas. The Electric Power exhibit was enclosed by 600 vertical aluminum prisms sculptured to float above a reflecting pool by Kenneth Snelson. These prisms were colorfully illuminated and a 12-billion candlelight projected from the center after dark.

Disney designed a 120-foot Tower of the Four Winds mobile sculpture for the exterior of Pepsi. Donald Delue's 43-foot-high bronze figure *The Rocket Thrower* and Paul Manship's 10-foot diameter *Sundial* were significant fair-commissioned sculptures. The Mormons exhibited a 9-ton replica of Bertel Thorvaldsen's famous statute, *The Christus*.

The evolution of film as an exhibit medium was advanced at fair theaters. Several shows developed multiple image techniques in motion pictures. Kodak's three-panel flexible screen movie, *The Searching Eye*, was produced by Saul Bass. Du Pont's film, *The World of Chemistry*, included interaction with an actor on stage. The Johnson's Wax movie, *To Be Alive*, by Francis Thompson and Alexander Hamid, won the 1966 Oscar for best documentary. Charles and Ray Eames perfected multiple-image projection with fifteen screens at IBM.

Several 360-degree and concave screens, which encircled the audience, were used at the fair. KLM-Cinerama produced a 360-degree show, *To the Moon and Back*, at the Travel and Transportation pavilion. New York State and the Port Authority both had 360-degree movies. General Cigar and Ireland exhibited 360-degree films projected onto the floor showing bird's-eye views of sports and Ireland.

Cinemobiles, combined rides and cinemas, moved viewers into spatial areas where films were projected on various arrangements of screens. The 435-seat "People Wall" lifted the audience up 60 feet into the IBM theater. The Bell System moving chair ride was a tour of communications history using movie and stage sets. The United States's *American Journey* by Cinerama transported viewers through sliding and rising screen tunnels.

Three-dimensional dioramas other than large animated General Motors and

Disney displays were also featured. Continental Insurance displayed an outdoor movie and indoor transparent screen dioramas. Thirteen dioramas traced "The Triumph of Man" from the first tools to space at Travelers Insurance. Coca-Cola visitors walked through five exotic world scenes.

The world's fair had entertainment from around the world. Most foreign and state exhibits offered ethnic food, music, dance, and merchandise. Folk festivals and programs honoring countries, states, and industries were staged throughout the fair. Other entertainment such as Louisiana's Mardi Gras parade jazz music and Oregon's timber carnival were also experienced. Cities Service provided the World's Fair Band of America. New York State promoted baton twirlers, and the city had an "Ice-Travaganza." Fashion shows appeared at the Better Living, New York, New England, Japan, and Spanish pavilions. Every evening around 10:00, a synchronized fountain, fireworks, music, and light show was presented at the Pool of Industry.

The Amusement Zone had a limited number of thrill rides and shows due to Moses's dislike for them. Rides included a monorail, aerial tower, Jaycopter, and a log flume. In addition, the Transportation Zone had an Avis antique car ride, a U.S. Rubber ferris wheel in the shape of a giant tire, and an automobile thrill show. A Swiss skyride stretched across the International Zone. The Long Island Railroad had a miniature train ride in the State Zone.

Most shows were located in the Amusement Zone. Two hundred and fifty figures were displayed at Walter's International Wax Museum. Florida had a porpoise show and in 1965 sponsored water skiing demonstrations. "To Broadway with Love" was produced by George Schaefer and Morton Da Costa at the Texas pavilion. "America Be Seated," an 1800s dinner show by Mike Todd, was staged on a Mississippi showboat. "Wonderworld" extravaganza included singers, dancers, swimmers, divers, comedians, and acrobats at the Amphitheater. The Amusement Zone also had a Continental Circus and a puppet show musical, *Les Poupes de Paris*, by Sid and Marty Krofft.

Exhibits and shows were simplified and reorganized in 1965 due to the financial problems of high costs and low attendance. The "Ice-Travaganza" and "Wonderworld" shows were closed. Additional thrill rides, a carousel, and an amphicar ride were added in the amusement area.

Visitors found in New York City a collateral experience of exhibits, entertainment, and events. Fair visitors were directed to sports events, the United Nations, and New York's great museums, zoos, and gardens. The new Lincoln Center for the Performing Arts sponsored a World's Fair Festival of concerts, ballets, and musicals. U.S. Olympic trials and the Amateur Athletic Union weightlifting championships were held at the fair. Operation Sail '64, a rendezvous of sailing ships from twenty nations, was organized in relation to the fair celebrations.

Inventions demonstrated at the fair were atomic fusion, computers, color television, satellite photos, and auto-animatronics. Communications inventions shown were facsimile machines, touchtone phones, picture phones, computer translations, and voiceprints. Rocket belts, exterior observation elevators, people movers, a monorail, and hydrofoils were used. Exhibits predicted space docking and shuttles, moon visits, vertical-lift planes, underwater resorts, laser cutting, desert irrigation, and auto traffic control towers. The Belgian waffle, a new food delight with whipped cream and strawberries, was promoted.

President Lyndon B. Johnson attended the opening ceremonies, which were microwaved by satellite for global color television broadcasts. Bad weather and threatened civil rights demonstrations resulted in negative publicity and low attendance from which the fair never recovered. Vice-President Hubert Humphrey opened the fair the second year when Olympic marathon winner Abebe Bikila ran in from Manhattan. Pope Paul VI came to the United States for the first time and visited the fair in 1965. Other dignitaries who visited were the shah and empress of Iran, President Chung Hee Park of South Korea, Deputy Prime Minister Chaerul Saleh of Indonesia, and Premier Gamal Abdel Nasser.

In 1964 there were 27,148,280 in attendance, and in 1965 there were 24,458,757, for a total of 51,607,037. The fair lost $20 million in 1964 and $1 million in 1965 despite a $64.3 million income each year. Note holders received only 62.4 cents of each dollar invested, but these same businesses earned large profits from services and tourist revenues. Hotel rates were raised by 40 percent during the fair. New York City gained millions of dollars in tax revenues, a restaurant above the park, the Hall of Science, a marina, the Singer Bowl Stadium, and various transportation improvements.

The successes and failures of the fair are related to the autocratic nature of Robert Moses and the authorities he controlled. Moses and his staff had many public projects under development at the same time as the fair. They had no expertise in organizing a world's fair and did not consult with outsiders. The Fair Corporation, through Moses, granted monopolies and expensive cost-plus contracts without competitive bidding. Exhibitors were required to use insurance, maintenance, garbage, trucking, and other services at inflated prices. Restaurant concessions were given to fair directors.

Moses's arrogance antagonized the Bureau of International Expositions (BIE), governments, private participants, and the press. The BIE did not sanction the fair and requested that its member countries not participate after Moses stated that the fair would not be subject to their rulings. H. L. Hunt of Texas withdrew from plans to build amusement rides and restaurants after disagreements with Moses. Moses's testimony before Congress and public comments created such outrage that only White House intervention saved federal exhibit funding.

As private corporations, authorities were not open to public scrutiny; however, the Fair Corporation was. Moses united the press against him with emotional lectures and attacks. News reporters retaliated with stories about exhibitors dropping out, added costs, and late schedules. News about disputes, incomplete work, and high costs helped contribute to the low attendance.

An extensive public relations effort, "Come to the Fair," included participation by giant corporations. These advertisements and press releases promoted the story of Moses and the fair. This publicity, however, could not overcome the news of conflict and anger that centered around Moses.

The fair staff, used to predictable revenues of authority tolls, continued a pattern of lavish spending and lax accounting. It took a long time for the accountants to realize that revenues were 40 percent below predictions. Eleven exhibitors filed for bankruptcy due to low attendance and high costs. The fair loaned its funds to help keep these exhibits open.

Fair finances looked better than they were because unused advance ticket sales were credited to the 1964 season. This accounting mistake was realized when 15 million visitors in the 1965 season had prepaid tickets. News of financial problems plagued the second year.

The fair was successful in developing unique architecture and exhibit rides, films, and shows. Walt Disney auto-animatronics exhibited today were advanced by corporate sponsorship at the fair. The remaining Unisphere served as an excellent logo and theme symbol. The unique exhibits and remaining elements of the fair continue to inspire future generations.

BIBLIOGRAPHY

The records of the New York World's Fair 1964–1965 Corporation, covering the period between 1959 and 1971, are housed in the New York Public Library's Rare Books and Manuscripts Division. These records include general files of corporate activity for administration, construction, maintenance, and promotion, including activity related to exhibitors. Films by Lowell Thomas and the various television networks are also included in this collection. Also at the New York Public Library are the papers of Robert Moses, the fair president. Series 12 contains correspondence, clippings, and printed matter related to his role in the fair. The Queens Museum in New York City promotes the study and preservation of documentation and memorabilia from this fair and published a catalog for an exhibit in the fall of 1989 commemorating the twenty-fifth anniversary of the fair.

Besides the film included in the corporation records, other visual records exist for this fair. The Queens Museum had a film, *To the Fair* (1964), which follows several visitors around the site. The museum also produced a film, *Beauty to Ashes* (1972), a history of Flushing Meadow Park from ash dump to world's fair site and beyond. *World's Fair* (1964), produced by John Campbell Films, Inc., and television station WNYC's film series on the fair are available at the New York Public Library.

The *Official Guide, New York World's Fair, 1964/1965* (1964, 1965), edited by Norton Wood, was produced in several different updated editions and is replete with maps and descriptions of each pavilion. Time-Life Books, *Official Souvenir Book, New York World's Fair 1964/1965* (1964), contains color photographs and drawings about exhibits at the fair, along with articles by celebrities. The *New York Times* and popular magazines of the day gave extensive coverage to the fair; references to specific articles may be found in the standard indexes.

While no scholarly monograph specifically dealing with the fair has yet been published, two secondary sources deserve mention. Robert A. Caro's critical biography of Robert Moses, *The Power Broker* (1974), includes a chapter on the fair and Moses's problems in the management of it. Walt Disney Productions published a celebratory work, *20th Anniversary, New York World's Fair 1964–1965, A Disney Retrospective* (1984), reviewing the Disney involvement at the fair.

Daniel T. Lawrence, A.I.A.

MONTREAL 1967
EXPO 67: UNIVERSAL AND INTERNATIONAL EXHIBITION OF 1967

Expo 67, held in Montreal from April 28 to October 29, 1967, was conceived as the major celebration of the one hundredth anniversary of Canadian confederation.

The idea of a world exhibition in Montreal was initiated at the time of the Brussels Exposition of 1958. The Bureau of International Expositions in Paris approved Canada's application for Expo 67 on November 13, 1962.

A site was selected opposite downtown Montreal on the St. Lawrence River at ile Sainte-Hélène, an old city park. This island was extended at both ends. A second island was created, known as ile Notre-Dame. Also included was a peninsula known as cité du Havre. Over the next year and a half, 17.6 million cubic yards of fill were taken from the river and transported by truck to the site; 297 acres of new land were thereby produced. The total site consisted of 988 acres, including lakes, canals, and parking lots. This magnificent acreage was developed into building sites with canals and lakes, a larger park on ile Notre-Dame, and the retention of the existing park on ile Sainte-Hélène.

The construction included a mass transit system starting at the main gate place d'Accueil on cité du Havre and terminating at La Ronde, a 135-acre amusement park built for Expo 67 on ile Sainte-Hélène. This transit system, known as the Expo-Express, consisted of eight computer-controlled trains of six cars each and cost $18.3 million. This transit facility was a full-sized heavy rail electric rapid transit line, using cars similar to those of the Toronto subway system. The system carried approximately 44 million passengers during the exhibition. The cost of unlimited travel on the Expo-Express was included in the price of admission. In addition to the Expo-Express, secondary transport was provided by three minirail systems. The minirails, approximately 6 miles in length, passed around and through many pavilions. The Blue minirail connected ile Sainte-Hélène with ile Notre Dame and passed through the U.S. pavilion. Admission fee for the Blue minirail was 50 cents. Two other transit systems, known as the Yellow minirails, had previously been used at the Swiss National Exposition of 1964. One of these systems served ile Sainte-Hélène and the other La Ronde. Admission for each of these systems was 25 cents. There were 60,845 participants, including 60 foreign national governments, 3 U.S. states, private pavilions, sponsors, lenders, and concessionaires in structures covering 121 acres of floor area.

Expo 67 officially opened to the public on April 28, 1967. On April 27 the official opening ceremonies were held at place des Nations, followed by a preview of the exposition in the late afternoon and evening for friends of Expo, employees, and exhibitors. The largest single one-day attendance (530,000) occurred on April 30. The grounds were hopelessly clogged that day, resulting in modifications of transit services that were utilized throughout the rest of the exposition period.

The islands of the exposition site were connected by several spectacular bridges, one of which won architectural and engineering awards. The longest bridge, the Concordia, connected the cité du Havre and ile Sainte-Hélène. Another, the Bridge of the Isles, connected ile Sainte-Hélène and ile Notre-Dame.

Expo 67 was the first exposition situated on a multi-island site. The pavilions were located in several areas of the site and were not grouped by type (private/ international) as had been the case in past expositions. This method of grouping made possible an unusual variety in architecture and design. The street furniture was also specially designed for Expo 67 and consisted of a modular triangular system of waste baskets, telephone booths, and street lamps. The street lamps were particularly interesting in that they consisted of cylindrical elements that projected light from the top onto white disks, which then reflected the light at different angles.

Expo 67 was one of the first expositions to have a standard sign system that is still frequently used today. A standard sign manual for this signage system was published.

The theme of Expo 67 was Man and His World. At most previous expositions, the theme had been expressed by a physical symbol, usually a single structure of futuristic and/or flamboyant design. In the case of Expo 67, this concept was discarded in favor of a series of theme pavilions developed by the Canadian Corporation of the 1967 World Exhibition. Many scholars and officials from around the globe contributed concepts for the theme. The theme was inspired by *Man and His World*, by Antoine de Saint-Exupéry.

The theme of Expo 67 was carried out in nine buildings with seventeen sub-themes. Man the Creator included art, contemporary sculpture, industrial design, and photography. This subtheme was expressed in a major international art exhibit in a new museum building, which still exists in Montreal. The sculpture exhibit on ile Sainte-Hélène was beautifully laid out in a garden setting. On cité du Havre adjoining the art museum, an international exhibition of photography and industrial design was installed.

The Man the Producer building, on ile Notre-Dame, included the subthemes of Resources for Man and Man in Control. The Man the Explorer complex on ile Sainte-Hélène covered Man, His Planet, and Space; Man and Life; and Man and the Polar Regions. The Man the Provider complex on ile Notre-Dame included agriculture and farming. Man and His Health, on cité du Havre, connected with the Man and His Community pavilion, included the Meditheater. Man and the Community included Cinerama, Electronic Community, Work a Day Community, and Enchanted City. The Labyrinth on cité du Havre adjoined Man and His Community. The Labyrinth, one of the most popular exhibits at Expo 67, consisted of a film produced by the National Film Board of Canada telling the essential story of humanity, dramatized in two chambers with a mirror maze.

Habitat 67, a 158-unit apartment complex of prefabricated concrete boxes, was also one of the most popular features. The Dupont Auditorium of Canada housed a series of lectures and films.

The design of the pavilions at Expo 67 was of high quality. The Canadian government pavilion was designed by Ashworth, Robbie Vaughn and Williams, Schoeler, Barkham and Heaton/Z. M. Stankiewicz on an 11½ acre site. The major element of this pavilion was a 100-foot-high inverted pyramid called Katimavik—taken from the Eskimo word for gathering place. The promenade around the top of the Katimavik's slopes offered one of the best vantage points to view Expo and Montreal. The Canadian pavilion consisted of a series of exhibits highlighted by the Land of Canada, the People of Canada, the Growth of Canada's Resources and Energy, Transportation and Communications, and Changing Times. The pavilion also contained an extensive art exhibit, library, and post office. A theater and bandstand featured a continuous program of special events. A children's creative center was also in operation.

The U.S. pavilion, designed by R. Buckminster Fuller along with Fuller & Sadao Inc. and Geometrics Inc., consisted of a geodesic dome 250 feet in diameter and 200 feet high. The framework of the dome was constructed of welded steel tubing, forming a hexagonal grid on the inside and pointing outward in the form of pyramids. There were approximately 1,900 tinted concave acrylic panels inserted in these hexagons; these constituted the skin of the structure. A series of platforms, connected by stairs and escalators and supported by concrete columns, were built within the pavilion to provide exhibit areas. The pavilion, featuring the theme Creative America, contained exhibits including a life-sized space display. *Mercury*, *Gemini*, and *Apollo* components were suspended from the dome frame. A moon landscape with a full-scale excursion module and surveyor was presented. The American spirit was depicted by folk artifacts such as Indian ornaments, dolls, and coats and by a wide variety of American paintings ranging in size up to 50 feet. The American cinema was represented by photo enlargements of Hollywood stars such as Gary Cooper and Humphrey Bogart and by props such as the chariot used in *Ben Hur* and a Checker taxi cab.

The Federal Republic of Germany pavilion, designed by Frei Otto and Rolf Gutbroad, consisting of a free-flowing tent structure using 120 foot-high masts, was an ingenious lightweight construction. The technique was a breakthrough in contemporary architectural design and was completely prefabricated in Germany and shipped to Expo.

Both Man the Explorer and Man the Producer complexes were designed by Affleck, Desbarats, Dimakopoulos, Lebensold Sise. These structures, tremendous steel space frames of truncated tetrahedrons, created totally flexible and spectacular spaces for the theme exhibits.

The Quebec pavilion, designed by Papineau, Gerin-Lajoie, Leblanc and Durand, was an understated but handsome structure consisting of 50-foot-high glass walls enclosing a truncated pyramid 160 feet by 160 feet. Exhibits illustrated Man and His Environment in Quebec.

The United Nations pavilion, designed by Eliot Noyes and Associates, in-

MONTREAL 1967. This overview shows a variety of pavilions at this exposition, including Habitat, a new concept in urban housing, designed by Moshe Safdie, and seen in the background. (Courtesy Peter M. Warner)

cluded a 300-seat theater, a 140 foot by 110 foot plaza containing flagpoles for each member nation and a round exhibit pavilion. This pavilion housed a U.N. post office, and special U.N. stamps in Canadian denominations were issued for use at this pavilion.

The pavilion of Belgium, designed by René Stapels, was a handsome building of Belgian handmade brick and tinted glass based on a modular parallelogram grid system.

The Man and The Community Pavilion, designed by Erickson and Massey, was a hexagonal pyramid of wood that formed a graceful and light concave cone.

The Labyrinth Building, designed by Blaud, Lemoyne, Edwards, Shine, was a reinforced concrete square structure containing galleries and film-viewing chambers with overhead film projection systems. The film exhibition and the architecture were well integrated.

The pavilion of Czechoslovakia, a steel and glass building designed by Miroslav Repa and S. Pylka, devoted an entire section to children. The World of Children featured a tiny theater with 2,000 puppets. Other exhibits illustrated the country's history, culture, and industry.

Habitat 67, the apartment complex on cité du Havre, consisted of a prefabricated construction of 354 concrete boxes manufactured on the site and erected by a rail-riding derrick. The project contained 158 apartments and cost $20 million to build. This complex, designed by Moshe Safdie and David Barott, was conceived as an innovative method for building prefabricated low-cost housing. The exhibit was meant to show the possibilities for high-density development functions. Many of the apartments were furnished and were on public display during the exposition. Several others were used by exhibitors. The crane and construction techniques for this complex were also on display.

All of the exhibits of Expo 67 were contained in national or commercially sponsored pavilions. There were no multiple exhibitor pavilions as had been the case at many previous expositions. Expo 67 was a first-category universal exposition, registered by the Bureau of International Expositions. This type of exposition requires that participants construct their own pavilions and exhibits on land leased from the exposition corporation, thus allowing for many innovations in architecture and design.

The World Festival, an integral part of Expo 67, was probably the greatest program of international entertainment presented in one city during a six-month period. The festival consisted of opera, ballet, theatrical productions, musical programs, and other events held both on the Expo site and offsite. A special Expo theater was built on site for this exposition. More than 20,000 performances were held in this program, with an aggregate audience of 16.5 million. The festival was one of the most memorable events of Expo 67 and was copied by most subsequent expositions.

In late September, a transit strike in Montreal halted all city buses and the new Metro system but not the Expo-Express. Official reports stated that this strike cost Expo approximately 5 million admissions. The strike lasted thirty days and put tremendous pressure on the main gate (place d'Accueil), which became the only entry facility into the exposition, since the others were served by the city transit system. Special train services were provided from downtown Montreal to a location near the main gate.

There were many innovations at Expo 67. One of the most striking, which has been copied at all subsequent world expositions, was the introduction of a new type of admission ticket known as the "passport." This idea was developed for Expo 67 because of the theme, Man and His World. Visiting a world exposition is really a trip around the world. Visitors' tickets were printed in the form of a passport booklet resembling an actual passport and containing a photo. The passports were made available for weekly and season admissions. The visitor, when entering each exhibit, could have the passport stamped by the exhibitor. This innovative form of admission became a special souvenir for each visitor. The single-day admission was a regular ticket. Many subsequent expositions have used passports strictly as souvenirs, and not as admission tickets.

Expo 67 was an outstanding success, with 50,306,648 admissions in six months, the largest attendance at such an event in North American history. Although the pavilions at Expo 67 were scheduled for demolition immediately after, this did not occur. At the suggestion of Mayor Jean Drapeau of Montreal, they were donated to the city of Montreal, which for many years thereafter operated them as an annual exhibition known as Man and His World. Habitat, the apartment complex, still stands today and is now a cooperative. The site on ile Notre-Dame was used for the 1980 Floralies Exposition. Some events of the 1976 Olympics were also held on ile Notre-Dame. The ongoing benefits of Expo 67 include the naming of the Montreal Expos baseball team, the staging of the 1976 Summer Olympics in Montreal, and a tremendous increase in tourism and economic benefits for Canada and Quebec. The city underwent massive renewal at the time of Expo. The construction of the long-planned Metro transit system was accelerated for the opening of Expo. La Ronde, the amusement area, continues to be operated in the summer by Montreal and is heavily patronized by the local citizenry. It has been continually upgraded since Expo 67.

Expo 67 was the first Universal Category exposition staged in North America and only the third such exposition registered by the Bureau of International Expositions up to that time. The essential goal of a world exposition is to bring people and their ideas together and to foster international understanding. Expo 67 was highly successful in this respect.

BIBLIOGRAPHY

The records of the Canadian Corporation for the 1967 World Exhibition, or Expo 67, are housed at the Public Archives Record Center in Montreal. The corporation published a five-volume report on its activities, *General Report on the 1967 World Exhibition* (1969). It contains attendance records, financial reports, reports of each corporate department, and a wealth of other detail in its more than 2,000 pages, and it stands as the basic research tool for the study of this exposition. The *Official Guide Expo 67* (1967) covers the basic details needed by the average visitor to the fair.

Other general works include Jean-Louis de Lorimor, ed., *Expo 67 Memorial Album of the First Category Universal and International Exhibition, Montreal* (1968). This massive slipcased volume covers the details of each pavilion and includes magnificent color photographs, as well as essays of the development, history and theme of the exposition. Two far more modest pictorial publications are *Album Souvenir Book* (1967) in two versions, one with photographs and one with drawings, and Robert Fulford, *This Was Expo* (1968), which appeared after the fair had ended.

The significant architecture of Expo 67 was surveyed in a number of contemporary journal articles. See, in particular, "The Architect's Expo," *Progressive Architecture* 48, no. 6 (June 1967): 126–67; "Brilliantly Ordered Visual World: Expo 67," *Architectural Record* 142 (July 1967): 115–26; and the *Architectural Review* and *Japan Architect*, both of which devoted their entire August 1967 issues to Expo 67.

A few guidebooks to specific exhibits are worthy of mention. Philip J. Polock, *The Camera as Witness* (1967), is the illustrated catalog of the theme photography exhibit. The sculpture exhibit catalog is Guy Robert, intro., *International Exhibition of Contemporary Sculpture* (1967). The exposition art exhibit catalog was *Man and His World–International Fine Arts Exhibition* (1967).

Peter M. Warner

SAN ANTONIO 1968

HEMISFAIR '68: A CONFLUENCE OF CULTURES OF THE AMERICAS

On April 4, 1968, Martin Luther King, Jr., the prophet of peace and understanding, was assassinated. While much of the American nation mourned, the city of San Antonio, Texas, prepared to celebrate its 250th birthday with a world's fair dedicated to strengthening understanding and unity among the nations of the Western Hemisphere. The idea had originated ten years earlier with San Antonio businessman Jerome Harris's suggestion that an international exposition would boost the city's stagnant economy and publicize its unique Spanish heritage. That suggestion set the stage for an outpouring of civic pride and support that forever dispelled the city's image as a lethargic remnant of Texas's past vitality.

Harris's idea for a celebration of hemispheric relations quickly captured the attention of the political elite. Governor John Connally led the lobbying effort for official sanction and state and federal funding. As commissioner-general of the fair, he traveled to four continents to line up exhibitors. Connally was joined in his lobbying efforts by Senator John Tower, Congressman Henry Gonzalez, and Lieutenant Governor Ben Barnes. On the local level, Mayor Walter McAllister lent his support, and a group of businessmen headed by construction magnate H. B. Zachary pledged $10 million to begin construction. The townspeople responded favorably as well. In 1964, San Antonio voters approved a $30 million bond issue by a two-to-one margin. Two years later, voters consented to an additional $5.5 million bond issue.

Despite this broad support, significant problems surrounded the choice of a site for the fair. The decision to locate the fair in the heart of an urban renewal area in downtown San Antonio led to a five-year battle between ''progressives'' desirous of removing unwanted obstacles and ''preservationists'' committed to protecting the city's heritage. In the end, some twenty historic houses were restored and turned into restaurants and boutiques. Their local flavor and Spanish ambience provided one of the most charming features of the 92.6-acre HemisFair '68 complex.

The compact size of the site created minor logistical problems in housing some fifty-five exhibitors representing twenty-four nations and nineteen corporations. The fair had the largest contingent of Latin American participants. To promote unity and solve space problems, the Central American states shared a pavilion, as did several smaller members of the Organization of American States. Also to alleviate potential congestion, the fair promoters created a multifaceted transportation system. The San Antonio River was rerouted to flow into the convention center complex and allow access via waterways. In addition, elevated walkways, a minimonorail, and a skyrail were created to cut down on internal traffic congestion.

While the housing and transportation arrangements were creative, the remainder of the site showed little imagination. The site was built around a rather conservative $13.5 million convention center composed of three separate buildings and filled with state-of-the-art equipment. The focal point of the fair grounds was the 622-foot Tower of the Americas with a revolving restaurant and magnificent observation decks. Since this was a special category fair, exhibits were set up in standard fair-provided space rather than the elaborate pavilions associated with larger fairs. The focal points of the exhibition area were the Institute of Texan Culture and the U.S. pavilion. The Women's pavilion chronicled women's role in the development of the Americas and highlighted achievements in government, the arts, and the sciences.

HemisFair '68 opened officially on April 6, 1968. The U.S. flag flew at half-staff in memory of Martin Luther King, Jr. In its six-month run ending October 6, some 6,384,842 paying guests were treated to a varied program of exhibitions and entertainment. Highlights included a performance of the Bolshoi Ballet, an exhibition of priceless Spanish art never before shown outside Spain, and a visit by President Lyndon B. Johnson. One of the most popular exhibits was "The Magic of a People," featuring some 10,000 items from American designer Alexander Girard's Latin American folk art collection.

HemisFair '68 received considerable acclaim, but it was not a financial success. The six-month run cost approximately $158 million, leaving the city of San Antonio with a $5.5 million deficit. Several factors may account for this. Heavy spring rains delayed construction, increased costs by $3 million, and limited attendance during the first two months. Periods of national mourning over the deaths of Dr. King and Robert F. Kennedy and damaging publicity from a minimonorail derailment helped keep attendance down to 85 percent of the anticipated number. Legal fees and damages associated with the derailment also limited profits.

Yet despite the significant deficit, HemisFair '68 was considered a major success for the city of San Antonio. It employed some 8,000 people directly and stimulated growth in the hotel and retail sectors. The restored buildings, the convention center, and the Institute of Texan Cultures remained as permanent assets. The site was reopened in March 1969 as a city-operated, income-generating amusement park. Most important, HemisFair '68 propelled San Antonio into the international spotlight and allowed it to display its special charm. San Antonio's world's fair provided a major boon to its tourist industry and a boost to civic pride.

BIBLIOGRAPHY

Primary sources for HemisFair '68 are limited. The location of official fair records is unknown, although some material can be found in the John Connally Papers at the

University of Texas, Austin. Other useful information is available from prominent boosters, including former governor Connally, Congressman Henry B. Gonzalez, former lieutenant governor Ben Barnes, and former senator John Tower, particularly with respect to the issues of acceptance and funding.

Fair publicity guides provide details of the layout, exhibits, and site development. The best are *HemisFair 1968: Official Souvenir Guidebook* (1968) and "HemisFair '68," an eighty-page supplement to the *San Antonio Express News*, April 2, 1968. Helpful overviews include Jim Davis, "San Antonio's Big Show," *Humble Way* 7 (First Quarter 1968): 1–8, and Keith Elliott, "HemisFair," *Texas Parade* 18 (April 1968): 12–19.

Excellent coverage appears in the *San Antonio Express News* and the *New York Times* between March and October 1968. The fair's problems are succinctly highlighted in Juan Vasquez, "Troubled HemisFair Becomes Amusement Center," *New York Times*, October 20, 1968. The immediate impact of the fair is best expressed in Kemper Diehl, "Fair Ends—Was It Worth It?" *New York Times*, October 6, 1968. Statistical data are compiled in "San Antonio Fair: A Statistical Study," *New York Times*, May 5, 1968. Two articles dealing with the important urban renewal aspects of this fair are James L. MacKay, "HemisFair '68 and Paseo del Rio," *American Institute of Architects Journal* 69 (April 1968): 48–58, and Roger Montgomery, "HemisFair '68: Prologue to Renewal," *Architectural Forum* 129 (October 1968): 84–89. An interesting retrospective and assessment appears in the *San Antonio Express News*, April 7, 1988.

Shirley M. Eoff

OSAKA 1970

JAPAN WORLD EXPOSITION (EXPO '70)*

Japan's desire to stage a world's fair goes back as far as London's Crystal Palace of 1851 when Asia was not considered significant in the world. Later, at the 1867 Paris Exposition universelle, Japan appeared for the first time with a pavilion and a representative display of products. World's fairs soon became important to Japan's industrialization; it wanted to stage one as early as 1877 to show its own progress. It received little encouragement.

A fair scheduled for 1912 was canceled after the death of Emperor Meiji, and plans for a 1940 world exposition in Tokyo were well underway when war broke out in Europe. However, all surviving tickets were honored at Expo '70. When the Bureau internationale des expositions (BIE) met in Paris in 1965 to choose a location for the 1970 world exposition, Japan formally applied to host it.

Partly because of the canceled 1940 fair and partly because of the great success of the 1964 Summer Olympics in Tokyo, Japan's proposal was accepted in September 1965. It became the third nation since World War II to host "a general exhibition of the first category."

The Japan World Exposition was registered on May 11, 1966, in accordance with BIE regulations. It was the first world exposition to be held in Asia and only the fourth to be held under the official sponsorship of BIE, after Paris 1937, Brussels 1958, and Montreal 1967 and the special exhibitions in Seattle 1962 and San Antonio 1968.

Expo '70 ran from March 15, 1970, to September 13, 1970, attracting 64,218,770 visitors during its 183-day run. Of these, 62 million were Japanese (in a nation of 103 million), and 1.7 million (2.7 percent) were foreigners. Among foreign visitors, there were 52 percent American, 7 percent Indian, 5 percent Chinese, 4 percent Filipino, 3 percent Canadian, 3 percent Korean, 2 percent Thai, 2 percent Australian, 2 percent German, 2 percent from Hong Kong, and 1 percent British. The maximum turnout for a single day (September 5) was 835,832 visitors. There were also 55 marriages, 17 deaths, a birth, 47,000 lost children, 44,000 lost adults, 60 workers' strikes, 1,800 thefts, 126 fires, and 1 typhoon.

Expo '70 was prepared and operated by the Japan Association for the 1970 World Exposition. It was organized and financed by the government of Japan

*The author of this essay gratefully acknowledges the assistance of Richard Fitz, Helen Amabile, and Nelia Dunbar in USIA's Library Programs Division; John Coppola, Eileen Finnigan, Kathleen Kalb, and James Ogul in USIA's Expo Office; David Webb, U.S. Department of Education, who was able to share both his memories of the fair and his pictures; and Margaret Manning. The views expressed in this essay are those of the author and not of the United States Information Agency.

with the cooperation of the Osaka prefecture and the city of Osaka. Kenzo Tange, probably Japan's best-known architect at the time, conducted the overall planning but designed no individual buildings.

The fairgrounds covered 815 acres in Suita City, one of the satellite cities surrounding Osaka City in Osaka prefecture, in a region known as Kansai ("west of the barrier") that was originally bamboo groves and rice fields. It cost the Japanese government $2 billion to improve transportation facilities and to develop this site, which was larger than Brussels or Montreal but more compactly laid out.

Tange planned the expo site in a tree pattern with "trunk," "branches," and "blossoms" to provide physical continuity to a vast collection of highly individualized buildings and to interrelate a varied group of elements into a model of future urban design. The "trunk" was the open plaza or Symbol Area, which extended from the main gate and embraced the Theme pavilion, an art museum, and a computerized information control center. The "branches" were the automobile lanes and tubular moving sidewalks, and the "blossoms" were the pavilions.

The transportation system was one of the principal merits of the fair. It featured a computerized monorail that took visitors the 2.7 miles around the fair site in 15 minutes; battery-powered cars able to accommodate six persons; and tubular moving sidewalks that traveled 1.5 miles per hour. These devices greatly curtailed walking and helped eliminate visitor fatigue.

Japan formally invited 126 countries (77 accepted) and 21 international organizations (4 accepted: United Nations, Asian Development Bank, Organization for Economic Co-operation and Development, and European Community) to participate along with 10 provincial and municipal governments, and 32 domestic exhibitors. This was more than at any previous world's fair.

Canada was the first nation to accept and to complete every phase of its planning. Bulgaria, Malta, and Portugal made their world's fair debuts. Chile, the first South American country to apply for participation, took part in its first expo since 1889. Spain and Yugoslavia did not come. Israel accepted but withdrew because of domestic problems. Afghanistan accepted after King Mohammed Zahir Shah inspected progress at the expo site during a 1969 state visit to Japan and immediately announced his country's participation. East Germany, North Korea, North Vietnam, and the People's Republic of China were not invited since they had no diplomatic relations with Japan. And the United States and the Soviet Union, in the choicest and largest sites available to foreign nations, continued their rivalry from Expo 67.

Japan had prepared for Expo '70 by sending representatives to earlier world's fairs to observe their organization. The final design was distinctly Japanese with some innovative and imaginative results. The buildings were arranged around seven plazas, named for the days of the week, to make it easier to locate the pavilions.

Expo '70's central theme, Progress and Harmony for Mankind, had four subthemes: "Toward Fuller Enjoyment of Life," "Toward More Bountiful Fruits from Nature," "Toward Fuller Engineering of Our Living Enjoyment," and "Toward Better Understanding of Each Other." The huge central theme area, the Symbol Zone, was designed by Tange and stretched north and south from the main gate. It was a unified plan containing a number of different facilities, including the Festival Plaza and the Theme Space. South of the main gate was the International Bazaar, a collection of shops selling products from many lands, and the Operations Control Center, the headquarters for the grounds management. Expo Land, the amusement park, was located to the east, and the specially built bus and subway stations were placed to the west.

The Tower of the Sun, a giant cone thrusting upward through the Festival Plaza roof with a brass face resembling an Aztec sun god, was designed by painter Taro Okamoto and defended by Tange against vigorous opposition from most of his architectural collaborators during the planning and construction phase. The enormous transparent roof of the Festival Plaza, resting on six gigantic pillar supports, covered 340,000 square feet, weighed 6,000 tons, and rose 98 feet. This was an impressive engineering feat, but it appeared to cut the saucer-shaped Expo '70 site in half. Inside the Festival Plaza area, there were facilities for full arena events and intimate theater productions.

The pavilions were designed to fit a model city of the future theme and were grouped in three major categories: Japanese government, Japanese commercial, and foreign. Modern architectural trends emphasized building materials of concrete, glass, and steel, little applied color or decoration, and no bright color schemes.

Japan's government pavilion, designed by Nikken Sekkei Komu Co., Ltd., consisted of five drumlike elevated structures surrounding an 80-meter (260-foot) tower. From above, it resembled a cherry blossom, Expo '70's emblem and the Japanese national flower. The Japanese government earmarked $17 million (6.1 billion yen) for its pavilion, the largest of the government pavilions. There were also twenty-four private pavilions, including such Japanese industrial giants as the Fuji Group pavilion (reminiscent of a red and yellow American covered wagon), Hitachi, Mitsui Group, Mitsubishi, Sumitomo (called a Fairytale pavilion), and Takara (called a Beautilion for its theme, "Joy of Being Beautiful").

The Soviet Union's pavilion, designed by Mosproject M. V. Posokhin, A. N. Kondratjev, and V. A. Svirski, resembled an immense red and white paper airplane capped by the hammer and sickle. At 357 feet, it was the expo's tallest building. It displayed numerous exhibits, including a centenary observance of Lenin's birth, a salute to the socialist life, and a space exhibit (*Soyuz* spaceship, *Proton* flying laboratory). Along with the Cuban pavilion, this was the most political display at the fair. Cuba's mostly pictorial exhibit highlighted the achievements of Fidel Castro and Che Guevara and depicted the country before, during, and after the revolution. In contrast, the Vietnamese pavilion was completely nonpolitical, concentrating on the country's history and culture, with no mention of war or U.S. troops. All these pavilions reflected an atmosphere of nationalistic fervor, which tended to be stifling, rather than international cooperation. The same could be said about many other national pavilions, including the Burmese dragon-king boat, the Hong Kong junk sails, and even the Swiss Tree of Light.

Switzerland's popular Tree of Light was a series of vast aluminum pipe branches bearing 32,000 incandescent light bulbs that glittered from a central "trunk" of precisely designed "branches" denoting the Swiss characteristics of order, precision, and harmony. Willi Walter, the designer, won the R. S. Reynolds Memorial Award from the American Institute of Architects for his creation.

The U.S. pavilion was built underground with an innovative air-supported fiberglass dome that seemed as big as two football fields but was actually 274 feet by 465 feet. It was the largest of its kind ever built and the only Expo '70 structure supported by both cables and air. Yet there were misgivings in Washington that it would be an unsuitable exhibition structure, and it was much criticized. Still, the architectural firm, Davis, Brody, Chermayeff, Geismar, de Harak Associates, won an honor award from the American Institute of Architects for "achievement of excellence in architectural design."

The U.S. exhibition, Images of America, was divided into seven sections: photography, painting, sports, space activities, folk art, contemporary art, and architecture. The U.S. space exhibit, containing moon rock samples and Mercury, Gemini, and Apollo space capsules, and its sports corner, with Babe Ruth's uniform and locker, were among the most popular at the fair. There were also three state pavilions (Alaska, Hawaii, Washington) and two city pavilions (Los Angeles and San Francisco).

Canada's pavilion, built around a "youth" theme and designed by Erickson/ Massey Architects and Planners, used wood throughout the interior and four mirrored pyramids on the exterior with the cooling effect of a central courtyard pond and plants to develop a calm and pleasant mood. The Japanese Architects Association considered it the outstanding building at Expo '70. Canada was also represented with pavilions for the provinces of British Columbia, Ontario, and Quebec.

Australia's unusual building was a curving concrete tower that ended in a "sky hook" and a 260-ton free-hanging circular roof that appeared to float above the ground. The tower, which resembled a huge wave about to break, was modeled on the famous Japanese Hikusai woodcut, *The Wave*.

The British pavilion, which consisted of four exhibition halls suspended from four bright orange steel shafts over 120 feet high, was designed in the shape of the Union Jack with the British flag painted on the roof. The Belgian pavilion was a small cream-colored structure with a red-tiled roof, set in a garden of white roses and an orchard of real Belgian apples.

Portugal, the first Western country to establish relations with Japan in 1543, had a replica of the monument on Tanegashima Island that symbolizes the

OSAKA 1970. Looking much like a giant pincushion, the U.S. pavilion featured an innovative air-supported fiberglass dome.

friendship between the two nations and the firearms first introduced into Japan by Portuguese sailors.

The Scandinavian countries (Denmark, Finland, Iceland, Norway, and Sweden) maintained a joint pavilion, designed by Vent Severin, with an exhibition that did not highlight any one country. Projectors threw pictures onto angled screens supported from the ceiling and onto the floor of the pavilion. As visitors entered, they were handed a piece of white card illustrated with the flags of the five participating Scandinavian countries, which they held a certain way to read messages projected down from the ceiling. The Dutch pavilion, a blue, silver, and orange structure shaped like box units arranged stairstep fashion in a T form, used an extensive multiple screening technique to give a many-sided and vivid impression of life in the Netherlands.

The Czech pavilion, very popular at Expo 67, was a flat, one-story structure with an intricate geometric design and walls of traditional Czechoslovakian glass. Its exhibit contrasted modern sculpture with folk art of St. George and his dragon in painted wood and a "glass river" that flowed 40 feet.

France reflected the originality of the French personality with a pavilion composed of four white domes—three overlapping and one set apart. Inside a Franco-Japanese museum honored relations between the two countries dating from the seventeenth century. Germany's contribution was the "Gardens of Music," a continuous celebration of contemporary German composers in the Music Auditorium under a fluorescent dome.

Vatican City cosponsored a Christian pavilion, the first joint venture by the Catholic and Protestant churches in Japan. Its exhibit included rare treasures from the Vatican Library, including a fourth-century Bible manuscript, the Vatican Greek Codex 1209, the Raphael tapestries with biblical motifs, and the world's largest bamboo pipe organ. The Vatican's participation was considered an important contribution to the ecumenical movement.

Many of the smaller nations were housed in six communal pavilions called International Place. These pavilions included Africa (Central African Republic, Gabon, Ghana, Madagascar, Mauritius, Nigeria, Sierra Leone, Tanzania, Uganda), Asia (Afghanistan, Cambodia, Laos, Nepal, United Arab Republic, Vietnam), Europe (Cyprus, Ireland, Malta, Monaco), and Latin America (Costa Rica, Dominican Republic, Ecuador, El Salvador, Nicaragua, Panama, Peru, Uruguay, Venezuela). The United Nations pavilion, a steel frame structure whose shape suggested a bowl carrying an imaginary globe, displayed the Japanese Peace Bell, which was donated by the U.N. Association of Japan in 1954 to represent humanity's prayer for peace.

When Expo '70 ended, most of the pavilions in the 815-acre fairground were demolished. Offers came to buy them, but interest died because of high maintenance costs. The expo site, now better known as being located in Senri Hills, was designated a national cultural park. It contains a Japanese garden, National Museum of Ethnology, National Museum of Art, Osaka Prefectural International Institute for Children's Literature, Commemorative Association for the Japan

World Exposition (a park service and expo fund administrative organization), Expo-Land Recreation Area, and various sports facilities, all open to the public.

The monorail was completely dismantled since it had been created only for transporting expo visitors; however, the idea of connecting Osaka International Airport and Sakai City, a satellite city south of Osaka, by a monorail system was developed. Part of it is expected to be completed between Senri Chuo and the expo park area in 1990. This new monorail system is intended for the rapid transit of passengers between Osaka International Airport (which is expected to have only domestic flights in the future) and the new Kansai International Airport (international flights only), which will be completed in 1993.

Expo '70 also made a significant contribution to the Osaka-Kobe area with major improvements to the Meishin and Kinki expressways and to rapid railway systems and subway networks in the eastern suburbs surrounding Osaka.

The fair began with perfumed confetti, booming guns, swirling fountains, smoke-blowing electronic robots, and colorfully dressed children and hostesses (called Expo Flowers and Expo Angels) from the participating nations. Canada, host for Expo 67, led the parade, followed by South Korea and the United States. Then Emperor Hirohito and Premier Eisaku Sato each formally opened the fair with congratulatory speeches less than 30 seconds long. On the same day, eighty fairgoers were trapped high in the air for several hours on a ferris wheel or "gondola snackbar" (so-called because riders could eat and drink on it) before they were rescued; the revolving doors to the U.S. pavilion broke down from too many eager visitors; and leftist demonstrators protested Expo '70 and the U.S.-Japan security treaty.

Crown Prince Akihito, honorary president of the Japan Association for the 1970 World Exposition, formally closed the fair September 13 amid cascades of unperfumed confetti, brass bands, colorful costumes, and dancing. Premier Sato, also at the closing ceremony, characterized the exposition as a "place for global dialogue."

In his opening day speech, Premier Sato expressed gratification that Japan finally had "acquired sufficient national strength to sponsor a world exposition and to discharge important responsibilities in the international community" (*New York Times*, March 17, 1970). The "strength" was Japan's growing economic power (third after the United States and the Soviet Union) in the world marketplace, which made it the first Asian nation rich enough to sponsor a multibillion-dollar exposition. Many of the nations that built pavilions hoped that such participation would increase their trading power with Japan.

Expo '70, bigger than any other post–World War II exposition, was a success, both in profit realized (19,439,402,017 yen or $146,160,918) and in attendance. It demonstrated Japanese industrial confidence and technical sophistication by offering more practical applications of technology already introduced to the public at earlier fairs, such as wide- and split-screen film techniques; it showed a few innovations and much experimentation by pavilion sponsors, such as Canada's multimirrored building and Switzerland's Tree of Light; and it developed Tange's multilevel network of moving sidewalks and computer-regulated monorails. None of these would have been investigated in the real world of practical building and city planning.

BIBLIOGRAPHY

There is an excellent collection of both published and unpublished works on the Japan World Exposition at the U.S. Information Agency, Washington, D.C., which has operational responsibility for official U.S. participation in all BIE-approved international expositions held outside the United States. The most complete source, especially on the U.S. role, is the agency's Historical Collection, which has congressional documents, fair guides, journal articles, newspaper clippings, official correspondence, and reports. The Library of Congress has guides and preliminary reports for both the fair generally and various national pavilions. Many of the official reports on the overall planning of the fair are in Japanese, while some of the pavilion reports are in that country's language.

Contemporary newspapers and journals covered the fair extensively. Two general descriptive articles are David Butwin, "Meet me at the Fair (If You've Got the Yen)," *Saturday Review*, September 13, 1969, 44–45, 96–97; and Bill Hosokawa, "Expo '70: SuperShow in Japan," *Reader's Digest* (January 1970): 149–53. John Allwood, *The Great Exhibitions* (1977), contains a good general descriptive chapter on the Osaka exposition.

For the architecture of the fair, see the entire issue of *Japan Architect* 45, nos. 5/6 (May–June 1970), which contains superb color photographs of fair buildings and commentary by some of the pavilion architects. Peter Blake, "Expo '70," *Architectural Forum* 132, no. 3 (April 1970): 30–41, is critical of most of the architecture, while Ervin Galantay, "Designing the Environment," *Nation*, August 31, 1970, 134–38, justifies the fair as an attempt by its planners to demonstrate why an urban environment need not be insufferable. A more extensive architectural review is *Structure, Space, Mankind: Expo '70* (1970), published by the editorial committee of the Second Architectural Convention of Japan. This work consists of one volume of text, including an essay by chief architect Kenzo Tange, and a volume of illustrations.

Among other contemporary articles, the more interesting include E. J. Kahn, "Letter from Osaka," *New Yorker*, June 6, 1970, 88, 91–94, 96–102, analyzing the fair's role in Japan's development and capturing the flavor of the event. Eleanor C. Munro, "The Orient Express," *ARTnews* 69, no. 4 (Summer 1970): 48–51, 72–75, found Expo '70 "automated, electronic and jangling with lights and music." The art at the exposition is criticized in "The Osaka Fair Expo '70" *Craft Horizons* 30, no. 3 (May-June 1970), by James Plaut, who noted that very few participating nations honored their national artistic heritage. Finally, "The U.S. Pavilion at Expo '70," *Art in America* 58, no. 2 (March–April 1970): 60–79, includes six essays on the U.S. contributions to folk art, painting, architecture, photography, and the "new technological art."

Martin Manning

SPOKANE 1974

EXPO '74: THE INTERNATIONAL EXPOSITION ON THE ENVIRONMENT

The Spokane World's Fair began as an effort by downtown business leaders to rejuvenate the decaying urban core of the city. They formed Spokane Unlimited in 1958 and commissioned consultants to create the blueprints for a "city reborn." The plan focused on massive downtown renovation anchored by restoration of the polluted Spokane River as it sliced through the central city. Civic leaders hired urban planner King Cole to spearhead the renewal effort. After a number of failed attempts to secure funding for the colossal project, activists seized the possibility of staging a world's fair. Consultants provided a theme for the fair (the environment) and checked with the prestigious Bureau of International Expositions (BIE) to discover there were no competing fairs in 1974. Delicate negotiations with railroads and other prime riverfront titleholders secured 100 acres on both banks of the Spokane River, as well as Havermale and Cannon islands. Business leaders voted to tax themselves to get the project underway, and as federal and state dollars began to pour into the city, voters approved needed bond issues. Construction began in 1972.

Expo '74 was the first U.S. world's fair to be sanctioned by the BIE since the United States joined in 1968. The fair's classification as a single theme or Category II Exposition by the BIE meant that the host city bore the responsibility for site development and construction. This allowed local architects and engineers to design functional, aesthetically pleasing pavilions that avoided the garish "bigger is better" mentality among exhibitors at other fairs. Planners color coded the site in zones of yellow, magenta, orange, red, and purple. The hue of each colorful sector was softer on the fringes but grew progressively brighter as fairgoers were drawn into the focal center of each area. Fifty pavilions provided homes for 103 exhibitors, including 10 nations, 43 commercial exhibitors, and a wide variety of states, Canadian provinces, and private organizations. The Folklife Festival, sponsored by the Smithsonian Institution, and the Afro-American pavilion were firsts for a world's fair. While exhibitors addressed issues of environmental concern from their own particular perspectives, it was by virtue of a series of international, national, and regional symposiums on the environment that Expo '74 had its most significant impact. The United Nations recognized the role Expo '74 played in promoting environmental awareness by designating the fair the center for World Environment Day activities on June 5.

Long before the gates closed for the final time at 6:00 P.M. on November 3, Spokane's World's Fair had already been heralded an overwhelming success. A total of 5.6 million visitors from all over the globe had passed through one of the five colorful gates since opening day on May 4, exceeding the break-even point by well over 1.5 million. The fair itself generated 4,000 jobs and an immediate economic return of at least $125 million. The estimated $699 million return to the Spokane area in revitalized downtown commerce and increased tourism over the ensuing decade was nearly nine times the cost for the exposition ($78 million).

The impact of the fair went far beyond the familiar measurement of dollars and cents. The environmental theme ("Celebrating Tomorrow's Fresh, New Environment") and related symposiums educated fairgoers and international experts alike. Spokane's world's fair officially opened the two-year American Bicentennial celebration and showcased the first bicentennial exhibit. Beyond these contributions to national and international concerns, Expo '74 transformed Spokane, the smallest city yet to host a world's fair. The Spokane Opera House and Convention Center emerged from Expo's Washington State Pavilion and Art Center. The site itself opened to a new function in 1976 as Riverfront Park, a 100-acre "living space" in the center of a city reborn. The Spokane River sparkled again, and the vibrant city anticipated a future bright with new possibilities.

BIBLIOGRAPHY

Manuscript collections pertaining to the Spokane world's fair are located at two different facilities in Spokane. The Eastern Washington State Historical Society Library at the Cheney-Cowles Memorial Museum is the repository for the records of the Expo '74 World's Fair Corporation (1965–1975) and of its president, King F. Cole (1968–1974). These papers contain incoming and outgoing correspondence, planning documents, financial forecasts, blueprints, audiovisual records, promotional materials, and other relevant documents. Library holdings also include manuscript records germane to Expo from the Northwest Mining Association, the Spokane Council of Churches, and the public interest group Save Our Station Fund. The Pacific Northwest Room at Spokane Public Library houses materials generated by the exhibitors and official published reports on the fair. Also included are environmental impact studies on the fair and an exhaustive collection of newspaper clippings and rare pamphlets on nearly every aspect of Expo '74.

The best secondary sources of comprehensive statistical and background information on Expo '74 are Claude Bekin's official *Report of the United States Commissioner . . .* (1974), Dawn Bowers, *Expo '74: World's Fair Spokane* (1974), which was underwritten by the Expo '74 Corporation, and the *Expo '74 Official Souvenir Program* (1974). William Stimson's recently published *A View of the Falls: An Illustrated History of Spokane* (1985) does an admirable job of placing Expo and its regional impact in the context of Spokane's twentieth century development. Willis B. Merriam's brief but informative pamphlet, *Spokane: Background to Expo '74* (1974), emphasizes the linkages between Expo and the urban renewal efforts of the late 1950s. The April 1974 issue of *Passages*, the magazine of Northwest Orient Airlines, contains numerous articles on the exposition, which provide various perspectives on the genesis and goals of Expo, as well as intriguing details on the pavilions. Dorothy Kienast examines the fair from an aesthetic vantage point in "Spokane and Expo '74: A Designer's Viewpoint" (*Creative Communicator*, 1974). These laudatory articles are somewhat balanced by a critical assessment of the environmental theme of the fair by Rosa Gustaitis in her feature article, "Expo '74: The

Environment as Commercial," *Washington Post*, May 12, 1974. Other articles high-lighting Expo '74 appeared in *Parade*, the *New York Times*, the *Chicago Sun-Times*, the *Miami News*, the *Milwaukee Journal*, and the *Baton Rouge Daily Star*. There are countless newspaper articles on Expo reaching back into the decade before the fair in the two Spokane newspapers, the *Spokesman-Review* and the *Spokane Chronicle*.

Arlin C. Migliazzo

OKINAWA 1975–1976
INTERNATIONAL OCEAN EXPOSITION

The International Ocean Exposition grew out of the Japanese government's desire to rectify, upon Okinawa's reversion to Japan in 1972, disparities with the other prefectures and to improve the basic social climate, utilizing the natural and cultural resources of Okinawa.

The exposition's 1 million square meter site on Motobu peninsula, about 80 kilometers north of Naha City, the prefectural capital, was chosen not simply because of the topography but also to maximize the benefits from the developments of the site and the highway linking Naha and Motobu. Including land with subtropical vegetation and sea with coral reefs, the site is roughly rectangular along the seashore, facing the three offshore islands of Ie, Minna, and Sesoko.

The International Ocean Exposition was the largest special exposition to date, with participation by thirty countries and four international organizations; another country participated unofficially. There were clusters of pavilions, each devoted to a particular theme, such as marine science and technology. Other pavilions housed exhibits from businesses and industries. The most spectacular attraction was the Aquapolis, touted as the future city on the sea. It was the world's largest floating structure—100 meters long, 100 meters wide, and 32 meters high. The Aquapolis weighed 16,500 tons and could accommodate 2,400 people. Other attractions at the fair included ethnic dance exhibitions, beauty contests, two international symposiums on the sea, and two transpacific yacht races.

Direct expenditures for the exposition came to about 90 billion yen, including 46 billion yen in operating expenses. In addition, another 250 million yen was spent on related public works. Although the total number of visitors, 3,480,000, was about 1 million fewer than anticipated, the exposition closed without a deficit. The International Ocean Exposition succeeded not only in boosting tourism but also in bringing needed improvements, such as highways, to Okinawa.

BIBLIOGRAPHY

Information on this fair may be found in various publications of the Japan Association for the International Ocean Exposition. See especially *Okinawa: Expo '75—A Review of the Okinawa International Ocean Exposition* (n.d.) and *Okinawa International Ocean Exposition* (1976). *Expo '75 Pictorial Report* (n.d.) is a convenient guide with bilingual captions. For the architecture of the fair, see *Japan Architect* 50 (October-November 1975): 18–102; the entire issue is devoted to the event.

Those conversant with Japanese may consult *Okinawa kokusai kaiyo hakurankai no koka* (n.d.), an economic and financial analysis; *Umi-sono nozomashii mirai, Okinawa kankei no ayumi* (1976) contains useful background information, statistics, and discussion of problems; and *Kaiyohaku-Okinawa kokusai kaiyohaku no gaiyo* (1972) provides a quick overview of the preliminary stages of the fair's planning. Japanese-language materials are located in the Okinawa Prefectural Library.

Mitsugu Sakihara

KNOXVILLE 1982

KNOXVILLE INTERNATIONAL ENERGY EXPOSITION

"Energy Turns the World" was the theme of Knoxville's world's fair, which occurred in 1982 after a decade of energy scarcity. Knoxville, although only the seventy-seventh largest city in the United States (182,161 population), considered itself a fitting location for an energy exposition for several reasons: it was within 20 miles of Oak Ridge's National Atomic Laboratory and its American Museum of Science and Energy; it was the home of the University of Tennessee's energy research facilities; it was at the center of the largest utility in the United States (Tennessee Valley Authority); and it was near the rich coal fields of the Cumberland Mountains. Knoxville, located at the intersections of interstate highways 75, 40, and 81, has the additional attraction of being within 30 miles of the glittering Gatlinburg–Pigeon Forge resort area and the Great Smoky Mountains National Park, the most popular of the national parks.

Early media accounts focused on pervasive skepticism about the fair. Then after unexpectedly high ticket sales, the attitude brightened and remained high until the October 31 closing. The $115-million budget was met, and some dire predictions about congestion, parking, and crime were never realized. Afterward, however, the failure of redevelopment plans tempered the midsummer euphoria.

Fair boosters had touted publicity, new jobs, urban redevelopment, improved roads, and increased tax revenues as reasons for bringing the fair to Knoxville, but only in the areas of improved roads and publicity did their hopes prove legitimate. Joseph Dodd of the University of Tennessee concluded that financially the success of the enterprise was restricted to businesses on the site itself. Knoxville businesses like restaurants, department stores, and camera shops— even those adjacent to the fair—suffered, and after the fair, plans for turning the former industrial slum into an attractive residential district fell through.

The $21.1-million U.S. pavilion could not be sold, and the federal government gave it to the city (for $1), which had no firm plans for the use of it. The symbol of the fair, the giant Sunsphere, was abandoned after its restaurants went bankrupt. Furthermore, the city had to absorb $35 million in bond issues, and city officials, who had projected as many as 17,000 permanent new jobs as a result of the fair, had to be content with only 200, according to a federal study.

Other problems included hotel overconstruction and irate consumers who, after cancelling room reservations, failed to receive refunds from the fair's Housing Board. Eventually the state attorney general distributed the fair's remaining funds among the complainants, who received sixteen cents for each dollar they had sent in as a deposit.

On the positive side, the $224 million in highway construction funds bore

KNOXVILLE 1982. The U.S. pavilion was one of the largest and most impressive at this fair. (Photograph by Peter M. Warner)

obvious fruit. Formerly known as "malfunction junction," Knoxville after the fair could boast of an efficient highway system. And on the site itself, the development of an "art park," including museums and studios, on 8 acres of the 72-acre site provided some consolation after postfair development failures.

Attendance topped the 11 million projected figure by more than 150,000, which made the Knoxville fair the most popular international theme fair in North American history. Only universal-class fairs like those at New York in 1964–1965 and Montreal in 1967 drew more.

Twenty-four nations, thirty corporations, and seven states sponsored exhibits at the fair. Japan displayed computers that talked in several languages; the United States dazzled fairgoers with robots and educational computer programs on energy; Saudia Arabia presented giant solar collectors; U.S. oil companies exhibited shale oil operations; and West Germany offered models of nuclear reactors.

But the most popular exhibits had little to do with energy, a fact that prompted criticism from the French, who brought a machine to dig minerals on the ocean floor and who demonstrated carbon dating of paintings. One heavily attended exhibit was the Egyptian display of 3,000-year-old chariots and equally ancient statues of private Egyptians. Peru, amid the glitter of Inca gold, unwrapped a 700-year-old mummy. Hungary's Dr. Erno Rubik presided over his country's exhibit of Rubik's cubes, and China brought bricks from the Great Wall, porcelain painters, and terracotta warriors and horses from the Qin dynasty.

These exhibits and an almost continuous round of shows and strolling musicians made the entertainment of the fair one of its high points. There were daily parades, fireworks displays, wandering clowns, marching bands, and world-class midway rides. Large numbers of big-name entertainers such as Bob Hope, Bill Cosby, Debbie Boone, Johnny Cash, and Victor Borge, and well as international symphonies and the Grand Kabuyki Theatre of Japan, highlighted special shows. Exhibition football (New England Patriots versus Pittsburgh Steelers) and basketball (Boston Celtics versus Philadelphia 76ers) drew crowds to the adjacent university stadium and coliseum.

The architecture and gently rolling terrain of the fair site added to the spectacle. Colorful yellow food stalls and blue exhibition halls provided a lively backdrop to the cantilevered glass and steel U.S. pavilion, whose extremely irregular roof lines contrasted with Knoxville's international-style office buildings on one side of the fair and the Tennessee River on the other. The Sunsphere, the 266-foot-tall globe of gold-tinted glass, housed restaurants and observation areas on five levels. But reviews of the Bruce Thompson structure were restrained, primarily because the concept was so similar to structural symbols of other fairs. The most pleasing of the fair's buildings were the restored Victorian L&N Railroad Station and Candy Factory, both of which housed boutiques and restaurants.

In retrospect, the Knoxville world's fair was not comparable to universal-class fairs, nor was it intended to be. Neither is it known for announcing innovations in the field of energy. It was, however, fortunate in attracting China, which had not appeared at a world's fair since 1904. It was also the first sanctioned world's fair in the American Southeast, a fact that allowed for a focus on distinctive southeastern folk culture (clogging, fiddling, chair caning, the making of mountain musical instruments). Finally the Knoxville fair may be remembered primarily for the fact that such a small, provincial city could host an international event drawing over 11 million visitors.

BIBLIOGRAPHY

Official records of the Knoxville International Energy Exposition are held in the McClung Collection of the East Tennessee Historical Center in Knoxville. Some financial and personnel records are still unavailable because of postfair litigation, but an extraordinary amount of material, including videotapes, slides, and papers, is open to researchers. Basic facts about the fair may be obtained from the *Official Guide Book, The 1982 World's Fair* (1982), and the role of the United States can be examined in U.S. Department of Commerce, *Final Report of the United States Commissioner General for the Knoxville International Energy Exposition . . . to the President of the United States* (1982).

Among publications evaluating the fair, Joseph Dodd, *World Class Politics: Knoxville's 1982 World's Fair, Redevelopment, and the Political Process* (1988), is probably the most valuable. Dodd demonstrates that although the Knoxville fair broke even and the organization set up to run the fair was "efficient," the long-term benefit to Knoxville was minimal because of inadequate postfair planning.

Other interesting works are Landrum Bolling, "Knoxville: Charged Up for a World's Fair," *Saturday Evening Post* (March 1982): 63–64, an upbeat description of Knoxville and highlights of the fair, such as the Health Pavilion; Jane O'Hara, "Greasing Up the Money-Go-Round," *Maclean's* April 26, 1982, 21–22, which recounts the financial wheeling and dealing that preceded the fair; and William Schmidt, "The Desolate Legacy of Knoxville's World's Fair," *New York Times*, May 18, 1984, which chronicles the collapse of redevelopment plans. Finally, several articles in *World's Fair* deal with the Knoxville fair. See especially Terry McWilliams et al., "Your *World's Fair* Guide to Knoxville, 1982," *World's Fair* 2, no. 2 (Spring 1982), and Terry McWilliams, "City on the River Showed the World a Thing or Two," *World's Fair* 3, no. 1 (Winter 1983).

Robert Doak

NEW ORLEANS 1984
LOUISIANA WORLD EXPOSITION

The initiative for what would become the 1984 Louisiana World Exposition began a decade earlier, in 1974. In October of that year, the Louisiana Tourist Development Commission, following up on a suggestion of state comptroller S. E. Vines, endorsed the idea of a world's fair at New Orleans in 1980. In December 1975, Governor Edwin Edwards appointed a committee of businessmen and politicians to develop such a project, claiming that a world's fair would attract 20 million visitors and generate $400 million for the city. In the summer of 1976, local businessmen formed a nonprofit corporation to produce an exposition and, a few months later, hired Ewen C. Dingwall, the former general manager of the 1962 Seattle fair, to do a feasibility study. In 1977, the state created the Louisiana Exposition Authority to represent Louisiana in fair-related matters; two years later, this group endorsed the concept of a world exposition in New Orleans in 1984. At about this time, Mayor Ernest N. Morial, speaking for the city of New Orleans, expressed his support for a fair provided it was coordinated with a new convention hall planned for the site. In addition, Morial demanded funds to reimburse the city for its site development expenses and insisted that the fair be compatible with the construction of a new Mississippi River bridge.

By this time, fair planners had incorporated themselves as Louisiana World Exposition, Inc. and applied to the Bureau of International Expositions (BIE) in Paris for sanctioning of a fair in 1984. A year later, the BIE granted the request conditionally provided that the local business community raise some $30 million to underwrite the event. Petr Spurney, the general manager of the exposition corporation, declared that the search for funding would begin immediately, and on May 13, 1981, he announced that backers of the fair had obtained more than $37.5 million in pledges, a figure the U.S. Department of Commerce had set as a requirement for federal approval of the event.

Although the initial financing hurdle was overcome, fair planners faced many more obstacles. The city government demanded more participation in planning the event and proposed that some $72 million in various capital improvements be funded in order to compensate the city for various losses in jobs and tax revenues. Eventually the state legislature appropriated $15 million for the city, a figure termed "better than nothing." By the end of 1981, the fair corporation had managed to arrange a $40 million line of credit through a consortium of banks, to lease the land for an 81.4-acre site, and to persuade the Reagan administration to send out official invitations for foreign participation in the fair.

Efforts to secure foreign participation proved frustrating. It was not until January 1983 that Japan became the first nation to accept; later in the year, perhaps through pressure on the State Department from the Louisiana congressional delegation, Australia, Canada, the People's Republic of China, Egypt, France, Italy, the Republic of Korea, Liberia, Mexico, Peru, and the Philippines agreed to sponsor individual pavilions, while other nations combined in jointly sponsored pavilions.

Even more frustrating were attempts to bring about corporate pavilions. Of some two dozen pavilions specified in the guidebook as corporate pavilions, five were actually sponsored by federal government agencies, and several others represented religious organizations or special interest groups. Of the ten or so corporate pavilions, the Chrysler effort was the most impressive. Covering some 20,000 square feet and shaped like a pentagon to resemble the company emblem, it contained a variety of displays extolling, as might be expected, the Chrysler company, its technology, and its vehicles. Another impressive corporate structure, although not identified as a pavilion, was the Liggett & Myers Quality Seal Amphitheatre. Partially underwritten by the Liggett & Myers Tobacco Company, this was a twelve-story structure that overlooked the Mississippi River and had a seating capacity of 5,500.

Although a theme tower had been contemplated as the central symbol for the fair and a competition had been held to choose a design for such a symbol, the developers abandoned the project for lack of sufficient financing. Instead, the fair's major architectural statement was the Wonderwall, a half-mile-long, multistoried midway featuring a hodgepodge of bright, many-hued architectural motifs with shops, stages, video arcades, food stands, and rest areas. Designed by California architects Charles Moore and William Turnbull in collaboration with the fair's principal architects, Perez and Associates, the Wonderwall cost an estimated $3.9 million and struck some critics as "vacuous kitsch," although fair visitors loved it. The fair also featured an aerial monorail system with fifty-six gondolas traveling between towers rising to 365 feet.

Financial problems increasingly burdened the fair as opening day approached. Management was tardy in hiring a vice-president for marketing, who would be responsible for procuring exhibits and concessions for the fair and selling the enterprise to corporations, travel agents, tour bus operators, and the general public. Fair officials believed their event was an "easy sell" and offended potential sponsors by driving unnecessarily hard bargains. In addition, the fair corporation was plagued by unexpectedly slow advance ticket sales. Despite early boasting that "no fair had ever gotten off to so good a start," fair managers scaled back their prediction of selling 129,000 season passes by the end of 1983 to just 40,000.

The financial problems were exacerbated by the rapidly growing cost of the fair's construction program, especially in the International Pavilion, a major project built over some wharves on the river's edge that was to become a shopping mall after the fair. In addition, slow advance ticket sales induced the management to add still more attractions, such as an Aquacade for water shows and a Watergarden, a spacious area with shallow pools and whimsical fountains. Projects such as these forced the construction costs, originally budgeted at $69 million, to $87 million by the end of 1983. The line of credit originally obtained from various banks had been exhausted, and the fair faced a crisis of imminent insolvency.

Some financial relief came in early 1984. In February, the city agreed to delay the collection of $5 million in taxes from advance ticket sales and donated $3 million toward the construction of a large parking lot for fair visitors. The local Dock Board released for the fair's use the $7 million it had earlier received from the fair as a guarantee that wharves the fair used would be restored to maritime use. In April, a new financial crisis arose when tour operators and others began demanding refunds for unsold tickets, blaming poor sales on the failure of the fair managers to mount a timely advertising campaign. (National press advertising began in January 1984; television advertising did not appear until March.) An appeal to the governor resulted in a $10 million loan from the state that would permit the fair to open on schedule.

Although it had been hoped that President Ronald Reagan would attend the opening ceremonies, he did not, and the fair opened on May 12 to a crowd of 62,746, well under the daily average of 70,000 fair managers had calculated as a break-even figure. Although the general tenor of press reports was optimistic, there were negative comments about the fact that many pavilions and attractions were still under construction and that the fair was an expensive outing for the average family; one survey estimated that a family of four would, on the average, spend $100 for a day at the fair, not including the price of admission. Only 30,555 attended the fair on its second day, which was also Mother's Day, and attendance failed to improve throughout the six-month run. In all, only 7.3 million visitors came to the fair, fewer than half the original projection, and the fair turned into a financial disaster unmatched in the annals of world expositions. In August, the local paper reported that city taxes collected by the fair had not been remitted to the state but had instead been used to cover fair expenses. And in November, the fair corporation declared bankruptcy; estimates of its losses range upwards of $120 million.

The *Times-Picayune* tried to analyze what had happened, suggesting that the fair's marketing plan was flawed, that the fair was undercapitalized, that New Orleans was too small a market, that the fair followed too closely the Knoxville fair, that New Orleans's hot, humid summers were a drawback. Some apologists tried to emphasize the artistic triumph of the fair or point to the residuals that would be left behind, most notably the Riverwalk shopping center, which a bankruptcy court estimated added $6.3 million to the fair's losses. As of November 1988, the Louisiana World Exposition corporation still existed, and the financial tangles of the fair had not yet been fully resolved.

BIBLIOGRAPHY

The most accessible and comprehensive source for the Louisiana World Exposition of 1984 is the *New Orleans Times-Picayune*, the city's major daily newspaper. (Because of a merger, the paper's name was *Times Picayune/States-Item*, from 1980 to 1986.) During the early years of planning and even after the opening, the fair obviously was less than a success. The paper, where at all possible, tried to put the best face on its exposition coverage; despite this, the newspaper remains the best single source on the subject. Newspaper researchers should begin by consulting the *Bell & Howell Newspaper Index to the Times-Picayune/The States-Item*, a comprehensive and detailed index for the numerous articles the paper devoted to the fair.

Another work of considerable value is the *1984 World's Fair, New Orleans: The Official Guidebook* (1984). Although poorly organized (it contains two paginations) and with a text that is sometimes repetitive and often difficult to follow, this work is nevertheless useful. Another official work, *Final Report on United States Participation in the 1984 Louisiana World Exposition* (1985), is a publication of the U.S. Department of Commerce.

Various other works, mainly studies prepared by consultants to the fair, may be useful to researchers. One of the best is the *Louisiana World Exposition, May 12–Nov. 11, 1984* (1984), apparently produced by the exposition itself. Most such works however, are heavily larded with promoters' jargon and hyperbole that limits their usefulness.

One of the most appealing works on the subject is Joshua Mann Pailet, *The World's Fair, New Orleans* (1987). While its text lacks serious substance, Pailet's splendid color photography creates a visual wonderland quite unlike the original subject. Pailet cites another book, *A Century of World's Fairs in Old New Orleans, 1884–1984* (1984?), by Paul F. Stahls, Jr., and a special "World's Fair Commemorative Issue" of *Louisiana Life* (May–June 1984), both of which may also contain information and photographs of interest.

World's Fair covered this fair thoroughly between 1983 and 1985, devoting numerous articles and editorial commentary to its planning, execution, and aftermath. Of particular interest are Winston Lill, "New Orleans Looks Ahead to 1984—and Back to 1884," *World's Fair* 3, no. 2 (Spring 1983); Alfred Heller, "Showboat Tonight!" and "People of the Fair," both in the Spring 1984 issue, and two articles by Bridget O'Brian on the financial problems of the fair: "The Fair Wasn't Broke—It Just Ran Short of Cash," also in the Spring 1984 issue, and "Going Bust: A Case History," in the Spring 1985 issue.

D. Clive Hardy

TSUKUBA 1985

EXPO 85

Dramatic progress in the twentieth century also produced the nuclear threat, environmental pollution, and rapid natural resource depletion. Consequently, the Japanese government planned EXPO 85 as a possible guide to improved environment management into the twenty-first century.

EXPO 85 was located in a rural belt near Tsukuba Science City, 50 kilometers northeast of Tokyo, an added impetus to the region's recent growth as a world science research center. The architecture of the fair was a colorful collection of massive geometric-shaped pavilions that looked dazzling when lit up at night. Its master site plan called for eight self-contained blocks, creating, in effect, fairs within a fair. Thus, the fine perspective vistas evident at the great Paris, New York, Brussels, and Osaka fairs were missing here. No innovative architectural symbols such as the Eiffel Tower, Trylon and Perisphere, Futurama or Aquapolis were unveiled at this otherwise well-designed expo.

Some impressive corporate exhibits featured the huge Fanuc robot (FUG-ITSU), animal and insect audiovisual view of the world (TDK), an all robot-performed stage musical (FUYO), a 25 by 40 meter Sony television (Jumbotron), High Speed Surface Transit (HSST) air-cushioned train (JAPAN AIR LINES), and the fair's tallest structure, an 85-meter ferris wheel (Technocosmos).

The numerous foreign exhibits, poor in quality, were housed in four groups of well-designed uniform modules. Architect Fumihiko Mako's foreign Block A design rejected conventional sharp-cornered surfaces for graceful eye-catching white tent structures. The B and F foreign blocks employed huge rectangular modules sporting Japanese and modern motifs. The G Block's highlight was its golden pointed arch roof. The United States displayed a highly technical preview of the next generation of robots, "Robots That Think," and the Soviet Union exhibited its usual scientific achievements. China stressed its culture and folk arts.

Japan's Theme and History pavilions portrayed advances in robotics, hydroponics, space, and housing. Its 40-meter (130-foot) Theme Tower afforded panoramic views. Its Children's Plaza instructed while delighting all ages with science gadgetry. Finally, its Expo Science Center, a permanent legacy of this fair and a part of the fair located offsite in downtown Tsukuba City, echoed Japan's science and technological advances.

The fair's well-designed transit systems were poorly employed. The Sky-Ride cable car crossed an uninspiring parkland, the Vista-Liner minirail passed through a small section of the fair, and the Mini-Bus traversed a dull route around expo's outer perimeter.

Expo's small amusement zone, Hoshimaru Land, had a few exciting rides, the best of which was the stand-up 360-degree loop roller coaster, Jet-Star. Expo's main events and entertainment took place in the 3,000-seat roofed outdoor Expo-Plaza, and the indoor Expo-Hall.

EXPO 85 attracted the greatest number of exhibitors and largest attendance for a special exposition. Using computer science, robotics and biotechnology in novel dynamic ways, it promoted public interest in science and sophisticated technology, especially among the young. It had a great impact on the Tokyo area and gave the Tsukuba region worldwide publicity.

BIBLIOGRAPHY

The most comprehensive publication on the Tsukuba fair is the *Official Report, Tsukuba Expo '85* (1986), published by the Japan Association for the International Exposition. Heavily illustrated, it contains maps, charts, and final statistics for the exposition. A detailed descriptive and illustrative account of all Japanese government exhibits at the fair may be found in *Japanese Government Exhibit, Expo '85* (1985), and the architecture of Tsukuba is surveyed in *Expo '85 Architecture* (1985), a publication of the Architectural Institute of Japan.

Beyond these volumes, an assortment of guidebooks comprises the main source of information for this exposition. See, for example, *Official Guide Book, Tsukuba Expo '85* (1985); *Press Guide Book, Expo '85* (1985); *"Quest," Tsukuba Expo Source Book* (1985), good for design and technological aspects; *Expo '85—High Technology Guide* (1985), with technical descriptions of the fair's major exhibits; and the *Official Guide Map, Tsukuba Expo '85* (1985), with a folded full-color three-dimensional map of the fair on one side and a map of Tsukuba Science City on the other. Most of these guides were bilingual publications, with text in English and Japanese.

The quarterly journal *World's Fair* covered the Tsukuba exposition thoroughly, running several articles in 1984 and 1985. See especially John Allwood, "Tsukuba," *World's Fair* 4, no. 1 (Winter 1984), and Alfred Heller, "Caution! You Are Approaching a Black Hole," *World's Fair* 5, no. 3 (Summer 1985).

Bernard Rosenfeld

VANCOUVER 1986

EXPO 86: THE 1986 WORLD EXPOSITION

The ostensible impulse behind holding a world's fair in Vancouver in 1986 was to celebrate the city's centenary. Like many other fairs, however, a mix of political and economic considerations underlay the decision. The provincial government, which assumed most of its $1 billion cost, sought to highlight the area's tourist potential and its location on the increasingly important Pacific rim. The fair suited the government's general strategy of regional megaprojects to pump up a provincial economy still mired in recession; 18,000 people worked at Expo, although mostly in low-paying service jobs. It also underlined the circus rather than bread priorities of the ruling Social Credit party, which was simultaneously cutting a wide range of health, education, and social programs under the guise of financial restraint but was not daunted by a projected $500 million loss. At the same time, the fair was intended to be the linchpin for the development of a section of downtown Vancouver, although it was never evident that a world's fair was necessary to generate such development. In purely partisan terms, Expo 86 was a last hurrah for the outgoing provincial premier, William Bennett, and served as an election symbol for his successor, William Vander Zalm.

Expo 86 was a Class II, Special Category Fair, with a traditional—some might say hackneyed—theme, "World in Motion—World in Touch: Human Aspirations and Achievements in Transportation and Communication." This fit the usual emphasis of world's fairs on transportation and communication—perhaps too well. In terms of architecture, displays, and audiovisual entertainment, there was a sense of déjà vu about the fair. The original architectural concept for the fair was formal and grand, but it was not carried out fully because of escalating costs. The modular structure used for most of the national pavilions was designed to provide flexible display space but was used unimaginatively and resulted in relative uniformity. Even the fair's symbol, the "gateway" building, a small sphere altered to resemble a geodesic dome, felt derivative after Buckminster Fuller's U.S. pavilion at Montreal in 1967. To some extent, the architectural blandness was masked by a bold color scheme, banners and site furniture, and the integration of midway booths and amusement rides with pavilions, and the excitement provided by the sheer masses of people crowded onto a relatively small site (175 acres versus Montreal's 1,000).

The fair was more successful at evoking nostalgia than a sense of future promise. Few new inventions were unveiled. The superpower displays suffered from impinging events: the U.S. pavilion was built around the space shuttle program in the wake of the *Challenger* disaster, and the displays from the Soviet Union incurred the metaphorical fallout of the Chernobyl nuclear plant explosion. Displays were generally competent but not technically innovative, relying for

VANCOUVER 1986. This geodesic dome, known as Expo Centre, represents a style of architecture first seen in the U.S. pavilion at Montreal 1967. (Photograph by Peter M. Warner)

the most part on films as the chief entertainment. The emphasis was on larger curved screens, some three-dimensional, and the kinetic split screen first popularized at Expo 67 and reprised in ever greater numbers at Tsukuba in 1985. As has become characteristic of many other world's fairs, the content of films was bland and platitudinous—most successful where humor was cultivated. An exciting exception, and easily the most popular pavilion, was *The Spirit Sings*, hosted by General Motors. An imaginative, and unexplained, combination of holography and performance, it included and acknowledged native people's forms of communication and transportation, which was otherwise lacking since, despite various efforts, there was no native people's pavilion at the fair.

More successful than the films was the array of arts and entertainment. The off-site World Festival of the Arts featured world-class fare, such as La Scala and Britain's National Theatre, but it also had a Pacific rim component, which included a Japanese version of *Medea*, the Beijing People's Art Theatre, an aboriginal play from Australia, the Royal Thai Ballet, and dance from Bali. In addition, the 14,000 free on-site performances added to the festive carnival atmosphere.

In fact, theme park or carnival would aptly describe Expo 86. And despite the unusual "first" of the combined presence of the United States, China, Cuba, and the Soviet Union, Expo 86 boasted nothing more substantial than hosting a lively party, complete with nightly fireworks. Fifty-four countries participated.

Expo's timing proved lucky. An expensive advertising campaign attracted millions of foreign visitors, especially from the U.S. West Coast—people looking for a safe and politically stable but relatively stimulating holiday destination. The summer was dry and sunny and conducive to repeat visits.

The fair was planned to run at a substantial deficit; the announced figure was $336 million. This official public debt was retired in two years out of government-run lottery funds. Additional debt was incurred in the speeded-up completion of a major highway, two bridges, and an advanced light rapid transit line.

BIBLIOGRAPHY

The official report on the Vancouver fair, containing most of the necessary factual data, is *General Report of the 1986 World Exposition, May 2–October 13, 1986* (1986). Basic information about the fairgrounds, the various pavilions, and the amenities can be found in *Expo 86: Official Souvenir Guide* (1986). *The Expo Celebration: The Official Retrospective Book* (1986) is a coffee-table picture book of the fair, while *Expo Design 86* (1986) is another semiofficial publication, as is *Expo: Something's Happening Here* (1986), a promotional videotape.

Robert Anderson and Eleanor Wachtel, *The Expo Story* (1986), published midway through the run of the fair, is the only detailed, critical book-length analysis of all the components leading up to the fair. Apart from the standard coverage of the fair in daily newspapers and popular magazines, four feature articles merit special mention. Robert Fulford, "Only Fair," *Saturday Night* (October 1986): 9–12, is a political appraisal of the fair from a Canadian perspective. E. J. Kahn, Jr., "Letter from Vancouver," *New*

Yorker, July 14, 1986, 73–81, is a descriptive and informative review by the same writer who covered the Knoxville and Tsukuba fairs. The architecture of the fair is discussed in K. D. Stein, "Vancouver: Better Than Fair," *Architectural Record* 174 (July 1986): 120–31. See also Robert Lindsay, "A World in Motion. A Wait in Line," *New York Times*, June 15, 1986. In addition, researchers should consult the quarterly journal *World's Fair*, which ran frequent articles on the Vancouver fair throughout the mid–1980s. Of particular interest are the articles published in the four 1986 issues of the journal.

Robert S. Anderson
Eleanor Wachtel

BRISBANE 1988

WORLD EXPO 88

World Expo 88 was the high point of the Australian bicentennial celebration. Brisbane and the rest of Australia took full advantage of it; Expo was everywhere. In addition, World Expo 88 marked the centennial of Australia's last major international exposition, held in Melbourne in 1888 (a smaller fair was held in Hobart, Tasmania, in 1894–1895).

The idea of organizing an international fair to highlight Australia's bicentennial first surfaced in 1978, and in 1981, Prime Minister Malcolm Fraser suggested to the Australian states that they consider hosting such an event. In 1983, Queensland took up the project, and in December of that year, the Bureau of International Expositions approved the fair as a specialized exposition based on the theme "Leisure in the Age of Technology."

In 1984, the Queensland government established a planning commission formally known as the Brisbane Exposition and South Bank Redevelopment Authority, or more commonly, the Expo Authority, which acquired a 98-acre site along the south bank of the Brisbane River. This area had long been the home of many brothels and dockyards, and postfair plans called for thorough redevelopment. Spared from the demolition were five historic structures, including the Ship Inn, the Plough Inn, and Collins Place. Site development, including $6 million worth of landscaping and the construction of twenty-seven cubical pavilions, continued through early 1988.

On April 30, 1988, Queen Elizabeth II formally opened World Expo 88. Although fair officials had expected only thirty international participants, by opening day, fifty-two nations had signed up, as well as more than twenty corporations, including IBM, Ford, Fujitsu, Cadbury, and Suncorp. The Expo Authority predicted a total attendance of 7 million to 8 million, but the fair proved popular, and by its close on October 30, paid attendance was 15,760,447.

The pavilions, as in other recent expositions, were temporary structures of little architectural interest, although much of the site was covered with eight large translucent canopies, called "Sun Sails." Designed to provide shade, these canopies became a distinctive landmark. Exhibits featured many aspects of leisure, ranging from reading to skiing. Leisure activities were displayed in still exhibits, film, and live performances, often involving the visitors themselves.

There was no lack of entertainment at the exposition. Among the Riverfront stage, the Amphitheatre, the Piazza, and the Aquacade, visitors could find some sort of performance at virtually any hour. Many pavilions had their own entertainment to amuse people waiting in line, and street entertainers added to the festivity. In addition, there was a $52 million amusement park, World Expo Park, filled with rides for young and old.

BRISBANE 1988. The tendency toward modular, prefabricated national pavilions at world's fairs is seen here with the U.S. pavilion at this Australian exposition.

In February 1988, a consortium, River City 2000, received the contract to redevelop the exposition site after the end of the fair. Along with the amusement park and the historic buildings saved from the fair and new public parkland, redevelopment plans call for an international hotel and trade center, a space science center, and commercial and residential areas. The future of the Sun Sails and the monorail that circled the fairgrounds is uncertain.

Planned as a self-supporting endeavor, World Expo 88 cost $420 million. Although attendance figures exceeded expectations, it is too early to tell whether the fair was profitable, although it did serve to enhance Brisbane's reputation as a major Australian city.

BIBLIOGRAPHY

Apart from the *World Expo 88 Media Guide* and the *World Expo 88 Official Souvenir Program*, both of which contain the essential descriptive facts about the Brisbane fair, there were a number of other publications available at or near the site. Louise Edgerton, ed., *Expo Entertainment* (1988), billed as the "ultimate pictorial souvenir program of World Expo '88," appeared about halfway through the run and contained chapters on the themes, entertainments, and special features of the fair. *The World Expo Collection 88* (1988), published by Philip Bacon Galleries, is a catalog of the international sculpture exhibition held in conjunction with the fair. *The Human Factor of World Expo 88* (1988) commemorates an alternative sculpture exhibit, created by John Underwood, a Brisbane sculptor and John Truscott, the fair's creative consultant, that emphasized a more whimsical form of sculpture. *Landscape of World Expo 88* (1988) is a record of the design and construction of the site and its more important pavilions and other physical features.

Three articles in successive issues of *World's Fair* give a good overview of the Brisbane Fair. Ian Gill, "Sir Joh and the Expo," *World's Fair* 8, no. 1 (Winter 1988): 2–8, discusses the influence of long-time Queensland premier Sir Johannes Bjelke-Petersen in the development of the fair. Gill also contributed "Making Peace with the Past," *World's Fair* 8, no. 2 (Spring 1988): 1–10, which places Brisbane 1988 in the context of the Australian bicentennial. And William Kahrl, "The Surprising Success of World Expo 88," *World's Fair* 8, no. 3 (Summer 1988), describes the fair midway through its run and accounts for its success. Finally, descriptive information about the fair can be found in major U.S. and British newspapers and magazines; see, for example, Sandford Brown, "Australia's Expo 88," *Lamp* 70, no. 2 (Summer 1988): 1–5.

Michael L. Gregory

GLASGOW 1988
GLASGOW GARDEN FESTIVAL

The Glasgow Garden Festival of 1988 neatly illustrates the changing emphasis of exhibitions. In 1888 Glasgow had hosted a great exhibition devoted, in the best nineteenth-century manner, to art and industry. In 1938, the city had been the setting for the last of the great empire exhibitions, a festival of raw materials, heavy industry, and engineering celebrating the imperial economic nexus. By 1988 the economy of western Scotland had been transformed: decline and recession had been weathered, at least in part, and Glasgow now celebrated a new type of future.

Garden Festival was to some extent a misnomer. There were gardens aplenty, but the 1988 show was a true exhibition with a significant international component. Like many of its predecessors, it was concerned with urban renewal, generated by sophisticated industries, a vigorous service sector, tourism in a leisured society, and embodying new approaches to the environment. The exhibition, appropriately, was laid out on 120 acres of Prince's Dock, one of the city's great docks, originally opened in 1900. With the decline of Glasgow as a port, the dock basins had been filled in, a fate that had already befallen the Queen's Dock on the other side of the River Clyde, where the Scottish National Exhibition Centre now stands.

The festival was divided into six sections: Science and Technology, Health and Wellbeing, Plants and Food. Landscape and Scenery, Water and Maritime, and Recreation and Sports. Some of the themes explored included new industrial developments, oil, science and nature, wind, solar power and other forms of natural energy, energy conservation, the reemergence of craftsmanship, healthy foods and natural medicines, modern approaches to agriculture, forestry, fish and shellfish farming, as well as new transport and engineering achievements. While the concern with new technology and more enlightened approaches to the environment looked to the future, past Scottish achievements were stressed through exhibits on maritime, fishing, canal, and railway heritage, agriculture and whisky distilling, steam power in human history, and the great Scottish travelers, particularly plant collectors.

The international component came from exhibits by the People's Republic of China, Hong Kong, New Zealand, Mexico, Israel, Pakistan, Finland, Australia, and Ireland. There was a United Nations Peace Garden and exhibits by the sister towns of Glasgow, Rostov-on-Don in the Soviet Union, Turin, Italy, and Dalian, China. Most used the garden theme as a means of displaying artistic or scientific achievement.

Glasgow has always had a strong civic pride, reemphasized in the late 1980s through the city's Miles Better campaign and the selection of the city by the European Community as the European City of Culture for 1990. The festival stressed the renovation of the remarkable architectural heritage of the city, its emergence as one of the most successful urban renewals in modern Britain, a tourist center of the first rank, and the greatest center of the arts outside London.

The festival closed on September 28, 1988, by which time it had recorded 4,345,820 visitors. The gross expenditure on the festival was £41.4 million, with a net cost after income from other sources of £18.7 million. It created 4,900 man-years of employment and resulted in an estimated private sector investment, on and off site, of £200 million. The site has been converted into a business park, housing development, marina, and public park. It had a significant effect in creating a new image for Glasgow and was both a symbol and an instrument of renewal, less grand, but more lighthearted, entertaining, and optimistic than its predecessors.

BIBLIOGRAPHY

Most basic factual information for this exhibition can be found in the *Official Guide* (1988). In addition, a number of articles in the *Times* (London) elaborate on some of the garden aspects of the event; see, in particular, the issues of April 24–25, May 13, 16, September 25, 27–28, 1988.

The Glasgow Garden Festival is given historical context and compared with other Glasgow exhibitions in Perilla Kinchin and Juliet Kinchin, *Glasgow's Great Exhibitions, 1888, 1901, 1911, 1938, 1988* (1988).

John M. MacKenzie

APPENDIXES

Appendix A: Bureau of International Expositions

Of the many eccentric attributes of the Bureau of International Expositions (BIE), the most notable is that unlike many other organizations, it does not seek simply to promote the medium it represents. On the contrary, the BIE was founded out of the need to restrict international expositions and has continued throughout its life to apply increasing constraints on the proliferation of these events. It is, of course, true that the process is designed to permit the raising of the quality and international significance of expositions. But the function of the bureau was conceived as a means primarily of reducing the diplomatic and financial embarrassment of too many host nations pressing the case for their cherished events.

As this book illustrates, in the years following the Crystal Palace exhibition of 1851, the number of expositions increased dramatically, first in Europe, then in the United States and worldwide. One has only to scan the chronological lists of events—at first at intervals of a few years, increasing to annually, thence to several expositions per year—to understand the motivation of the sixteen hard-pressed governments that gathered in diplomatic conference in Berlin in 1912. In a number of nations, committees had emerged that endeavored, on a national basis, to regulate the holding of expositions within their frontiers. The first was in France, in 1902; others quickly emerged, and these met and formed a permanent alliance (Fédération des comités permanents des expositions) in Brussels in 1908. But it was soon apparent that without full diplomatic cooperation, control was difficult, and the 1912 Berlin meeting was the result. Alas, the timing was inopportune. World War I intervened, and it was not until 1928 that the French government revived the issue. Forty-three nations participated in the 1928 convention in Paris, and five others (including the United States, which did not formally join until 1968) sent observers. From this convention emerged the agreement regulating the holding of international expositions, with the Bureau of International Expositions as its executive arm.

The convention of November 22, 1928, became international law on January 17, 1931. It specified the frequency at which expositions of differing categories were to be held, as well as setting out recommendations for the better control of expositions, many of which are still valid today. Fundamentally, it required the host government to act as a guarantor for the satisfactory application of the convention's various recommendations. These were designed to protect the interests of organizer and participant alike. For example, the question of the diplomatic privileges to be accorded to foreign nationals employed in pavilions was addressed.

Between the wars, the BIE was one of a number of international organizations that came under the authority of the League of Nations. Since it has not subsequently been accorded—nor has it sought—a similar relationship with the United Nations, the BIE remains one of the last of the League of Nations's surviving reminders. From its headquarters in the elegant avenue Victor Hugo in Paris, the BIE utilizes the services of the French government and external relations agencies to carry out its international contacts. The bureau's permanent staff is small and is headed by a secretary-general. The number of member states tends to vary around forty, the resignations and adhesions reflecting the stresses and strains of international relations throughout the years. The hardcore membership, predictably, is from the developed world, with a welcome movement toward membership by the developing nations. The cost of membership is not great and varies by means of a formula based on population and relative prosperity. Rather, there has been a move toward a larger share of the BIE's operating costs being contributed through registration fees required of nations organizing expositions; the amount varies according to the nature of the event being registered. The formal business of the BIE is transacted at winter and summer meetings at which the small, specialized international commissions (executive, budget, regulation, and information) convene during a week of hectic activity that culminates in the general assembly. The assembly hears reports from the commission presidents, and under the chairmanship of the BIE president, the business of the bureau unfolds in solemn review. Delegates and observers, numbering in all over one hundred, frequently come from embassies in Paris, although there is a sprinkling of exhibition specialists to add experience to the debate.

The 1928 convention has been modified on several occasions by the emergence of a new protocol—significantly by those of 1948 and 1966 and, most important, by that of 1972. These were designed to respond to the changing role of expositions in a sophisticated and shrinking world. Most evident of all was the desire to come to grips with the ongoing disagreement on the role of the smaller, more specialized expositions. It is clear that the BIE has been on more secure and rewarding ground in the control of the larger, universal fairs. These expensive manifestations lend themselves to the measured intergovernmental control mechanisms applied by the BIE. They were strictly limited as to frequency by the 1972 protocol to an interval of ten years—or twenty years in the same member state. The cost and scale—and the required lead time—of these projects imposed a discipline on the holder. But not so for the so-called specialized event, which even in the rigorous term of the 1972 convention could still take place each two years.

It became evident to a number of aspiring international organizers that they could take a specialized exhibition that was intended to be a serious study of a particular category of human endeavor and by the application of a carnival atmosphere and a somewhat carefree disregard of the official topic arrive at a commercially attractive product. These events grew larger and more sophisticated until they in turn became embarrassments to the world of diplomacy. This was so because what was needed to make the event international was the involvement at considerable cost of nations that sometimes found themselves under unreasonable diplomatic pressure to support the event. It was on this basis that only a few years elapsed after 1972 before the argument was reopened. As of 1989, yet another protocol was being devised to regulate the emergence of the "fake" universal exposition, no matter how successful or well ordered these may individually have been in some cases. The proposed new rules abandon the previous "universal" and "specialized" titles and specify instead only that one BIE-registered event of whatever character and lasting six months may be held each five years. Smaller events, strongly regulated and lasting normally a maximum of three months, may be recognized (but not registered) by the BIE. These are so controlled as to make them appeal more to the organizer genuinely seeking to serve a specialized audience.

In removing these anomalies, the BIE is continuing to serve the international community by protecting the medium from abuse, while at the same time seeking to raise the significance and quality of the medium.

Ted Allan

Appendix B: Fair Statistics

This appendix lists the opening and closing dates for the fairs included in this volume, the size of the site, the paid and total attendance, and the profit or loss incurred by the fair organizers. Although we have included what we believe to be the most accurate figures available, readers should be aware that substantial discrepancies abound in the literature. The date of the formal ceremony opening a fair may differ from the date the public was first admitted; generally, we have used the latter. Attendance figures vary considerably as well. It is not always clear whether they include free or discounted admissions, employees passing through the gates, tickets sold but not used, or artificial inflation carried out by the promoters. Where information was available, we have tried to distinguish between total attendance and paid attendance; unfortunately, this distinction is not often made in fair records. Profit and loss figures present even greater problems because of different accounting procedures over the years, whether the sale of fair assets are included in the final figures, and whether or not underwriters' guarantees are factored in. Therefore, these figures should be used with prudence.

Site/Year	Open Date	Close Date	Size (acres)	Attendance (+000) Paid	Total	Profit/(Loss)
London 1851	May 1, 1851	Oct. 15, 1851	19	6,039		£186,437
Dublin 1853	May 12, 1853	Oct. 29, 1853	2.5	956	1,156	£19,000
New York 1853–1854	July 14, 1853	Nov. 1, 1854	4		1,150	($300,000)
Paris 1855	May 15, 1855	Nov. 15, 1855	29	5,162		(FF8.3 million)
London 1862	May 1, 1862	Nov. 15, 1862	23.5		6,211	broke even
Dublin 1865	May 9, 1865	Nov. 10, 1865	17	956		£10,074
Paris 1867	April 1, 1867	Oct. 1, 1867	215	9,063		FF2.9 million
London 1871–1874	May 1, 1871	Sept. 30, 1871	100		1,142	£17,671
	May 1, 1872	Oct. 19, 1872	100		647	(£5,780)
	April 14, 1873	Oct. 31, 1873	100		498	(£12,126)
	April 6, 1874	Oct. 31, 1874	100		467	(£17,821)
Vienna 1873	May 1, 1873	Nov. 1, 1873	280	5,058	7,250	(15 million gldn.)
Philadelphia 1876	May 10, 1876	Nov. 10, 1876	285	8,004	9,789	($4.5 million)
Paris 1878	May 1, 1878	Nov. 10, 1878	185	13,000	16,032	(FF31 million)
Sydney 1879–1880	Sept. 17, 1879	April 20, 1880	24	850	1,117	(£103,615)
Melbourne 1880–1881	Oct. 1, 1880	April 30, 1881	21		1,459	(£277,292)
Atlanta 1881	Oct. 5, 1881	Dec. 31, 1881	19	196	290	loss
Amsterdam 1883	May 1, 1883	Oct. 31, 1883	62		1,439	
Boston 1883–1884	Sept. 3, 1883	Jan. 12, 1884	3		300	($25,000)
Calcutta 1883–1884	Dec. 4, 1883	March 10, 1884	22		1,000	profit?

Location	Opened	Closed				Result
Louisville 1883–1887	Aug. 1, 1883	Nov. 10, 1883	45	770	971	($470,000+)
New Orleans 1884–1885	Dec. 16, 1884	June 1, 1885	249		1,159	broke even
Antwerp 1885	May 2, 1885	Nov. 2, 1885	54.3		3,500	£5,555
Edinburgh 1886	May 6, 1886	Oct. 30, 1886	25		2,770	£34,642
London 1886	May 4, 1886	Nov. 10, 1886	24		5,551	
Adelaide 1887–1888	June 21, 1887	Jan. 7, 1888	18		767	$1,737
Barcelona 1888	May 20, 1888	Dec. 9, 1888	115		2,240	£41,000
Glasgow 1888	May 8, 1888	Nov. 10, 1888	70		5,748	(£238,000)
Melbourne 1888–1889	Aug. 1, 1888	Jan. 31, 1889	35		2,200	$600,000
Paris 1889	May 6, 1889	Nov. 6, 1889	228	27,722	32,350	£579
Dunedin 1889–1890	Nov. 26, 1889	April 19, 1890	12.5		625	(£4,500)
Kingston 1891	Jan. 27, 1891	May 2, 1891	23		303	$1.4 million
Chicago 1893	May 1, 1893	Oct. 30, 1893	686	21,477	27,529	profit
Antwerp 1894	May 5, 1894	Nov. 5, 1894	86.5		3,000	$66,851
San Francisco 1894	Jan. 27, 1894	June 30, 1894	160		1,356	loss
Hobart 1894–1895	Nov. 15, 1894	May 15, 1895	11		290	($25,000)
Atlanta 1895	Sept. 18, 1895	Dec. 31, 1895	189	780		
Brussels 1897	May 10, 1897	Nov. 8, 1897	148		6,000	loss
Guatemala City 1897	March 15, 1897	June 30, 1897	800			$39
Nashville 1897	May 1, 1897	Oct. 31, 1897	200	1,167		
Stockholm 1897	May 1, 1897	Oct. 3, 1897	514			

Site/Year	Open Date	Close Date	Size (acres)	Attendance (+000) Paid	Total	Profit/(Loss)
Omaha 1898	June 1, 1898	Oct. 31, 1898	200	1,778	2,614	
Paris 1900	April 15, 1900	Nov. 12, 1900	553	39,027	50,861	FF7.1 million
Buffalo 1901	May 1, 1901	Nov. 2, 1901	350	5,307	8,120	($3 million)
Glasgow 1901	May 2, 1901	Nov. 9, 1901	75		11,560	£35,216
Charleston 1901–1902	Dec. 1, 1901	June 1, 1902	160			
Hanoi 1902–1903	Nov. 16, 1902	Feb. 15, 1903	41			
St. Louis 1904	April 30, 1904	Dec. 1, 1904	1,271.8	12,804	19,695	$1.02 million
Liège 1905	April 27, 1905	Nov. 6, 1905	52		7,000	BF75,117
Portland 1905	June 1, 1905	Oct. 15, 1905	400	1,588	2,554	$84,840
Milan 1906	April 28, 1906	Oct. 31, 1906	250		5,500	
Christchurch 1906–1907	Nov. 1, 1906	April 15, 1907	14		1,968	(£81,430)
Dublin 1907	May 4, 1907	Nov. 9, 1907	52		2,750	(£103,345)
Jamestown 1907	April 26, 1907	Nov. 30, 1907	400	1,481	2,851	($2.5 million)
London 1908	May 14, 1908	Oct. 31, 1908	140		8,400	profit
Seattle 1909	June 1, 1909	Oct. 16, 1909	250	2,766	3,741	$63,676
Brussels 1910	April 23, 1910	Nov. 1910	220		13,000	(BF10,000)
Nanking 1910	June 5, 1910		90–100			
London 1911	May 12, 1911	Oct. 28, 1911	200+			loss
Ghent 1913	April 26, 1913	Dec. 1913	309		11,000	

San Francisco 1915	Feb. 20, 1915	Dec. 4, 1915	635	13,128	18,876	$2.4 million
San Diego 1915–1916	Jan. 1, 1915	Dec. 31, 1916	400		2,050 (1915) / 1,698 (1916)	profit
New York 1918	July 29, 1918		25			
Rio de Janeiro 1922–1923	Sept. 7, 1922	July 31, 1923	62	3,626		
Wembley 1924–1925	April 23, 1924 / May 9, 1925	Nov. 1, 1924 / Oct. 31, 1925	216 / 216	15,081 / 7,590	17,403 / 9,699	(£1.6 million)
Paris 1925	April 30, 1925	Oct. 15, 1925	72		14,000	
Dunedin 1925–1926	Nov. 17, 1925	May 1, 1926	65		3,200	(£16,217)
Philadelphia 1926	May 31, 1926	Nov. 30, 1926	1,000	5,853	6,408	($5.6 million)
Long Beach 1928	July 27, 1928	Sept. 3, 1928	63		1,100	broke even
Barcelona 1929–1930	May 19, 1929	Jan. 15, 1930	291.5			
Seville 1929–1930	May 9, 1929	June 21, 1930	494		1,500	
Antwerp 1930	April 26, 1930	Nov. 5, 1930	170.5	468		(BF7 million)
Liège 1930	May 3, 1930	Nov. 3, 1930	165			BF15 million
Paris 1931	May 6, 1931	Nov. 16, 1931	148	32,000	33,489	FF29,000
Chicago 1933–1934	May 27, 1933 / May 26, 1934	Nov. 12, 1933 / Oct. 31, 1934	427 / 427	22,566 / 16,486	27,703 / 21,066	$160,000
Brussels 1935	April 27, 1935	Nov. 6, 1935	250	20,000	26,000	BF45 million
San Diego 1935–1936	May 29, 1935 / Feb. 12, 1936	Nov. 11, 1935 / Sept. 9, 1936	185 / 185		4,785 / 2,004	$44,000
Johannesburg 1936–1937	Sept. 15, 1936	Jan. 15, 1937	100		1,500	(£70,000)

Site/Year	Open Date	Close Date	Size (acres)	Attendance (+000) Paid	Attendance (+000) Total	Profit/(Loss)
Paris 1937	May 24, 1937	Nov. 2, 1937	259	31,412	34,000	(FF495 million)
Glasgow 1938	May 3, 1938	Oct. 29, 1938	175		12,593	(£118,691)
New York 1939–1940	April 30, 1939 May 11, 1940	Oct. 31, 1939 Oct. 27, 1940	1,216.5 1,216.5		25,817 19,116	($18.7 million)
San Francisco 1939–1940	Feb. 18, 1939 May 25, 1940	Oct. 29, 1939 Sept. 29, 1940	400 400		17,042	($559,423)
Wellington 1939–1940	Nov. 8, 1939	Dec. 2, 1940	55		2,641	
Lisbon 1940	June 2, 1940					
Port-au-Prince 1949–1950	Dec. 8, 1949	June 8, 1950	65		250+	
Brussels 1958	April 17, 1958	Oct. 19, 1958	500		41,454	(BF3 billion)
Seattle 1962	April 21, 1962	Oct. 21, 1962	74		9,640	
New York 1964—1965	April 22, 1964 April 21, 1965	Oct. 18, 1964 Oct. 17, 1965	646 646		27,148 24,459	($21 million)
Montreal 1967	April 28, 1967	Oct. 29, 1967	988.7	50,306	54,992	(C$274 million)
San Antonio 1968	April 6, 1968	Oct. 6, 1968	92.6		6,384	($5.5 million)
Osaka 1970	March 15, 1970	Sept. 13, 1970	815		64,219	$146 million
Spokane 1974	May 4, 1974	Nov. 3, 1974	100		5,600	$47 million+
Okinawa 1975–1976	July 17, 1975	Jan. 18, 1976	247.1		3,480	
Knoxville 1982	May 1, 1982	Oct. 31, 1982	72		11,150	loss
New Orleans 1984	May 12, 1984	Nov. 11, 1984	81.4		7,300	($121 million)

Tsukuba 1985	March 17, 1985	Sept. 16, 1985	250	20,335	
Vancouver 1986	May 2, 1986	Oct. 13, 1986	175	22,000	(C$336 million +)
Brisbane 1988	April 30, 1988	Oct. 30, 1988	98	15,760	
Glasgow 1988	April 29, 1988	Sept. 28, 1988	120	4,346	

Appendix C: Fair Officials

This appendix lists the principal individuals responsible for the management and operation of each of the fairs included in this volume. Wherever possible, titles carried by those individuals are also indicated. In some cases, a lack of sufficient reliable information precluded the listing of more than one individual or the officials' titles for a particular fair.

LONDON 1851

Prince Albert, Chairman, Royal Commission
Henry Cole

DUBLIN 1853

William Dargan
Richard Turner

NEW YORK 1853–1854

Theodore Sedgwick, President of the Association (1852–1854)
Phineas T. Barnum, President of the Association (1854)

PARIS 1855

Prince Napoleon, Chairman of Exposition Committee
Frédéric Le Play, committee member
Michael Chevalier, committee member
Emile Pereire, committee member

LONDON 1862

Earl Granville, Royal Commissioner
Wentworth Dilke, Commissioner
Colonel Lawrence Shadwell, General Manager
William Fairbairn, Commissioner
Marquis of Chandos, Commissioner
Thomas Baring

DUBLIN 1865

Duke of Leinster
Lord Talbot de Malahide
Benjamin Lee Guinness

PARIS 1867

Frédéric Le Play, Commissioner General

LONDON 1871–1874

Prince of Wales, President of Royal Commission
Marquis of Ripon, Chair of General Purposes Committee
Earl Granville, Chair of Finance Committee

VIENNA 1873

Baron Wilhelm von Schwarz-Sendborn, General Director
Archduke Charles Louis, Fair Protector

PHILADELPHIA 1876

John Welsh, President of the Board of Finance
Joseph R. Hawley, President of Centennial Commission

PARIS 1878

Jean Baptiste Krantz, Commissioner General
Charles Dietz-Monnin, Director of the French Section
George Berger, Director of Foreign Sections
Marquis of Chennevieres, Director of Fine Arts

SYDNEY 1879–1880

Lord Augustus Loftus, President of the Exposition Committee

MELBOURNE 1880–1881

William Clark, Committee President
J. J. Casey, Executive Vice-President
James Munro, Executive Vice-President
Sir Graham Berry, Prime Minister

ATLANTA 1881

Hannibal Ingalls Kimball, Chairman, Executive Committee of the International Cotton
Exposition Association, and Director General
Joseph E. Brown, President of the International Cotton Exposition Association

AMSTERDAM 1883

Edouard Agostini, Technical Advisor
Oliver Claude Sainte-Foxe, French Commissioner

BOSTON 1883–1884

Nathaniel J. Bradlee, President
Charles Benjamin Norton, Secretary
Frederick W. Lincoln, Treasurer

CALCUTTA 1883–1884

Augustus Rivers Thompson, President of the Executive Committee
S. T. Trevor, Vice-President of the Executive Committee
Jules Joubert, General Manager

LOUISVILLE 1883–1887

J. H. Lindenberger, Committee Chairman
Bidermann du Pont, Exposition President
J. M. Wright, General Manager

NEW ORLEANS 1884–1885

Edmund Richardson, President
Albert Baldwin, Vice-President
William B. Smith, Vice-President
Edward A. Burke, Director General
F. C. Morehead, Commissioner General

ANTWERP 1885

Victor Lynen, President of the Executive Committee
Auguste Beernaert, Director of Central Committee

EDINBURGH 1886

Queen Victoria, Royal Patroness
Edward, Prince of Wales, Royal Patron
Marquis of Lothian, Honorary President
Sir James Gowans, Chairman of the Executive Council
Henry Anthony Hedley, Manager of the Exhibition
James Marchbank, Secretary
Thomas Gaff, Treasurer

LONDON 1886

Prince of Wales, President of Royal Commission
Sir Philip Cunliffe-Owens, Secretary to Royal Commission

Edward Cunliffe-Owens, Assistant Secretary

J. R. Royle, Assistant Secretary for India

ADELAIDE 1887–1888

Sir Edwin T. Smith, Vice-President

Sir Samuel Davenport, Executive Commissioner

Jonathan Fairfax Conigrave, Secretary

BARCELONA 1888

Francesc de P. Ruis i Taulet, President of Central Committee

Manel Girona i Agrafel, Royal Delegate

GLASGOW 1888

Sir Archibald Campbell, President

Sir James King, Chairman of the Executive Council

Henry Anthony Hedley, Manager of the Exposition

W. M. Cunningham, Secretary

Alfred Brown, Treasurer

MELBOURNE 1888–1889

George Higinbotham, President of the Exhibition Committee

Sir James MacBain, Successor of Higinbotham

Sir Graham Beny, Agent General

PARIS 1889

Pierre Tirad, Commissioner General

Charles Adolphe, Minister of Public Works

George Berger, General Manager of the Exposition

DUNEDIN 1889–1890

John Roberts, President

R.E.N. Twopeny, Executive Commissioner

Jules Joubert, General Manager

KINGSTON 1891

Governor H. Al Blake, President

S. Lee Bapty, General Manager

A. C. Sinclair, Promoter

CHICAGO 1893

Thomas W. Palmer, President of World's Columbian Commission
Harlow Higinbotham, President of World's Columbian Exposition Corporation
Daniel H. Burnham, Chief of Construction

ANTWERP 1894

Count of Ursel, Commissioner General
Count of Pret Roose of Calesburg, President of the Executive Committee

SAN FRANCISCO 1894

Michael H. de Young, President and Director General

HOBART 1894–1895

Jules Joubert, General Manager
William Moore, President and ex officio chairman of all committees
Russell Young, Solicitor

ATLANTA 1895

Charles A. Collier, President and Director-General
W. A. Hemphill, First Vice-President
Samuel H. Inman, Financial Director

BRUSSELS 1897

Adrien d'Outremont, Commissioner General
Emile Demot, Executive Committee member
Maurice Lemonnier, Executive Committee member
Nigor Thys, Executive Committee member
Senator Georges Dupret, Executive Committee member

GUATEMALA CITY 1897

Juan F. Ponciano

NASHVILLE 1897

John W. Thomas, President
V. L. Kirkman, First Vice-President
W. A. Henderson, Second Vice-President
John Overton, Third Vice-President

STOCKHOLM 1897

H.R.H. The Crown Prince, Chairman of the Central Committee
H.R.H. Prince Eugene, Chairman of the Art Exhibit Department
Governor Baron Gustaf Tamm, Chairman of the Administration Committee
Oscar Bjorck, Commissioner of the Art Exhibit
Arthur Thiel, Commissioner for the Industrial Arts

OMAHA 1898

Gurdon W. Wattles, President
Alvin Saunders, Vice-President
Herman Kountze, Treasurer
John A. Wakefield, Secretary
Edward Rosewater, Publicity

PARIS 1900

Alfred Picard, Commissioner General
Henri Chardon, Secretary-General
M. J. Bouvard, Director of Architecture and of Parks and Gardens
Ferdinand W. Peck, Commissioner General of the United States

BUFFALO 1901

John G. Milburn, President
William I. Buchanan, Director General
C. Y. Turner, Director of Color
Karl Bitter, Director of Sculpture

GLASGOW 1901

Lord Blythswood, President
Henry Anthony Hedley, General Manager of the Exhibition
James Hunter Dickson, Treasurer

CHARLESTON 1901–1902

F. G. Wagener, President

HANOI 1902–1903

Paul Bourgeois, Secretary of French Commission on Foreign Expositions
Guillaume Capus, Director General

ST. LOUIS 1904

David R. Francis, President

William H. Thompson, Treasurer

Walter B. Stevens, Secretary

LIÈGE 1905

Richard Lamarche, Commissioner General

Count of Flanders, President of Honor of the Superior Patronage Commission

Prince Albert, President of Exposition Commission

PORTLAND 1905

Henry Corbett, President (1902–1903)

Harvey Scott, President (1903–1904)

Henry Goode, President (1904–1906)

Theodore Hardee, Assistant to the President

John Wakefield, Director of Concessions and Admissions

Ion Lewis, Director of Architecture

Oskar Huber, Director of Works

Henry Reed, Secretary and Director of Exploitation

MILAN 1906

Senator C. Mangili, President of Executive Committee

Conte Crivelli Serbelloni, Vice President of Executive Committee

CHRISTCHURCH 1906–1907

Sir Joseph G. Ward, President

W. Hall Jones, Commissioner

DUBLIN 1907

Marquis of Ormonds, President

William M. Murphy, Chairman of Finance and General Purposes Committee

James Shanks, Chief Executive Officer

JAMESTOWN 1907

Fitzhugh Lee, President of Exposition Company

Henry St. George, Successor of Lee

LONDON 1908

Imre Kiralfy, Director of Exposition Company
John Belcher, Managing Architect
Marius Tondoire, Managing Architect

SEATTLE 1909

John E. Chilberg, Head of the Executive Committee
Ira A. Nadeau, Director General
John Langley Howard, Chief Architect

BRUSSELS 1910

Emile Demot, Presiding Officer of the Executive Committee
Eugene Keyon, Director General
Count Adrien van der Burch, Director General
Robert d'Ursel, Commissioner General

NANKING 1910

Tuan Fang, Governor-General
Chang Jen-chun, Successor of Fang
H. E. Chin Chi, Director General
Yang Shih-chi, Adjudicator General

LONDON 1911

Forbes Dennis, Honorary Secretary
Frank Lascelles, Master of the Pageant
H. W. Matthews, General Business Manager

GHENT 1913

Gerard Cooreman, President of the Executive Committee

SAN FRANCISCO 1915

Charles C. Moore, President
William H. Crocker, Vice-President
Reuben B. Hale, Vice-President
I. W. Hellman, Jr., Vice-President
M. H. de Young, Vice-President
Leon Sloss, Vice-President
James Rolph, Jr., Vice-President

SAN DIEGO 1915–1916

G. Aubrey Davidson, President
D. C. Collier, Director General
Frank P. Allen, Jr., Director of Works

NEW YORK 1918

Harry F. McGarvie, Director General
Captain A. M. Baber, Assistant Director
E. W. McConnell, Director of Works

RIO DE JANEIRO 1922–1923

Carlos Sampaio, Commissioner General

WEMBLEY 1924–1925

Prince of Wales, President
Lord Stevenson, Chairman of the Board
Sir Travers Clark, Chief Administrator
Sir John W. Simpson, Architect
Maxwell Ayrton, Architect
Sir E. O. Williams, Consulting Engineer

PARIS 1925

Fernand Davy, General Commissioner
Charles Plumet, Chief Architect

DUNEDIN 1925–1926

J. Sutherland Ross, President and Chairman
Charles Speight, Deputy Chairman
Charles P. Hainsworth, General Manager

PHILADELPHIA 1926

Erastus Long Austin, Business Manager, Controller, and Director in Chief
W. Freeland Kendrick, President of the Sesqui-Centennial Exhibition Association
Mrs. J. Willard Martin, Chair of the Women's Committee

LONG BEACH 1928

J. David Larson, General Manager
Paul C. Graham, General Chairman

BARCELONA 1929–1930

Sr. Marques de Foronda, Director
Sr. Don Eduardo Aunos, Minister of Work

SEVILLE 1929–1930

Sr. Don José Cruz Conde, Royal Commissioner of the Exposition
Sr. Don Nicolas Diaz Molero, Honorary President
Sr. Don Eduardo Aunos, Minister of Work

ANTWERP/LIÈGE 1930

Emile Dignefer, President
Baron Delvaux de Feuffe, Special Commissioner

PARIS 1931

Marshal Hubert Lyautey, General Commissioner
Governor General Marcel Olivier, General Delegate

CHICAGO 1933–1934

Rufus G. Dawes, President of the Fair Corporation
Charles C. Peterson, Vice-President
Daniel H. Burnham, Secretary
George Woodruff, Treasurer
Lenox R. Lohr, General Manager

BRUSSELS 1935

Adrien van der Burch, Commissioner General
René Fonck, Director General
Joseph van Neck, Chief Architect

SAN DIEGO 1935–1936

Frank G. Belcher, President
Zack Farmer, Managing Director
Philip Gildred, Managing Director
Wayne M. Dailard, Managing Director

JOHANNESBURG 1936–1937

Councillor Maldwyn Edmund, President
Major Colin C. Frye, Chairman of Executive Committee

PARIS 1937

Edmond Labbé, Commissioner General
Paul Leon, Commissioner General adjoint
Pierre Mortier, Director of Propaganda
Jacques Greber, Chief Architect

GLASGOW 1938

Earl of Elgin, President
Cecil M. Weir, convenor of the Administrative Committee
S. J. Graham, General Manager
Thomas S. Tait, Architect

NEW YORK 1939–1940

Grover Whalen, President
George A. McAneny, Chairman
Harvey D. Gibson, Successor of McAneny

SAN FRANCISCO 1939–1940

Leland W. Cutler, Exposition President (1939)
Marshall Dill, Exposition President (1940)
George Creel, U.S. Commissioner (both years)

WELLINGTON 1939–1940

The Hon. D. G. Sullivan, President
T.C.A. Hislop, Chairman of Directors

LISBON 1940

Captain Henrique Galvao, Organizer

PORT-AU-PRINCE 1949–1950

President Dumarsais Estime
Jean Fouchard, Commissioner General
John Shaw Young, U.S. Commissioner
Warren Kelchner, Deputy Commissioner
August F. Schmeidigen, Chief Architect

BRUSSELS 1958

Georges Moens Fernig, Commissioner General
Charles Everaerts de Velp, Secretary General
André Waterkeyn, Chief Engineer, Designer of the Atomium

SEATTLE 1962

Edward Carlson, Chairman of Century 21 Corporation

Ewen Dingwall, Director

James N. Faber, Assistant Director

NEW YORK 1964–1965

Robert Moses, President

Major General William E. Potter, Executive Vice-President

Brigadier General William Whipple, Jr., Chief Engineer

Thomas J. Deegan, Jr., Chairman of Executive Committee

Charles F. Preusse, Counsel to the Fair

MONTREAL 1967

H. E. Pierre Dupuy, Ambassador and Commissioner General

Robert F. Shaw, Deputy Commissioner General

Jean Drapeau, Mayor of City of Montreal

SAN ANTONIO 1968

John Connally, Commissioner General

Marshall Stevens, President

John H. White, Vice-President

OSAKA 1970

H.R.H. Crown Prince Akihito, Honorary President

Eisaku Sato, President

Toru Haguiwara, Commissioner General

SPOKANE 1974

King F. Cole, President

Petr L. Spurney, General Manager

Roderick A. Lindsay, Chairman of the Board

OKINAWA 1975–1976

Jiro Takase, Commissioner General of Japanese Government

Nobumoto Ohama, President, Japan Association

Takashi Ohki, Supervisor

KNOXVILLE 1982

Jake F. Butcher, Chairman of the Board
S. H. Roberts, Jr., President
Roger F. Hibbs, Treasurer

NEW ORLEANS 1984

Floyd W. Lewis, Chairman
Petr L. Spurney, President and Chief Executive Officer
Lester E. Kabacoff, Vice-President

TSUKUBA 1985

Katsuichi Ikawa, Commissioner General
Toshiwo Doko, Chairman

VANCOUVER 1986

Jimmy Pattison, Chairman
Patrick Reid, Commissioner General

BRISBANE 1988

Sir Llewellyn Edwards, Chairman
Sir Edward Williams, Commissioner General
Bob Minnikin, General Manager

GLASGOW 1988

Sir Robin Duthie, SDA Chairman
Iain Robertson, SDA Chief Executive
Laing Homes, Developers
Robert Reid, Public Relations

Appendix D: Fairs Not Included

This appendix lists, by year and city, fairs and exhibitions held after 1851 that fell short of meeting the qualifications to be included in the main body of this book. Many of them were very specialized in nature, while others lacked a suitable international scope. Yet each was important to its host city, and the list, taken as a whole, demonstrates the pervasiveness of such fairs, especially in the nineteenth century. The name of the fair is given in the language of the host country unless that language is not a common Western tongue.

Year	City (Country)	Name
1852	Cork	Irish Industrial Exhibition
1853	Brussels	Exposition d'art industriel
1853	Fredericton, New Brunswick	Native Industry Exhibition
1854	Christiania	Exhibition of Norwegian Arts and Manufactures
1854	Madrid	Exposición de Artes Industriales
1854	Melbourne	International Exhibition
1854	Munich	Allgemeine deutsche industrie Ausstellung
1855	Madras	Exhibition of Arts, Manufactures and Raw Materials of the Presidency
1856	Brussels	Exposition d'art Belge
1857	Bern	Exposition des Arts et des Manufactures Suisses
1857	Lausanne	Exposition industrielle
1858	New York	American Industry Exhibition
1858	Turin	Esposizione Nazionale de Prodotti d'Industrie
1859	Athens	National Exhibition
1859	Hannover	Industrie-Ausstellung
1860	St. Petersburg	Exhibition of Russian Products
1861	Florence	Esposizione Italiana
1861	Haarlem	Dutch Industries Exhibition

396   APPENDIX D

1861	Melbourne	Victorian Exhibition
1861–1862	Edinburgh	Exhibition of Industrial and Decorative Art
1862	Rome	Esposizione Nazionale
1863	Constantinople	Exhibition of Turkish Produce and Foreign Machinery
1864	Amsterdam	Exhibition of Dutch Produce, Art, and Industry
1864	Calcutta	Agricultural Exhibition
1864	Lucknow, India	Agricultural Exhibition
1864	Valletta, Malta	Exhibition of Local Arts and Industry
1864	Merseburg, Thüringen, Germany	Industrie-Ausstellung
1864	Turin	Esposizione del Cotoni Italiani
1865	Birmingham	Metals and Trades Exhibition
1865	Bordeaux	Exposition industrielle et artistique
1865	Boulogne	Exposition internationale de pêche
1865	Cologne	Landwirtschaft und gartenbau Ausstellung
1865	Dunedin	New Zealand Exposition
1865	Freetown, Sierra Leone	Industrial Exhibition
1865	Oporto, Portugal	Exposição das Artes, Fabricantes, e Agricola
1865	Stettin, Prussia	Industrie-Ausstellung
1866	Copenhagen	Danish Industrial Exhibition
1866	Melbourne	Intercolonial Exhibition
1866	Rio de Janeiro	Exposição das Materias Primas
1866	Saigon	Cochin China Exhibition
1866	Stockholm	Scandinavian Industries Exhibition
1866	Vienna	Landwirtschaft Ausstellung
1866–1867	Melbourne	Intercolonial Exhibition of Australasia
1867	The Hague	Fishery Exhibition
1868	Bucharest	National Exhibition
1868	Le Havre, France	Exposition maritime internationale
1868	Santiago	Exposición de Productos de Chile
1869	Amsterdam	International Exhibition of Domestic Economy

1869	Beauvais	Exposition d'agriculture et d'industrie
1869	Chartres, France	Exposition d'art et d'industrie
1869	Hamburg	Industrie- und Gewerbeausstellung
1869	Naples	Esposizione Marittimo
1870	Gujarat	Indian Cotton Exhibition
1870	Liège	Exposition internationale d'art industriel
1870	London	Workmen's International Exhibition
1870	St. Petersburg	Russian Industrial Exhibition
1870	Sydney	Intercolonial Exhibition
1870	Turin	Esposizione de Prodotti d'Italiane
1870–1871	Córdova	Exposición Nacional Argentina
1871	Georgetown	Exhibition of Natural Products
1871	Lima	Exposición Nacional de Perú
1871	Naples	Esposizione Internationale Marittimo
1871	Turin	Esposizione Industriel de Prodotti Naturale
1872	Athens	National Industrial Exhibition
1872	Bogotá	Exposición de las Productos de América Sud
1872	Copenhagen	Scandinavian Art and Industry Exhibition
1872	Dublin	Arts, Industries, and Manufactures Exhibition
1872	Kyoto	Japanese Exhibition
1872	Louisville	Industrial Exhibition
1872	Melbourne	Exhibition of Natural Products and Works of Art
1873	Nashville	Industrial Exposition
1873	Chicago	Interstate Exposition
1873	Madrid	Exposición de Productos Naturales
1874	Brussels	Exposition d'Art Industriel
1874	Cincinnati	Industrial Exhibition
1874	Marseille	Exposition d'inventions modernes
1874	Rome	Esposizione de Prodotti d'Industrie Italiano
1875	Geneva	Exposition internationale
1875	Kyoto	Exhibition of Japanese Manufactures

1875	Melbourne	Intercolonial Exhibition
1875	Santiago	Exposición Internacional de Chile
1875–1876	Algiers	Exposition Universelle
1875–1876	Montevideo	Exposición Nacional
1876	Helsinki	Finland Universal Exhibition
1876	Munich	Deutsch-österreichische Kunst-und Industrie Ausstellung
1876	New Orleans	Southern States Agricultural and Industrial Exposition
1876	Thurso, Scotland	Exhibition of Arts and Industry
1877	Capetown	South African International Exhibition
1877	Hamburg	Internationale Milchwertschafts-ausstellung
1878	Ballarat, Victoria, Australia	International Exhibition
1879	Milan	Esposizione Internazionale
1880	Berlin	Internationale Fischerei-Ausstellung
1880	Brussels	Exposition nationale
1881	Adelaide	International Exhibition
1881	London	International Medical and Sanitary Exhibition
1881	Milan	Esposizione Industriale Italiana
1881	Paris	Exposition internationale d'electricité
1882	Biella, Italy	Esposizione Generale
1882	Bordeaux	Exposition de produits industriels et agricole
1882	Christchurch	New Zealand International Exhibition
1882	Edinburgh	International Fisheries Exhibition
1882	Lille	Exposition internationale d'art industrielle
1882	Munich	Internationale Elektricitats-Ausstellung
1883	Caracas	Exposición Nacional de Venezuela
1883	London	International Fisheries Exhibition
1883	Madrid	Exposición de Minería y Metalurgia
1883	Prague	Industrial and Electrical Exhibition
1883	Vienna	Internationale Electrische Ausstellung

1883	Zurich	Schweizerische Landes-Ausstellung
1883–1884	Marseille	Exposition internationale maritime
1883–1884	Nice	Exposition internationale
1884	Brussels	Exposition d'art industriel
1884	Charleston, South Carolina	Industrial Exposition
1884	Edinburgh	International Forestry Exhibition
1884	London	International Health Exhibition
1884	Melbourne	Intercolonial Exhibition
1884	Philadelphia	International Electrical Exhibition
1884	Turin	Esposizione Generale Italiana
1885	Budapest	Hungarian National Exhibition
1885	Konigsberg, Prussia	Internationale Ausstellung für Polytechnik und Industrie
1885	Montenegro	Universal Exhibition
1885	Montevideo	Exposición Nacional de Uruguay
1885	Nuremberg	Internationale Ausstellung
1886	Edinburgh	International Exhibition of Industry, Science, and Art
1886	Liverpool	International Shipping Exhibition
1887	Atlanta	Piedmont Exposition
1887	Le Havre, France	Exposition internationale maritime
1887	Liverpool	Royal Jubilee Exhibition
1887	Manchester	Royal Jubilee Exhibition
1887	Parma, Italy	Esposizione Industriale e Scientifica
1888	Berlin	Landes Ausstellung
1888	Bologna	Esposizione Internationale
1888	Brussels	Grand concours internationale des sciences et de l'industrie
1888	Copenhagen	Nordiske Industri-Landbrugs og Kunstudstilling
1888	Minneapolis	Industrial Exposition
1888	Jacksonville	Sub-Tropical Exposition

1888	Richmond	Virginia Agricultural, Mechanical, and Tobacco Exposition
1889	Ocala	Florida Inter-National and Semi-Tropical Exposition
1890	Boston	International Maritime Exhibition
1891	St. Etienne, France	Exposition d'art et d'industrie
1891–1892	Detroit	International Fair and Exposition
1891–1892	Launceston	Tasmania International Exhibition
1891–1892	Palermo	Esposizione Nazionale
1892	Buffalo	International Exposition
1892	Kimberley	South Africa and International Exhibition
1892	London	International Horticulture Exhibition
1892	Madrid	Exposición Histórico Americana
1894	Luxembourg	Exposition du travail
1894	Lyons	Exposition internationale
1894	Manchester	British and Colonial Industrial Exhibition
1894	Milan	Esposizione Internationale
1894	Odessa	National Exhibition
1895	Amsterdam	International Exposition
1895	Dublin	Arts and Crafts Exhibition
1895	Kyoto	National Japanese Exhibition
1895	Rio de Janeiro	Exposição Nacional
1896	Berlin	Industrie-Ausstellung
1896	Budapest	Hungarian Millenary Exposition
1896	Geneva	Exposition nationale suisse
1896	Kiel	Internationale See-Ausstellung
1896	Nizhni Novgorod	Pan-Russian Exhibition
1897	Arcachon, France	Exposition international
1897	Brisbane	Queensland International Exhibition
1897	London	Imperial Victorian Exhibition
1897	Madrid	Exposición de las Industrias de España
1898	Dijon	Exposition universelle et internationale
1898	London	Universal Exhibition

1898	Turin	Esposizione Nazionale Italiana
1899	Coolgardie	Western Australian International Mining and Industrial Exhibition
1899	Ghent	Provincial Exhibition of East Flanders
1899	Philadelphia	National Export Exhibition
1899	Venice	Esposizione Internationale
1900	London	Women's International Exhibition
1901	Calcutta	Indian Industrial and Agricultural Exhibition
1901	Ponta Delgada	Exposição Internacional
1901	Riga	Jubilaums-Ausstellung
1902–1903	Cork, Ireland	International Exhibition
1902	Lille	Exposition de Lille
1902	Turin	Esposizione Internazionale de Disegno
1902	Wolverhampton	International Exhibition
1903	Osaka	National Industrial Exposition
1905	London	Indian and Colonial Exhibition
1906	Marseille	Exposition coloniale
1907	Bordeaux	Exposition internationale maritime
1909	London	Imperial International Exhibition
1909	Quito	National Ecuadoran Exposition
1910	Buenos Aires	Exposición Internacional de Agricultura
1910	London	Japan-British Exhibition
1911	Glasgow	Scottish National Exhibition
1911	London	Coronation Exhibition
1911	Rome	Esposizione Internazionale d'Arte
1911	Turin	Esposizione Internationale d'Industria e de Laboro
1912	London	Latin-British Exhibition
1914	London	Anglo-American Exhibition
1915	Panama	Exposición Nacional de Panamá
1921	Riga	Jubilaums-Ausstellung
1923	Gothenburg	Gothenburg Tercentennial Jubilee Exposition
1925	La Paz	Exposición Industrial

1925	Tel Aviv	Palestine and Near East Exposition
1930	Dresden	Internationale Hygiene Ausstellung
1931	Berlin	Internationale Baugewerbe Ausstellung
1931	Rio de Janeiro	Exposição Internacional
1932	Bucharest	International Children's Exposition
1933	Tokyo	Women's and Children's International Exhibition
1934	Oporto	Exposição Internacional
1936	Cleveland	Great Lakes Exposition
1936	Dallas	Texas Centennial Central Exposition
1951	London	Festival of Britain
1954	São Paulo	Fería Internacional Comercial do São Paulo
1955–1956	Ciudad Trujillo, Dominican Republic	Fería Internacional para el Paz y la Fraternidad
1967	Fairbanks	Alaska 67 Centennial Exposition

Appendix E: Fairs That Never Were

From time to time, major world's fairs have been planned but never held. Reasons for these nonoccurrences range from the onset of a world war to the realization that the financial demands of the fair were beyond the ability of the host city and other sponsors to meet. This appendix provides brief histories of a number of these fairs that once seemed so promising to their planners yet died as dreams.

NEW YORK 1913

In early 1910, the New York Advancement Company suggested that a world's fair be held to celebrate the three-hundredth anniversary of the settlement of Manhattan. In June, Mayor William Gaynor appointed a committee headed by John Clafin to look into the feasibility of a 1913 fair for the city. The committee met later that month, with most members opposed to the idea, asserting that there were too many taking place, that New York could not afford a fair that would match the recent St. Louis exposition, and that a fair would bring no permanent benefits to the city. After further study by a subcommittee, Clafin recommended to the mayor that a fair not be held. Proponents then began talking about a permanent world's fair, similar to Earl's Court in London, but the advisory committee also declined to endorse this idea. Still others suggested that New York host a spectacular reception to "parliaments of the world," an event that would be hosted by a giant committee composed of New Yorkers, New Jerseyites, and 100 others appointed by the president. This idea failed to generate any enthusiasm, and the *New York Times* editorialized in December 1910 that New Yorkers would be perfectly content to get along without the bother and expense of hosting a fair.

BALTIMORE 1914

Talk of a major world's fair to celebrate the centennial of the "Star-Spangled Banner" and the successful defense of Baltimore in the War of 1812 was relatively short-lived, and civic leaders instead put on a week-long celebration centered around Fort McHenry, then in a state of considerable neglect. It was hoped that the celebration, to include events such as religious services, parades, and an appearance by the president (the secretary of state came instead), would generate enough interest to restore the area and make it into a national landmark.

NEW ORLEANS 1915

New Orleans had hoped to host a world's fair to celebrate the completion of the Panama Canal. The city mounted a large publicity campaign to win public support for its fair, basing its case on the fact that it was the U.S. port nearest to the canal. San Francisco, however, won the battle, and the New Orleans fair was never held.

TOKYO 1917

A world's fair planned for Tokyo in 1912 had been postponed until 1917, when a larger exposition, formally titled the Grand Exhibition of Japan, was to be held. It was cancelled because of World War I.

PORTLAND 1930

A Portland (Oregon) exposition company was chartered in 1925 but failed to raise sufficient capital to begin preparations for the fair, which was to have been called the Pacific American International Exposition. The Great Depression halted further planning after 1930, and the company was dissolved in 1945. The only tangible result of this effort was the striking of a commemorative medal, using bronze from the U.S.S. *Oregon*, then berthed in Portland and used as a museum.

HAVANA 1932

A French syndicate proposed to the Cuban national tourist commission that a fair be held in Havana between December 1931 and April 1932. Mayor Tirso Mesa of Havana liked the idea and appointed a committee of ten prominent businessmen to carry on the planning. The site was to be a parcel of reclaimed land at the foot of the Prado that would extend along the harbor, similar to the manner in which the Paris colonial exposition of 1931 had extended along the Seine River. Eight nations were to participate, and the plans called for a Parisian restaurant and an amusement park. A lack of preparation time, the worldwide economic crisis, and political instability in Cuba conspired to keep this fair from happening.

NEW YORK 1932

In 1927, a world's fair organizing committee revealed plans for a major world's fair to commemorate the two hundredth anniversary of George Washington's birth. The site chosen was the 2,000-acre Marine Park, at the south end of the Flatlands in Brooklyn, on Jamaica Bay. The committee's plans included digging a 30-foot channel in front of the site to accommodate visits of large warships. In addition, 5 million square feet of exhibition space, a stadium seating 200,000, and a bid for the 1932 Olympic Games were all contemplated. Planners anticipated participation by over forty nations, as well as Puerto Rico, Alaska, Hawaii, and the Philippine Islands. Postfair projections included a permanent marine park on the site, as well as an ongoing international exposition and possibly an airport. After a round of initial enthusiasm and preliminary planning, the organizing committee ran into difficulties, first from civic leaders in Chicago, upset about the possibility of their Century of Progress fair, set for 1933, being upstaged, and then from the Merchants Association of New York City. This important organization announced its opposition to the 1932 fair in December 1929, two months after the stock market crash, asserting that technological advances of the 1920s—movies, radios, and automobiles—had made world's fairs all but obsolete and that, given the lack of time for proper planning and the competition from Chicago, a New York fair in 1932 was certain to fail. This viewpoint was echoed by the George Washington Bicentennial Commission of New York State. In a report published during the summer of 1930, the commission sought suggestions for appropriate bicentennial celebrations but clearly stated that no national or international expositions would be held. In February 1931, Sol Bloom, the treasurer of the original organizing committee, announced that no world's fair would take place but that the bicentennial would be celebrated across the nation throughout the year 1932. In the end, the Washington bicentennial was celebrated with a series of smaller events, such as pageants, parades, and colonial balls, around the country, and with the issuance of a set of twelve commemorative stamps and a new twenty-five cent piece, all portraying Washington's likeness.

VANCOUVER 1936

In 1930, plans were announced for the first great Canadian world's fair, to be held in Vancouver in 1936. Prime Minister Mackenzie King, various provincial premiers, and officials of the Canadian National Railroad and the Canadian Pacific Railroad expressed their initial support for the endeavor. The principal object of this fair was to focus the benefits of Far East trade to North America, and especially to the Pacific coast ports of Vancouver, Seattle, San Francisco, and Los Angeles. The estimated cost of the fair was $15 million, but planners were certain that this would be an excellent investment.

LOS ANGELES 1940

A permanent "World Mart and Exhibition" was to have been built in Los Angeles harbor, but the onset of World War II forced the abandonment of plans. The fair, called the Pacific Mercado, was to have included all the nations of the Western Hemisphere in an effort to promote a spirit of friendship and cooperation based on mutual trade. A similar venture, the "First Great Exposition Featuring the Pacific Basin and the Americas," was planned for 1942. It was to have been open year round and have foreign consulates, an international office complex, and administrative space in permanent buildings. The war undermined these plans as well, and no buildings were ever constructed.

TOKYO 1940

Japan had been interested in hosting an international exposition since the beginning of the century. Plans for fairs in 1912 and 1917 had not materialized, and after World War I, it was hoped to host a fair in conjunction with the Tokyo Peace Memorial Exposition in 1922, but preparations could not be made in time. The exposition date was then pushed forward to 1940, with the fair, called the Grand International Exposition of Japan, to be held in conjunction with the Twelfth Olympiad. The fair was to be sited in both Tokyo and Yokohama, and it was planned around the celebration of the 2,600th anniversary of the accession of the Emperor Jinmu. Once again war intervened and caused plans to be postponed indefinitely. Tickets sold for the 1940 exposition were honored at the Osaka 1970 fair.

ROME 1942

Originally to be known as E42, this fair was planned for Tre Fontano, a site 3 miles south of Rome. Formally titled the Esposizione Universale di Roma, it was to have commemorated the twentieth anniversary of the fascist march on Rome, and Benito Mussolini planned to make it a great showplace of his political philosophy. The principal architect of fascist Italy, Marcello Piacentini, designed the fair buildings, highlighted by a concrete arch over 300 feet high. Work began in 1938, and some of the major buildings were constructed, including a church, the Palazzo dell Civilita (also known as the Square Colosseum), and the Palace of Congresses. The war halted further development, and the site was vandalized in the immediate postwar years. In 1951, the buildings were restored, and the rest of the buildings in Piacentini's original plan were constructed. The giant sports arena was used in the 1960 Olympics, and many of the other buildings became museums.

ST. LOUIS 1953

An exposition to commemorate the sesquicentennial of the Louisiana Purchase aroused no particular opposition when it was first announced in 1948. When a site in Forest Park was chosen, however, most city officials objected on the grounds that such a fair would aggravate the housing shortage, and a citizens' group, led by Mrs. William A. Schubert, protested the use of any parkland for a world's fair.

PARIS 1955

In May 1950, the government announced that Paris would host an international exposition in 1955 to mark the centennial of the first Exposition universelle. Six months later, however, the date of the proposed fair was pushed back to 1961 because of the higher priorities of the government in reconstruction, modernization, and rearmament that would preclude any financial commitment to a world's fair.

HOUSTON 1956

A state-chartered philanthropic organization known as Houston's World's Fair, Inc. revealed plans in 1953 to hold a fair in Houston three years later. The corporation bought 935 acres of land adjoining the San Jacinto battlefield, 25 miles east of Houston, and announced that the fair would promote peace and the restoration of free trade among all nations. In addition, the fair would display the achievements of the atomic age and bring to the city important economic benefits.

SAN FRANCISCO 1956

In 1954, George Christopher, a member of the San Francisco Board of Supervisors and candidate for mayor of the city, proposed a world's fair that would celebrate the centennial of the official establishment of the city and county and observe the fiftieth anniversary of the great earthquake and fire. Civic, business, and financial leaders, however, felt that such a fair would be a financial disaster, citing a lack of preparation time and unfavorable world political conditions. In addition, critics noted problems that had plagued the San Francisco fair of 1939–1940 and suggested that world's fairs were obsolete.

PHILADELPHIA 1976

Planning for Philadelphia's participation in the national bicentennial began with the appointment of a citizens' committee in 1962. A major part of early planning was an international exposition, an "occasion where the dual goals of celebrating the past and recognizing the future can be brought together." Philadelphians felt their city was the most logical place for such a fair, given its historical legacy and its central location. To that end the Philadelphia Bicentennial Corporation was formed. Initial plans called for the fair to be sited in the city on the west bank of the Schuylkill River, centered on Penn Central's Thirtieth Street station, where up to 390 acres were available. There were to be no national pavilions but rather a "total environment that is responsive to the theme." Planning for the fair was to be coordinated with many other civic improvements underway for the bicentennial—renovating of historic sites, constructing a tourist center, scheduling numerous international conferences. International performance was to be emphasized, and there would be performance pavilions rather than country pavilions.

For more than six years, the bicentennial corporation wrestled with its plans, moving the proposed fair to a second site at Port Richmond and debating over many other details. Further complications arose in early 1972 when newly elected mayor Frank Rizzo rejected the Port Richmond site in favor of one of 240 acres in Fairmount Park, with additional land in Society Hill and along the river. In May 1972, all fair plans were buried by the American Revolution Bicentennial committee, which refused to sanction the event on the grounds of cost, too little preparation time, and the fact that poor people would not be able to afford the cost of admission. The committee recommended that 1976 bicentennial observances resemble those of 1932—a national celebration made up of a large number of small events.

LOS ANGELES 1981

Planning for an international exposition to be held in 1981 at the Ontario Motor Speedway, 40 miles from downtown Los Angeles, began in the early 1970s, and the proposed fair received the sanction of the Bureau of International Expositions in November 1976. By 1977, however, planners were encountering major financial difficulties. A $38 million bond issue proposal seemed dead in the state legislature, and efforts to raise private funds lagged badly. City and county money was not forthcoming either, although governments of both had endorsed the concept of a fair, which would commemorate the two-hundredth anniversary of the city's founding. Opponents pointed to major environmental and public transportation problems in and around the site and accused promoters of using the idea of the fair to bail out the financially troubled speedway. In May 1978, the Los Angeles fair received a death blow when Commerce Secretary Juanita Kreps announced that she did not support the fair and that the Carter administration would not send out official invitations to foreign nations to participate.

PARIS 1989

The idea of celebrating the bicentennial of the French Revolution and the centennial of the 1889 exposition with another world's fair was first suggested in September 1981 and gained parliamentary approval in July 1983. Original plans called for the fair to have four themes: the sources of liberty, the solidarity of mankind, biology, and living in the year 2000. Planners located two sites—one in the west end and one in the east end of the city—for the fair and envisioned some of it on a giant floating island in the Seine River. Shortly after winning parliamentary approval, however, the proposed fair was abruptly cancelled by French president François Mitterand, who blamed popular Paris mayor Jacques Chirac's opposition to the fair as too costly and disruptive.

CHICAGO 1992

The idea for a world's fair to celebrate the quincentennial of the discovery of America and the centennial of the World's Columbian Exposition was first publicly suggested by Chicago architect Harry Weese in 1977. In 1980, a group of prominent Chicago business leaders began discussing the idea seriously and in 1981 organized themselves as the Chicago World's Fair—1992 Corporation, with Thomas G. Ayers, the recently retired head of Commonwealth Edison Company, as chairman. Working in considerable secrecy and with haste, the Fair Corporation put together a specific proposal for a universal category fair for 1992 that would be sited south of the Chicago Loop, near the location of the Century of Progress fair, that would draw over 54 million people and would earn an $8 million profit. Over the next two years, however, the planners hurt themselves with a condescending attitude toward anyone who dared criticize or question their plans and by their inability to refute veiled hints that their plans concealed a substantial degree of potential profiteering on property development in and around the fair site. Although Mayor Jane Byrne was very much in favor of the fair, Mayor Harold Washington, who entered office in 1983, was far more skeptical, as was the city council in his administration. By this time, a public action group, the 1992 Committee, had also been formed to demand public accountability on the part of the fair planners; this group eventually became an important lobby in opposition to the fair. Questions were raised about the financing for the fair, the choice of a site, the number and quality of jobs that would be created, and, perhaps most important, whether public funds could be better spent on a variety of neighborhood improvement projects. Although the fair corporation hired John Kramer, a young and dynamic publicist, as general manager and scaled down its plans somewhat, important questions still remained unanswered. Some answers were revealed by an independent advisory committee appointed by state House Speaker Michael Madigan, which reported in June 1985 that there was every likelihood that the fair would lose hundreds of millions of dollars and that the fair was far too risky a proposition for the city to take on. When Governor James Thompson and most city officials endorsed the Madigan report, the fair corporation abandoned its plans.

Appendix F: Fairs Yet to Come

OSAKA 1990: INTERNATIONAL GARDEN AND GREENERY EXPOSITION

This fair, scheduled to run from April 1 to September 30, 1990, will pursue the objective of helping visitors to appreciate the value of gardens and greenery to human life, with the hope that the lessons taught will carry forward to make a more pleasant twenty-first century. The exposition will be located on some 340 acres of parkland, divided into a mountain area, a fields area, and a city area, each featuring a different topography and varieties of plant life. Exhibition halls will be located in the city area, featuring displays of flowers and other plant life from Japan and other participating nations. A main event hall will be used for opening and closing ceremonies and national day ceremonies. A number of outdoor exhibition zones will also be developed. Osaka 1990 was registered by the Bureau of International Expositions as a specialized exposition in June 1986.

SEVILLE 1992: COLUMBUS QUINCENTENNIAL EXPOSITION (EXPO '92)

Based on the theme "The Age of Discovery," this exposition will be the first universal-class world's fair in Europe since Brussels 1958 and will commemorate the five hundredth anniversary of the discovery of the New World by Christopher Columbus. The fair will run from April 20 to October 12, 1992, and closing ceremonies will mark the day of that discovery. Recognized by the BIE as a first-class international exposition, the first such since Osaka 1970, and approved by the European Parliament on October 14, 1988, Expo '92 will have more than eighty countries and many international organizations and corporations participating. Some 40 million visitors are expected. The fair will be located on a 540-acre site on a island in the Guadalquivir River, near the center of the city of Seville. The ceremonial headquarters for the fair will be the old Carthusian monastery of Santa Maria de las Cuevas, a place where Columbus often came to consult with a monk who knew much about navigation and astronomy. The site will be divided into five areas: the Area of Spain, including the monastery; the Area of Discovery; the Area of the Future; the Area of National and International Pavilions; and a special event and amusement zone. The total cost of the fair is estimated at $800 million, to be covered by admission charges, television and franchise rights, and commercial sponsorships. The hope is that the exposition will be self-sufficient. The U.S. pavilion, tentatively planned as a star-shaped structure of 50,000 square feet, will showcase exhibits based on the theme "Re-Discover the USA." Costs of U.S. participation are estimated at $30 million, half from private sources and half from federal funds.

Expo '92 was originally scheduled to be held in tandem with an international exposition in Chicago, but plans for the latter collapsed (see appendix E). The fair is being held in conjunction with a specialized exposition in Genoa, Italy, however (see below).

GENOA 1992: GENOA EXPO '92

This fair, based on the theme "Christopher Columbus: Ships and the Sea," will be held from May 15 to August 15, 1992, in Genoa, the city of Columbus's birth. A 12-acre site near the center of the city will be used for the fair, and exhibits will be housed in an existing hall. The event received BIE sanction in December 1987 and is to be sponsored by the Italian Ministry of Cultural and Environmental Wealth and the Italian national commission, together with a number of local and regional organizations.

U.S. participation has been approved, and the United States will have a 10,000 square foot exhibit in the exhibition hall on the Genoa waterfront. It is not yet certain how many other countries will participate.

VIENNA/BUDAPEST 1995

This venture, jointly sponsored by the capitals of Austria and Hungary, will mark the first time a fair spread simultaneously over two sites in different cities will occur. Approved by the BIE in the spring of 1989, the fair will celebrate the 1100th anniversary of the founding of Hungary, the 999th anniversary of Austria's creation, the fiftieth anniversary of the reestablishment of the Austrian republic after World War II, and the twentieth anniversary of the signing of the Helsinki accord on European cooperation and security. It will invoke memories of the grandeur of the old Austro-Hungarian empire, but it may also serve to strengthen economic ties between the European Economic Community and Comecon, its counterpart among Warsaw Pact nations.

The theme of the fair, "Bridges to the Future," reflects the desire of planners for a greater degree of East-West economic cooperation and can be demonstrated in plans for a new high-speed railroad between Vienna and Budapest and inquiries by North American entrepreneurs concerning the construction of hotels and other tourist facilities in Budapest.

MIAMI 1995

This city, long interested in hosting a fair, had also requested the BIE to sanction a 1995 world's fair. The city has the backing of the U.S. Department of Commerce, which oversees U.S. government participation in domestic fairs. The BIE decision to sanction the Vienna-Budapest fair, however, leaves Miami the choice of hosting a nonsanctioned fair or postponing its plans for several years.

HONG KONG 1997

A world's fair to coincide with the return of this city to China has been proposed, but plans are very indefinite.

HANNOVER 1998 or 2000, TORONTO 2000, VENICE 2000

Each of these cities has applied to the BIE to host a fair during the year indicated.

GENERAL BIBLIOGRAPHY

BIBLIOGRAPHIES AND CHECKLISTS

In searching out primary and secondary material for research on world's fairs, the place to begin is Robert W. Rydell, *Books of the Fairs* (1990). This long essay, published as part of a Smithsonian Institution project, "The Books of the Fairs," to gather together and microfilm its holdings of some 2,000 books, pamphlets, and journals on world's fairs and expositions between 1834 and 1915, constitutes a comprehensive and analytical discussion of exposition bibliography. Rydell's work, divided into three major sections, first traces the general evolution of fairs. The second section concerns itself with the historiography of fairs and expositions and contains commentary on a wide variety of published works. The final section deals with the literature of fairs as found in the Smithsonian and other archival and manuscript collections. The Smithsonian project, published in four stages by Research Publications, Ltd., in 1989 and 1990, includes Rydell's bibliography as an introduction.

Other bibliographies and checklists are far less comprehensive. The Library of Congress's Division of Bibliography published *A Selected List of References on Fairs and Expositions, 1928–1939* (1938); it is very complete for those years and also includes mention of some general works, but is of limited usefulness because of its short time span. Julia Finette Davis, "International Expositions, 1851–1900," in volume 4 of *American Association of Architectural Bibliographers* (1967), contains short summaries of major nineteenth-century fairs with substantial bibliographies, including some archival sources following each. As might be expected, the emphasis is on architecture. Alva W. Stewart and Susan J. Stewart, *World's Fairs since 1960: A Bibliographic Overview* (1983), covers seven fairs between 1962 and 1982, listing, without annotation, bibliographic citations for each. Another bibliography dealing with recent fairs is John Hill and Beverley Carron Payne, comps., *World's Fairs and Expos: The Modern Era* (1982), a publication of the Canberra College of Advanced Education. This work lists sources for fairs between 1962 and 1982, without annotation and with a strong emphasis on planning, construction, traffic, architecture, and residual use.

ARCHIVAL HOLDINGS

U.S. Government

Material related to world's fairs and expositions may be found in at least four different federal repositories. The most extensive body of information is to be found in the Smithsonian Institution archives, since the Smithsonian and the U.S. National Museum, whose records are in these archives, were responsible for preparing U.S. exhibits for most of the fairs between 1876 and 1939. The records at the Smithsonian, described more fully in *Guide to the Smithsonian Archives* (1983) and in Rydell's *Books of the Fairs* (1990), are primarily found in Record Groups 70 and 192 and consist of documents illustrative of the financial and technical aspects of exhibiting at world's fairs. In addition, there are several collections of photographs; particularly valuable are those relating to Chicago 1893, Atlanta 1895, Nashville 1897, and Buffalo 1901.

The U.S. National Archives contains some fair records, principally within Record Group 46 (Records of the United States Senate) and Record Group 223 (Records of the United States House of Representatives). Here researchers may find official reports from U.S. commissioners to various fairs, mandated by Congress at the time money was appropriated for U.S. participation in the fair. Accompanying these reports may be correspondence, State Department reports, and other documents concerning the political and diplomatic aspects of U.S. participation.

A number of manuscript collections in the Library of Congress contain material relating to various world's fairs. Of particular significance are the papers of Frank Lamson Scribner, a botanist and exhibit specialist, who was instrumental in preparing the U.S. exhibits for the Department of Agriculture between 1900 and 1934 and who was a technical adviser at a number of U.S. fairs. Other important collections include the papers of Frances B. Johnston, a photographer at the Chicago 1893 and St. Louis 1904 fairs, and thepapers of William John McGee, who was the director of the history and anthropology exhibit at the St. Louis 1904 fair.

Since 1958, the U.S. Information Agency (USIA) has been responsible for U.S. participation in foreign expositions while the Department of Commerce has handled domestic expositions. The USIA maintains a historical collection that includes official material on those fairs in which the agency had a role; this includes final reports, guides, clippings, survey questionnaires and reports, and internal correspondence. The material in the collection is quite extensive for the Brussels 1958, Osaka 1970, and Okinawa 1975 fairs. In addition, the agency maintains a more generalized clippings file, with material from all fairs, domestic and foreign, since 1958.

State, Local, and University Archives

The locations of the records of many individual fairs are noted in the annotated bibliographies for those fairs, as supplied by their authors. This section deals with archival holdings that contain information on a number of different fairs, although if a particular collection has a particularly strong representation for one fair, it may also be included in the bibliography for that fair.

The best collection of world's fair material outside Washington, D.C., is the Donald G. Larson Collection of Expositions and Fairs, 1851–1940, housed in the Special Collections Department, Henry Madden Library, California State University at Fresno. This collection consists of printed material concerning world's fairs during the time period indicated, including guidebooks, catalogs, maps, and pamphlets, as well as academic work on fairs, including dissertations and theses. In addition, the Larson Collection contains fair-related items of material culture—photographs and glass negatives, awards, souvenir medals, postcards, and badges, for example. Altogether, there are some 6,300 cataloged items in the collection.

The Hagley Museum and Library, near Wilmington, Delaware, which emphasizes science and technology in its holdings, contains a substantial amount of fair-related material in its various sections. The library is rich in material on pre-1851 mechanics' institutes in the United States and also boasts much on the early Paris expositions— technical reports, official reports, and proceedings of scientific congresses and conferences. There are more than fifty books and pamphlets on the Paris 1878 fair alone. The Hagley Photography Archives contains a number of items from the Chicago 1893, Paris 1900, and New York 1939–1940 fairs, while the Manuscripts Department, which contains the papers of the large du Pont family, has material of interest to researchers on the New York 1853 and New York 1939–1940 fairs, among others.

Near the Hagley Museum is the Winterthur Museum and Library, whose holdings include a large number of commercial exhibit catalogs and advertisements, especially from the Philadelphia 1876 and Chicago 1893 expositions. The archives at Winterthur is another good source for material on the Chicago 1893 fair; the card catalog lists over 900 items, including a large number of photographs.

The Robert A. Feer Collection of World Fairs of North America is located at the Boston Public Library. Donated by a private collector, this collection includes books, articles, prints, and memorabilia from fairs between 1853 and 1968. Earl R. Taylor, comp., *A Checklist of the Robert A. Feer Collection of World Fairs of North America* (1976), is a useful finding aid.

Other repositories containing world's fair materials include the University of Maryland Architecture Library, whose collection is strongest in late nineteenth-century fairs, the University of Maryland, Baltimore County Special Collections, which has a small selection of material, also dealing with late nineteenth-century fairs, and the Henry Ford Museum and Greenfield Village, near Dearborn, Michigan, which houses a selection of brochures, souvenir booklets, and memorabilia from a variety of fairs. Researchers should consult individual libraries or archives for specific details of holdings.

World's Fair Organizations

At least two national organizations cater to persons having an interest in the subject of world's fairs. Principally, these are collectors' organizations, but individuals with a serious historical interest in fairs may also be collectors, and the quarterly newsletters of these organizations often contain articles (or reprints of older articles) of interest to students of world's fair history. For further information, contact the Exposition Collectors and Historical Organization (ECHO), 1436 Killarney Avenue, Los Angeles, California 90065, and the World's Fair Collectors Society, c/o Peter M. Warner, 106 Castle Heights Avenue, Nyack, New York 10960.

GENERAL WORKS

The most recent and comprehensive book on world's fairs and expositions is John Allwood, *The Great Exhibitions* (1977). This book, now out of print and hard to find, touches on some seventy fairs up to and including Osaka 1970, with interesting and insightful commentary and an abundance of excellent illustrations. There is also an appendix on the Bureau of International Expositions and a checklist of international exhibitions with an array of statistical information. Allwood's book also contains a short bibliography, which concentrates on the most important fairs.

Another important general work is Kenneth Luckhurst, *The Story of Exhibitions* (1951). This survey is particularly useful on the art and industrial exhibitions and the French national exhibitions prior to 1851. The book contains a chapter on national, local, and specialized exhibitions and another on exhibition buildings and display techniques.

A number of general works deal only with nineteenth-century fairs. The most recent of these is Werner Plum, *World Exhibitions in the Nineteenth Century: Pageants of Social and Cultural Change* (1977), a Marxist analysis of early expositions, described by the author as "pageants of the world of rising bourgeois-industrial society, as it prepared itself for the universal expansion of its technology, its economic sinews, and its political power." Less analytical is Christian Beutler, *Weltausstellung im 19. Jahrhundert* (1973), a heavily illustrated catalog of buildings and decorative art exhibits for the ten major world's fairs between 1851 and 1893.

Two volumes in French contain useful information for the generalist researcher. *Le Livre des expositions universelles, 1851–1989* (1983), a publication of the Paris Museum of Decorative Arts, is a coffee table book on twenty-nine expositions held between 1851 and 1970, with many illustrations and short articles on the specific aspects of each fair. The book also contains a more substantial chapter on general world's fair topics such as architecture, the sciences, and organization, and concludes with a chapter on the prospects for a 1989 Paris world's fair. René Poirier, *Des Faires, des peuples, des expostions* (1958), written for the Brussels 1958 exposition, is a survey of fairs from 1851 to 1939, with additional chapters on the origins of fairs, national and colonial fairs, the organization of fairs, and the "social and spiritual" life of fairs.

Earlier works on nineteenth-century fairs include C. B. Norton, *World's Fairs from London 1851 to Chicago 1893* (1890), a survey of the major fairs since the Crystal Palace with some good engravings of various fair buildings. The book also previews the upcoming World's Columbian Exposition of 1893. William Phipps Blake, "Great International Expositions . . . ," an address delivered before the American Centennial Commission and published as a pamphlet in 1872, contains a good deal of information, especially about the Paris 1867 fair, meant for those planning the Centennial Exhibition in Philadelphia but useful to historians of a later time. An article, "International Exhibitions from 1851 to 1874: A Retrospect," in *Practical Magazine* 4 (1875): 448–54, contains a good discussion of the topic, with particular emphasis on British fairs but some mention of smaller, more obscure fairs held in the 1850s and 1860s. An early effort to work world's fairs into the mainstream of historical scholarship on nineteenth-century America is Merle Curti, "America at the World Fairs, 1851–1893," *American Historical Review* 55 (1950): 833–56. Curti's article emphasizes how the exhibits sent to these early fairs reflected the "emergence of a new and powerful America" that won praise from Europeans earlier than had been presumed. Finally, the *Encyclopedia Britannica*, in its earlier editions, contained excellent articles on world's fairs and expositions under the heading "Exhibitions." See the Ninth Edition (1889), vol. 8, pp. 803–5, and the Eleventh Edition (1911), vol. 10, pp. 67–71.

Other general works that may merit consultation are H. W. Waters, *History of Fairs and Expositions: Their Classifications, Functions, and Values* (1939), and George Jackson, *History of Centennials, Expositions, and World Fairs* (1939). Both books, published in conjunction with the New York World's Fair of 1939–1940, contain a hodgepodge of information on fairs of various kinds. Waters's book combines some superficial history with practical information on promotion and organization of fairs and discusses state fairs, trade fairs, and agricultural fairs, in addition to world's fairs. Jackson also discusses some of the practical aspects of fair management; his book, moreover, contains Rufus Dawes's report on the Century of Progress Exposition in Chicago in 1933–1934 and short chapters on both the New York and San Francisco fairs of 1939–1940.

Among other publications, *The Great World's Fairs and Expositions* (1986) is an illustrated catalog of the Mitchell Wolfson, Jr., Collection of Decorative and Propaganda Arts, exhibited in 1986 at Miami-Dade College, Miami, Florida. Colin Simkin, *Fairs* (1944), is a special publication of the Travelers [Insurance Company], containing a short essay, "Fairs Past and Present," by Simkin, along with many pictures and ephemeral information. Maurice Isaac, *Les Expositions internationales* (1936), is an exhaustive three-volume analysis of the organization and regulation of fairs by the Bureau of International Expositions and of what the author calls the "judicial milieu" of fairs. Finally, Robert K. Landers, "World's Fairs: How They Are Faring," *Editorial Research Reports*, April 18, 1986, 291–308, includes a brief survey of past fairs, with emphasis on those of the 1980s and their financial problems.

With the advent of video recording, a number of fairs have become generally available in a visual format. The most important video source is the episode, "Come to the Fair!" from *A Walk through the Twentieth Century with Bill Moyers* (1985). This hour-long documentary includes film clips and commentary on most major fairs from Buffalo 1901. In addition, privately produced videotapes are available for a number of individual twentieth-century fairs, including San Francisco 1915, New York 1939–1940, New York 1964–1965, Vancouver 1986, and Brisbane 1988.

COLLECTIVE AND THEMATIC WORKS

Several books dealing with fairs in one location have been published and provide a convenient source for comparative history. Adolphe Demy, *Essai historique sur les Expositions universelles de Paris* (1907), is a general work on world's fairs through 1908, although it contains separate chapters on each of the five great Paris fairs between 1855 and 1900 and only briefly mentions other fairs. A more recent work is Pascal Ory, *Les Expositions universelles de Paris* (1982), which surveys each of the six major Paris fairs (1855–1900 and 1937) and includes a final chapter on the legacies of these fairs.

For the various Belgian fairs, consult A. Cockx and J. Lemmens, *Les Expositions universelles et internationales en Belgique de 1885 à 1958* (1958). Written for the 1958 Brussels fair, this short volume surveys the Belgian fairs that preceded it, with separate chapters for each of the twentieth-century events. Glasgow's five exhibitions are described in Perilla Kinchin and Juliet Kinchin, *Glasgow's Great Exhibitions: 1888, 1901, 1911, 1938, 1988* (1988), a recent book graced with many illustrations and site plans.

Two significant articles discuss the world's fairs on the 1930s but from different points of view. Robert W. Rydell, in "The Fan Dance of Science: America's World's Fairs in the Great Depression," *Isis* 76 (December 1985): 525–42, discusses the efforts made by promoters and particularly the National Research Council to popularize science and its achievements at world's fairs. In "Utopia Realized: The World's Fairs of the 1930s," an article in Joseph J. Corn, ed., *Imagining Tomorrow: History, Technology, and the American Future* (1986), Folke T. Kihlstedt notes how fairs of the 1930s, especially the New York World's Fair of 1939–1940, stressed the future in terms of optimism and material progress within the context of corporate capitalism and individual opportunity. For visitors, the future was actualized by forward-looking architecture and industrial design.

Several books concern themselves with architectural and design aspects of world's fairs. The most recent and comprehensive is Wolfgang Friebe, *Architektur der Weltausstellungen, 1851 bis 1970* (1983), also available in an English edition, *Architecture of World's Fairs, 1851–1970*. This is a heavily illustrated book highlighting architectural innovations at many world's fairs and including site plans for a number of those fairs. Wolfgang Clasen, in *Expositions, Exhibits, Industrial and Trade Fairs* (1968), cites noteworthy pavilions and well-designed exhibits that have appeared at various world's fairs and lesser events. In an article on fair architecture, "Seven Eras of World's Fairs," *Progressive Architecture* 55 (August 1974): 64–73, L. G. Zimmerman establishes a seven-part taxonomy for fairs: the Crystal Palace era, 1851–1876; the Centennial era, 1876–1889; the Neoclassic era, 1889–1893; the Art Nouveau era, 1893–1925; the Modern era, 1925–1940; the Atomic/Pop Art era, 1940–1967; and the Expo era, 1967–1976. John R. Mullen, *World's Fairs and Their Impact upon Urban Planning* (1972), is primarily a bibliography, but in a short introductory essay, Mullen emphasizes the role fairs can play in bringing about urban benefits. In "American Technology at World Fairs, 1851–1876" (master's thesis, University of Delaware, 1962), Monte Allen Calvert describes the displays of American technology at the early fairs and notes how U.S. representation clearly improved over the years, reflecting the nation's growing "industrial maturity."

A recent book that covers several different themes with respect to world's fairs is Paul Greenhalgh, *Ephemeral Vistas: The Expositions Universelles, Great Exhibitions, and World's Fairs, 1851–1939* (1988). Although there is an underlying constant of nationalism, seen in chapters devoted to imperial display and "human showcases," Greenhalgh's book also considers such diverse topics as fair origins, funding, women, and fine arts.

The participation of women at world's fairs was the subject of Virginia Grant Darney's 1982 Ph.D. dissertation at Emory University. In "Women and World's Fairs: American International Expositions, 1876–1904," Darney notes how the fairs of that era reflect women's progress from "gender segregation" to "gender integration and individualism." Jeanne Madeline Weimann, *The Fair Women* (1981), deals principally with the Women's Building at the 1893 World's Columbian Exposition in Chicago but also mentions briefly women's participation at other fairs.

Robert W. Rydell discusses the manner in which American fairs between 1876 and 1916 were used to confirm the prevailing anthropological notion of Anglo-Saxon racial superiority in his monograph, *All the World's a Fair* (1984). His book treats twelve different fairs, giving particular attention to the zoolike displays of nonwhites that visually stressed the social and cultural differences among the races. Another work that is highly anthropological in nature is Burton Benedict, ed., *The Anthropology of World's Fairs* (1983). While much of this work deals with the Panama-Pacific International Exposition in San Francisco, Benedict's lengthy introductory essay does mention numerous other fairs in his discussion of the "rituals" and "rules" governing world's fairs and their exhibits.

Edo McCullough treats the entertainment aspects of fairs informally in *World's Fair Midways* (1966), a book that discusses not only the entertainment areas but also the nature of the entertainment. The use of fairs by filmmakers to showcase innovative cinematic techniques is surveyed in Marc Mancini, "Pictures at an Exposition," *Film Comment* 19 (January-February 1983): 43–49. In a well-illustrated book, *Glass from World's Fairs, 1851–1904* (1986), Jane Shadel Spillman surveys the glass exhibits from eleven major fairs. Finally, William J. Bomar, *Postal Markings of United States Expo-*

sitions (1986), presents an exhaustive survey of special cancellations used either to promote upcoming fairs or to cancel postcards and letters at exposition postal stations. The book also contains information on specially printed envelopes, postcards, and seals used in conjunction with fairs.

INDEX

Page numbers set in **boldface** indicate the location of the main entry.

ABOUT THE EDITORS AND CONTRIBUTORS

CARL ABBOTT is professor of urban studies and planning at Portland State University. He has published extensively on the history of American urban development and planning. He is particularly interested in the changing role of world's fairs as land development projects.

TED ALLAN is senior vice-president of the Bureau of International Expositions in Paris and a contributing editor to *World's Fair*. He has been connected with every world's fair since Brussels 1958 and was the British commissioner general at Vancouver 1986.

ROBERT S. ANDERSON is an associate professor in the Department of Communications, Simon Fraser University, Burnaby, Canada. With Eleanor Wachtel, he edited the *Expo Story* (1986) on the Vancouver 1986 fair.

PAUL ASHDOWN, a professor of journalism at the University of Tennessee, observed the construction of the 1982 world's fair from his office window in Knoxville. That fair's inspiration was the 1962 Seattle fair, the subject of his contribution. Earlier, his father had told him stories about the Crystal Palace in London.

R. REID BADGER is associate professor of American studies at the University of Alabama. He is the author of *The Great American Fair: The World's Columbian Exposition and American Culture*, several essays on American literature and early jazz, and is coeditor of *Alabama and the Borderlands: From Prehistory to Statehood*.

LINDA BASTYR is a preservation planner with an interest in Victorian houses. She holds a master's degree in urban planning from the University of Illinois at Urbana-Champaign.

BURTON BENEDICT is professor of anthropology and director of the Lowie Museum of Anthropology at the University of California at Berkeley. He has done research on second-generation Chinese in Boston, Muslims and Buddhists in London, Indians in Mauritius, Creoles in Seychelles, and world's fairs.

KAYE BRIEGEL is a lecturer in the Oral History Resource Center at California State University, Long Beach. She has researched and written about various aspects of Long Beach history, including "A Centennial History of the Alamitos Land Company" published in the *Southern California Quarterly* (Summer 1988).

RICHMOND F. BROWN is completing his Ph.D. work in Latin American history at Tulane University. His dissertation research centers on nineteenth-century Guatemala.

ROBERT W. BROWN, who received his degree from Duke University and is an associate professor of History at Pembroke State University, recalls from the New York world's fair of 1964 foot weariness and glimpses of futuristic technology. He specializes in the intellectual and cultural history of nineteenth-century Europe.

FELICITY CAIRD is a graduate student in history at the University of Canterbury in Christchurch, New Zealand. When she is not traveling in the United States and Great Britain in search of elusive research materials, she works in the New Zealand Room of the Christchurch Public Library.

KEN CARLS is an associate professor of graphic design at the University of Illinois at Urbana-Champaign, where he teaches the history of design since industrialization.

EDWARD CAUDILL is an assistant professor of journalism at the University of Tennessee, Knoxville. His teaching areas are writing, editing, history, and mass communications theory. Caudill's research focuses on the history of ideas in the press. He is working on a book-length project, tentatively titled, "Darwin in the Press: The Evolution of an Idea."

ARTHUR CHANDLER is professor of humanities at San Francisco State University. His favorite courses to teach are the Biography of a City series: San Francisco and Paris. In 1976 he won the National Fels Award for Non-Fiction for his "The Faustian Infinite: Western Mathematics and the Humanities of Endless Space."

YVONNE M. CONDON holds undergraduate and graduate degrees in history and education from Webster University. As a museum educator at the Missouri Historical Society, she lectures on the St. Louis world's fair. She also served on the planning team for the exhibit on the 1904 fair titled "Places in the Park."

MARY E. DALY lectures on modern Irish history at University College, Dublin. She is the author of *A Social and Economic History of Ireland since 1800; Dublin: The Deposed Capital, 1860–1914;* and *The Famine in Ireland*, and is completing a book on industrial policy in the Irish Free State, 1922–1939.

CATHERINE DIBELLO received her Ph.D. from Indiana University, Bloomington. She majored in English literature and minored in Victorian studies. She teaches in the English department of Shippensburg University of Pennsylvania.

ROBERT DOAK is professor of English and communications at Wingate College, Wingate, North Carolina. He is also the editor of the *Popular Culture in the South Newsletter*.

RUSSELL DUNCAN is a 1988 graduate of the University of Georgia, where he is an instructor in history. He is the author of *Freedom's Shore: Tunis Campbell and the Georgia Freedmen* (1986). He is working on a study of race, class, party, and the corruption of the American creed.

SHIRLEY M. EOFF earned a Ph.D. at Texas Tech University and teaches in the history department of Angelo State University, San Angelo, Texas. Her area of specialization is twentieth-century U.S. history.

JOHN E. FINDLING teaches U.S. history at Indiana University Southeast and has attended four world's fairs since Montreal 1967. He is the author of a *Dictionary of American Diplomatic History* and a lifelong Chicago Cubs fan.

MAURICE GENDRON was born and raised in Montreal and received his Ph.D. in French literature from the University of California. His area of specialization is the nineteenth century and especially the belle époque, which prompted his interest in French and Belgian world's fairs of that era.

DAVID GLASSBERG is assistant professor of history and director of the public history program at the University of Massachusetts at Amherst. A native Philadelphian, he is the author of several articles exploring popular images and uses of history, as well as a book, *American Historical Pageantry*.

LEWIS L. GOULD is Eugene C. Barker Centennial Professor in American History at the University of Texas at Austin and is the author of *The Presidency of William McKinley* (1980).

PAUL GREENHALGH is a tutor on the V&A/RCA Course (history of design), run by the Victoria and Albert Museum and the Royal College of Art. He wrote *Ephemeral Vistas* (1988), on great exhibitions and fairs, and has contributed articles to many journals, including *Art History, Art Monthly, Ceramic Review*, and *Leonardo*.

MICHAEL L. GREGORY graduated from Western Michigan University in 1987 with a history major. His interest in world's fairs began in 1987, and since then he has spent much of his time researching many expositions and fairs. He has been to four expositions since 1975 and enjoys collecting souvenirs from all of the expositions.

JOY H. HALL's attraction—although her research has concentrated on French socialism—to the history of the early Third Republic began with a graduate study of the Paris Exposition of 1889. Dr. Hall teaches at Auburn University at Montgomery, Alabama, and is writing a monograph on socialist involvement in the exposition.

D. CLIVE HARDY is the archivist in the special collections department of the Earl K. Long Library at the University of New Orleans. He enjoys Mardi Gras and spent a good deal of time at the New Orleans fair of 1984.

ALFRED HELLER is editor of *World's Fair*, a quarterly journal published in Corte Madera, California, since 1981. He has attended thirteen world's fairs, beginning with the Golden Gate International Exposition in 1939.

DWIGHT W. HOOVER directs the Center for Middletown Studies and is a professor of history at Ball State University, where he has taught for thirty years. He is very fond of county and state fairs, having shown farm animals at both, but he has never attended a world's fair.

CHRISTOPHER JEENS is the archivist and records manager of the London borough of Hammersmith and Fulham. Previously he has worked for the Church Missionary Society, cataloging China mission papers, and as a freelance writer and editor.

SANDRA MONTGOMERY KEELAN earned a bachelor's degree in economics and history from Duke University and a master's degree in Latin American history from Texas Tech University. Keelan now manages outside contract labor for Northern Telecom's installation department.

CARL E. KRAMER is president of Kentuckiana Historical Services, a public history consulting firm in Clarksville, Indiana, and an adjunct lecturer in history at Indiana University Southeast and the University of Louisville. He received his Ph.D. from the University of Toledo and is the author of *Capital on the Kentucky: A 200-Year History of Frankfort and Franklin County, Kentucky* (1986).

MARC LAGANA, born in Versailles, France, in 1943, graduated from the University of Wisconsin-Madison with a Ph.D. Interested primarily in contemporary French social and colonial history, Lagana is a history professor at the University of Quebec at Montreal.

DONALD G. LARSON attended the Golden Gate International Exposition in 1940. A graduate of the University of California at Berkeley, he is a history instructor at Fresno City College, Fresno, California. His World's Fair Collection is housed at the California State University at Fresno in the Special Collections Department of the Henry Madden Library.

DANIEL T. LAWRENCE is an architect and a consultant for Rutgers University. Previous work includes John Hopkins University, Rockville, Maryland; Urban Mass Transit Administration Study, Atlantic City, New Jersey; Urban Development, Akron, Ohio; Metropolitan Hospital, Philadelphia; Mountain Lakes Subdivision, Princeton, New Jersey; and solar homes. He lives in Hawley, Pennsylvania.

GARY W. MCDONOGH teaches anthropology at New College, University of South Florida. His Barcelona interests range from elite imagery and power in his *Good Families of Barcelona* to study on Barcelona's portside ghetto and the ideology of space and marginalization. He attended his only world's fair in New York, 1964.

JOHN M. MACKENZIE is the author of *Propaganda and Empire* and *The Empire of Nature*, coauthor of *The Railway Station, a Social History*, and editor of *Imperialism and Popular Culture* and *Imperialism and the Natural World*. He edits the Studies in Imperialism series for Manchester University Press and possesses a large collection of ephemera relating to exhibitions and imperialism.

RONALD J. MAHONEY is the curator of the Donald G. Larson Collection of International Expositions and Fairs, 1851–1940, and head of the Department of Special Collections, Henry Madden Library, California State University, Fresno. The Larson Collection is one of the largest of its kind in the United States.

MARTIN MANNING is historical librarian, U.S. Information Agency, Washington, D.C., which has responsibility for U.S. participation in all BIE-approved international expositions held abroad. Manning was born in Boston, Massachusetts, not far from the site of the 1883 American Exhibition of the Products, Arts and Manufactures of Foreign Nations, and has degrees from Boston College and Catholic University.

SUSAN M. MATTHIAS is associate professor of fine arts at Indiana University Southeast, where she teaches printmaking and drawing. An active studio artist, Matthias has exhibited in Poland, West Germany, and Australia, as well as throughout the United States. Her interest in twentieth-century decorative art provided her the impetus to research the 1925 Paris exposition. Now she says, "I'd love to have been in Paris in 1925."

ARLIN C. MIGLIAZZO is associate professor of history at Whitworth College, Spokane, Washington. Migliazzo received his Ph.D. from Washington State University and has done postdoctoral study at the University of Michigan. He first visited Spokane as the Expo '74 site was under construction and returned as a fairgoer in the summer of 1974.

MICHAEL MULLEN is a writer-artist, author of *Pictures*, and *City and Sayings* (both forthcoming) whose interest in the 1930s led naturally to the New York World's Fair. He is at work on a pop-up book about the fair and other articles and reviews.

TONI OPLT received her B.A. and M.A. degrees from Southern Illinois University, Edwardsville, where she is a lecturer in the Department of English. Her article "Reading, Thinking, and Writing" appeared in the Spring 1985 issue of the Illinois Association of Teachers of English *Bulletin*.

TIMOTHY PALMER attended his first world's fair—HemisFair '68 in San Antonio—when he was ten years old. Twenty-years later the HemisFair was the subject of his master's thesis in American civilization at the University of Texas at Austin. Palmer is a public relations executive and freelance writer in Dallas.

KIMBERLY PELLE is completing her studies in French and sociology at Indiana University Southeast. Although she has never attended a world's fair, she is probably the only person connected with this project who has lived in Mozambique.

JOHN POWELL, assistant professor of history at Hannibal–LaGrange College, has combined research interests in Victorian politics and culture to publish articles on Matthew Arnold and others in *Recusant History, Quarterly Review of Historical Studies,* and *Nineteenth Century Prose.* He is working on a biography of Lord Kimberley.

THOMAS PRASCH is a doctoral candidate in English history at Indiana University. Having completed two years' work as editorial assistant and managing editor at *Victorian Studies*, he is currently doing dissertation research in England on representations of the working class in Victorian graphic art and photography.

BARRIE M. ʾRATCLIFFE is Professeur titulaire en histoire contemporaine de l'Europe at the Université Laval in Quebec. He is researching the urban history of Paris in the first half of the nineteenth century.

BERNARD ROSENFELD is a lifelong world exposition researcher. Rosenfeld has attended fifteen world's fairs (New York 1939 to Vancouver 1986), several lesser fairs, and sites of most past expositions. He belongs to and contributes numerous world's fair reports for the newsletters of the World's Fair Collectors Society and the Exposition Collectors and Historians Organization. He designed the logo for and held offices in the former.

RONALD O. ROTH, a historical preservation consultant, grew up near the site of the Bronx International Exposition, in the vibrant, ethnically mixed neighborhood of the East Bronx. In a misguided name change—or did he miss an earthquake?—it became the South Bronx. At the Parker Pen pavilion of New York's mid-sixties world's fair, the Turkish pen pal offered to him didn't respond, so the Brazilian operator invited him to a party of her compatriots.

JAMES M. RUSSELL is professor of history at the University of Tennessee at Chattanooga. He has published several articles on Atlanta history and most recently, *Atlanta, 1847–1890: City Building in the Old South and the New* (1988). He is working on a book dealing with homicide and violent crime in Charleston, South Carolina, from 1821 to 1930.

ROBERT W. RYDELL is the author of *All the World's a Fair* (1984) and the forthcoming *Books of the Fairs* (1990). He has taught at the University of Michigan, served as John Adams Professor of American Civilization at the University of Amsterdam, and is currently associate professor of history at Montana State University in Bozeman, Montana.

MITSUGU SAKIHARA is the most appropriate author for the Okinawa 1975 fair as he traces his ancestry to Motobu, the Expo site, but he is quite saddened by the transfiguration of his ancestral village into a gaudy resort town. He obtained his B.A. and M.A. at the University of Oregon, and his Ph.D. at the University of Hawaii, where he teaches the only Okinawan history course in the United States.

LEILA G. SIRK grew up in postwar Stuttgart, Germany. At age twenty, she decided to improve her knowledge of English by traveling and studying in the

United States. Eventually she married and settled down in San Francisco. Presently, she is working on her master's degree in humanities at San Francisco State University.

PHILLIP T. SMITH, B.A. (Texas), M.A. (Indiana), M.Phil. and Ph.D. (Columbia), is chairman of the History Department at Saint Joseph's University, Philadelphia, where he teaches the history of Britain and the British empire. He is the author of *Policing Victorian London: Political Policing, Public Order, and the London Metropolitan Police* (1985).

RAYMOND STARR (A.B. and Ph.D., University of Texas) has spent his entire academic career at San Diego State University, where he focuses on local history methods and San Diego history. His publications include *San Diego: A Pictorial History* (1986) and articles in *Public Historian, Historian, California Historian,* and *Journal of San Diego History.* He also serves as book review editor for the *Journal of San Diego History.*

IVAN D. STEEN was born, raised, and educated in New York City. Following completion of his doctoral studies at New York University, he taught at Hunter College. Since 1965 he has been a member of the Department of History at the State University of New York at Albany.

VLADIMIR STEFFEL is associate professor of history and chair of the honors program at the Ohio State University campus in Marion. He has published widely in the urban history of Victorian Britain and is active in the Ohio Academy of History.

DAVID THOMSON is a recent university graduate with a strong family background in Dunedin. He was a research assistant and tutor in the Otago University History Department for two years. Since then he has forsaken regular employment to travel on a shoestring budget through India, Europe, and Africa. His present whereabouts are unknown.

WRAY VAMPLEW is a reader in economic history at the Flinders University of South Australia. His research centers on the social and economic history of sport. His most recent book is *Pay Up and Play the Game: Professional Sport in Britain 1875–1914,* which won the 1989 book award of the North American Society for Sport History.

ELEANOR WACHTEL is a Montreal-born writer and broadcaster with the CBC Radio. Her work appears regularly in national magazines and literary journals. She is also the coeditor of *The Expo Story,* a critical analysis of Vancouver's Expo'86 that was published at the start of the fair.

PETER M. WARNER, world's fair historian and collector, has attended twelve world expositions. His collection, begun in 1958, has grown into a major research resource on world's fairs from 1851 to date. Warner is the founder and past president of the World's Fair Collectors Society, Inc.

RAYMOND L. WILSON is a regular contributor to the professional literature on American art. His *Painting in California 1806–1940* is forthcoming.

ANDREA WITCZAK is a student of design history, graduating from the University of Illinois at Urbana-Champaign with an MFA in graphic design and design history and teaches at the University of South Carolina. She has a special interest in designers and craftsmen from the American arts and crafts movement and is a Frank Lloyd Wright fan.

ARAM A. YENGOYAN is professor of anthropology at the University of California, Davis. His Sydney essay is part of a larger comparative and historical interpretation of the cultural and ideological underpinings of world expositions in England, France, and the United States from 1851 to the present.